Leather Bound BOOKS

IDENTIFICATION
&
VALUES

Arthur
Boutiette

COLLECTOR BOOKS
A Division of Schroeder Publishing Co., Inc.

Front cover:
Bunyan's *Pilgrim's Progress* edited by Sir Walter Scott, 1801, page 167, $750.00.
A Night of Cleopatra by Theopile Gautier, 1880, page 136, $900.00.
Poetical Works of Robert Burns, 1870, page 89, $350.00.
Aurora Leigh by Elizabeth Barrett Browning, 1872, page 86, $425.00.
Her Letter, His Answer and His Last Letter by Bret Harte, 1905, page 146, $750.00.

Back cover:
The Complete Angler by Izaak Walton and Charles Cotton, 1875, page 244, $425.00.
Leaves of Grass by Walt Whitman, 1915, page 248, $275.00.
Life of Napoleon by John Holland Rose, 1913, page 210, $280.00.
Poems by Alfred Lord Tennyson, 1880, page 232, $375.00.
The Works of William Shakespeare, 1870, page 217, $285.00.

Cover design by Beth Summers
Book design by Christen Byrd

COLLECTOR BOOKS
P.O. Box 3009
Paducah, Kentucky 42002-3009
www.collectorbooks.com

Copyright © 2006 Arthur Boutiette

The current values in this book should be used only as a guide. They are not intended to set prices, which vary from one section of the country to another. Auction prices as well as dealer prices vary greatly and are affected by condition as well as demand. Neither the author nor the publisher assumes responsibility for any losses that might be incurred as a result of consulting this guide.

Searching for a Publisher?

We are always looking for people knowledgeable within their fields. If you feel that there is a real need for a book on your collectible subject and have a large comprehensive collection, contact Collector Books.

Proudly printed and bound in the
United States of America

Contents

Acknowledgments

I would like to thank my wife, Melanie, and my two children, Nicole Marie and Grant Alexander Boutiette, for their encouragement and support of my interest in and passion for collecting and selling leather bindings and books.

A special thanks to Edie Reynolds and Dan Gaeta, owners of the John Bale Book Company in Waterbury, Connecticut, for their assistance and critique of this work and for their extraordinary involvement over the years in helping to build my personal library. They are some of the most honorable book dealers I have had the pleasure of knowing and I thank them for their friendship.

I would also like to thank and acknowledge Dennis Melhouse, owner of First Folio Books, Richard Williams, Delane Goodwin, Bobbi Patterson, Susan and Jordon Jacuzzi, and Lisa Fischer for their assistance and involvement in this work. Without them this book would not have been possible.

Books & Bindings as an Investment

When I became involved in the book business some twenty-five years ago, my wife and I would visit book dealers, book shows, and bookstores from one end of this country to the other. We often traveled to Europe asking book dealers if they had any leather bound books. Most of the dealers and shop owners we dealt with in those days were mortified with our query. Some even seemed insulted by our questions. A typical reply from very perturbed book dealers would go something like this, "Sir, we do not have leather books per se. We do not deal in just leather books, for what we are interested in is the content of the books, not the type of covering or binding...." This kind of reaction underscores what we encountered for many years. Our feeling, and the feeling of very few others at that time, was that the leather bindings of many of these books would be worth far more than the actual content of the books. To most, this was simply a bibliophile kind of heresy!

Since our early days of buying books and fine bindings, we have seen this field of collecting leather bindings simply explode with interest, and with this interest the reality of "supply and demand" emerges. As more people became interested and involved in collecting these fine leather books, fewer fine leather bindings were available. As a result, in the past several decades in particular, a field all of its own emerged — the field of antique leather bindings. The past twenty-five years have seen antique leather books change from simply things of beauty to one of the hottest antique collectibles. This has created significant value and return for those who have invested in fine antique leather bindings. Collecting them has indeed become a business all its own within the vast book trade. This book is primarily written to address the investment value of leather-bound antiquarian books and to provide the reader with a comprehensive guide for assessing value.

In the past, collectors traditionally placed a premium on specific types of books such as first editions, signed books, illuminated manuscripts, and the like.

These types of specialties were, and are still, highly sought after. There has always been keen interest in extraordinary fine bindings, particularly well-preserved examples of a master binder's work. Those items still command premium prices, in most cases more than ever before. What is different is that regular antique leather bindings and sets have also become extremely desirable and rare. Books, that just ten or fifteen years ago could be purchased for little or nothing, have now seen an unprecedented rise in popularity and value.

Again, it's the old story of supply and demand. No one doubts or questions the beauty of antique leather bindings. One merely has to walk into a room where the bookshelves are aglow with the beauty of fine calf and Moroccan leather bindings, and the warmth of the room simply embraces you. Even when one walks into a room and there is simply a grouping of leather books, less than a shelf full, your eye is automatically drawn to "the look" of the fine leather bindings. To pick up a book and to feel the supple leather and examine the fine artistry and craftsmanship is a wonderful experience in and of itself.

Now, because of the tremendous interest in collecting leather books and the scarcity of these fine leather bindings found in good or better condition, they are becoming increasingly more difficult to obtain with each passing year. Add to this fact that many of the fine leather bindings that came from larger sets often have missing volumes, making their investment value near worthless. Also, many of the fine bindings of the past 100 or 200 years have not been cared for and therefore have rotted or disintegrated. Again, "supply and demand" takes over. Those fine specimens that are now left and that are complete and that are in wonderful condition, are sought after by more and more private collectors. Because of this, the value of these books continues to rise. The good news is that there are still fine leather books and fine leather bindings available for purchase at affordable prices. However, we believe the window of opportunity is closing, and closing fast. During the next decade many of these fine leather books and sets will be cost prohibitive for most collectors.

I believe that the next few years will be your last opportunity to purchase these books at any affordable price. After that, they will mostly be in private collections or museums or will be too costly for most of us to afford. And if we can afford them, they will still be very difficult to find and obtain. If you like the look and the feel of fine leather bindings, rest assured that the investment value is one of the best in the antique field. This is the time to learn more about them and to start your own collection as there are still great opportunities to get involved in collecting these "treasures" but those opportunities are now and not tomorrow.

Almost any old leather binding that has been cared

for and preserved, and especially sets of leather bindings that are complete, have become antique collectibles. There is, however, a criterion that we believe one must follow to insure that what you purchase is of an "investment quality." The following pages present criteria that we have put together for our customers. It is a plan that we have followed for many years and has paid handsome dividends. From my experience most antique leather bindings which follow the guidelines that I will outline have, and will continue to, double in price every three to five years. That's a substantial return and makes a fine investment to consider.

Our experience shows that there are generally three reasons why people collect antique leather books. One reason is simply because of the content — some people actually read them! After all, these books cross the spectrum of every imaginable and interesting subject. The world is full of avid readers so why not read something that you enjoy and that also just happens to be something of value. Some very collectible subjects are religion, history, literature, poetry, medicine, etiquette, botanicals, philosophy, and the great authors, just to mention a few.

Another reason people collect these types of books is they like "the look" of antique leather books. A fine leather binding is generally a beautiful thing to look at, and it adds beauty to any home. Many collectors are now building their own private libraries full of these works of art and beauty.

Finally, others collect because fine leather books are rapidly disappearing. They have seen that bindings are no longer readily available in the market place and have either been closeted away in personal collections

and institutions, or have been damaged. Because of their scarcity, they are rapidly appreciating in value, and these collectors are making an investment in these books with the purpose of selling them at a later date or with the intent of passing something of great value on to loved ones in future generations. I actually have customers who have a percent of their portfolios invested in leather bound books that follow the criteria that I am about to suggest. In other words, they are approaching the field as if they were investing in property or fine art, assessing value and anticipating a return on their investment.

So the three most common reasons for collecting fine bindings are (1) content, (2) investment, and (3) beauty.

Regardless of the reason that one collects leather books, I have found that there are six general guidelines that are extremely important, and I believe if you follow them they will pay great dividends for you or your descendants. When these guidelines are followed, the value of these leather books increases very rapidly. In the past two years alone, I have seen them increase in price by over one third. In the past five years, they have more than doubled. As a dealer in fine antiquarian books, I suggest that if you are a novice and you want to collect leather books that you should follow these six simple rules to help guide your purchases.

CONDITIONS FOR INVESTMENT

1. Buy English language books. Most fine bindings you collect should be written in English, unless you are an avid collector or sophisticated bibliophile or really know what you are doing with foreign language books or authors.

2. Buy older books. As a general rule most should be dated prior to the 1900s (except fine signed bindings between 1900 and 1935).

3. Buy books in the finest condition possible. The condition should be "fine," "near fine," or "very good" (see explanation in "definitions of conditions" found later in this chapter). Don't let a bargain trick you into choosing an imperfect copy over a more expensive copy, even if you must wait for the better copy to show up.

4. Buy complete items. Many titles were issued in two or more volumes, so always be certain that the book is complete. Also, be sure to check that no illustrations or plates have been removed.

5. Buy books that fall into a collectible or interesting

category. Remember, you are buying books as an investment, so try to avoid subjects that do not have a wide appeal but rather will depend on activity in a limited segment of the book market in order to appreciate.

6. Buy books *in leather*. Avoid books bound in faux leather or decorative cloth.

To give you a solid understanding of the six guidelines, let's look at each of them in more detail.

GUIDELINES

1. Stick with English. Why? Because the market for foreign language books is limited, and we are attempting to develop an investment quality collection that will have a ready market when offered for sale. This is not to say that books in foreign languages are worthless, but only that the resale market is more refined. Also, it has been our experience that many foreign books sold today by decorators, flea markets, antique shops, and the like are incomplete books or sets, and that they are generally of a poor quality leather. These books will never be worth anymore than you paid for them. Most of these books cost between $15 and $38. You can usually purchase a nice investment quality leather book in the $75 to $100 price range that will serve the same decorative purpose, and yet it will increase in value. Which one would you want to own?

Some investors will, however, be comfortable buying books written in languages other than English, especially when they are beautifully bound or examples of early printing. For those who are determined to purchase foreign language books, remember that the other guidelines still apply: always keep the basics in mind. English language books and bindings from before the eighteenth century are increasingly difficult to buy in original bindings, so it is natural that anyone interested in owning books from this period will have to invest

in foreign language books. A word of advice: Be sure to purchase these from reputable book dealers. We have listed in the Resource Chapter a number of dealers we have had first hand experience with who are knowledgeable, and above all, honorable. I would be happy to help anyone that would like to be involved in collecting other types of books and manuscripts that are not written in English, which have great appreciating value.

2. Old or antiquarian. In most cases, try to purchase books that are from before the twentieth century. There are still many seventeenth and eighteenth century books with original leather bindings available for purchase. Bindings from the nineteenth and twentieth century generally are more attractive and are, in particular, becoming difficult to obtain, especially in full leather, highly gilt sets. There are, however, a lot of extremely fine leather books that were made with fine bindings after the turn of the century between 1900 and 1935. Many of these fine bindings are called "signed bindings," which means that the binding is signed with a company name or the name of the individual binder, either on the inside front or back covers or on the endpapers of the book. Also sometimes the name is inconspicuously placed on the spine or cover itself. Although these books were printed by one company they were many times bound by a different company. Some examples of a few of the better names to look for during this period are Sangorski & Sutcliffe, Riviere, Zaehnsdorf, and Bayntum. These great bindings are an exception to the pre-1900 rule. (See a listing of other seventeenth, eighteenth, and nineteenth century binders within the Binding Chapter.)

3. Condition. The books you purchase need to be in "very good" or better condition. The old saying in the book business is that "condition is everything." It is a bit of an overstatement but not by much. If the book you purchase has had a board broken off, or piece of the tail or headband is gone, or hunks of leather are missing, or if the leather is discolored or stained, then its value is impeded. If pages are torn, or signatures are loose, or the binding is "shaken" then the value is impeded. If labels are missing and the gilt is worn away or hinges are "starting" or cracked, then the value is impeded. The Antiquarian Booksellers Association of America (www.abaa.com) has compiled the following definitions of the conditions of books which are used universally by most book dealers.

DEFINITIONS

a. *Fine condition* — refers to books that are perfect, in as-issued condition with no defects.

b. *Near fine condition* — perfect, but not as crisp as those graded fine. They show only little wear from reading, such as very small marks on the binding, etc. These books have no major defects.

c. *Very good condition* — books may show some minor wear but must have no tears on the pages or binding, no foxing and are overall in great condition.

d. *Good condition* — applies to an average used book that has all of its pages, yet may have a few major defects. However, its text must be complete.

e. *Ex-library* — should always be indicated as such and may be found in any condition. These are books that were previously owned by a public library showing labels, stamps, pockets, etc.

f. *Read or well-read books* — these generally are books that are bought for content only and their condition is poor. (Often referred to as "reading copies," or "binding copies.")

4. Complete. One of the most important investment quality rules is that the book (or books) be complete. It may sound silly or obvious, but you will be surprised by how many books or sets of books are not complete. For example, you're looking at a set of books that has three volumes. Let's say the title of the books you are looking at is *The Life of Napoleon.* The first thing you would do is look at the title page of the first volume. If it says "in 4 volumes" then you know it is not a complete set. If you buy incomplete books then most often you have purchased what is termed "furniture" or

"decorator" books, meaning books that you can place in your home for decorative purposes only. They most likely will never appreciate in value because they are not complete.

Now let's say that when you looked in the front of the book it does not say "in 4 volumes." It says nothing about how many volumes, then you need to look for other clues to determine whether the set is complete or not. One way is to look in the end of whatever you can determine is the last volume. If the volumes are numbered, it's easy. Usually at the very end of the last volume it will either say "finis" or "the end," often with an index or appendix or something that is different from what is in the end of the other volumes in the set. If none of these is present you should be suspicious, as there is a good chance that the set is not complete.

What about the times there are no clues? Sometimes, especially in large sets of novels, the books will not be sequentially numbered. You therefore won't know where to look for the last volume to find an appendix or the words "the end." Even if you did determine the last volume, it probably won't have an appendix because in these large sets they didn't have appendixes or say "finis." They usually had nothing in the end of the volume except the end of the story. Sets like the works of Dickens, Scott, Cooper, Twain, and hundreds of other authors who wrote many novels don't have very many clues. Let's say you have a set of James Fenimore Cooper, and you look in the end of his novel *Last of the Mohicans.* At the end of the volume, it might say "the end," but the other 24 volumes in that set will probably also say "the end." So, with these large sets you would have to have a list of the author's works (which you could obtain at the public library or on the Internet) to help determine if the set was complete. Another method is to write down the date of the book, the title, and who printed the book, and go to the reference section of your library and look them up in the *American Book Prices Current.* This is a set of reference books that will give you a listing of books sold, for how much, when, and a listing of how many volumes it should have. This is also a great reference to tell you what your books are worth, because it lists the actual selling price from many auction houses and other sources and when the books sold. More information on this reference book can be found in the chapter on "Book Terms."

Having said all of this, there is a gray area concerning what is and is not complete. This gray area is usually in the literature category. So let's say you are looking at three volumes on a shelf, and each volume has a top and bottom label. The top volume says "Works of Irving"; the bottom label says "Christopher Columbus." The first thing to do is to determine whether these three volumes are the complete story of Christopher Columbus's life. If it is complete, then what you have is a wonderful complete set of the life of Columbus, but since the top label says "Irving's Works" you know you can't possibly have all the works of Irving as he wrote many books. You do, however, have a set which is called "Complete In Itself" because it's the complete story of Columbus. Since you don't have the complete works of Irving (major or minor works), then these books won't be a great investment quality set, but they do have value. As mentioned earlier, the Columbus set only had two of the three volumes, and if you still went ahead and purchased them, then you would have no investment. You would simply have two furniture or decorator books that will not appreciate.

Understand the difference between the complete works of someone and a complete set. Complete set means that everything the author wrote up to the time the books were printed, or all the volumes the printer decided to print, are in the set. Many printers didn't print everything an author wrote. Sometimes they did this because some of the works may not have been very popular, or failed to sell well when others tried to print them. But more often than that, because they did not want to take a bigger financial risk by printing all of the works, they printed just some of them to see how they would sell. Many times, if the sales went well, they would add more titles to the printing a few months or even a few years later.

Some printers pre-sold their books so they would not experience financial disaster if the books didn't sell well. These printers sold by "subscription only," and many times printed the names of the buyers in the front of the book before they printed them.

Remember that complete set also means you have all the volumes the author wrote at the time of the printing. This means you may purchase a set of books in 1875 and at the time of the purchase it was a complete set of everything the author had written up to that time. Then say in 1876 or 1890 the author wrote several other books. You still have a complete set as printed, but not everything the author penned.

Complete works typically means you have all the books the author wrote.

Remember to purchase your antiquarian leather books from an established and honorable dealer! Experienced and reputable dealers will know whether a set of books is complete, and whether they're a good investment. They will also refund a purchase that is not as described. We have provided a list of dealers who have always been honorable to us in the Resource Chapter of this book (page 56).

5. Interesting or collectible subjects. Any book you purchase should be a collectible subject. Generally, as mentioned earlier, books on history, poetry, novels, medicine, botanicals, etiquette, science, literature, cooking, gardening, fore-edge paintings, books with hand-colored illustrations, etc., are books that you may want to seek. However, general encyclopedias, state law books, bound leather magazines, periodicals, annuals, sets like Stoddard's Lectures and the Harvard Classics just to mention a few, are, as a rule, titles that you should avoid, as they do not generally appreciate in value. The ones that do are for the expert collectors to determine. Here are examples of some of the more difficult sets to obtain in

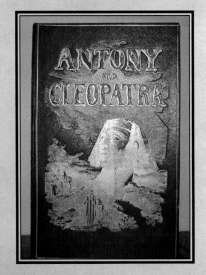

leather: Mark Twain, Arthur Conan Doyle, Thomas Hardy, Henry James, the writings of Jefferson, Thomas Paine, Henry David Thoreau, the complete works of Darwin, and James Fenimore Cooper just to mention a few. Many people also collect the American authors like Lowell, Emerson, and Hawthorne. Whether you decide to collect all authors, novels only, just British or American works, or if you are like me and want to collect across the board, be sure that the majority of your purchases are recognizable authors and titles, and usually not those that are insignificant or obscure.

6. Leather. Since this entire book is mostly about leather bindings, then the last guideline should be obvious . . . the book should be bound in leather. Leather books come in various sizes, shapes, and colors. There are many types of materials used for leather bindings, but the vast majority of them will fall into two types. One is goat skin, called Moroccan leather, and the other is made of cowhide, called calf leather. (An extensive explanation of the different types of leather is outlined in the Binding Chapter.) Also, all leather books have leather spines. However, the covers vary greatly. Sometimes the entire book is covered in leather. This, of course, is called a "full leather binding." A book with just the spine and tips of the four corners of the covers in leather is called a "three-quarter leather binding" (usually by Americans), or a "one-half leather binding"

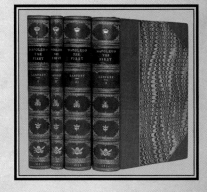

(usually called this by the English). Others describe ¾ and ½ by the amount of leather that covers the corners of the boards. Under Book Terms, we describe ¾ leather bindings as having wider leather back and corners covered in leather than ½ leather. And ½ is when the spine and outer corners are of leather while the rest of the sides are covered with cloth or paper (often marbled). When the cover tips are not finished with leather and just the spine is covered with leather, it is called a "one-quarter leather binding." It doesn't matter whether the book is one-quarter, one-half, three-quarter, or full, the book is considered leather and has investment value if it meets the other guidelines. But remember, the leather needs to be old, preferably contemporary. In the book world "contemporary" does not mean new, but rather that it is the same or similar age as the book itself. Recent bindings, especially machine produced mass market items such as Franklin Press and Easton Press titles, do not qualify as investment grade bindings, even though of interest to many buyers.

If you follow these simple guidelines, you will make intelligent investment quality purchases. Leather book collecting can be a most profitable and fun endeavor. Even if you are not collecting for investment purposes, you will have the security of knowing that the books in your library will never go down in value and will most likely continue to appreciate. That's a pretty good feeling to have with anything that one owns. So remember . . . .

To Be Investment Quality:
1. Written in English
2. Old
3. Very good or better condition
4. Complete
5. Collectible subject
6. Leather

To gain an appreciation of the book as an artifact of beauty, let us take a little time to review its history before going further into how to purchase fine bindings as an investment.

History of Printing

There have been many influential people in the history of the world. Certainly, Johann Gutenberg, the father of printing, can be characterized as one of the most influential men in the last millennium. Mark Twain once said there could be no doubt that Gutenberg's invention was "the incomparably greatest event in the history of the world." Actually, Johann Gutenberg was not his real name. His name was Johannes Gensfleish, which in English literally translated into "goose flesh." He was often taunted by his name, so he took on the name Gutenberg, based on the area in Germany where his family lived, Zun Gutenberg. Born around 1398, Gutenberg was the son of a merchant in the large town of Mainz, Germany.

Gutenberg's invention, the printing press, revolutionized the world. Although printing was reported in places like China in the eighth century, it was a very time consuming process utilizing engraved wooden blocks. The blocks had to be carved by hand and generally could only be used once. Gutenberg's contribution was the development of reusable, movable type. The movable type was a system where pieces of metal made up single letter type that could be assembled and reused. Ink was rolled over the raised surfaces of the hand set letters. The letters were held together by a wooden form and then pressed against the paper, transferring the ink and printing to both sides of the paper. The significance of this was enormous. First, prior to this invention books were hand written, meaning scribes sat and tediously wrote or copied the words by hand. Needless to say, it was incredibly time consuming and therefore not many books were available. Upon the completion of the printing press literacy skyrocketed worldwide. Prior to the press, only the very wealthy could afford books, whereas after its invention, it would be possible for almost anyone to own a book.

The printing press made it possible for millions to receive the written word absolutely transforming learning. It profoundly impacted the political and religious climates of the time. Many believe it even led to the Industrial Revolution. Equally important was the Protestant Reformation, also following on the heels of the printing press, and leading to dramatic changes in the Catholic Church. In fact, no area of human endeavor was left untouched by Gutenberg's invention.

The Gutenberg Bible was printed in 1455 or 1456. At the time of printing, it is estimated that less than 5% of the German population could read. Within thirty to forty years, over 40,000 copies of the Bible were printed. Gutenberg himself printed almost 180

copies. Fewer than 50 copies of the original 180 are now believed to be in existence. The Bible had 282 pages. It was also known as the "Forty-Two Line Bible," referring to the number of lines on each page. An original copy can be found at the Library of Congress in Washington, DC. Today, a Gutenberg Bible coming on open market would sell for several million dollars. Individual pages, when available, sell for around $50,000.

Other than the Bible, Gutenberg and his partner, Johann Fust, cannot be credited with the printing of any other completed work. The date attributed to the printing of the first Bible is somewhat controversial. However, based on one of the few surviving copies, historians believe it can be dated with some certainty to 1456. A surviving copy exhibited at the Royal Library in Paris contains a memorandum written by Henry Cremer, Vicar of St. Stephin's Mentz, stating that it was illuminated and rubricated by him on St. Bartholomew's Day (August 24), 1456. In a second surviving copy there is a similar memorandum by the same person, stating that it was illuminated, bound, and finished by him on the Feast of the Assumption of the Virgin, August 15, 1456.

Tragically, Gutenberg died penniless. Shortly after printing his Bibles he lost everything due to a dispute with his partner Fust. Knowing little about printing, Fust began his relationship with Gutenberg as an investor in the development of the printing press, loaning a signifi-

cant amount of money to him. Eventually Fust became tired of waiting for repayment. He waited for nearly eight years. Fust lent money on three different occasions. The first time Gutenberg borrowed 150 gulden. When he went back a second time, he needed an additional 800. It was at that time Fust made Gutenberg sign a document making Fust an equal partner. Fust realized the potential of the investment and the possibility of seeing a great profit following the completion of the press. Fust insisted that the investment was not to fund Gutenberg's publishing ventures but to produce the Bible. As collateral, Gutenberg was forced to sign his equipment and the Bible itself over to Fust in case of a default on the loan or on its interest. In all, Gutenberg borrowed approximately 1,750 gulden. This was equivalent to about fifty-eight years of income for an average worker. Obviously, it was a significant amount of money. When Gutenberg finally printed the Bible in 1456, Fust called the note due. Gutenberg, not having sufficient funds to repay the debt, fought his creditor in court but eventually lost. In doing so, he lost all that he had, including his print shop and

his invention. Fust went on to make a fortune selling Bibles. Gutenberg's financial situation was so bad that he even received a yearly food subsidy from the Town of Mainz. The people of the town were happy to keep him alive due to the notoriety he brought to their town. He lived to be around 68 years old, and died in 1468.

From the early clay tablets to the invention of the printing press, man has come a long way in the development of the written word. To give you an idea of just how far, let's take a look back to the beginning of writing.

The earliest known books were on clay tablets. In 3500 BC clay tablets were used to communicate in Mesopotamia. This is the first known example of the written word. Years later, thousands of clay books on every imaginable subject were discovered in the Library of Nineveh.

Eventually, man began experimenting with other materials that could be used for writing. One of the major discoveries was the use of the papyrus plant in producing a writing surface. The term "paper" is derived from the Egyptian word papyrus. A technique was developed utilizing the papyrus plant, and began the journey that eventually led to the development of modern paper. Of all the writing and drawing materials people have used throughout history, paper is the most widely used around the world.

The Egyptians were pioneers in the development of papyrus, using the reeds growing along the banks of the Nile River. However, the papyrus plant is only one of the predecessors of paper. Other writing surfaces primarily made from the bark of mulberry, fig, and daphne trees, along with papyrus, are collectively known by the generic term "tapa," a writing surface used by ancient Egyptians, Greeks, and Romans. Extensively found in nearly every culture, the use of papyrus, or tapa, is considered the oldest papermaking technique. Recent archaeological excavations in China revealed some of the oldest tapa ever found. This discovery leads to the possibility that paper was being produced in China before western records began.

Papyrus itself was derived from the stems of the papyrus plants. The stems were cut into strips which were placed perpendicular to each other. The stems were then pressed together forming a scroll. Lastly, a stick was placed at the end of the scroll and hieroglyphics were written upon it. The scrolls had to be read only on the one side and therefore the reader had to unroll one side and roll up the other as he read. This was difficult to do and very cumbersome to use. Because of the cumbersome nature of scrolls, they were only used during the first several centuries for literary works. Early scrolls date back to 2500 BC, while the Dead Sea Scrolls are dated 150 BC – 40 AD. Throughout this time the quality of the scrolls continually improved.

Man's yearning for the printed word continued to inspire inventions. With each invention improvements were made in the development of the written word. The parchment codex was one of these ground-breaking inventions. Sheets of parchment were bound together much like a modern notebook. While good parchment appeared in the first and second century in the form of the scroll, this new, more convenient codex form largely replaced the scroll. It was another milestone in the progress of book printing itself. The parchment codex was favored for a variety of reasons. It was convenient to travel with, it saved tremendous space in the libraries of the world, and it was easier to read. But even with these benefits it did not catch on very easily, and the scroll continued to be popular. It was not until 300 AD that the codex achieved any type of notoriety at all. The codex, without question, was much more economical because both sides of the surface could be used. The amount of papyrus needed to create a codex was less than half of that needed

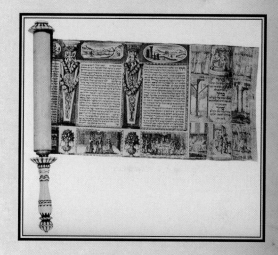

to form a scroll. The codex form of a book was easy to stack, easy to shelve, and easy to store. It was also much easier to handle, and the contents of the writing were easier to see and much more accessible to the reader. The shift from the roll to the codex was inevitable.

Among the first people to use the codex were early Christians dating back to the times of the Apostles. Only Christian books used the codex form where Arabic or Jewish books did not. Even with all the benefits, it took several hundred years to make the switch from the scroll to the codex form of the book. It is believed that the switch came due to the widespread use of books by Christians and the sweeping impact of Christianity in those days across the world. But the scroll continued to survive.

During Pope Gregory's days, around 1590, the papyrus, the scroll, the wax tablet, and the parchment codex were all used in book production. The Romans used wax tablets, which were books made from wood boards hollowed out so that wax could be layered into the wood. Indentations were then made in the wax with metal tools. Pope Gregory was tremendously committed to the written word and therefore to books. Because of his influence there was a great demand for books throughout Rome and beyond. Rome also began exporting books to other countries, and so the history of the book continued to grow.

By the ninth century, books and book production were a major part of cultural and educational life in Europe. In the Middle Ages paper became more common. Although less durable and harder to write on than parchment, paper was certainly a lot cheaper. By the fourteenth century it was available to anyone who wanted it at a very inexpensive price. Paper was made from rags, usually a linen cloth. The rags were left to rot for four or five days and then placed into a mill. The rotting rags changed into a pulp which had long fibers. Hundreds of gallons of the pulp would then be switched to a large vat where it was kept stirred and warm. The pulp would then be drained through a mold which left matted fibers that would form newly made pieces of paper. In those days, two men could produce 3,000 pieces of paper a day. With the abundance and increasing use of paper, a proliferation of writing emerged that dramatically raised the literacy of the middle class. Then came Gutenberg, and the rest is history.

Many of the techniques and inventions used throughout history contributed to the development and refinement of the written word. Gutenberg combined many of these technologies using paper, ink, and a press to revolutionize the world through the invention of the printing press. His invention of reusable type allowed for mass production of the printed word and for the first time in history, the written word was available to the masses.

The earliest printed books were called incunabula, a biblical word taken from the Latin that means swaddling clothes or infancy. The book trade frequently refers to its meaning as "from the cradle." The term incunabula has become the term to describe books printed from the birth of printing in 1455 or 1456 to around 1501.

The following chronological table will give you a more complete history of the evolution of the printed word and of the book.

CHRONOLOGICAL LISTING OF BOOKS & PRINTING

3500 BC The clay tablets of the Babylonians and Assyrians are among the earliest known books. A triangular stylus was used to press the cuneiform alphabet into the clay. They were often stored in clay envelopes that protected them much like modern book covers do today.

2500 BC The Papyrus Scroll, made from the Cyperus papyrus plant found growing on the banks of the Nile River, was used by the Egyptians to write their hieroglyphics using a pen made from cyperus reeds. The scroll was made by cutting the Cyperus plant stems into thin strips that were laid, slightly overlapping, side by side. They were pounded together to form sheets that were glued together and wound around a wooden stick to form a scroll.

2400 BC Animal skins, because of their pliable nature, replaced the brittle papyrus scroll moving us toward the modern style of the book, known as the codex form.

950 BC Leather becomes a primary source for scrolls and writing.

600 BC Mediterranean cultures collaborate to develop a common writing system. Reading and writing will be done in a left-to-right fashion.

295 BC King Ptolemy I Soter I called for the collection of all known books in the world. All sovereigns and governors were requested to turn over works in all areas of literature, including poetry, history, medicine, and many others. Originals were confiscated and kept in the Alexandria library, and only transcripts were eventually returned to the owners.

200 BC Wax Tablets, a form of books used by the

Romans, were made from pieces of wood with a slight hollow indentation layered with blackened wax. An iron stylus, shaped much like a pencil, was used to make carvings in the wax. The wood pieces or tablets could then be joined together like a three-ringed binder. The Latin name for this was codex from the word for wood.

150 BC   Hebrew and Aramaic documents known as the Dead Sea Scrolls were found sealed in ceramic pots in caves near the Dead Sea in 1957. The approximate dates of the scrolls are 150 BC – 40 AD.

100 BC   The codex book form began to replace the scroll.

47 AD   The Library of Alexandria, said to contain copies and translations of all known books, was heavily damaged by fire. Tens of thousands of documents were lost.

100 AD   Ts'ai Lun of China is known as the father of true paper. Ts'ai Lun developed and refined the process of making paper from macerated hemp fibers suspended in water.

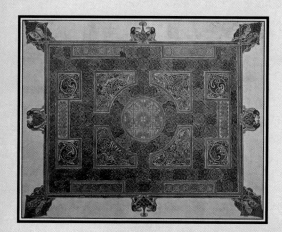

687 AD   An actual manuscript copy of The Gospel of St. John was buried with the body of St. Cuthbert, a bishop near Lindesfarne. Two hundred years later the wooden casket was opened by Danish invaders revealing the perfectly preserved manuscript. This stands as one of history's most sensational book exhumations. Known now as the Lindesfarne Gospels.

750 AD   Between 750 AD and the eleventh century papermaking spread through many coun-

tries. By 950 AD it had reached Baghdad, Damascus, and Cairo. It reached Spain in the eleventh century and Italy in the thirteenth.

751 AD   Papermaking reached the Islamic world.

868 AD   The first book was hand printed on paper originated in China. The book contained Buddhist scripts printed in block letters.

1250   The first fore edge painting appeared on a French Psalter manuscript.

1276   Watermarking was developed at one of the Fabriano Mills in Tuscany. This important invention allowed a product to have a branded trademark of its own. A collection of Fabriano watermarks contains watermarks dating from 1276 until modern times.

1373   The Bibliotheque Nationale is founded. The library consists of approximately 1000 titles housed in the Louvre.

1418   The oldest known specimen of a woodcut is dated to 1418.

1456   Gutenberg printed his 42 line Bible in Mainz, Germany, on the highest quality paper. In 1476 William Caxton introduced printing to England. The following year, England printed the first color illustrated book in St. Albans, a Mainz Psalter by Fust and Schoffer.

1465   The first dry point engraved prints appear in the *Master of the Housebook* in Germany.

1468   On February 3, Gutenberg dies.

1469   For the first time the roller appeared in German bookbinding.

1472   The first printed edition of Dante's *Divine Comedy*.

1477   *Monte Sancto di Dio*, the first book containing intaglio illustrations, was published in Florence.

1493   Daniel Hopfer is the first to use the technique of etching.

1517   The differences between Martin Luther and the Roman Catholic Church become widespread. Many believe this is due to the mass printing and distribution of revolutionary ideas for the first time including the printing of the Bible in German.

1521   The Cambridge University Press is founded.

1537   All books printed by French presses were required to deliver a copy to the royal library, The Bibliotheque Nationale.

1549   The first complete edition of the Book of Common Prayer is printed.

1642	Ludwig von Siegen invented the mezzotint, or half-tint.
1690	The first American paper mill was established in Germantown, Pennsylvania.
1709	England introduced The Copyright Act.
1734	Jean-Baptiste Le Prince invented the process of aquatint. Francois Janinet first employed it for color prints. Later it was often combined with etching, dry point, and line engraving. It was a favorite technique of Pablo Picasso in the twentieth century.
1738	Gottfried Engelmann was born. He became a lithograph printer and later invented the technique of chromolithography in 1836.
1753	The national Library of Britain is founded.
1755	William Edwards of Yorkshire founded the Edwards of Halifax binding firm. The firm went on to patent transparent vellum bindings and popularized the art of fore edge painting.
1765	Joseph Nicephore Niepce, the future inventor of photography (1822), was born.
1770	The first English handmade paper is developed by James Whitman.
1787	Louis Jacq. Mande Daguerre (1787 – 1851) develops the daguerreotype process.
1798	Senefelder invents lithography.
1799	The Rosetta stone is cut containing the same text in Greek and Egyptian hieroglyphic. Discovered in 1799 near the mouth of the Nile, the stone led to the decoding of ancient Egyptian works.
1800	The Library of Congress is founded in Washington, DC.
1804	George Baxter patented the letterpress process for color printing.
1811	The Chiswick Press is founded.
1812	The Cylinder Press is built by Friedrich Konig in Britain.
1816	Joseph Zaehnsdorf was born. He later became a craftsman bookbinder.
1817	The first machine to make paper in America was built at Brandywine, Delaware.
1829	America manufactured the Fourdrinier paper machine for the first time.

1829	Braille is invented and introduced by Louis Braille.
1832	Philip Watt of London invented the sewing machine. Eventually this became an important instrument in bookbinding.
1837	Chromolithography is used for the first time.
1838	A unique method of color printing was patented by Charles Knight. Blocks of wood or metal rotated and impressed images onto sheets of paper.

1843	Wood is used for paper making for the first time.
1852	America introduced its first coated stock paper.
1854	The first American wood pulp paper was made in Buffalo, New York.
1860	The first use of buckram for book covers is recorded.
1863	A rotary useful letterpress is invented by Bullock.
1878	The typecasting machine is invented by Wicks.
1884	The Grolier Society is founded.
1889	Meggendorfer popularizes pop-up and moveable illustrations and books.
1906	The International Antiquarian Bookseller Association is established.
1947	International League of Antiquarian Booksellers (I.C.A.B.) is established.
1949	The A.B.A.A. — Antiquarian Booksellers Association of America is established.

A Brief History of Bookbindings

The art of bookbinding began over two thousand years ago, long before the first printed book appeared. Originally, bindings were designed to protect handwritten manuscripts. Over time, as the method of printing evolved, so did the art of bookbinding. The bindings became increasingly sophisticated, durable, and ornate, taking many different forms. In fact, bookbinding took on a life of its own, becoming a unique art form.

Some of the earliest bindings were made of papyrus boards. The boards consisted of several layers of papyrus paper pressed together forming a thick protective covering for the written manuscript. As bindings developed, a variety of materials were used to create the boards including wood, different types of paper, and even rope. Rope bindings or roll board, became very popular and quite common.

Exquisite bindings were crafted from ivory, brass, copper, and expensive jewels. Many bindings were even made of gold. Italian and French craftsman created exquisite gold leaf bindings. Fabrics including silk and velvet became popular and these bindings were often further adorned with expensive jewels, such as rubies, emerald, amethyst, and pearls.

Egyptians and the Coptic Church of Egypt are credited with the perfection of early bookbinding. Their bindings not only represent some of the finest craftsmanship ever seen, they also showcase the finest materials known to man. These bindings were adorned with jewels, gold, silver, and ivory. In time, the art of bookbinding spread to other cultures and continents as well.

As bookbinding migrated from Central Asia to Iran, and on to the Arabian Peninsula and Anatolia, each region characterized its bindings by using motifs unique to its culture. More frequently used designs included arabesques and motifs as seen on doors of mosques. In fact, by the fifteenth century, most bindings were done by monks within monasteries.

When calligraphy developed, copies of religious works proliferated. These works were protected by beautiful bindings, maintaining a high degree of refinement and elegance. Due to the superb quality of the bindings, the cost of books remained beyond what the middle and lower classes could afford, limiting ownership to only the very wealthy.

Eventually, bindings were made affordable to a larger percentage of the population. European countries used wood, mainly oak, for their bindings. The American colonies relied on birch, maple, and sometimes oak in binding production. In the late seventeenth century, paste boards were often used by publishers in book production due to the low cost of boards. As this became popular, they continued to be used as an inexpensive way to bind books. Now buyers could take these books to a binder of choice and request a specific type of binding. To keep cost down, many collectors repeatedly chose designs and bindings that were similar, if not the same, as previously purchased bindings.

Leather, another excellent binding material, was seen as early as the fifth century. Eventually, special crafting tools were developed solely for the purpose of enhancing leather bindings. The popularity of leather bindings expanded in the late seventeenth century and became the preferred binding material for many reasons. Foremost, it is durable and withstands many types of environments. It is flexible, lightweight, and most of all, abundant. Leather skins being prepared for use as bindings were lined, de-haired, vetted and finally immersed in a tanning solution. After tanning, leather is a pale, honey-colored shade. Once bound, leather can be enhanced and colored in a limitless variety of ways.

The popularity of leather was also due in part to the large variety of leather types. The most common types of leather were Oasis Goat and Levant, a heavy, coarse-grained Moroccan leather. Vellum, a type of leather made from the skin of calf, lamb, or goat, was also used. While not undergoing the tanning process, the vellum was degreased and treated in a special way.

The Industrial Revolution ushered in technology that allowed and resulted in massive book production. With the invention of the printing press, the availability and popularity of the printed book spread throughout the world. Demand for books dramatically increased, resulting in an explosion of printing businesses. Printers, bookbinders, and designers increased in number at an astronomical rate. Individual practitioners of the trade established their own businesses, producing fine books and bindings at an affordable rate. As the number of printed books increased, naturally, the art of bookbinding increased as well. Around the globe, many gifted craftsman took up the trade of bookbinding.

When Johann Gutenberg changed the world with the invention of the movable type printing press, mankind received one of the greatest gifts of all time. Through the printed book, information and knowledge were made available to all. By the late 1400s, it is estimated that between six and seven million books had been printed.

TYPES OF LEATHER

Leather for binding is done by soaking raw animal skin, calf or goat, in a bath of oak bark. This process is called canning. The following is a list of different types of leather:

BUCK LEATHER. It is suede finished and oil tanned. It is soft and strong.

CALF SKIN. Calf skin has a smooth, dense surface and a fine grain. The hair follicle pattern is intermittent. It is usually vegetable tanned. It is often dyed, wrinkled, and splattered for different effects. Because it takes dyes well, it has been used extensively for bindings.

CHAMOIS. Leather made from the skins of wild animals and tanned by rubbing different types of oils or fat into the skin. This leather is generally yellow and very supple.

CRUSHED LEATHER. Crushed refers to morocco leather that has been pulverized, or crushed, to make it very smooth.

GOAT SKIN. Goat skin leather is characterized by parallel rows of hair pores lying in the grooves of the grain, which is very pronounced. Wide varieties of pigments and stain can be used on goat skin.

LEVANT LEATHER. A heavy coarse-grained leather, originally made from large Moroccan goats, which are now extinct. Levant leather seen today is from large goats from the Cape of Good Hope, and these bindings have been called Cape Morocco bindings.

MOTTLED LEATHER. Leather stained with wax or ferrous sulfate to create a mottling effect that looks like animal or cat paws or blotches.

NIGER LEATHER. Leather made from the skins of small Nigerian goats. A tough flexible goatskin that has a fine grain.

OASIS LEATHER. Morocco leather from African goats. A second quality niger morocco.

OOZE LEATHER. A calf skin or split sheepskin made to look like velvet or suede. Has a smooth glove-like feel.

PERSIAN LEATHER. Leather made from a small goat in Persia characterized by a small grain. It is very soft but not very durable.

PIG SKIN. This leather has a follicle pattern made up of groups of three that are easily seen upon inspection. The grain is weak. Over time this leather becomes tough, brittle, and difficult to work on. Therefore it is not used as often as other skins. Used usually for covering heavy books.

RUSSIAN LEATHER OR DICED CALF. A term used for calf leather that is tanned with willow bark and birch tar oil. It is characterized by a finished checked pattern. This tanning process originated in Russia, giving it its name. Because of the birch bark oils used, the leather has a unique odor. Once dyed, the leather is usually red or reddish brown.

SEAL SKIN. Takes many types of processing easily, resulting in many different looks, such as acid marbling. It is known for its shiny appearance.

SHEEP SKIN. Sheep skin leather has a smooth surface and a less pronounced grain. Hair pores are arranged in groupings rather than in rows. While very soft with minimal grain, sheep skin is easily scuffed or marked.

SPRINKLED LEATHER. Leather sprinkled with dye, ink or acid, giving it a sprinkled effect or speckled surface.

STAINED LEATHER. Leather tanned using a wide variety of dyes resulting in many different looks. Bookbinders became creative in designing different types of bindings by using this process.

STRAIGHT GRAINED LEATHER. Leather with the grain running in only one direction. Usual colors were red, green, black, and blue.

TREE PROCESS. Calf leather processed with acid to create a wood grain or tree trunk effect. Often referred to as tree calf, it looks like burl wood or roots from a tree. In the mid 1800s it evolved into producing the form of an entire tree on the binding itself. This process continued with tree calf bindings until about 1925.

VELLUM. The skin of a young calf, goat, or lamb used for the pages or binding of books. Its durability made it the choice material for books that received much use, such as school books and bibles. Heavier books made from wood were often covered with vellum and then decorated with beautiful blind tooling, hand-painted ornaments, or jewels. Many bindings were finished with a brass clasp.

PERIOD BINDINGS

Many bindings appearing in this book fall within specific periods of time, like the Neoclassic period seen during the time of Napoleon. In France it was the

Empire, in England, the Regency. American motifs on bindings are referred to as the Federal period. These type bindings feature laurels, Greek keys, and other designs of the specific periods. The styles remain popular still today. The beauty of mosaic bindings are seen in the intricate patterns of leather inlays, exhibiting different colors and geometric designs. Some mosaic bindings have geometric designs with borders of gold. Mosaics decompose rapidly and are therefore rare. The bindings of the Romantic period exhibit a swirling, ornate design. Many colors, onlays, and designs depicting paintings and floral patterns on the bindings were unique to the Vogue period. The Art Deco period predictably showcased many geometric designs.

CRAFTSMANSHIP

Ultimately, the quality of bookbinding comes down to the quality of craftsmanship. The binding often is worth more than the book itself. Creating and designing bindings is time consuming and a unique form of art and, as this book demonstrates, has a value all its own. Even today, often the binding, not the writing, determines the value of a book.

Throughout history books have been a treasure to many famous people. Different materials used in creating the bindings appealed to different taste. Monarchs became very involved and interested in bookbinding and even seem to have favorite types of bindings. Henry VIII was fond of beautiful leathers and velvet bindings. George III had a fondness for calf and sheep skin bindings. Napoleon was known to favor vellum. Queen Victoria was partial to inlayed and jewel encrusted bindings. Wealthy buyers preferred Moroccan leather styled with gold and elaborate designs. Often, price was of no concern to book collectors.

There were many sought-after craftsmen in bookbinding. Two superb craftsmen that immediately come to mind are William Edwards of Halifax and Roger Payne. Edwards specialized in Etruscan and vellum bindings. He created some of the finest, most beautifully simplistic bookbindings ever seen. In 1785 he patented a method of making vellum transparent and he and his sons revitalized the art of fore-edge painting. Payne, a native of Windsor and a London bookbinder, introduced richly tooled corner pieces and ornamental doublures. He also invented the graining of Morocco known as straight grain. Both Payne's and Edwards's books are in great demand to this day.

As the number of bookbinders increased, lower and lower standards began to emerge. In response to this decline in quality, a group of artists and craftsman, led by William Morris, began to set up their own businesses designing and publishing books of a superior quality. This practice continued into the 1900s when many private book presses emerged. Although most of these private presses were more involved in the printing aspect of books, they were often associated with master binders. Today, these books command premium prices.

The following are names of the more prominent private presses up to 1935, along with the year they were founded:

Appledore Press — 1870 in Connecticut
Argonau Press — 1926
Ashendene — 1894 by St. John Hornby
Ballantyne Press — 1796 by James Ballantyne
Beaumont Press — 1917. Specialized in hand-printed editions.
Boars Head Press — 1930 by Sandford
Bremers Press — 1911
Cayme Press — 1923 by Humphrey Toulmin. Specialized in heraldic and genealogical books.
Caradoc Press — 1899
Chiswick Press — 1811
Cloister Press — 1921 by Charles Hobson.
Clover Hill Press — 1931 by Douglas Cleverdon

Cranach Press — 1912 by Von Kessler
Cuala Press — 1903 by Elizabeth Corbert Yeats
Doves — 1900 by T.J. Cobden-Sanderson. Focused on the beauty of the letterforms and structure of the letters.
Einhorn Press — 1909 by Melchior Lechters
Elston Press — 1900 by Clarke Conwell
Eragny Press — 1894 by Lucien Pissaro
Essex House Press — 1898 by C.R. Ashbee
Favil Press — 1920 by P. Sainsburg
Flying Fame Press — 1912 by Claude Lovat Fraser
Florence Press — 1908
Golden Cockerel Press — Founded in 1923, specializing in the blending of text with original wood engravings. Golden Cockerel produced some of the finest illustrated books of the twentieth century, most notably with The Canterbury Tales (1929 – 31) in four volumes.
Golden Hind Press — 1927 by Arthur Wisner Rushmore
Grabhorn Press — 1919 by Edwin & Robert Grabhorn
Gregynog Press — 1927 by D. Cohen & A. Myers
Hand and Flower Press — 1939
Harris Press — 1890 by Charles Harris
High House Press — 1924 by James Masters
Hogart Press — 1917 by L. and Virginia Woolf
Hours Press — 1928 by Nancy Cunard
Kelmscott Press — 1891 by William Morris and Emery Walker
Kunera Press — 1910
Mall Press — 1916 by Emery Walker
Marion Press — 1896 by Frank Hopkins, this was an early American press.
Mosher Press — 1891 by Thomas Bird Mosher
Nonesuch Press — 1923 by Sir Francis Meynell. Dedicated to making books as attractive as possible in a very exclusive way.
Oriole Press — 1926 by Joseph Ishill
Ovid Press — 1919 by John Rodker
Pear Tree Press — 1899 by James Guthrie
Pelican Press — 1916 by Francis Meynell
Perpetua Press — 1911 by David Bland
Polidori Press — 1840 by Gaetano Polidori
Purington Rollins Press — 1911 by Carl Purington Rollins
Raven Press — 1931
Riccardi Press — 1909
Rochester Press — 1888 by Henry Houghton
Roycroft Press — 1856 by Elbert Hubbard
Rupprecht Press — 1914 by Fritz Helmut Ehmcke
Sale Hill Press — 1904 by G. A. Hammond
Shakespeare Head Press — 1904 by A.H. Bullen.

Stanbrook Abbey Press — 1876 by Benedictine Monks
Swan Press — 1921 by Sydney Matthewman
Temple Sheen Press — 1911 by Arthur Sabin
Three Mountains Press — 1922 by William Bird
Trovillion Press — 1908 by Hal Trovillion
Unicorn Press — 1895 by Ernest Oldmeadow
Vale Press — 1894 by Charles Ricketts
Westminster Press — 1878 by Archibald Doughlas
Zilver Distel Press — 1910

SIGNED BINDING

The familiar expression "signed binding" indicates that a book contains the printed or stamped name of the original binder and/or company somewhere on the book. It may appear on the dentelle (the inner gilt border on the inner edge of the cover), on the doublure (the inside lining of the cover), on the top or bottom corner of the end papers (the extra leaves added to the front or back of the book), or even tooled into the leather binding itself in an inconspicuous place. See the diagram on this page for an example of a binder's imprint.

Binding Signature Detail
THE ROSE BINDERY-BOSTON

Many book collectors look for these types of bindings. Depending on the craftsmanship or fame of the binder, the signature can add significance and value to the book. Listed are some of the better known eighteenth, nineteenth, and twentieth century binders. Look at some of your books for these binders' names. You will be surprised to find that you already own some of their fine work.

Period Binders Bath. England.
Signature Detail

BINDERS

There are hundreds of great binders. Here is a listing of some of them.

Adams	Lewis
Alman	Leightonson & Hodge
Andrews	Maclehose
Atelier	Marcourt
Bayntun	Mercier
Benett	Moore
Bentley	Morley
Blackwell	Morrell
Bickers & Son	Morrell, Harrison & Sons
Birdsall & Son	Nutt
Blacket, J.	Old Monastery Hill Bindery
Bone, W. and Son	Orrock & Son
Bookends Bindery	Oxford
Booklovers Bindery	Parsonnet
Boston Bookbinding Co.	Payne
Bowes & Bowes	Ramage
Bradstreet	Relfe Brothers
Carss & Co.	Remnant & Edmonds
Cross	Reynolds
de Coverley	Riverside
Dent	Riviere
Drake, R. Ingram	Roach
Edmund & Remnants	Root
Edwards	Rose
Frost & Company	Sangorski & Sutcliffe
Genova, A. of Venice	Schulze, Otto
Hale & Roworth	Seton & MacKenzie
Hanson & Sloan	Sickles
Hatchards	Simpson & Renshaw
Hawes	Smith, R. W.
Henderson & Biggett	Sotheran & Company
Henry Botheran	Stikeman
Henry Young & Sons	Strong
Herring	Tout
Himbaugh & Browne	Trow, John F. & Son
Hoach	Truslove
Hogg	Truslove & Hanson
Holloway	Tucket
Hood, S.	Wallis
Kalthoeber	Wilbee
Larkins	Wright
Lauder	Young
Lauder & MacDonald	Zaehnsdorf
Lawrence	

Armorial Binding, from the
Dolinsky collection.

Cambridge Binding.

Cathedral Binding.

Cosway Binding.

Cottage Binding. From the
Dolinsky collection.

The following is a list of some different types of bindings and an explanation of each. Examples of many of these bindings are in the price guide section of this book.

TYPES OF BINDINGS

ARMORIAL BINDING. A binding adorned with the coat of arms, usually in gilt, of a previous owner (either the original or a subsequent owner). The term also includes bookplates incorporating the owner's arms. It also describes armorial decorated books. *See example.*

BRADEL BINDING. A temporary binding with uncut edges. The spine is usually of linen or leather.

BUCKRAM BINDING. A hard-wearing waxed cloth binding.

CAMBRIDGE BINDING. An English style binding. Features two different colors of brown leather which are created by using an acid wash on the leather in order to leave a rectangular panel surrounded by a leather frame. *See example.*

CAMEO BINDING. Books with an inset or a stamped cameo, coin, or artifact on the covers or inside covers.

CATHEDRAL BINDING. Bindings decorated with cathedrals or Gothic architecture. *See example.*

CHAMPLEVÉ BINDING. Book covers that are enameled. Designs were cut in thin sheets of gold or copper, and the area between these thin sheets and the wooden boards were filled with enamel. Made mostly in the thirteenth century, although copied in the 1800s.

COSWAY BINDING. Cosway bindings first appeared in the twentieth century. These bindings, usually made of Moroccan leather, were adorned with hand-painted ivory or porcelain miniatures inset on the book boards. The ivory could appear on the inside or outside of the boards and were protected by a sheet of glass covering the ivory. J. H. Stonehouse developed a series of designs and then commissioned the Riviere bindery to produce some fine bindings with these designs. In the early 1900s, C. B. Currie designed miniature paintings resembling the style and use of watercolors of Richard Cosway. Ms. Currie is well known for her work on fore-edge paintings which remain in great demand today. She often signed and numbered her work in books, further enhancing their value. An example of her work appears on page 167 of this book. *See example.*

COTTAGE BINDING. The framework of a design that was tooled on a cover resembling the gable of a house. It was used mostly in the mid-1600s to the 1700s as a book decoration and became very popular in England. *See example.*

DICED BINDING. A ruled pattern of diamonds on the leather covers. *See example.*

Diced Binding.

EMBOSSED BINDING. Covers of leather which before being attached to the book had a design impressed on the sides and the spine — a process called bas-relief. It was done with a heated dye and a counter dye. Many European publishers of Bibles and prayer books began using these bindings. Embossed bindings in Morocco became very popular. *See example.*

Embossed Binding.

EMBROIDERED BINDING. Bindings covered with velvet, silk, or canvas that have designs which were done in gold or silver thread and colored silks. Sometimes they even had pearls or sequins. The earliest known English embroidered cover is from the thirteenth century. In the sixteenth and seventeenth centuries, embroidered bindings became popular in England, especially bindings under the Tudors and Stuarts. They were also known as needlework bindings or textile bindings. *See example.*

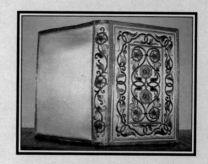

Embroidered Binding.

ETRUSCAN BINDING. These were decorated with patterns of Etruscan vases and other classical ornaments, usually from calf skin. Panels on each cover are encased by borders of various classical designs. This was perfected by William Edwards of Halifax in the 1700s. The method was to brush acid on the calf skin, thus burning the design into the leather. *See example.*

Etruscan Binding.

EXTRA BOUND BINDING. The boards were laced by cords with a hollow back and a morocco cover. All the edges were gilt. End papers were usually outstanding. Great detail was done in perfecting the head bands. Special attention was paid to details. The more gold tooling the better. *See example.*

Extra Bound Binding.

Flame Stitch Binding.

Fore-edge Binding.

Geometric Binding.

Gutta Percha Binding.

Ivory Binding.

FAN BINDING. The central design on the board of the book was an opened fan. These were found in France and Italy in the 1700s and early 1800s.

FLAME STITCH BINDING. A design etched in the covers with acid to form a "flame" pattern, similar to some early tree calf books. *See example.*

FORE-EDGE BINDING. The fore edge is the edge of the book, opposite the spine. A fore edge binding has a hand-painted painting or design drawn on this edge. They are extremely popular and quite expensive. These books have become very rare since there were not very many of them made. Original examples are hard to find, and there are thousands of reproductions that have flooded the market. Most of these fore edge reproductions are being produced on old books. Even these fore edge books have value. However, the older fore edge books are worth between $400 and $10,000 each. Under the book term section, please look at two definitions entitled "Edwards of Halifax" and "Fore Edge Paintings" for more information on fore edge books. *See example.*

FOREL BINDING. Oak boards were covered with roughly dressed unsplit sheep skin. They were used primarily by monks going back as far as the eighth and ninth centuries in England.

GEOMETRIC BINDING. A binding whose covers are designed with geometric patterns. *See example.*

GIFT BINDING. A leather binding done for presentation. Sometimes these are done for schools, Christmas presents, and for books given annually.

GOUACHE. Bindings which have a chalking appearance — often beautiful, hand-painted scenes are painted onto these bindings. Water-soluble paints differing from watercolors in that gouache uses glue to bind the pigments and the lighter tones contain white pigment, which means they're opaque rather than transparent. The bindings have a see-through depth in appearance.

GOLD BINDING. Very expensive and rare bindings. Few examples are available. These are bindings of which the boards were overlaid with panels of thinly beaten gold that were inlaid with silver, enamel, or jewels. These bindings were made as early as the seventh century.

GUTTA PERCHA BINDING. Gutta percha comes from the guttiferous tree found in the Pacific Rim, particularly around Singapore. There is much confusion as to what gutta percha actually is. Literally, it describes a residue from latex, dried after collection from different types of guttiferous trees; it is basically a rubber based material. It was one of the first natural plastics to be exploited by man. It is chemically the same as rubber, but the shape of its molecule gives it a different property. This substance was used in making bookbindings in the 1600s. However, it wasn't very popular or practical. A similar product called caoutchouc, pronounced "cow-chook" replaced the gutta percha and was easier to use and more practical. It was basically a rubber gum and was considered to be an adhesive binding. The bindings that we now call gutta percha are really not gutta percha, but are caoutchouc bindings. Since no one ever stopped calling them gutta percha bindings, we continue to call these caoutchouc bindings gutta percha. *See example.*

IVORY BINDING. Often made of all ivory but also with mixed materials. An example of an ivory, gold, celluloid, and bronze binding on a Jewish prayer book is shown. *See example.*

JANSENIST BINDING. French binding with richly tooled doublures but little if any decoration or ornamentation on the outer boards.

JEWEL BINDING. Examples of these bindings by Sangorski & Sutcliffe or Riviere are rare and command large prices. Some took an artist as long as 13 months to make and generally are "one of a kind." They are original, as usually just one was commissioned or produced. Bindings sometimes were of gold, silver, or silver gilt that were encrusted with semi-precious stones, many times surrounded by an ivory plaque. They date back as far as the seventh century. These bindings became more available in the twentieth century. Binders such as Sangorski and Sutcliffe made jewel bindings where the jewels were set in metal cups with small base plates. The plates were pasted to the mill board, the bases being hidden by the leather of the cover which was cut so that only the jewel and the rim of its cup could be seen. Several examples of these twentieth century bindings are available online with www.abebooks.com, and are listed between $10,000 to $75,000. *See example.*

Jewel Binding.

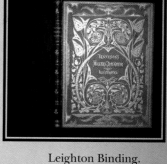

Leighton Binding.

Limp Binding.

Mauchline Binding.

Mauchline Binding.

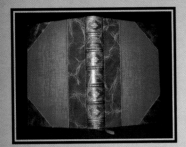

Marbled Binding.

Marbled Binding.

Mottled Binding.

OnLay Binding.

Painted Binding.

Papier Mache Binding.

LACE BINDING. Binding made of rare French lace. They used elaborate tooling of broad lace-like borders covering most of the cover and often had a small space in the center of the board for a shield or armorial decoration or an artifact. These bindings date back as far as the eighth century. They were created by the French. Nearly all early examples have disintegrated. Copies that are available cost as much as $80,000.

LACQUERED BINDING. Usually from Persia, Turkey, or India. Boards were given seven coats of lacquer, and then gold colors were painted on the cover and sometimes miniature designs were included.

LEIGHTON BINDING. A binding created by the hand of John Leighton (1822 – 1912), one of the most productive and creative designers of bookbindings in the nineteenth century. He was particularly famous for his ability to detail groups of objects or designs within small areas. His work was signed with his initials. *See example.*

LIMP BINDING. A style of binding books with thin, flexible covers usually made without boards and limp in your hands unlike the stiffness of most leather bindings. *See example.*

MAUCHLINE BINDING. A binding usually made of sycamore and decorated with decals of famous places or things. *See examples.*

MARBLED BINDING. A binding where a pattern etched with acids gives a marbled effect on the boards. *See examples.*

MONNIER BINDING. Mosaic inlaid Chinese landscapes, or birds and scenes. Invented by Louis Monnier.

MOSAIC BINDING. A binding which began in the 1500s. Its decoration is based on formal geometric designs with a centrally placed medallion, square, or rectangle on the front or rear board as a background for arms or monograms. Mosaic bindings also had leaves and flowers in onlays of colored leathers, and they were usually displayed around a central oval. These books were decorated with inlays and onlays of leather.

MOTTLED BINDING. A binding which has been given a mottled effect by staining the leather with blots or flecks by using an acid. *See example.*

ONLAY BINDING. From the Art Nouveau era, onlay is the use of thin leather strips or pieces applied on top of a substrate. When you onlay a binding you decorate the binding with thin, multicolored pieces of leather which gives a mosaic effect. *See example.*

PAINTED BINDING. A binding whose front or back board is hand painted with a design or scene. *See example.*

PAPIER MACHE. A grayish substance made from paper pulp. When hardened it could be used in forming boards for bookbinding. Even though it is a French sounding name, papier mache was not made in France until the mid seventeenth century. Papier mache actually originates from China. They used it to make helmets, which they toughened by many layers of lacquer. Papier mache is French for "chewed paper." Famous English bookmaker John Baskerville, well known for his fine quality books, began to copy the lacquered pieces from Japan in 1740. His assistant, Henry Clay, invented a way to produce papier mache so strong that it was equally as durable as wood and began using it for bookbinding. *See example.*

PEASANT BINDING. Crudely made bindings generally from Germany. Usually found on Bibles sold to the masses. Many have religious scenes painted on the boards and occasionally colored paper scenes were pasted on. Used during the 1600s.

PRESENTATION BINDING. Generally a binding that was presented to someone to commemorate an occasion or to honor someone. An inscription or name is usually engraved in the front cover. *See example.*

PRIZE BINDING. Books that have been given to students for high marks in a certain subject. The school will usually paste a paper plaque in the inside cover with the student's name and what his achievement is. These bindings will usually have the logo, inscription, or motto of the school embossed or stamped on the front cover. *See example.*

PUBLISHERS BINDING. A cased binding or an edition binding supplied by the publisher to the trade. *See example.*

RELIEVO BINDING. A process whereby leather is softened, then formed and deeply embossed. A raised surface or image is created. Relievo, of Italian origin, means "relief." *See examples.*

Presentation Binding.

Prize Binding.

Prize Binding.

Publishers Binding.

Relievo Binding.

Relievo Binding.

Royal Binding.

Sprinkled Binding.

Sterling or Silver Binding.

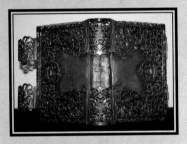

Sterling or Silver Binding. From the Dolinsky collection.

Tartan Binding.

RETROSPECTIVE BINDING. A binding which is a copy, imitation, or reproduction of a binding that was used or created years before.

ROYAL BINDING. A term used to describe bindings that have a sovereignty coat of arms or initials. It may or may not have belonged to a member of the Royal Family. An example is the Book of Common Prayer which is a Royal Binding from one of the Royal Chapels. *See example.*

SCORED CALF BINDING. Calf treated by a compression process that produces a crinkled effect, looking like a coarse straight-grain Morocco.

SOMBRE BINDING. Blind tooled black velvet or black cloth with the edges blackened. Found in Bibles before 1750.

SPRINKLED BINDING. Used primarily on calf bindings and it means the binding is colored with small specks or spots. It can also be done on the page ends. *See example.*

STERLING OR SILVER BINDING. Bindings made of 92% silver are sterling. 90% silver is called coin silver bindings and 80% silver usually originates from France or Germany. Usually very elaborate and reticulated in design. *See examples.*

SUEDE BINDING. Used primarily in the late nineteenth and early twentieth centuries.

TARTAN BINDING. Usually made with sycamore wood as is the mauchline binding. This binding is decorated with Scottish patterns usually in red or green. *See example.*

TORTOISE SHELL BINDING. A rare binding made from the shell of a tortoise.

TRADE BINDING. No frills bindings that were generally very plain calf or sheep bindings. It's also another name for the publisher's binding. A publisher of a book usually bought the book, which was unbound, and called it the trade binding or enclosed it in wrappers and took it to their own binder to have it bound in a more elaborate binding. Used extensively in the 1700s and 1800s. *See example.*

TREE CALF BINDING. A calf binding that has the boards stained by mixing copperas and pearl ash to a design of a tree or tree trunk. Used in books printed in the late 1700s, to resemble veneer of furniture or roots. Popular from 1840 to 1925. *See example.*

Trade Binding.

TRANSPARENT BINDING. Bindings treated with pearl ash to make them look transparent. They were covered in vellum. This was patented by Edwards of Halifax around 1780.

VELLUM BINDING. Made from the skin of a young goat, calf, or lamb. *See example.*

VELVET BINDING. A favorite of Henry VIII, these are bindings covered with velvet. They were mostly popular with the English, and have been around from the 1500s through the 1800s. They are used primarily for prayer books. In most examples the velvet has faded. Usually purple or dark blue in color. An example of a velvet binding in perfect condition can be seen. *See example.*

Tree Calf Binding.

VENETIAN BINDING. They were made of goat skin or Morocco. Wood was sometimes used. They usually featured a leaf motif; sometimes they had small dolphins in blind and in gold. They originated in Venice and began around 1560. They often displayed Oriental designs. They are very rare and costly.

Vellum Binding.

VOTIVE BINDING. Highly decorated bindings, usually containing the Gospels with religious scenes.

WHEEL BINDING. A binding which has a design where the center of the boards are decorated with circular wheel patterns and where the spokes spray outward to the edges of the cover. Developed by the Scottish and popularized in the eighteenth century.

WOOD BINDING. Durable bindings made of a variety of woods like oak, beech, birch, etc. Impressive nineteenth century examples were hand carved. *See example.*

Velvet Binding.

WOODCUT BINDING. Where a woodcut decoration was applied to the boards by pasting several layers to form a wrapper. Very delicate. Few examples exist.

Wood Binding.

General Book Knowledge

The following pages provide valuable insight into the components of a book, including types of edge, marbling, different types of illustrations, and the necessary information on book "lingo." This information is especially useful when bidding in book auctions or understanding abbreviations and terms used to describe a book. It is important that you become familiar with book nomenclature whether to aid your auction bidding or to help you peruse catalogs and pricing information. In addition, an explanation on how to read Roman numerals and define the anatomy of a book is provided.

BOOK EDGES

Books have many different types of book edges. For example, many times the book has gold gilding on all three edges: the top, the bottom and the fore edge or outer edge of the book. Generally this is for looks and protection. Many books have just the top edge with gold gilt and the other two edges are not gilded. This was done for one of two reasons. One, because the top edge many times was the only edge of the book to be seen, therefore saving money by gilding the top edge only. Second, the top edge was the only edge exposed to dust. Gilded edges are much easier to clean than a rough or ungilded edge of a book.

Another type of edge is rough cut, deckle edge, or uncut, which refers to uneven pages in a book. An "unopened" edge refers to books that actually had to be cut open with book knives in order to separate the pages. Gauffred (or gauffered, or goffered) edges are gold or silvered edges decorated by the impression of heated tools, most often called a pointillé. Lastly, a book's

Rough Cut

edges may be marbleized. This process was done by hand, leaving a painted design on the three edges of the book. Marbled paper is made by lowering a sheet of paper onto a bath of gum or size, on the surface of which colors have been induced out with a rod or comb. It was found in Japan as early as 1118 in a process called Suminahashi. (See marbling information.)

Gauffered Edge

BOOK PLATES

The time honored tradition of book plates is still practiced today. However, a book collector, or book purest, prefers owning books with no marks, signatures, or book plates. The value of the book is usually highest when the book is in its purest state. There are, of course, exceptions. For example, a book having the bookplate of Isaac Newton could help authenticate the book as belonging to or coming from his personal library. Therefore a book plate authenticated as being the book plate of Sir Isaac Newton could lead to the belief that the book at one time was owned by Sir Isaac Newton. This will dramatically increase the value of the book. However, we are speaking of your books and your collection and your decision as to whether to put your own book plate in the book. My personal opinion is that it is bet-

Book Plate of
Alexander Hamilton

ter not to unless, of course, you have decided to become a very famous person or you plan to develop an awesome library that one day the auction house would advertise. The ad would look something like this, "we are selling the Boutiette Collection, or Library of the Witt Collection, or the Dolinsky Collection, or the Ed Carnes Library," etc. The preference for average collectors is avoid marking the book in any way. If you must, design it yourself. Avoid store bought book plates.

MARBLING

Marbling is the art of creating colorful patterns by sprinkling different kinds of pigments into water then transforming what emerged onto a piece of paper. Historians differ as to when the process was developed. Most agree it began in Japan and later, independently in Turkey. Actual evidence exists dating its origins back over 2000 years ago to the Tang Dynasty in China. We do know that marbling was used in Japan in the twelfth century. It is called Suminahashi, which translates to "oceans ink floating." Most marbling patterns did not look anything like marble. They looked like rocks or clouds. Craftsman dropped circles of black or indigo blue into water, and with a blow, would move the water on the surface to produce ring like patterns. The paper was then submerged in the water. And as the ink rose to the surface, an unusual pattern would appear. On their own in the twelfth century, the Turks developed a type of marbling in the city of Bukhara called ebru. The word ebru translates as "cloud." This marbling actually looks like a floating group of clouds. Whether the Chinese, Japanese, or Turks are given credit is irrelevant. What is important is that the process is an integral part of bookbinding. The marbling process was used almost exclusively in the binding of books. Although it did have some secondary uses, such as providing backgrounds for official state documents and signatures, it was used with text to help protect the erasing of signatures and forgeries. Initially, in bookbinding, marbling papers were used to cover the fold strings glue marks of the binding. It was also used as background for coats of arms. In the sixteenth century marbling was used on expensive book edges so that missing pages were easily spotted due to the break in the marbling pattern. The Dutch used a more scientific approach. Concentric circles were formed, aligned in rows, then columns, and then applied with the colors. Marbling became so popular that guilds were developed by some marbling craftsmen.

These guilds existed to vigorously protect the secrets of how marbling was done. Marbling techniques were closely guarded family secrets for generations. Even marbling apprentices were not trusted with the formulas. If they were, it was only after many years of service. In England, marbling became so popular that the government began to tax its importation. This put the cost out of reach for many, so the English developed a creative way to smuggle in marbled paper by wrapping presents or other goods with the paper. When the binders received the goods or presents, they took the marbled wrapping paper off, pressed it out, and used it in their bookbindings. The following is a brief description of how the marbling process took place.

1. Some aluminum sulphate, which is a color binder called alum, is dissolved in water. Then it is sponged onto the sheets of paper to be marbleized. The alum is what will bond the color to the paper. Then it is hung up to dry.

2. A liquid called size is made by blending gelatin carrageenan with water.

3. The size is poured into a tray.

4. Different colors of paint or ink are splattered onto the surface of the size. The colors float on the surface, because they are lighter than the thickened water.

5. A rod is used to stir the floating colors. Combs and rakes may also be run through the colors to make more detailed designs.

6. A sheet of the alum-treated paper is carefully laid onto the surface of the size, and it sucks up the floating colors.

7. The paper is lifted off, rinsed, and hung up to dry.

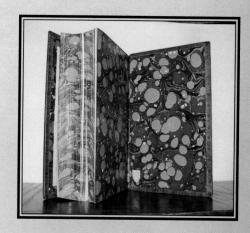

Marbled Edges and Endpapers

ENGRAVINGS AND ILLUSTRATIONS

Engraving is the art of duplicating an image. The art is similar to painting. Engraving used in books is a relatively new art form in relation to its history. In prehistoric times it was used in stone and on pottery. It has been used through the centuries for expressing something by figures, or as an artistic expression. The Chinese used engravings as early as 870 BC. Engraving spread through Europe with the advent of the printed word. The following is a listing of different types of engraving procedures:

AQUATINT. An etching technique identified by an unlimited series of gradations from pale gray to velvety black made from copper or zinc.

BLOCK BOOK. A book in which the text and illustrations are entirely printed by wood engravings or woodcuts, made to actual reproduction size, one block to a page. They were done by hand; this was a form of duplicating manuscripts before the invention of printing with movable type.

CHROMOLITHOGRAPH. An early term for color images and the forerunner to color printing from which modern lithography developed. Also called a chromo, it is almost always printed on one side of a piece of paper. It often has a shellac or varnish look on the finish of the image. *See example.*

COLOR LITHOGRAPHY. A multicolor lithograph is made from a series of lithograph stones, one for each basic color that is to be printed.

COPPER ENGRAVING. An engraved or etched copper printing plate. Also can refer to a print made from a copper plate or piece of copper. *See example.*

DRYPOINT. An intaglio printing process in which a copper or zinc plate is inscribed directly with a pointed needle of steel. Prints are made by this process as well.

ENGRAVING. The process of incising a design, or inscription, using a sharp tool on a hard surface. Usually done with copper, metal, or wood.

HALFTONE. An area of ink that is broken up into dots. The dots vary in size and density according to the value of the halftone. More white space between black ink dots give the area a lighter appearance, which then looks like another color.

HAND COLORED. An artist was paid to color an existing engraving or illustration by hand. *See example.*

MEZZOTINT. A relief printing process in which the entire surface of a copper or steel plate is heavily abraded with a special tool called a cradle. It prints as velvety black. The areas to be white in the print are rubbed with a burnisher and engraver's scraper, which smooth and depress those areas so that they do not take the ink in relief printing. This process extrapolates the whites from the blacks.

PHOTOENGRAVING. A photomechanical process for making line cuts and halftone cuts by photographing an image on a metal plate and then etching. *See example.*

PHOTOGRAVURE. A process for making prints from an intaglio plate prepared by a photographic process. *See example.*

STEEL ENGRAVING. The process of engraving on steel, or an impression taken from an engraved steel plate. *See example.*

STIPPLE ENGRAVING. Engraving, etching, or wood engraving in which the design areas are made up of small dots or flecks.

WOODCUT. A relief printing technique in which the printing surface is carved with special woodcut tools from a block of wood. The woodcut block is cut from a smoothed plank cut longitudinally from the tree trunk so that the grain runs in parallel lines in the block. *See example.*

WOOD ENGRAVING. A relief printing technique in which a block of wood is incised with a tool to create a printing surface. The blocks used in wood engraving are transverse cuts of the hardest woods.

ILLUMINATE

In early bookmaking, to illuminate a book was to place large letters, called ornamental capitals, on the pages of the book. A craftsman would also hand decorate and paint flowers and other ornamental patterns or devices on the margin of the book. Gold leafing was used extensively in the process as was vivid color painted by hand. Red paint, or "rubricate" as it was called, was used to make smaller capitals or letters. The handwork continued to the headings of the chapters and to the beginning of paragraphs. Very large initials were drawn and colored by hand.

AUTOGRAPHED / TIPPED IN / FLAT SIGNED

For a book to be flat signed, meaning that the author signed the book on an existing page, generally adds significant value to a book. In addition, many books may have a signature or a letter from the author that has been tipped in, meaning added to an existing

page. Although not as good as being flat signed, a tipped in letter, signature, or manuscript generally adds value to the book.

AMERICAN BOOK SIZES

Book sizes are usually referred to as octavo, quarto, folio, and so on. However, there is quite a range of sizes within each of these names. For example, a crown octavo book is 7½ by 5 inches and a demioctavo book is 8 by 5½ inches, but it gives a broad idea that an octavo is usually about a 7 inch book up to a 10½ inch book. They may say it's a large octavo instead of giving the specific sizes. If you see a specific name like thirtysixmo, you can look at this chart and know the exact size.

Name	Inches
Thirtysixmo	4 x 3⅓
Medium Thirtywomo	4¾ x 3
Medium Twentyfourmo	5½ x 3⅝
Medium Eighteenmo	6⅔ x 4
Medium Sixteenmo	6¾ x 4½
Cap Octavo	7 x 7¼
Duodecimo	7½ x 4½
Crown Octavo	7½ x 5
Post Octavo	7½ x 5½
Medium Duodecimo	7⅔ x 5⅛
Demy Octavo	8 x 5½
Small Quarto (usually less)	8½ x 7
Broad Quarto (varies up to 13 x 10)	8½ x 7
Medium Octavo	9½ x 6
Royal Octavo	10 x 6½
Super Royal Octavo	10½ x 7
Imperial Quarto	11 x 15
Imperial Octavo	11½ x 8¼
Atlas Folio or Elephant Folio (largest folio size)	17 x 26

BRITISH BOOK SIZES

For hundreds of years, the British used the following definitions as sizes for their books. In 1969 they changed those sizes to a metric equivalent.

Name	Inches
Pott Octavo	6¼ x 4
Foolscap Octavo	6¾ x 4¼
Crown Octavo	7½ x 5
Large Post Octavo	8¼ x 5¼
Demy Octavo	8¾ x 5
Medium Octavo	9 x 5¾
Royal Octavo	10 x 6¼
Super Royal Octavo	10 x 6¾
Imperial Octavo	11 x 7½
Foolscap Quarto	8½ x 6¾
Crown Quarto	10 x 7½
Large Post Quarto	10½ x 8¼
Demy Quarto	11¼ x 8¾
Medium Quarto	11½ x 9
Royal Quarto	12½ x 10
Foolscap Folio	13½ x 8½

If all of that has you seeing double, then here is a list of three basic sizes that will take care of ninety percent of the books you come in contact with.

TABLE OF AVERAGE BOOK SIZES

Folio. 17½ inches (444.5 mm) by 11¼ inches (285.8 mm). Large, upright volumes are commonly the size used for atlases. Larger folios from larger sheets are called atlas or elephant.

Quarto. 11¼ inches (285.8 mm) by 8¾ inches (222.3 mm). Large square volumes (the typical coffee-table book). When larger than quarto they may be called royal or imperial quarto.

Octavo. 8¾ inches (222.3 mm) by 5⅝ inches (142.9 mm). The common novel-sized volume often called a demyoctavo. Smaller volumes are listed as post or crown octavo, and larger ones may be royal or imperial octavo.

COLLATION IN BIBLIOGRAPHIES

Each gathering in a book is given a signature letter A – Z. Each leaf in the gathering is also numbered, and this means that any one particular leaf can immediately be described by bibliographers. Instead of saying "the leaf on which unnumbered pages 3 and 4 are printed is torn, page 3 stained," one can say "A2 torn, recto stained." (Recto is the top or front of the leaf and verso the back — thus in any open book the page on the left will be verso and that on the right a recto.)

ABBREVIATIONS

When purchasing an antiquarian book from a catalog, book auction house, or dealer, you will often see all kinds of crazy abbreviations, which are used to save both time and space. Here is a listing of many abbreviations for your use.

ABA	Antiquarian Booksellers' Association
ABAA	Antiquarian Booksellers' Association of America
abbr.	Abbreviation(s)
add.	Additional, addition(s)
a.e.g.	All edges gilt
aft., aftw.	Afterwards
A.L.	Autograph letter
A.L.S.	Autographed letter signed
anon.	Anonymous
BAR	Book Auction Records
B.C.	Before Christ
bdg.	Binding
bds.	Boards
bister (bistre).	A dark brown color. "Sepia tone."
bk.	Book
B.L.	Black letter
BMC	British Museum Catalogue
bnd.	Bound
c.	Circa, about
c. & p.	Collated and found perfect
cancels.	Leaves replaced by corrected extra leaves
cat.	Catalog
CBEL	Cambridge Bibliography of English Literature
cf.	Calf
cent.	Century
chap.	Chapter(s)
cl., clo.	Cloth
cl. bds.	Cloth boards, i.e., boards covered with cloth
col.	Column(s)
col.(d)	Colored
comp.	Complete
cont.	Contemporary
Cr. 8vo.	Crown octavo size
Crown Octavo.	About 5 by 7½ in.; -4to, 7½ by 10 in.
d. e.	Deckle edges
D.S.	Document signed
dec.	Decorated
Demy 8vo.	Demy octavo, 5½ by 8¾ in.; 4to, about 8¾ by 11 in.
d.j.	Dust jacket
doc.	Document
d.w.	Dust wrapper
DNA	Dictionary of National Biography
e. d. l.	Edition de luxe
e. i.	Extra-illustrated
el. fo.	Elephant folio. (About 14 in. tall)
emb.	Embossed
engr.	Engraving
enl.	Enlarged
e.p.	End-paper
etch.	Etching(s), etcher
ex-lib.	Ex-library
f.	Folio (30 cm. and over)
facs.	Facsimile
fcp.	Foolscap size
f. e. p.	Fore edges painted
ff.	Leaves (i.e. folios)
flex.	Flexible
fol.	Folio size
foolscap octavo.	About 4½ by 6¾ in.; quarto, about 6¾ by 8½ in.
for. (forrel).	Heavy rough parchment used on old books
front.	Frontispiece
foxed.	Brown spotted
Fr.	French
g. e.	Gilt edges
g. m. e.	Gilt marbled edges.
g. l.	Gothic letter
g. t.	Gilt top
g. t. e.	Gilt top edges
Ger., Germ.	German
glt.	Gilt
Gr.	Greek
h. c.	Half calf
hf. bd.	Half-bound
hm.	Half morocco
I. p.	India paper
ILAB	International League of Antiquarian Booksellers

ills.	Illustrations	parch.	Parchment
illum.	Illuminated	phot.	Photograph(s), photogravure(s)
imp.	Imperial	pict.	Pictorial
impft.	Imperfect	pl.	Plate(s)
imp. fol.	Imperial folio	plts.	Plates
Imperial octavo.	About 11 by 7½ in.; -quarto, about 15 by 11 in.	pol.	Polished
		port.	Portrait
inscr.	Inscription	prelims.	Preliminary leaves
Ital.	Italian	pres.	Presentation copy
J. p.	Japan paper	priv. pr.	Privately printed
J. v.	Japanese vellum	pt.	Part
jt.	Joint	pub.(d)	Published
l.	Leaf	Q.	Quarto (2" to 12")
l. p.	Large paper	r. e.	Red edges
l. s.	Letter signed	R. e.	Royal edition
law calf,		r. f.	Rough finish (paper)
law sheep.	Plain uncolored leather (calf or sheep)	R. O., r. 8vo.	Royal octavo
lea.	Leather	Rect., ro.	Recto (right-hand page). Front of printed leaf
lev.	Levant		
lex.	8vo. Lexicon octavo	rev.	Revised, revision
lge.	Large	Rom.	Roman
ll.	Leaves	roy.	8 vo. Royal octavo. About 6 by 10 in.; -4to, about 10 by 12½ in.
m. e.	Marbled edges		
medium 8vo.	About 9½ by 6 in.; -4to, about 12 by 9½ in.	Rus.	Russ. Russia
		s. a.	Sine anno (without date of publication)
-mo.	Size mark	s. e.	Special edition
mor.	Morocco leather	s. l.	Sine loco (without place of publication)
ms.(s)	Manuscript(s)	s. n.	Sine nominee (without name of printer)
mut.	Mutilated	s. p.	Small paper
NCBEL	New Cambridge Bibliography of English Literature	ser.	Series
		sgd.	Signed
n. d.	No date	Sh.	Sheep
n. ed.	New edition	Sig.	Signature
n. p.	Depending on context: no publisher; no printer; or no place (of publication)	sm.	Small
		sm. 4o or 4to	
n.y.	No year (of publication)	or Q.	Small quarto
O. v.	On vellum	soc.	Society
Ob.	Oblong	SOED	Shorter Oxford English Dictionary
Oct.	Octavo size	spr.	Sprinkled
OED	Oxford English Dictionary	STC	Short-Title Catalogue
orig.	Original	sup. ex.	Super-extra, "de luxe"
p. o.	Post octavo	swd.	Sewed
p. o. f.	Painted on fore edge	t. e. g.	Top edges gilt
p. o. r. p.	Printed on rice paper	t. p.	Title page
p. o. s.	Printed on silk or satin	tabby.	Watered (moiré) silk
p. p.	Proof plate	thk.	Thick
pa.	Paper	t.l.s.	Typed letter, signed

TLS	Times Literary Supplement
unbd.	Unbound
unopened	Folds of leaves not opened
v.	Volume(s)
v. d.	Various dates
v. g.	Very good copy
v. y.	Various years
vel., vell.	Vellum
vers.	Verso (left-hand page), back of printed page
vig. T.	Vignette title
vign.	Vignette(s)
vo.	Verso
vol(s).	Volume(s)
w.	Water stained
w. a. f.	With all faults
wormed	Worm-eaten
wraps	Wrappers

ROMAN NUMERALS

A system of dating is found on most books before 1800. Each numeral has to be added mentally to arrive at the total. Here is the formula for the Roman Numeral numbering system.

M = 1,000	I = 1	VI = 6
D = 500	II = 2	VII = 7
C = 100	III = 3	VIII = 8
L = 50	IV = 4	IX = 9
	V = 5	X = 10

Some examples:

X = 10
XX = 20
XXX = 30
XXXI = 31
XXXVI = 36
MCCCCLXXXIV = 1484
MDXXXXV = 1545
MDCXLVIII = 1648 (the X before the L has to be subtracted)
MDCCLXXX = 1780
MDCCCXIII = 1813

Another way to explain this is as follows:

A numeral is a symbol used to represent a number. Each letter used in Roman numerals stands for a different number. A row of letters means that they should be added together. For example, XXX = 10 + 10 + 10 = 30, and LXI = 50 + 10 + 1 = 61. If a smaller value is placed before a larger one, you must subtract instead of adding. For example, IV = 4 (i.e., one subtracted from five).

These rules will be handy in writing Roman numerals. Just convert one digit at a time. Here is an exercise to try: convert 963 to Roman numerals. 963 = 900 + 60 + 3 = CM + LX + III.

There are a few rules in converting Roman numerals to Arabic numbers. They are:

• Subtract only powers of ten, such as I, X, or C. Writing VL for 45 is not allowed: write XLV instead.

• Subtract only a single letter from a single numeral.

• Don't subtract a letter from another letter more than ten times greater. This means that you can only subtract I from V or X, and X from L or C.

BOOK ANATOMY

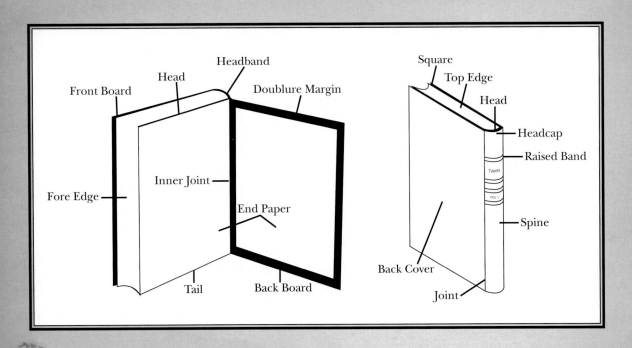

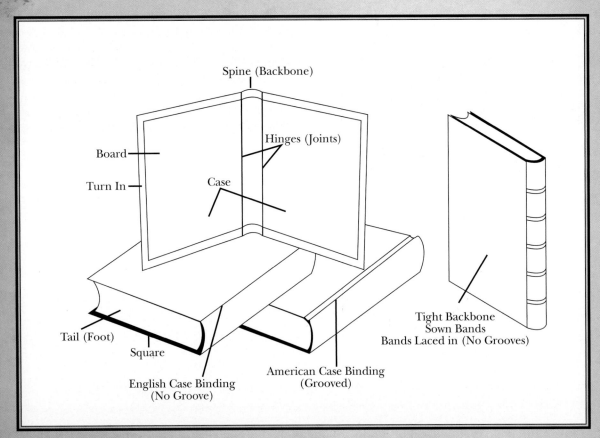

Book Care

When beginning or maintaining a book collection, it is essential that you become familiar with the information that will help protect and preserve your library investment for generations to come.

Books are far more fragile than most people realize. Unlike art, porcelain, or furniture, the materials used in bookmaking and binding are more expendable. The pages themselves can tear, mildew, and even rot. The hemp cord and threads, along with the glues and adhesives used in bookmaking are prime targets for rodents and insects. A poor climate condition is one of the main causes of book damage and leather disintegration. The number one killer of books is the improper handling of them.

It is important to educate yourself with a few simple things that can be done to prevent damage and preserve your collection. The leading causes of book damage fall into the following categories: poor climate and atmospheric conditions including excessive heat, moisture, and light, improper book handling, and insect damage.

CLIMATE AND ATMOSPHERIC CONDITIONS

Poor environmental conditions are a leading contributor to book damage. Extreme heat, moisture, or light will cause rapid deterioration of the book's natural materials.

Heat, when excessive, can cause your books to crack, flake, or become brittle. Never allow books to be in the direct flow of any heating ducts. The constant flow of hot air will dry out your bindings resulting in brittle and cracked leather. Avoid displaying books near windows, radiators, and fireplaces as well.

A damp environment will cause paper to cockle and encourage chemical activity potentially resulting in mold, mildew, or pest damage. Very dry conditions are problematic as well; without enough moisture, the book's natural materials can become brittle leading to pages that will become weak and easily torn. When the bindings themselves become dried out, they start to crumble and split. Either extreme heat or moisture will lead to rapid deterioration of the book's paper. Stable conditions created through the proper levels of temperature and atmospheric moisture are essential in preserving the integrity of the books materials.

The perfect condition for books and leather bindings is when the environment's relative humidity is about 50%, and the temperature is between 66 and 72 degrees. Excessive humidity begets moisture, and moisture begets mold and mildew causing foxing, or the browning and blackening of pages. The appearance of brown or reddish spots is the first indication of mold and mildew damage. Often you can detect a musty odor as well. Books displayed in areas of too much moisture can be protected by investing in a good dehumidifier which will control most moisture problems. In addition, during the winter months, duct work systems containing a humidifier can also pump too much moisture into the air further leading to book damage. Once again, a dehumidifier will control these potential atmospheric problems. Humidity is the weight or mass of water vapor in a certain volume of air. Never allow the relative humidity to exceed 70%. When you are trying to prevent items from becoming brittle you would be adding moisture to the air by means of a humidifier. When you need to take moisture out of the air to prevent books or papers from getting foxed or mold or mildew, you do that with a dehumidifier. You can measure the humidity in your room or library by purchasing an instrument called a hygrometer. Below is an example of foxing.

Light eventually fades inks and even leather. It quickens the chemical decomposition of many materials. The U (ultraviof discoloration and fading in a relatively short period of time. When the quality of paper is poor, this can happen in a matter of a few days. Room lighting can also contribute toolet) component of light is the source of much of this damage. A book left open in daylight will show signs this problem. Windows and artificial light sources may need UV protection, like screens or filters, which have to be changed periodically. Below are bindings that have been faded by light.

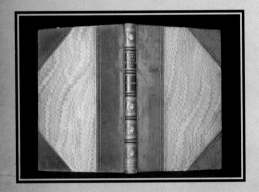

When displaying books, it is a good practice to keep those that have the same bindings together. For example, if you have a four volume set of Napoleon's works and separate them for decorative purposes, you might discover significant changes in the conditions of the books in a few months. The separated books could show a difference in the toning or color of the leather on the binding due to the different amounts of natural or room lighting in which they have been exposed. The differences become very noticeable when the books are put back together. Therefore it is always a good idea to keep like bindings and sets together.

AMBIENT LIGHT. When overexposed to light, some leather bindings will fade as well as individual colors that fade more easily than others. For example, green and purple bindings are notorious for turning light brown. Many times you will see a set of green or purple books where the boards are still green or purple, but the exposed spines will have turned brown. Spot lights and strong artificial lights also contribute to significant fading of books. Visible radiation should be no more than 200 lux. UV radiation should be under 75 lux. Incandescent light is the lighting source that will create fewer problems, but one must be careful because it passes off more heat than other forms of lighting. Fluorescent lighting throws off much more UV radiation than does the incandescent.

In addition, it is important to note that leather bindings are very sensitive to atmospheric pollutants such as sulphur dioxide. Basements, cellars, garages, and attics are not the place to store or keep books of any value. Nitrogen dioxide, sulfur dioxide, and chlorides are gaseous air contaminates which can affect the condition of books. Most gaseous pollutants can be eliminated with an activated carbon filter. Smoking should never be allowed around books as the tar and nicotine are damaging to the pages and over time will darken the pages and bindings.

BOOK HANDLING

The single greatest contributing factor to book damage is poor or improper handling of your books. When handling leather bindings or antiquarian books, hold the book in the center of your palm so that when opened, the covers rest against your thumb and fingers. Never let the boards (i.e. the covers) of the book drop open. They must be supported at all times. The hinge or gutter of a book cover can actually crack or tear causing the cover to actually break off of the book. Books, when dropped, will break. If you carry too many at one time and drop one on the floor, the likelihood of the cover snapping off is very high. Boards and spine covers that are yanked, pulled, or pried open too far will create too much stress on the hinge points of the bindings and cause them to break. Never open a book beyond the point of resistance. Forcing a book open flat will break its back.

DO NOT. Do not pull a book this way, as it will damage the headband.

DO. Do support the spine, but don't open the book all the way!

DO. This is the correct way to pull a book from the shelf.

When removing a book from the bookshelf, be sure to pull the book from the center of the spine. Never pull a book from the top or the headband. The majority of people do exactly that, causing the leather headband to break, tear, or pull loose. A fingernail can scuff or tear the headband or the leather around it as well. To properly remove or pull a book, simply push the surrounding books to the right and left of the one you are about to pull, allowing you the room to grasp the center of the spine on the targeted book or place your hand or finger over the top of the book and reach to the back (i.e. the fore edge of the book) and gently pull the book forward. The diagram on this page demonstrates the "how to" and "how not to" pull a book from a shelf. With folio size books or books that are very heavy, use both hands. Always be sure your hands are clean.

Good shelving is a must when storing books. Rough cut boards or unfinished wood can damage the sensitive leather on the bindings. Be sure your shelving does not have a lip or beading on the edges that will bump your bindings when pulling books off the shelf. Check for splinters, nails, staples, or any other protruding objects that could damage your books. Make sure

the surface of your shelving is adequate. Tacky shellac, varnish, or poor quality, chalky paint will damage leather bindings as well. There should be enough space between each shelf to allow at least three inches of air flow space over the tops of the books. In addition, the depth of your shelves should accommodate the depths of your books.

Avoid squeezing too many books onto one shelf. When packed too tightly, book hinges tend to break down. On the other hand, too few books on a shelf can also create problems, such as allowing the books to fall too easily. A sagging shelf will force books to sit unevenly and will contribute to the break down of the binding.

INSECTS

Insects are another major contributor to book damage when books are improperly cared for. Vermin love books. Among the worst villains are cockroaches, beetles, woodborers, silver fish, and moths. Certain materials present in the construction of books attract insects. There are easy precautions you can take to prevent insect damage to your books.

A book's natural materials usually attract a variety of insects. For instance, the sizing or the paste in books is made from wheat, attracting vermin also known as cellulose eaters. Preventative measures will go a long way in helping to protect your library from insect attack. Never leave food lying around. Always keep your library clean. Be sure cracks in the floor are sealed, holes in the wall or bricks are filled, and that your vents and duct work don't have broken seams. Do not leave windows open without window screens. If you do develop a problem, take care of it immediately. If you see moths flying in the air three or four times a week, then you may have an infestation near or in one of your books. Often these moths come from grocery sacks that you have carried home. Moths lay eggs in the bags, you carry the bag home, the eggs hatch, and before long you have a major infestation problem. Usually, after finding the source, the problem can be easily eliminated. The location of the problem determines if it is an isolated situation or if many books are affected. Infestations can often be treated by wrapping the problem books and freezing them. Ask your conservator if it's okay to freeze the affected book(s). If the book is multi-layered, like the boards of ½ and ¾ leather bindings consisting of several layers of cardboard like materials, they will have different stretching or shrinking limits and freezing should not be done. If a binding is hand painted the paint will flake off if frozen. However, most bindings can be treated this way, killing the bugs within 36 hours.

Cockroaches and silverfish can do extensive damage to a book by eating the book's paste. Usually found on the surfaces of the books, they love the starchy adhesives. The woodborers, commonly known as "book worms," tunnel through the pages and even the leather bindings. Upon seeing signs of cockroaches, silverfish, or woodborers on or near your books or shelving, contact an exterminator immediately. Usually this problem can be easily solved by a professional within 60 days. Beetles can be a nuisance and occasionally eat on books, but normally they are more interested in animal matter. Boric acid can dramatically reduce insect infestation. A little sprinkle on the shelves behind the books is most helpful.

In addition to insects, rodents are also partial to books. These pests destroy books, not so much for their nutritional appeal but simply because they love to chew and sharpen their teeth. They usually attack the covers of the leather bindings or the fore edges of the book. If you see any signs of animal droppings on your shelves, call the exterminator immediately.

MOLD, SMOKE, MILDEW, AND SOOT

Evidence of mold or mildew like pink, reddish brown, or black spots on the pages of your book(s) indicate damage, and immediate action should be taken. First, try to determine if these spots have been there for many years, and it is an old problem which is now dormant or inactive. If the books are damp then wrap them in foil or plastic wrap and place them in a freezer (with the exceptions that we previously mentioned). If the books are soaking wet from water damage, then they should be dried out by blowing cool or slightly warm air across them. If the damaged books are valuable, then seek the help of a professional. A list of professionals appears on page 58. If the books are not valuable, then it is not cost effective to restore the books. Restoration can cost more than the books  themselves. But in any event, be sure to isolate these books from the rest of your collection. If you have a weather disaster or a plumbing accident at your home, contact an expert immediately. A list of reputable conservators of bindings can be found in the Resource Chapter.

Remember to act quickly. Mold starts to grow within 24 to 36 hours. Gently clean them with undyed cotton cloths or paper towels. If your books are very wet, attempt to dry them out by passing air over the pages while waiting for assistance. Spread the book open in front of a fan that will pass air back and forth over the pages. If you can, stand the book upright and partially open. If it is waterlogged this can be heavy and awkward. Make sure that it does not pull apart under its own weight. As the book dries, check for signs of mold growth.

Do not attempt to pry apart the pages of a wet book. They will separate as they dry out. However, the shiny art paper used for printing illustrations is an exception. They contain china clay, and if left to dry, the pages will stick together in a solid block. Try to separate sheets of art paper from each other and from text paper as they dry with wax paper or silicone release paper. One of the more recent remedies is to have a professional freeze dry your books.

Remember when displaying your books at home or in your library to be mindful of where the water sources are located. It is never a good idea to display your books near a bathroom that may be located above or adjacent to your book display. A water source of any kind should be far removed from your books. Too often tubs have overflowed, showers leaked, or toilet tanks cracked, causing water leaks to the floor below, damaging many wonderful collections. If you display books in such areas it is a recipe for disaster!

GENERAL CARE

DUST. It is important to dust your books several times a year. Dust is not only abrasive, it can even soil the inside or outside materials of your book. When dusting, use a feather duster or a dry, lint-free rag. Never use chemicals on the rag or feather duster. Never use commercial products like Pledge or Endust. When used gently, mini-vacuums can also be very handy. Be sure to cover the end of the hose or tube with a soft linen or muslin rag ensuring that if a small piece of leather is loose on your binding that it won't get sucked into oblivion.

PACKING. Many customers purchase leather books simply for investment purposes and never display them. Some display them, but eventually run out of room, forcing them to store a portion of their books. When storing books, do not lay them on their side. When shipping books, the opposite is true. Laying the books on their side is actually preferred since it will be for a short time only. Books stored for lengthy periods of time will have a tendency to warp if laid flat. So, whenever possible, store them in basically the same way you would if you had them on a library shelf, straight up. Do not lay them on their spine or on their fore edge. And remember, never expose your books to extreme heat or moisture, therefore avoid attics, basements, and cellars.

PRESERVATION

Opinions vary regarding book preservation. There are several book dealers who disagree with what I am about to tell you. However, I believe the vast majority would agree. Leather is made from animal skins, the skins of mammals. Leather has been around a long time, evidenced by a leather pre-historic bowl recently found dating back more than 5,000 years. Although leather is durable, through modern technology and industrial developments in the past three or four hundred years, mankind has added many airborne pollutants that contribute to the break down of the once, almost indestructible leather. We must now take preventive measures to protect leather bindings. There are two basic, but very different, techniques used in book preservation. First is to apply some type of treatment that helps prevent your books from drying out and cracking, and secondly, is to add pigment if necessary. Some book dealers believe that a book should remain as is. I do not hold that view. When a painter finished his work, a hundred, or even five hundred years ago, he probably had no idea that his painting would be enjoyed by countless people two or three hundred years later. This painting most likely would never have lasted to the twenty-first century had it not received some type of treatment. Museum paintings, in the Louvre or at the Sistine Chapel, have all had conservatory work done to them. The pollutants in the air darkened them so that you couldn't see the paintings themselves, so they had to be cleaned or restored. Books, especially leather bindings, are not unlike paintings. They may need preservation treatment as well. Unless, of course, they are already in excellent condition and you keep them in the environment that we have written about.

"Red rot" is a common and significant form of chemical damage affecting leather book bindings. The fibers break and completely turn to a brick-red powder. It is easily identifiable by the red dust coming off the binding. It is often noticed on clothes or a cloth the books are sitting on.

Air pollution leads to chemical damage of bindings. A good example is combustible gas given off by a fireplace. This has been evidenced when one sees spines of books that had been untouched in a bookcase for a long time. The spines exhibit a higher acidity and higher sulphur content than the boards that have been protected by being against each other. Sulphur dioxide absorbed by the leather from the atmosphere is converted into sulphuric acid in the presence of an oxidant and erodes the book's leather. Another form of chemical damage is photochemical degradation of leather. As we mentioned earlier in this chapter, light in general, and more specifically, UV sunlight, contributes significantly to the aging of organic material, leading to the decay or changing color of the leather.

Another cause of damage to book bindings is the stretching and shrinking of the leather due to changes in relative humidity. Cracks may appear, and the grain will separate. This happens often to books bound in sheepskin. As the leather continues to breakdown, its ability to absorb or give up moisture decreases. So in an environment with lots of changes in temperature and relative humidity, this may lead to leather disintegrating.

Since this book is about leather bindings and their values, it is important to understand what things can affect their values. Due to climatic conditions, leather bindings can have a tendency to dry out. If your book or books are dried out then you may consider treating your books with a solution containing 40% neatsfoot oil and 60% anhydrous lanolin. Neatsfoot oil is a lubricator used and recommended for use by book binders and conservators for many years. Lanolin, a wool fat, is also a lubricant, but more importantly, it has water retention qualities as well. One of the most popular leather dressings was developed by H. J. Plenderleiths and is called the British Museum Leather Dressing. Its basic ingredients are 200 gram lanolin, 30 ml cedar oil, 15 gram beeswax, and 350 ml hexane. Sometimes 60% of the lanolin was replaced by neatsfoot oil. For years well informed dealers or bibliophiles have suggested everything from beeswax to Vaseline, saddle soap, coconut oil, olive oil, and paraffin, but

most of these are too viscous to penetrate the leather deeply. Some actually seal off the leather so it can't breathe, causing more damage than good. This is why it is important to use the proper kind of book treatment or preservative. We recommend the Museum Leather Dressing, listed in the Resource Chapter, along with other product information. We also recommend the more available Triple Crown Leather Formula, also found in the Books Resource Chapter.

When applying a dressing or treatment, the chemicals in these preparations can actually cause dust and dirt to penetrate even further into the leather. Therefore, be sure to remove any and all dust, dirt, and grime from the bindings before treatment begins. If your bindings are exceedingly dirty and have surface grime or dirt, a surface cleaning agent can be used to remove fixed dirt. The cleaner should be whipped to a foam

before using, allowing the dirt or soiling to be cleaned by the foam. When only the foam is used, the leather suffers very little humidification. Use cotton or a cotton cloth when cleaning leather. The formula for cleaning solution is:

    996 gram distilled water
    2 gram neutral (non-ionic) soap
    2 gram carboxymethyl cellulose (CMC), medium
    viscosity

Mix the soap and CMC. Add to water. Shake. Whip the mixture till a layer of foam is formed on the surface. Use only the foam. If you don't want to be bothered by this process, you can order a good book cleaner from a book supply company like Talas whose address can be found in the Resource Chapter.

In applying a treatment to books you should be very careful not to darken the color of the leather. Ninety percent of books will not darken. The camel or butterscotch colored bindings, blonde and very light colored bindings, and white vellum may have a tendency to darken. You may want to try an application of the treatment on a small area of the book that is not close to the spine and see how it looks. This treatment is important for the preservation of the book. When applying, give extra attention around the moveable hinges of the book.

Now that you feel that you have a handle on book treatments, let me throw you a curve ball. Recently the Library of Congress warned that what they and many bibliophiles believed for years may not now be true. They state that if one has little experience in treating books or uses the wrong materials, it may do more harm than good. They caution that if too much dressing is applied or applied too often, the surface of the book could become tacky or sticky. Some dressings have been known to soak through the leather and stain the paste downs or end papers of the book, so be careful. Use sparingly, and when in doubt ask questions first. If your books are cared for properly and protected from harmful humidity, heat vents, and the like, then chances are they will be better off being left alone. However, if your humidity is not at around 50%, your temperature is not between 68 and 72 degrees or if they are already dried out or cracking, then you may need to be pro-active and treat your books.

The second factor to consider in preservation is pigment. Many leather bindings in existence today have been scuffed, leaving the leather finish raw in small places. Raw leather, when exposed to air, has a tendency to rot more quickly. It has no protective coating and therefore is very susceptible to disintegration. There are book leather pigments similar to pigments found in shoe polish that can be used in the preservation and treatment of books. However, shoe polish itself often contains acid and should not be used on book leather. You may ask, well if it's good for a leather shoe, why isn't it good for a leather book? The reason is leather books are tanned differently, and the leather process for developing a book is vastly different than that for a leather shoe. However, the principle is the same. There are products that do not contain destructive elements and high acidity, but have proper color. These products can be used to put pigment back into your leather book. These products come in ten different colors which are effective on most leather bindings. The colors include dark brown, brown, medium beige, camel, red, red mahogany, green, navy blue, and neutral. Often, the pigment color of the original leather is faded on portions of a book that

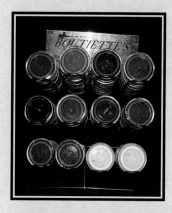

have been overly handled or rubbed, causing the protective coating of the leather to wear off. This leaves the leather with a raw, course appearance. Common areas where this occurs are the bottom edge of the book's tailband and covers. By simply applying a tiny bit of matching pigment to your finger and rubbing it on the affected areas, you replace the protective coating and preserve your book from rotting. You can find more information on these products in the Resource section.

DON'TS

When building and preserving your library, there are some important "don'ts" to remember when handling your books. Following these tips will help ensure your books longevity and preservation for years to come. Most of the following list is just common sense, although you will find many that you haven't heard about, and some that will surprise you.

• Don't write in your books. If you absolutely must write, never use ink, but instead a No. 1 (soft) pencil. Never write near the page corners. In the future, you may want to erase writing, and if it's too close to the corner, it is highly likely you will damage it when erasing.

• Don't lick your fingers to turn pages. Saliva breaks down organic materials and causes mold. It is also unsanitary.

• Don't put tape of any kind on your binding or pages of your book.

• Don't loan your books to others.

• Don't handle your books with dirty hands.

• Don't eat or drink near your books.

• Don't display your books on or near windows, strong UV rays, or spotlights.

• Don't let the mist from a central humidifier system spray directly onto your books.

• Don't place your books in the path of any hot air, such as air ducts.

• Don't pull books from shelving by their headpiece or headband.

• Don't carry too many books at one time.

• Don't overweight a shelf with books.

• Don't have too high or low humidity.

• Don't have the temperature above 72°.

• Don't separate or breakup your sets of books when displaying.

• Don't have shelves with beading, tacks, staples, or any other sharp objects that will damage your books.

• Don't overpack your book shelf.

• Don't underpack your book shelf.

• Don't let books dangle over the edge of your book shelf.

• Don't place your books on any shelving with rough or tacky surfaces.

• Don't lay books down flat on their boards for storing.

• Don't lay books on their fore edge or spine.

• Don't handle books with very long fingernails. They will gouge the book and damage the leather.

• Don't let dirt, dust, or grime remain on your books.

• Don't use any chemicals to clean your books.

• Don't allow mold to grow on your books.

• Don't allow insects to invade your book perimeter.

• Don't leave unscreened windows open near your books.

• Don't place your books near any water source.

• Don't place your books near a fireplace opening.

• Don't allow your books to dry out. This will leave them hard and brittle.

• Don't set anything on your books. It could leave a permanent mark or stain.

Book Terms & Notable People

ADDENDUM. Addition/additions to the book after it has been printed.

ALL EDGES GILT (OR GILDED). All three outer edges of the leaves (pages) of the book have been cut smooth and gilded with gold leaf.

ALL PUBLISHED. The book or set was never completed.

A.L.S. Autograph letter, signed.

AMERICAN BOOK-PRICES CURRENT (ABPC). The title of a publication that is produced annually with 30,000 to 40,000 new entries. A well respected and essential tool for book dealers and collectors. It has been published annually since 1895. It is divided into two sections: (1) printed books, maps, charts, and broadsides, (2) autograph letters and manuscripts. It lists thousands of books and autographs that have been sold at reputable book sales and auctions each year. It will give the reader the exact prices of books that sold for over $50, giving the reader a guideline on what this copy of a similar book might sell for. In January 1994, ABPC was made available on CD ROM, with over half a million entries dating back to 1975. An annual subscription fee is charged. Although the title ABPC implies the list is exclusive to American sales, in fact, it encompasses sales worldwide.

ARABESQUE. Islamic decorations or ornamentation emanated from vines and acanthus leaves.

ARMORIAL. A binding adorned with the coat of arms, usually in gilt, belonging to the original or subsequent owner. The term also refers to bookplates incorporating the owner's arms, and encompassing armorial decorated books as well.

AS ISSUED. A term used to emphasize the original condition the book was produced or sold in, often used when some individual feature contradicts normal expectation, e.g. edges trimmed, as issued.

ASSOCIATION COPY. A copy of a book in which the main interest of the book has a connection to its previous owner, usually the book's author.

BASKERVILLE, JOHN. Born in 1705. His presswork was among the finest.

BACKSTRIP. The spine of the book.

BALLANTYNE PRESS. 1796 – 1908. Founded by James Ballantyne.

BANDS. The cords or hemp to which the folded sheets of the book are attached.

BASIL. Artificially grained unsplit sheepskin used to copy expensive leather.

BAXTER, GEORGE. A very early color printer. His illustrations are sought after. In 1836, he patented a color printing process.

BEVELED BOARDS. Thick boards or covers with chamfered edges, giving the book a sloping edge.

BEWICK, THOMAS. 1753 – 1828. Sought after British engraver.

BIBLIOPHILE. A lover of books.

BLAKE, WILLIAM. A very collectible British illustrator.

BLANK LEAVES. Leaves with no printing on it.

BLIND. An impression made in the leather or cloth by a tool, die-stamp, or roll, without any addition of gold or color. This process is similar to how a notary seal works.

BLOCKING. Cover decorations applied in a press with a metal plate.

BOARDS. The wood, paste-board, straw-board, or other non-leather base material used to create the sides of hardbound or cased books.

BOOK OF HOURS. A book of prayers for personal use printed from the eleventh through the sixteenth century. These books contained hand-illuminated artwork.

BOOK LABEL. A label of ownership usually found on one of the book's front endpapers. It is normally smaller than a book-plate, usually listing the owner's name.

BOOKPLATE (or EX LIBRIS). A paper or leather plate usually pasted in a book as a sign of ownership. It gives clues to the provenance of the book. Many book authorities consider it to lower the value of a book. However, it is usually agreed that if the bookplate identifies a notable person, it usually will increase the book's value.

BOOK STAMP or LIBRARY STAMP. An ownership stamp of metal or rubber applied in ink or blind to the endpaper or fly-leaf of a book. A stamp can also be impressed on the books cover in gilt or blind by using a metal die.

BOUND. A book in which the gatherings are sewn onto horizontal cords, which are drawn through holes in the book's board and firmly attached so that leaves and binding become a structural entity.

BREAKING UP. Books whose color plates have been split or broken up, and are subsequently sold separately, most likely for framing.

BROADSIDE. A single sheet of paper most often printed on one side.

BUCKRAM. A hard-wearing waxed cloth binding.

C. or CA. Circa, Latin, meaning about or around, giving an approximate date. C1890 means printed around 1890.

CALF. A smooth leather with no perceptible grain. Its natural color is pale biscuit, butterscotch, or honey, but it can be dyed almost any shade. It is leather made from the hide of a calf and one of the most common leather used in bookbinding.

CALLED FOR. A book that should be present in a complete copy and has everything it is supposed to have.

CANCELS. Any part of a book substituted for what was originally printed.

CARTOUCHE. A round, oval, or decorated area on labels often found on covers of bindings. In ancient times it was a tablet for inscription or ornament.

CASED. A book in which a block of stitched signatures, held together by a strip of canvas (called the mull) attached to their backs, is inserted into a ready-made case by machinery. The text block is attached by gluing the overlaps of the mull to the inner edges of the boards over which the end papers are then pasted down.

CATCHWORD. A word printed at the foot of one page and then repeated as the first word on the following page. This system aids in collation of the book.

CATHEDRAL BINDINGS. Bindings decorated with Gothic architectural motifs of cathedrals and churches.

CAXTON, WILLIAM. Born in 1420. England's first printer.

CHAIN LINES. Widely spaced lines visible in the paper's texture, imprinted by the wire mesh of the book's/paper's original mold.

CHROMOLITHOGRAPHY. A printing process producing colored lithographies. It was commonly used in Victorian books.

CLASPS. A device on the board or covers of the book which snaps into a catch on the opposite board or cover that is used to keep a book closed. Clasps are similar to bosses used on medieval bindings. The bosses were made from metal, brass, copper, or leather.

CODEX. Originally the trunk of a tree, then a wooden tablet, finally a book. Originally wax covered wooden writing tablets which were hinged together to form a book. The common form of a book in the Western world after ca. 350 AD, with pages, gatherings, and a binding taking the place of a roll.

COLLATION. A term referring to the number of leaves in each of the books gatherings. A description of a book by its signatures or the number of quires.

COLOPHON. An inscription at the end of a book, usually at the foot of the last page. It normally gives publication facts or shows the trademark of the publisher.

COMPLETE IN ITSELF. A book is a complete story in and of itself, even though it came from a larger set of books.

COMPLETE WORKS VS. COMPLETE AS PRINTED. A complete set contains ALL the works of an author. Other sets contain only his/her major works. And complete at printing refers to all works up to and including work in question.

CONJUGATE. Leaves that are joined at the inner fold are said to be conjugate.

CONTEMPORARY BINDING. The original binding dating from the time period the book was published.

COPPERPLATE. Etched or engraved illustrations in books made from a piece of copper.

COUNTERMARK. A second watermark which often identifies the mill and/or quality of paper.

CROWN. A popular paper size measuring about 7½ x 5 inches. Also the upper extremity of a book's spine.

CRUSHED MOROCCO. Morocco leather which has been so thoroughly ironed, pressed, or rolled that the grain of the original skin has been almost obliterated. The characteristic high polish is given after the volume is bound.

DECKLE EDGES. Usually handmade paper using leaves with uncut edges.

DECORATED INITIAL. A pattern of foliage. An abstract design with no figures or story. Also an initial

letter that is ornamentation and is usually larger than the other letters.

DECORATOR. A person who does pen work decoration with colored ink. Usually the ink is red or blue.

DEMY. A term referring to a book's paper size. A book in demy octavo (8vo) may be up to 8¾ inches.

DENTELLE. A gilt border with a lacy pattern on the inner edge.

DEVICE. A printer's mark.

DIAPER. A lattice pattern of diamonds or lozenges.

DISBOUND. Having lost or having been removed from its binding.

DICED. A ruled pattern in the form of diamonds on the leather covers.

DOUBLE-COLUMN. Two side by side columns printed on each. Double columns are often used in Bibles.

DOUBLURE, DOUBLÉ. The paste-down or inside lining of the book covers that are made of leather or silk and are usually decorated.

DROP TITLE. The title is placed at the head of the first page of text rather than on a separate title-page.

DRY POINT. Writing without ink; cf. stylus.

DUOTONE. An image printed in two colors, like black and dark blue.

DUST JACKET (or DUST WRAPPER). The paper jacket wrapped around most modern books to protect the cloth covers. Many times this jacket is worth more than the book itself.

EDGES. The edges of a volume may be colored (usually red), sprinkled with red paint spots, gilt with gold leaf, marbled, trimmed, or uncut (left untouched by the binder).

EDITION. All the copies of a book produced, at any time, from the same setting of type.

ÉDITION DE LUXE. Any book produced primarily for its appearance rather than the content. Books that had extra features added.

EDWARDS OF HALIFAX. William Edwards, a book binder in Halifax, England, had five sons, all of whom were involved in his business. Three of his sons later opened their own businesses. The elder Edwards rediscovered and popularized the art of fore-edge painting in the late 1700s. It became a very popular art form. His son Thomas went on to perfect the fore-edge process, later opening his own business. William and Thomas also developed Etruscan bindings in 1785. By rendering vellum transparent, and painting or drawing the designs on the underside, the covers of a volume were protected from wear and tear. Many bindings were developed by Edwards of Halifax, and occasionally you will see them attributed to him. Original fore-edge paintings by Edwards of Halifax are rare, sought after, and usually costly.

EMBLEMATICAL. A term describing ornaments or symbols on leather bindings (e.g. hunting horns for Surtees, ravens for Edgar Allan Poe volumes, bees and eagles for Napoleonica, harps for Ireland).

ENDPAPERS, ENDLEAVES. The double leaves added to the front and back of the book cover by the binder. The outer leaf of each is pasted to the inner surface of the cover known as the paste-down. Endpapers are not usually part of the book as printed.

ENGRAVING. An illustration or decorative device printed from a metal plate or the end grain of a wooden block.

EPHEMERA. Book dealers commonly use the term in reference to paper goods other than the book. The actual Greek meaning refers to printed matter of passing interest.

ERRATA. Mistakes and misprints discovered after the book has been printed.

ETCHING. An image printed from an acid-etched intaglio plate.

ETRUSCAN STYLE BINIDNG. Calf bindings decorated by acid staining. The decorations typically depict a classic ornament such as Greek vases or Palmettes. Often they are used as a border around a plain tree-calf panel.

EXEMPLAR. A book from which another is copied.

EX-LIBRARY. This term refers to a book which at one time had been in a lending library.

EX-LIBRIS. Book plate.

EXTRA. A binder's term for a copy which has been bound and "finished" in the most elegant style, with all edges gilt and generally with an abundance of gilt decoration.

EXTRA ILLUSTRATED. A book with extra plates added to those originally issued.

F.E.P. The front endpaper.

FIRST EDITION. Generally means the first appearance of the work in a printed form.

FIRST EDITION THUS. Not the original edition, but the first of a new edition containing a new feature to the book (i.e., a new illustration).

FIRST ENGLISH EDITION OR FIRST AMERICAN EDITION. The first edition of a book published in England or America that had previously been published abroad.

FLYLEAF. A binder's blank addition to, and following, the free front endpaper. It is often used on the free front endpaper itself.

FLY TITLE. A second half-title is found many times in books from 1750 to 1890. It is placed between the last page of the prelims and the opening page of the text. A flytitle is also known as a bastard title.

FOLIATION. The consecutive numbering of the folios (or leaves) of a volume.

FOLIO. A leaf of paper or parchment in a loose or bound book numbered only on the front. The front and back of the leaf are respectively referred to as recto and verso. Folio also refers to a book or manuscript of the largest size. A large sheet of paper folded in the middle making two leaves or four pages is also called a folio.

FOOLSCAP. A small paper size. At 17 x 13½ inches (43 x 34 cm): when folded into octavo (8vo) format this will give a book 6¾ inches.

FORE EDGE. The edge of a book opposite the spine.

FORE-EDGE PAINTING. This refers to any painted decoration on the fore edge of a book. This technique was popularized in the eighteenth century by John Brindley and Edwards of Halifax. The fore edge of the book was fanned out and then decorated with painted views, usually famous places or structures like churches or castles. When the pages are gilded, the painting remains concealed while the book is closed. When the fore edges are spread or fanned open the painting will reappear.

FORMAT. The shape and size of a book. The size of a volume in terms of the number of times the original sheet has been folded to form its constituent leaves. Folio (fol. or 2) = folded once; quarto (4to or 4) = folded twice; octavo (8vo or 8) = folded three times; duodecimo (12mo or 12) = folded four times, etc.

FOXED, FOXING. Paper damaged due to poor environmental conditions becomes marked with spots known as foxing. The spots take on a variety of colors including brown, yellow, or black, and are normally associated with mold or mildew.

FRONTISPIECE. An illustration facing the title page of a book.

GATHERING. When one sheet has been printed on both sides, folded and sewn into the book, the leaves from that sheet belong to one gathering. It is then sewn through the center fold, and each gathering in the book is given its own signature letter.

GAUFFERED (or goffered) EDGES. Gilt (or silvered) edges decorated by the impression of heated tools, usually of the pointillé type. The formal designs or ornamentation are found on the page ends of a book.

GIFT BINDING. A leather binding styled exclusively for presentation. Common examples include school prizes and Christmas gifts.

GILT EDGES. This means that all three edges of the book have been cut smooth and gilded. The initials AEG are also used.

GILT TOPS or TOP EDGES GILT. Interchangeable terms meaning that only the top edges have been gilded.

GROOVES. The space or depressions between the boards and the spine are called grooves.

GUTTER. The gutter is the point at which the folded writing material meets the spine of a codex. Gutter also refers to the white space formed by the inner margins of two facing papers.

GROLIER, JEAN. 1479 – 1565. An important French book collector.

HALF BOUND. When the spine and outer corners of a book are made of leather, while the remaining sides are cloth or paper.

HALF TITLE. The leaf in front of the title page which carries on its recto the title of the book with no other information.

HAND COLORED. Book illustrations individually hand colored after the book or illustration are printed.

HARD-GRAIN MOROCCO. Goatskin used for binding that has a close, pebbly texture.

HEADBAND. A decorative cloth band placed inside the back strip at the top of the spine.

HEADCAP. Headcap refers to the top of the spine. The head cap breaks down or chips when books are improperly handled or pulled from the top of the spine.

HEADLINE. A line of type at the top of a page, above the text.

HEADPIECE. A type ornament or vignette at the head of a chapter or division of a book.

HINGES. Usually refers to the inside gutters or junctions of a book. The term joints most often refers to the outside gutter, however the terms are used interchangeably. For example, when you read that a book has been re-hinged or re-jointed it means the books have been reinforced with new gutters and hinges.

HISTORIATED INITIAL. A letter or initial containing figures or a story within the initial.

HOLLOW BACKS. A binding with recessed cords not glued to the spine. This allows a book to lie flat when opened, pulling the recessed cords up, forming a semi-circular space at the leather back.

HOLOGRAPH. A document written entirely in the author's own hand.

ILLUMINATION. Generally the hand-applied work is in gold, silver, or colored paint. The art of decorating a text with designs or letter.

IMPRESSION. All the copies of a book printed at the same time, in a single printing, from the same type.

IMPRIMATUR. A mark of official approval or license to print or publish a book. The Latin phrase "let it be printed" or "it may be printed" is often used as the imprimatur. Usually used by the Catholic Church.

IMPRINT. A statement of names of the persons (publishers, printers) responsible for the book, including the date and place of publication.

INCUNABULA. A book printed during the infancy of printing from movable metal type before 1500.

INDIA PAPER. An abbreviation for India Proof Paper used for proofs of engravings.

INK FOR PRINTING. A pigmented liquid used for printing. The two ingredients found in printing ink are varnish, made from boiled linseed oil, and different colors or pigments.

INK FOR WRITING. A pigmented paste initially made of soot and gum that is unstable in quality. Over time the ingredients changed to iron gall, made of gall nuts, gum, and copperas. It is permanent and has a brown appearance.

INSCRIBED COPY. A copy with a note or inscription to the recipient in addition to the author's signature.

INTAGLIO. A method of printing using an engraved or designed metal plate pressed onto paper, leaving the impression or design on the paper. The incised die produces a design in relief.

JAPANESE VELLUM. Paper, rather stiff, with a smooth glossy surface similar to vellum, but thinner. It is often used for deluxe editions.

LABEL. Leather labels usually made of very thin morocco have been used since the 1750s. A leather or paper square placed on the spine of a book usually containing the author, title, or volume number of the book.

LAID DOWN. Backed with a stronger paper or material.

LAID PAPER. Shows the characteristic parallel wire marks of early papers made in a mesh frame by hand.

LARGE PAPER. Special copies of a book printed on larger paper than the rest of the edition.

LEAF. A piece of paper comprising a page on its front side (recto, obverse) and another on its back (verso, reverse).

LEVANT. Loose-grained morocco leather, highly polished and attractive. The most sought after type, originating from the Near East.

LIBER. A book.

LIMITED EDITION. Limited to a specific number of copies, which is usually noted in the first few pages of the book.

LIMP BINDING. A flexible or flimsy binding, usually made of suede or leather that is sometimes without boards.

LINE ENDINGS. Decorative patterns used to fill up the space left by a short line of text.

LINSON. A paper used in binding that is often grained to look like cloth or even leather.

LITHOGRAPH. Invented by Alois Senefelder in 1798, lithography is a process of printing from a plane smooth surface like stone or metal on which the image to be printed is ink receptive and the blank area ink repellant.

MANUSCRIPT. A book or document written by hand. Abbreviated MS.

MARBLED. Marbled paper is made by lowering a sheet of paper into a bath of gum or size, on the surface of which colors have been drawn out with a comb and stirred into a pattern. It is of Japanese origin, and is over 1,000 years old.

MARBLED CALF. A pattern etched in calf bindings with acids, sometimes giving a marbled effect or look.

MAUCHLINE BINDING. Mauchline is the name used to describe wooden items, usually made of sycamore, that were everyday items made in England and Scotland between 1800 and 1933. Mauchline is named for the Ayrshire town of Mauchline, Scotland, where it was originally made. It is usually decorated with a decal transfer of a familiar scene or famous homestead from a wood engraving and applied to a lacquered wooden object. By 1860 even photographs were being applied. Ferns were later added to give a three-dimensional view. When decorated with Scottish Tartan patterns, Mauchline becomes tartanware. Tartanware became very popular during the mid-nineteenth century when Queen Victoria created a rage for all things Scottish, which developed with her continued fascination with Scotland. See examples of both on pages 25 and 28.

MEISENBACH, GEORGE. Inventor of the halftone reproduction in 1881.

MEZZOTINT. A distinctive form of engraving, deeply black and textured, in which the plate has been worked from dark to light. Used many times for portraits.

MINIATURE. Any volume 3" or less is considered to be a miniature.

MINT COPY. A perfect copy — to be the same as the day it was issued.

MISBOUND. Bound in the wrong order or wrong place.

MOROCCO. A leather made of goat-skin that is able to absorb dye easily. It is Islamic in origin and comes in various types, such as Levant. Hard-grain and niger refer to differences of grain, pattern, or texture in the actual skin when tanned and dyed. Straight-grain and crushed morocco refer to its treatment before it is put on the book.

MOSAIC BINDINGS. Bindings decorated with contrasting colors that are inlaid, onlaid, or hand painted.

MOTTLED CALF. Calf given a mottled effect by staining the leather with blots or flecks of coppers, a type of acid.

NIGER. A type of morocco (goat-skin) from West Africa. It is a soft skin with a variable grain. It was native dyed, often in crimson, red, green, or natural buff. Usually it appears uneven in color.

OASIS. A smooth African goatskin usually tanned and dyed in America.

OBLONG. A book is oblong when its width exceeds its height.

OCTAVO. The most traditional and common format of a book in the seventeenth century. It is based on a sheet folded three times, giving eight leaves, equaling sixteen pages. Usually written simply 8vo. Octavo also refers to a book of between seven inches and ten inches in height.

OFFSETS, OFFSETTING. Brown staining found on the page opposite an engraved plate and mirroring the engraving. This often results when something is left in the book causing the engraving to transfer itself to the opposite page.

ONLY. A note of warning indicating a set of books is incomplete. For example, if a catalog describes a set of books as being 12 volumes (only) it means one volume or several volumes are missing.

PADDED. When leather bindings have cotton inserted between the leather and boards, they are padded.

PAGINATION. The sequence of figures used to number the pages of a book. These are known individually as page numbers, collectively as pagination.

PANEL, PANELLED. In book binding it means a rectangle formed of single, double, or triple fillets (ruled lines), that are gilt or blind on the sides or between the bands on the spine of the book.

PAPYRUS. Thin sheets from the stem of the papyrus plant, found on the banks of the Nile River. Made by laying strips side by side, with another layer of similar strips crossing them. Then soaking them and smashing them, then letting them dry to form a writing surface.

PARCHMENT. The dressed undersplit of sheepskin, used for writing or binding.

PARTS. A once popular method of publishing a book in installments, individual parts, or numbers, later to be bound together on completion.

PASTEDOWN. The half of the endpaper lining the inside cover.

PAYNE, ROGER. 1738 – 1797. A master binder whose books are very desirable.

PICKERING, WILLIAM. 1796 – 1854. A well-respected bookseller and printer.

PLATES. The illustrations in a book. They may be copperplates, steel engravings, lithographs, or wood engravings.

POINT. The slight variations between different copies of a book, enabling distinctions to be made between different issues or states. For example: Book is a first edition, second state.

POINTILLÉ. Gold-tooled decoration on leather bindings producing a dotted effect. This is accomplished through the repetition of single dots or the use of tools with dotted outlines.

PRELIMINARY LEAVES, or PRELIMS. All the pages (title page, contents, preface, list of illustrations, etc.) preceding the main body of the text.

PRESENTATION COPY. A book copy given by the author to someone, usually as a gift.

PRESSMARK. A notation in or on a book indicating where it should be placed in a library.

PRIVATE PRESS (PRESSES). A traditional hand press owned and operated in the interest of fine printing and high quality products.

PRIVATELY PRINTED. Most often refers to books printed from private presses or books that were for closed or private distribution.

PRIVATELY PUBLISHED. Done so at the author's expense.

PRIZE BINDING. Usually given by a school or university for a student achieving excellence in a subject. The book will usually have a pasted down paper plaque on the inside front cover, and the cover of the book will often have the logo of the school stamped on the front cover.

PROVENANCE. The history of a book's previous ownership. This may be clearly marked by the owner's name, coat of arms, bookplate, or other evidence in the book itself. It may take some detective work from other sources such as auction house records or booksellers' catalogs to establish the provenance of the book.

ROAN. A thin sheepskin used for bookbinding.

ROYAL. A larger paper size — 25 inches x 20 inches, a royal octavo (8vo) is a full 10 inches tall.

QUARTER BOUND. Leather appears on the spine of a book only, while the sides are covered with cloth or paper.

QUARTO. A book that appears square in shape and is somewhere between a folio and octavo size. A long ledger or a telephone directory is about quarto size.

QUIRE. A gathering.

RAISED BANDS. One of the most important parts of the inner structure of a binding. Looking at the spine it is a group of bands, usually crossing the spine.

REBACKED. The binding of a book has been given a new back strip or spine.

RECASED. Referring to a book that has been loosened or removed from its cover and subsequently reinstalled into the same cover.

RECTO. The right-hand page of a book or the front side of a leaf.

REJOINTED. A book whose joints have deteriorated and then been repaired. Often repairs are unnoticeable when performed by an exceptionally talented binder.

REMBOÎTAGE. The transferring of a book from one binding to another. The new bindings are usually more elaborate, contemporary, original, or appropriate for the book.

RUBBED. On the leather books it is when the joints, head or tailpieces, or corners are scuffed or chaffed.

RUBRIC, RUBRICATED, RUBRISHER. A rubric is a heading to a book chapter or section, written or printed in red; rubric meaning red.

SANGORSKI AND SUTCLIFFE. A renowned bindery founded in 1901 by Francis Sangorski and George Sutcliffe. This high quality British bindery specialized in elaborately bound copies of the Rubaiyat and many other fine books.

SCORED CALF. Calf skin treated by a compression process, which produces a crinkled effect that looks like a coarse straight-grain morocco.

SEXTODECIMO. A small format book made from printed sheets folded four times to give sixteen leaves. Although small in size, it is not considered a true miniature.

SHAKEN. A term explaining or describing a book whose pages are coming loose or falling out of a binding.

SIGNATURE. The letter assigned to a gathering or section of printed pages. It is found at the foot of the first page of the first leaf of any gathering.

SIGNED BINDINGS. Usually a name will be printed on the inside front or back cover, or at the top or bottom of one of the fly leaves, indicating the name of the person or company who bound the book. This generally adds value to the book, especially the higher-ended books.

SLIPCASE. An open-ended protective sleeve which has three sides used to house a book.

SPINE. The part of a book visible when standing upright on a shelf. The back of the book.

SPRINKLED. This process is used primarily on calf bindings. The binding is colored with small specks or spots, and can also be done on the pages ends.

STRAIGHT-GRAIN MOROCCO. Morocco with an induced grain patterned of straight lines, giving it a smoother texture.

SUNNED. Refers to bindings faded from exposure to UV or natural light. Green and purple leather are the easiest colors to fade.

TAIL. The foot of the back strip or bottom margin of the leaf.

TAILPIECE. A decorative piece or item at the end of a chapter.

TAUCHNITZ, LEIPZIG. A printing firm known for inexpensive reprints of British books.

T.E.G. Top edge gilt.

THREE-QUARTER BOUND. A book with a leather back and corners.

TIES. Tapes or ribbons slotted into the binding for tying the volume shut.

TIPPED IN. A separate illustration or map which is cut to the page size and placed in the book. More commonly the term is used to mean a signature, note, or letter, attached to one of the free-end papers.

TITLE PAGE or TITLE LEAF. The page at the beginning of a book giving details of the author, publisher, date of publication, and address or city where the book was produced.

T.L.S. Typed letter, signed.

TOOLING. Decorative marks, indentions, or impressions made in leather bindings.

TREE CALF. A calf binding that has the boards (covers) stained by mixing of copperas and pearl ash to resemble the design of a tree or tree trunk.

TRIMMED. Trimmed means that the edges of a book's leaves have been cut smooth.

UNBOUND. Has no binding.

UNCUT (of edges). A book is uncut if the edges of the paper have not been cut with a plough or guillotine. It is actually a good problem, because it usually means the book was never read or used.

UNOPENED. The folded sheets that make up the book have not been severed at the folds, leaving some leaves still joined along the outer edges.

VAN GLIDER. A very fine quality of paper used in bindings.

VARIANT. Copies of the same impression exhibiting unexplained variations.

VELLUM. (1) Usually unsplit calf with the hair follicles visible on the spine and cover. The boards of these books spread and easily warp. (2) Can also refer to the skin of a calf, lamb, or goat, untanned but de-greased, treated, and then used for leather bindings.

VERSO. The back or reverse side of the leaf.

VIGNETTE. A small ornamental or decorative design used on a title page or as a head- or tailpiece to a chapter.

VOLUME. A book may run to many volumes but remain a single book. A single volume may, however, contain several books bound together.

W.A.F. Stands for "with all faults," meaning "sold as is," without any guarantee as to condition or completeness.

WATERED SILK. Having a wavy pattern. Used often for doublure and pastedown.

WATERMARK. A mark or device used to identify or distinguish paper in the process of paper making. Usually seen in the finished product when the paper is held against the light.

WHATMAN PAPER. Handmade English paper, used on fine editions.

WOODCUT, WOOD ENGRAVING. An illustration printed from a piece of wood. One of the earliest forms used to create an illustration.

WORMHOLES. The tunnels or holes made in paper or leather and sometimes in the boards of the book.

WRAPS. Paper covers.

ZAEHNSDORF, JOSEPH. A well-respected book binder who produced very fine bindings. Although born in Budapest, he started his bindery in London.

YAPP, YAPP EDGES. A style of binding leaving overlapping flaps on all three edges. Yapp edges refers specifically to the flaps. This style of binding, introduced in 1863, is named after its creator, Johnathan Yapp.

Resources & Accoutrements

WHERE TO FIND INVESTMENT QUALITY LEATHER BINDINGS

The following is a list of reputable dealers with whom I have dealt for years. They are knowledgeable, fairly priced, and above all, honorable. Whether you want to buy investment quality leather books or sell your collection, the following seven dealers come highly recommended as great resources for you.

THE JOHN BALE BOOK COMPANY
Dan Gaeta & Edith Reynolds
158 Grand Street
Waterbury, CT 06702
203-757-2279
www.thejohnbalebooks.com

BOUTIETTE ANTIQUARIAN BOOKS
Arthur Boutiette
11724 Fairway Drive
Little Rock, AR 72212
501-258-1442
Sorry, we couldn't resist including ourselves!
e-mail: arthurbout@aol.com

FIRST FOLIO BOOKS
Dennis Melhouse
1206 Brentwood
Paris, TN 38242
731-644-9940
www.first-folio.com

D & D GALLERIES
David Carlson
P. O. Box 8413
Somerville, NJ 08876
908-874-3162
www.dndgalleries.com

TAMERLANE BOOKS
John Freas
516 Kathmere Road
Havertown, PA 19083
610-449-4400

RULE'S FINE BOOKS
Jim Rule
218 Kingsrow Drive
Little Rock, AR 72207
501-664-1170

GIBSON GALLERIES
Gordon Gibson
14 Kramer Avenue
West Caldwell, NJ 07006
973-403-9377

BOOK CATALOGS

This is a partial list of book dealers or people who sell books, among other things, and offer free catalogs. These catalogs are an excellent resource when ordering books. Additionally, they provide valuable insight on the pricing of books you may already have in your collection.

D & D GALLERIES
P. O. Box 8413
Somerville, NJ 08876
908-874-3162
www.dndgalleries.com

BOUTIETTE'S ANTIQUARIAN BOOKS
11724 Fairway Drive
Little Rock, AR 72212
501-258-1442
e-mail: arthurbout@aol.com

RESOURCES & ACCOUTREMENTS

BAUMANS RARE BOOKS
1215 Locust Street
Philadelphia, PA 19107
www.baumanrarebooks.com

GEORGE BAYNTUN
Manvers Street
Bath
BA1 15W, United Kingdom
www.georgebayntum.com

BOW WINDOWS BOOK SHOP
175 High Street
Lewes, East Sussex
BN7 1YE, United Kingdom
www.bowwindows.com

PHILLIP PIRAGES
2205 Nut Tree Lane
McMinnville, OR 97128
www.pirages.com

ADRIAN HARRINGTON FINE BOOKS
64 A Kensington Church St.
Kensington, London
W8 4DB United Kigdom
www.harringtonbooks.co.uk

R & R AUCTIONS
Specializing in autographs
e-mail them for a catalog at
kay@rrauctions.com

HERITAGE BOOKSHOP
8540 Melrose Avenue
Los Angeles, CA 90069
www.heritagebookshop.com

IMPERIAL FINE BOOKS
790 Madison Avenue, Suite 200
New York, NY 10021
www.imperialfinebooks.com

DENNING HOUSE ANTIQUARIAN BOOKS
P. O. Box 42
31 Orrs Mills Road
Salisbury Mills, NY 12577
www.denninghousebooks.com

J. N. BARTFIELD
30 West End Avenue
New York, NY 10023
212-496-7856

SWANN GALLERIES
104 East 25th Street
New York, NY 10010
www.swanngalleries.com

ABRAHAM LINCOLN BOOKSHOP
357 West Chicago Avenue
Chicago, IL 60610
312-944-3085
www.alincolnbookshop.com
e-mail: staff@alincolnbookshop.com

ANTONIO RAIMO GALLERIES
700 Miami Circle N.E.
Atlanta, GA 30324
www.antoniogalleries.com

THE 19TH CENTURY SHOP
1047 Hollins Street
Baltimore, MD 21223

JOHN WINDLE ANTIQUARIAN BOOKSELLER
49 Geary Street, Suite 233
San Francisco, CA 94018
415-986-5826
www.johnwindle.com

BOOK AUCTIONS

The following book auction houses can be an excellent venue for acquiring leather bindings.

PBA GALLERIES
www.pbagalleries.com

SWANN GALLERIES
www.swanngalleries.com

SOUTHEBY'S
www.southebys.com

CHRISTIE'S
www.christies.com

NEW ENGLAND BOOK AUCTION
413-665-3253
www.nebooksauctions.com

WAVERLY
www.waverlyauctions.com

SKINNER
www.skinnerinc.com

BLOOMSBURG BOOK AUCTION
www.bloomsburg-book-auct.com

BALTIMORE BOOK AUCTION
410-659-0550

DOMINIC WINTER BOOK AUCTION
www.dominicwinter.co.ok

JOHN NICHOLSONS
www.auctionsatjohnnicholsons.com

BONHAMS
www.bonhams.com

BONHAMS & BUTTERFIELDS
www.butterfields.com

CHEFFINS
www.cheffins.co.uk

DOYLE NEW YORK
www.doylenewyork.com

STRIDES
www.stridesquction.co.uk

RUPERT TOOVEY & CO.
www.rupert-toovey.com

BOOK BINDERS

IMG BOOK BINDERY
21114 Walton
St. Clair Shores, MI 48081
586-777-6928
imgbook@c3net.net

STARR BOOKWORKS
Chris Starr
1297 N. Roadrunner Road
Apache Junction, AZ 85219
480-390-2681

AND BOOKS TOO
Dennis Gouey
36 Main Street
Torrington, CT 06790
203-542-5063

SANGORSKI & SUTCLIFFE
1751 Bermondery Street
London SE1

TOLLBRIDGE HOUSE/ PERIOD BOOKBINDERS
Tollbridge Road
Batheaston, Bath
BA1 7DF United Kingdom
jemma@periodbookbinders.co.uk

CRAFT BOOKBINDING COMPANY
2525 Ebright Road
Wilmington, DE 19810
302-475-1534
info@bookrestoration.net

BOOK INSURANCE

As the saying goes, if you have more than two of something, you have a collection. But have you ever thought that you may need to insure that collection? And how do you go about it? I hope to provide some answers to those questions and give you information needed to make an informed decision concerning insurance for your collection.

There are an estimated 90 million collectors in the United States and over 2,000 general collecting categories and millions of book collectors. The antique and collecting industry is estimated at $25 billion per year. The investment in antiques, art, and collectibles has outperformed many other investments. Although we invest time, money, and space in our collections, the majority of us do not carry insurance for our collections, and we are unaware of our policy's limitations. A recent survey conducted by Chubb Insurance, underwriters of PBS's

Antiques Road Show, found that many people did not know the limitations of their coverage nor what the policy would actually pay if an item was lost, broken, or stolen.

If you have homeowner's insurance, would it replace that collectible you recently purchased if you accidentally dropped it? If you mail a few pieces for repair, and they are lost in transit, would your policy cover the cost of replacement? If you do have insurance, it's important to talk to your agent to understand your coverage, its limitations, and on what basis a claim will be paid. If you don't have insurance coverage, you should consider it. What would happen if a bookshelf collapsed, or you dropped a valuable book and the cover snapped off in the cleaning process? Consider that your collection is no longer just a hobby, but also an investment.

TYPES OF INSURANCE

Insurance policies covering privately owned collections are often referred to as "scheduled personal property floaters." These policies are specifically designed to provide coverage for collectibles. Floater policies often provide very broad coverage. For example, coverage is often provided on an "open causes of loss" basis. This includes risks of loss including fire, theft, breakage, and natural disaster. Read the policy carefully to determine the causes of loss insured, the excluded exposures, and the conditions of coverage.

Floater policies offered through insurance companies are classified as either "admitted" or "non-admitted." Admitted insurance companies are licensed by a state insurance department to conduct business in the particular state and, generally, the coverage forms and rates are required to be submitted to the state insurance department for review and approval. Your homeowner's insurer is most likely an admitted insurance company. In contrast, non-admitted (also known as surplus lines) insurers are authorized by the state regulator to conduct business in the particular state, but the coverage forms and rates are not regulated. Because the coverage forms and rates used by non-admitted insurers are not regulated, these insurers have the flexibility to design insurance policies that can be used to cover unique or unusual types of property.

There is another difference between admitted and non-admitted insurers. If an admitted insurer becomes financially impaired or insolvent, most state insurance departments have the authority to take over the operation of the company, and most states have a guaranty fund in place to provide payments for covered claims to help mini-mize the financial loss to policyholders resulting from an insurer's insolvency. However, state insurance departments do not have the authority to take over the operation of a non-admitted insurer, and the state's guaranty fund does not respond to insolvencies of non-admitted insurers.

Before obtaining an insurance policy, call your state's insurance department. Make sure the company is licensed to do business in your state, and request additional information such as the length of time the company has been licensed, types of insurance provided, and any complaints against the company.

POLICY FEATURES AND COVERAGE

Depending on what you want to spend, the following items could be included in any collectibles insurance policy:

* Specific coverage should include theft, vandalism, accidental breakage, fire, lighting, windstorm, flood, water damage, earthquake, and shipping coverage.

* Additions to the collection should be automatically covered for a short time until you can add them onto the existing policy.

* An inflation guard feature that automatically increases the value of your collection each year.

* A reasonable deductible.

* Replacement cost coverage, so that you will be paid the current market retail value of the loss, and not what you originally paid for it.

* Affordable rate of premium to coverage value.

* Detailed inventories or professional appraisals should not be required.

In addition to the above, you may also wish to consider automatic travel and exhibit coverage (note that this does not include coverage for dealers) and moving coverage.

VALUATION, APPRAISAL, AND INVENTORY

For most collections, the insurer should not require a detailed inventory or professional appraisal in order to obtain coverage. However, the company may require a list of individual items with a stated value. This is not uncommon and easily provided if you have kept receipts for your purchases. Although an inventory may not be required, it is still up to you to place a value on your collection. This may be difficult if you have inadequate records or lack an inventory.

An appraisal is one way of determining the value of your collection. This is a good idea, particularly if you have no idea of its value. Generally, an appraiser will need to be present at the time the collection is viewed, measured, documented, and photographed. The appraiser will then research your collection, and ultimately provide you with a written appraisal report. This report will contain information concerning the purpose and type of appraisal conducted. It should also contain a complete description of each item, including size measurements, markings, characteristics, and value. In addition, a photo of each item is included, as well as a glossary of terms and bibliography of materials used to research and determine value.

An appraiser should be certified by the American Society of Appraisers or the International Society of Appraisers. Values should be determined within the guidelines of the Uniform Standards of Professional Appraisal Practice and in some cases in deference to the appraisers many years of experience. For example, in appraising a book collection, a reputable dealer who has over 25 years of experience would be considered a qualified source. Average cost run from $90 to $120 an hour. Some, however, will quote a flat fee based upon their estimate of time required. Normally, appraisal fees include any travel expenses required but never a percentage of value placed on your collection.

An inventory of your collection provides you current valuation, records of purchases, spending, and the length of time each item has been in your collection. More importantly, it can assist you with proof of loss when you have a claim. All insurers require some proof of loss, other than your say so. Some documentation of the item, or a sample of the item, will be required.

Remember, an inventory of your collection is essential. You need not invest in any software; all you need is pencil and paper. At a minimum, you should track the following information for each item:

- Date purchased
- Name of seller and location
- Category of item (manufacturer, type, etc.)
- Good description of item, color, markings, and other unique features
- Size
- Purchase price
- Current value
- Picture of the item (not required but a really good idea)

Finally, assign each item a unique identifier, such as a number or series of letters that will readily lead you to the inventory description. Keep all purchase receipts in a folder and note the inventory number on the receipt. In the case of an actual loss, an inventory description and receipt can be easily found.

For those of you who are computer savvy, and like to keep things in order on a PC, it's fairly easy to create a database in Access or a spreadsheet in Excel or an equivalent software. In addition, there is inventory software specifically designed for collections which are available for purchase online. These include Collection Master (www.nortica.com); Q Collector, "The Computer program for Book Collectors, www.gbooks.com; The Collectibles Database, www.collectiblesdatabase.com; and Collectible Manager, www.ultimediasoftware.com, but you may find more by doing a general search.

A number of websites regarding insurance for collectibles are available and very helpful. Do some research and obtain information about several insurance companies before you purchase a policy.

This insurance information that you have just read was based on an article by Bonnie S. Salzman. A special thanks to Bonnie for this very informative and useful article and for granting us permission to share it with you. Bonnie can be reached at bsalzman@msn.com.

While there are many insurance companies from which to choose, often your current homeowner's policy is sufficient for your collectibles. Just remember to compare several options before choosing. Chubb Insurance, one of the leading collectible insurance companies, offers these pointers.

- Itemized coverage. This option allows you to determine the insured value of each of your possessions. In the event of a total covered loss of an item, you will receive 100% of the insured value. There is no deductible, no depreciation, and no surprises.
- 150% replacement cost. Chubb's valuable articles policy provides safeguards for items that appreciate. If the market value (before the loss) of an item lost or damaged in a covered loss is greater then the itemized amount listed on the policy, they will pay the market value up to 150% of the itemized coverage amount for the item.
- Breakage protection. Coverage for breakage or damage to fragile items is automatically included. This coverage is typically restricted or excluded in homeowners' policies.
- Coverage for "mysterious disappearance." Many homeowners' policies don't cover valuable items that are lost or misplaced, especially when they disappear away

from the home. A Chubb valuable articles policy provides coverage in these situations.

• Worldwide coverage. Your valuables are automatically covered wherever you take them — anywhere in the world.

• Hassle-free appraisal requirements. Unlike many other insurance companies, Chubb does not require an appraisal for every piece that you itemize. For most possessions, they simply need a description of the item and a value. They generally require an appraisal only for fine art worth more than $100,000, jewelry worth more than $50,000, and any other item valued over $25,000.

• Coverage for pairs and sets. If a piece of an itemized pair or set (like earrings or a set of silver) is lost or damaged in a covered loss, you have the option to provide them with the remaining piece(s), and you will receive the coverage amount for the entire set. (This is a great insurance feature for book collectors.)

• Cash settlement. Unlike other insurance companies, you are not required to replace itemized valuables in the event of a loss. You can choose a cash settlement or replace your valuables with the dealer of your choice. The decision is yours.

• Coverage for newly acquired items. If you acquire a new item and already have similar items insured with itemized coverage, your new item is automatically covered for 90 days for up to 25% of the total itemized coverage for those similar articles (maximum $50,000).

For more information about Chubb's coverage or to get a quote, contact www.Chubb.com or call the Chubb Customer Care Team at 866-324-8222.

Here is a list of several other insurance companies that you might want to research:

www.antiqueandcollectible.com
www.collectors.org
www.americancollectorsins.com
www.collectinsure.com
www.collectorsresources.com

ASSOCIATION OF INSURANCE ADMINISTRATION
P.O. Box 4389
Davidson, NC 28036
1-800-287-7127

COLLECTIBLES INSURANCE AGENCY
P.O. Box 1200
Westminster, MD 21158
888-837-9537
info@insurecollectibles.com

WHAT ABOUT COST

Recently I reviewed insurance cost online. One site www.collectors.org, which offers replacement cost coverage and an "all risk coverage including, fire, lightning, windstorm, vandalism, theft, accidental breakage, flood, earthquake, and shipping coverage," posted a chart giving you an idea of how much they charge per thousand dollars worth of coverage. For example:

$20,000 worth of coverage for $50.00 a year
$50,000 worth of coverage for $125.00 a year
$100,000 worth of coverage for $175.00 a year
$200,000 worth of coverage for $275.00 a year

There is much to consider when purchasing adequate insurance coverage for your books. This information should assist you in making an informed decision concerning your insurance needs.

Your homeowners' already affords you adequate coverage under a standard replacement cost clause. However, read your policy carefully to be absolutely certain that your collectibles are included. If you want coverage for accidental damage from dropping your book, water damage, insect damage, your standard homeowners' policy will most likely required additional coverage.

BOOK APPRAISERS

Although many insurance companies do not require an appraisal on each and every book, it is preferable to have one for your own purposes. To provide the insurance company with enough information when determining adequate coverage, you must know the total value of your collection.

Additionally, many insurance companies only give your "basis" in the event of a loss, i.e., what you paid for the items, unless you prove what the current value is. For example, you have a book that you have owned for ten years and you purchased it for $30. Let's say the current value of the book is $400. So your basis is $30 but your replacement cost if $400. It is essential to have at least replacement value. The appraisal will be helpful in proving that the replacement value is in fact $400.

There are several ways to obtain such an appraisal. One is to find someone locally who has been in the business of selling rare leather bindings for many years. Another is the ABAA organization website which lists dealers specializing in bindings. Also you can solicit the help of the dealers listed below. They can provide a professional evaluation and certified appraisal. With a high quality, detailed scan of the book, an appraiser can both evaluate the book's condition and determine the type of binding. Then, upon listing the author, title, publisher date, and other significant details, the appraiser will be able to provide the highest quality service. And remember, the Internet can provide many additional references.

JOHN BALE BOOK CO.
Dan Gaeta & Edie Reynolds
158 Grand Street
Waterbury, CT 06702
203-757-2279
jbbks@yahoo.com

BOUTIETTE'S ANTIQUARIAN BOOKS
Arthur Boutiette
11724 Fairway Drive
Little Rock, AR 72212
501-258-1442
arthurbout@aol.com

FIRST FOLIO BOOKS
Dennis Melhouse
1206 Brentwood
Paris, TN 38242
731-644-9940
firstfol@bellsouth.net

CONSERVATORS

CONSERVATION LABORATORY
New York Public Library
42nd Street & 5th Avenue
New York, NY 10018
212-930-0549

PAPER STAR ASSOCIATES
543 Illington Road
Ossining, NY 10562
914-941-8166

UK INSTITUTE OF CONSERVATION
6 Whitehorse Mews
Westminster Bridge Road
London
W14 8A5 United Kingdom

BRIDWELL CONSERVATION LABORATORY
SMU University
Dallas, TX
214-768-3733

YALE UNIVERSITY CONSERVATION DIVISION
P. O. Box 208240
Yale Station
New Haven, CT 06520

ETHERINGTON CONSERVATION CENTER, INC
7609 Business Park Drive
Greensboro, NC 27409
336-665-1317
336-665-1319
www.donetherington.com

CONSERVATION MATERIALS

CLEAN COVER GEL
A soft cleaner for cloth and paper book covers. Can restore original color and appearance. $11.65 per quart from Talas. E-mail them at info@talasonline.com.

TALAS LEATHER DRESSING
Made only with lanolin and neatsfoot oil. Formula was developed by the New York Public Library. $20.00 from Talas. Located at 20 West 20th Street, 5th floor, New York, NY 10011. E-mail them at info@talasonline.com.

MUSEUM LEATHER DRESSING
Developed in 1946 by H. J. Plenderleith. Used by the British Museum for treatment of leather bindings. E-mail them at information@britishmuseum.ac.uk.

TRIPLE CROWN LEATHER FORMULA
A leather treatment for bindings. $20.00. Available through Boutiette Antiquarian Books. E-mail them at arthurbout@aol.com.

LEATHER BOOK POLISH/PIGMENT
Excellent for scuffed books where the pigment has been rubbed away. Will restore color and pigment. Available in ten colors through Boutiette's Antiquarian Books. The following colors or combination of colors will cover almost all color shades of leather bindings: red, red mahogany, black, navy, brown, dark brown, green, camel, medium beige, and neutral.

Each color is $10.00 per jar. Seven or more colors are $7.50 each. Postage is not included in price. E-mail them at arthurbout@aol.com.

PIGMENT & POLISH VIDEO
A video demonstrating different techniques and uses of this leather polish is available for $25.00. E-mail arthurbout@aol.com.

MISCELLANEOUS BOOK PRODUCTS

THE LIBRARY SHOP
New York Public Library
42nd Street & 5th Avenue
New York, NY 10018
212-930-0041

CONSERVATION MATERIALS
1395 Greg Street, Suite 110
Sparks, NV 89431
702-331-0582

BOOK ACCROUTREMENTS
BOOK PLATES

AMERICAN SOCIETY OF BOOKPLATE
COLLECTORS & DESIGNS
605 North Stoneman, #F
Alhambra, NY 10507

EX LIBRIS
405 Adams Street
Bedford Hills, NY 10507

BOOK CASES

ARISTOCRAFT
P. O. Box 420
Jasper, IN 47546
812-482-2527

HAAS CABINET CO.
625 W. Utica Street
Sellerburg, IN 47172
800-457-6458

BOOK / LIBRARY LADDERS

PUTNAM ROLLING LADDER CO.
32 Howard Street
New York, NY 10013
212-226-5147

LEVENGER CATALOG
P. O. Box 1256
Delray Beach, FL 33447
800-545-0242

LIBRARY LIGHTING

AMERICAN LIGHTING ASSOCIATION
435 North Michigan Ave.
Chicago, IL 60611
800-274-4484

THE ILLUMINATING ENGINEERING
Society of America
120 Wall Street
New York, NY 10005
212-248-5000

YEARLY BOOK FAIR CALENDAR

JANUARY OF EACH YEAR:

Austin Texas Book Fair
Palmer Auditorium
Austin, TX
Phone: 409-935-3016

New Jersey Antiquarian Book Fair
130 Route 10 West
East Hanover, NJ
Contact: Gary Austin
Phone: 800-556-3727

New York Book Show
68 Lexington Ave.
New York, NY
Phone: 215-862-5828
www.mancusoshows.com

FEBRUARY OF EACH YEAR:

California International Antiquarian Book Fair
Concourse Exhibition Center
Phone: 415-962-2500
E-mail: info@winslowevents.com

Columbus Ohio Book Fair
Veterans Memorial Hall
Columbus, OH
Phone: 614-781-0070
www.columbusproductions.com

Delaware Antiquarian Book Fair
Univ. of Delaware Campus, Arsht Hall,
2700 Pennsylvania Ave.
Wilmington, DE
Phone: 302-655-3055

New York Greenwich Village Fair
Phone: 212-675-8151
www.gvabf.org

Westchester Antiquarian Book & Ephemera Fair
670 White Plains Road
Tarrytown, NY
Contact: Michael Gannon
Phone: 518-861-5478

MARCH OF EACH YEAR:

Akron Antiquarian Book Fair
48 East Bath Road
Cuyahoga Falls, OH
Contact: Andrea Klein
Phone: 330-865-5831

Connecticut Antiquarian Book Fair
421 Bantam Road
Litchfield, CT
Contact: Bruce Gventer
413-528-2327

Florida Antiquarian Book Fair
535 Fourth Ave. N.
St. Petersburg, FL
Contact: Larry Kellogg
Phone: 727-563-9922

Indiana Book and Paper Show
Beech Grove High School
5330 Hornet Ave.
Beech Grove, IN
Phone: 765-966-3056

M.A.R.I.A.B. Boston Antiquarian Book Fair
539 Tremont Street
Boston, MA
Contact: Michael Gannon
Phone: 518-861-5478

Raleigh Antiquarian Book Fair
NC Fairgrounds, Gov. Kerr Building
Raleigh, NC
Phone: 336-218-8055

Vermont Antiquarian Book Fair
South Burlington, Vermont
Clarion Hotel
802-527-7243
www.valley.net/~vaba

Washington D.C. Antiquarian Book Fair
Holiday Inn Rosslyn
Arlington, VA
Phone: 301-654-2926
E-mail: dduff@wabf.com

APRIL OF EACH YEAR:

Albuquerque Antiquarian Book Fair
1634 University Blvd. NE
Albuquerque, NM
Contact: Alan Shalette
Phone: 505-291-9653

Great St. Louis Book Fair
8433 Mid County
Vinita Park, MO 63114
Phone: 314-533-0671

Long Island Antiquarian Book Fair
Field House
295 Stewart Ave.
Garden City, NY
Phone: 631-261-4590
E-mail: flamingoshows@aol.com

Michigan Antiquarian Book Fair
Lansing Center
333 East Michigan Ave.
Lansing, MI
Phone: 517-332-0112

New York Antiquarian Book Fair
Park Avenue & 7th Street
New York, NY
Contact: Lana Zepponi
Phone: 212-777-5218

MAY OF EACH YEAR:

Connecticut Antiquarian Book Fair
153 South Main Street
Torrington, CT
Contact: Bruce Gventer
Phone: 413-528-2327

Gold Rush Book Fair
Nevada County Fair Grounds
Grass Valley, CA
Contact: John Hardy
Phone: 530-470-0189

New England Antiquarian Book Fair
Concord, NH

Philadelphia Antiquarian Book Fair
Fort Washington Expo Center
Phone: 215-757-1132
E-mail: tjmccauley1@comcast.net

Washington Antiquarian Book Fair
Holiday Inn Rossley at Key Bridge
1900 Fort Myer Drive
Arlington, VA
Phone: 301-654-2626

JUNE OF EACH YEAR:

Chicago Printers Row Book Fair
1727 S. Indiana, #104
Chicago, IL 60616
Phone: 312-987-1980

Cooperstown Antiquarian Book Fair
Susquehanna Avenue
Cooperstown, NY
Contact: Ed Brodzinsky, Willis Monie
Phone: 607-638-9962
            800-322-2995

The Portland Book, Print, and Paper Show
239 Park Avenue
Portland, ME
Contact: Bruce Gventer
Phone: 413-528-2327

JULY OF EACH YEAR:

Great Barrington Antiquarian Book Fair
John Dewey Academy at Searles Castle Main Street
Great Barrington, MA
Phone: 413-441-1010
E-mail: BBSHOWS@aol.com

Stockbridge Berkshire Antiquarian Book Fair
Main Street (Rt. 7 and 102)
Stockbridge, MA
Contact: Bruce Gventer
Phone: 413-528-2327

AUGUST OF EACH YEAR:

Austin Book Fair
Palmer Auditorium
Riverside Drive at South 1st Street
Austin, TX
Phone: 409-935-3016

Granite State Book and Ephemera Fair
JFK Coliseum
Manchester, NH
Phone: 631-261-4590
E-mail: flamingoshows@aol.com

Rocky Mountain Antiquarian Book Fair
Denver, CO
Phone: 303-480-0220

SEPTEMBER OF EACH YEAR:

Rochester Antiquarian Book Fair
Corner of Calkins and East Henrietta Rd.
Rochester, NY
Contact: Franlee Frank
Phone: 585-325-2050

OCTOBER OF EACH YEAR:

Boston International Antiquarian Book Fair
Hynes Convention Center
900 Boyleston Street
Boston, MA
Contact: Commonwealth Promotions

Seattle Book Fair
Seattle, WA
Phone: 206-323-3999
www.seattlebookfair.com

NOVEMBER OF EACH YEAR:

Buckeye Book Fair
212 East Liberty Street
Wooster, OH 44691
Phone: 216-264-1125

Kentucky Book Fair
P. O. Box 715
Frankfurt, KY 40602
Phone: 502-875-7000

New York Holiday Book Fair
The Altman Building
135th West 18th Street
New York, NY

Midwest Bookhunters Fair
Gentile Center, Loyola University
Chicago, Illinois
773-989-2200
www.midwestbookhunters.org

Be sure to call, write, e-mail, or check the Internet to get updated dates and locations.

BOOKS ONLINE

An excellent resource for purchasing bindings online is abebooks.com, most likely the world's largest resource of books. There are over 12,500 dealers from around the world offering over 50 million books for sale. Some, of course, will be leather bindings. Also check out: bookfinder.com, bibliofind.com, and alibris.com.

SUBSCRIPTIONS

An interesting magazine to subscribe to is *Fine Books & Collections*, a wonderful publication full of interesting articles and general book information. It will keep you up to date on happenings in the "book world." To subscribe, write to:

Fine Books & Collections Magazine
4905 Pine Cone Dr., #2
Durham, NC 27707
919-489-1916, ext. 120

BOOK ASSOCIATIONS AND CLUBS

Library of America: A publisher and organization founded to preserve the best of American writing, both collections and individual works. Explore American authors and preserve our best literature at the same time. Contact them at www.loa.org.

Antiquarian Bookseller Association of America: The premier bookseller's association with over 500 dealers. Write them at 20 West 44th St., New York, NY 10036. Phone number is 212-944-8291. Or contact them at www.abaa.com.

ABAA Newsletter: Subscribe to the ABAA newsletter at $20 a year for 4 issues. Send checks to ABAA, 20 W. 44th St., 4th Fl., New York, NY 10036.

Leather Bound Antiquarian
Book Price Guide

The following 2,500 listings, descriptions, and prices are intended to provide you a guide in determining the value of leather bindings and books. We have attempted to provide you with a cross-section of values ranging from common to difficult to obtain and from inexpensive to costly. Keep in mind that condition is extremely important. Ninety percent of the books and bindings that you will find in the following pages are in "near fine" or "fine" condition. The same book in good or very good condition will be worth significantly less.

Most of the books and bindings listed are written in English and all the listings are considered to be complete. In regards to size, we have attempted to list half of the books in inches, and for the experienced bookman, we have listed the remaining sizes in technical book terms.

We are hopeful the following pages will be of benefit to you when you are contemplating purchasing similar or like books, when trying to determine the value of books or bindings that have been left to you or that you have purchased, or for insurance purposes.

A'BECKETT, Gilbert Abbott. *The Comic History of England*. London: Punch, 1847. Two volumes. Full butterscotch calf by Morrell. All edges gilt. Illustrated by John Leech. Ten hand-colored plates, 120 woodcuts in each volume. First edition. Fine. $850.00

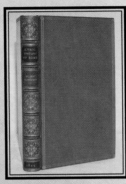

A'BECKETT, Gilbert Abbott. *The Comic History of Rome*. London: Bradbury and Evans, 1849. Full butterscotch calf by Morrell. All edges gilt. Illustrated by John Leech. Ten hand-colored plates. First edition. Fine. $425.00

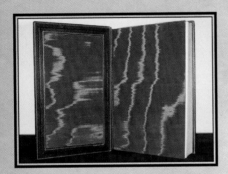

A'KEMPIS, Thomas. *The Imitation of Christ*. London: John Nimo, 1886. Full chocolate calf crushed French levant by Putnam. Top edges gilt, leather dentells and doublures, silk moiré endpapers. Each page is illustrated with a border surrounding the text. 8" tall. Near fine. $575.00

ABBOTT, Edwin A. Flatland. *A Romance of Many Dimensions*. London: 1884. Original full calf. Square octavo. Illustrations by the author. First edition. Near fine. $490.00

ABBOTT, George. *Brief Description of the Whole World*. London, 1624. Early eighteenth century half brown sheep. Small square octavo. Illustrated with frontispiece portrait of the author. Sixth edition. Near fine. $1,150.00

ABBOTT, Charles C. *Clear Skies and Cloudy*. London and Philadelphia: J.B. Lippincott, 1899. Two volumes. Three-quarter teal morocco. Highly gilt spine, top edges gilt. Illustrated with photogravures. 7" tall. Near fine. $375.00

ACKERMAN, Rudolph, and GERNING, Baron Johann Isaac von. *A Picturesque Tour along the Rhine, from Mentz to Cologne*. London, 1820. Folio, mid-twentieth century full red morocco gilt. First edition, with 24 hand-colored illustrations and folded map outlined in color. Near fine. $4,400.00

ADAIR, James. *The History of the American Indians; Particularly Those Nations Adjoining to the Mississippi, East and West Florida, Georgia, South and North Carolina, and Virginia*. London, 1775. Twentieth century full navy morocco gilt by Zaehnsdorf. Gilt decorated spines and dentelles. First edition. Near fine. $2,400.00

ADAMS, George. *Essays on the Microscope*. London, 1787. Two volumes. Text volume: quarto, modern half calf; plate volume: oblong folio. First edition, with 32 fine folio engravings. Near fine. $3,600.00

ABBOTT, Evelyn. *Hellenica*. New York, Bombay and Calcutta: Longmans, Green and Co., 1907. Full tree calf by Bickers. Prize binding with marbled edges. 7½" tall. Nearans, fine. $240.00

ABBOTT, John S.C. *History of Napoleon Bonaparte.*
New York: Harper & Brothers, 1855. Two volumes.
Three-quarter red morocco. Top edges gilt. Profusely
illustrated. 9" tall. Near fine. $390.00

ADDISON, Joseph. *Addison's Works.* London: J.
McCreery, 1811. Six volumes. Full calf. Marbled edges.
Fine. $750.00

ADAMS, John Quincy. *Oration on the Life and Character of
Gilbert Motier de Lafayette.* Washington: Gales and Seaton,
1835. Contemporary full straight-grain red morocco.
Octavo. First edition. Near fine. $2,800.00

ADAMS, John. *A Defense of the Constitutions of Government of the
United States of America.* London, 1787. Three-quarter
brown morocco. Octavo. First edition. Near fine. $2,600.00

AESOP. *Fables.* London: John Stockdale, 1793. Two volumes.
Full red morocco, all edges gilt, gilt panels. Near fine.
$1,700.00

AESOP. *Fabvlae.* 1619. Late sixteenth century red morocco
gilt. Flat spine gilt with oval floral garlands and oval
morocco label in the center. Illustrated with 60 small
woodcut illustrations in the text. Near fine. $2,400.00

ALCOTT, Louisa M. *Little Women.* Boston, Little Brown & Co.,
1922. Little Brown & Company. Color illustrations by
Jessie W. Smith. Red morocco gilt. Near fine. $950.00

ALIGHIERI, Dante. *The Divine Comedy of Dante Alighieri.* Translated by Henry Wadsworth Longfellow. Boston: James R.
Osgood & Co., 1871. Three royal octavo volumes. Contemporary three-quarter red morocco gilt with raised
bands. Near fine. $475.00

ALIGHIERI, Dante. *The Vision: Hell, Purgatory and Paradise.*
London: Frederick Warne & Co., circa 1886. Three-quarter tan calf gilt. Raised bands, ornate spines, and marbled
boards and edges. Translated by Rev. Henry F. Cary.
Near fine. $275.00

ALIGHIERI, Dante. *The Vision: Hell, Purgatory, and Paradise.*
London: John Taylor, 1831. Three volumes. Full tan calf,
gilt panels, 4to. Translated by Rev. Henry Cary. Near
fine. $550.00

ALISON, A. *History of Europe. From the Commencement of the
French Revolution, to the Restorations of the Bourbons.* London, William Blackwood & Sons, 1839. Ten volumes, full
tan calf, red and green labels. Near fine. $1,300.00

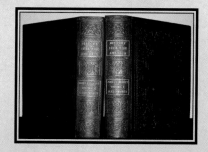

ABBOTT, John S.C. *The History of the Civil War in
America.* New York: Henry Bill, 1863. Two volumes. Full
brown calf with marbled edges. Illustrated. Light foxing
on edges of plates. 10" tall. Near fine. $625.00

AINSWORTH, William Harrison. *The Works of
Ainsworth.* London: George Routeledge and Sons, 1895.
Sixteen volumes (only four shown). Three-quarter tan
calf with marbled edges. Illustrated with woodcuts. 8½"
tall. Near fine. $1,600.00

ALIGHIERI, Dante. *The Vision of Hell.* London: Cassell, Petter and Galpin, circa 1870. Full black calf. All edges gilt. Dore illustrations. 15" tall. Very good. $850.00

ALLESTREE, Richard. *The Ladies Calling. In Two Parts.* Oxford: At the Theater, 1677. With: *The Whole Duty of Man.* London: Robert Pawlet, 1682. Two octavo volumes. Contemporary full burgundy morocco gilt. Gilt decorated spines and covers with raised bands. Near fine. $2,400.00

ANDERSEN, Hans Christian. *Danish Fairy Legends and Tales.* London: William Pickering, 1846. Half calf gilt, small octavo. First English edition. Near fine. $1,275.00

ANDERSEN, Hans Christian. *Fairy Tales and Sketches.* London: 1887. Full brown calf gilt. Octavo. Illustrated. Near fine. $450.00

ANDERSEN, Hans Christian. *Fairy Tales.* London: Hodder and Stoughton, 1924. Full vellum gilt. Quarto. First edition, one of only 500 copies signed by the illustrator, Kay Nielsen. Near fine. $2,400.00

ALOE (pseudo TUCKER, Charlotte Maria). *Hebrew Heroes A Tale Founded on Jewish History.* London: T. Nelson and Sons, 1900. Full green morocco by Relfe Brothers. Prize binding with marbled edges. Twenty-eight illustrations. 7½" tall. Near fine. $175.00

ANDERSEN, Hans Christian. *Hans Andersen's Fairy Tales.* London: Constable & Co., 1913. Full blue morocco gilt. Small quarto. Gilt-decorated spine with raised bands. Illustrated by W. Heath Robinson including color plates and black and white full-page and in-text illustrations. Near fine. $975.00

ANDERSEN, Hans Christian. *Stories from Hans Anderson.* London: Hodder & Stoughton, 1911. Original full vellum with gilt cover. Small folio. First edition, one of only 750 copies signed by the artist, Edmund Dulac. Near fine. $1,650.00

ANDERSEN, Hans Christian. *Stories from Hans Anderson.* London: 1911. Full vellum. Folio. Gilt-decorated spine and covers, top edge gilt. Illustrated and signed by Edmund Dulac, with 28 color plates. Near fine. $2,800.00

ANONYMOUS. *A Century of French Romance.* New York: D. Appleton & Co., 1902. Twenty volumes. Three-quarter red morocco. Gilt decorated spines. Illustrated. Limited edition, one of only 250 sets. Near fine. $2,200.00

ANONYMOUS. *British Sports and Sportsmen includes Golf, Tennis, Hockey & Winter Sports.* London: Sports and Sportsman Ltd, circa 1800. Full red morocco. Gilt decorated spine. Illustrated. Near fine. $475.00

ANONYMOUS. *Half Hours in the Holy Land.* Travels in Egypt, Palestine and Syria. London: James Nisbet & Co., circa 1890. Full tree calf. Near fine. $250.00

ANONYMOUS. *Napoleon In Time.* Printed for Subscribers only, circa 1890. Three-quarter green morocco. Ribbed spine, gilt decorated with marbled boards. Illustrated. Near fine. $175.00

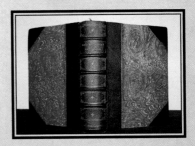

ANDERSEN, Hans. *Hans Andersen's Fairy Tales.* New York: Scribner and Welford, 1882. Three-quarter black calf with marbled edges. Original illustrations and thirty full-page plates printed in color. 7½" tall. Near fine. $1,250.00

ARCHER, Thomas. *Pictures and Royal Portraits Illustrative of English and Scottish History.* **London: Blackie & Son, 1878. Two volumes. Full red morocco. Illustrated. First editions. Frank Deering bookplates. Fine. $950.00**

ANONYMOUS. *The Cathedrals of England and Wales. Their History, Architecture & Associations.* London: Cassell & Co., 1906. Two volumes. Full purple morocco gilt. Illustrated. Near fine. $575.00

ANONYMOUS. *The Court and Camp of Buonaparte.* London: John Murray, 1831. Small 8vo. Half maroon calf, ribbed gilt decorated spine. Includes folding genealogical table of the Buonaparte family. Near fine. $180.00

ANONYMOUS. *The Court and Camp of Buonaparte.* London: John Murray, 1829. Three-quarter tan calf. 12mo. Near fine. $275.00

ANONYMOUS. *The Odes and Epodes of Horace, Introduction, Life and Essays.* Boston: Bibliophiole Society, 1901. Nine volumes. Full brown morocco. Gilt spines and covers. Top edges gilt. Limited edition. Near fine. $590.00

ANONYMOUS. *The Sacred Books and Early Literature of the East with Historical Surveys of The Chief Writings of Each Nation.* New York: Parke Austin, 1917. Fourteen volumes. Three-quarter brown morocco. Gilt spines. Illustrated. Near fine. $1,150.00

ANONYMOUS. *The Travels and Surprising Adventures of Baron Munchasen.* London: William Tegg, 1868. Full red morocco by Bayntun. Gilt decorated spine and covers. Illustrated by George Cruikshank. Near fine. $675.00

ANSON, Adrian C. *A Ball Player's Career.* Chicago: Era Publishing Co., 1900. Three-quarter calf. Octavo. Illustrated with photographic plates. First edition. Near fine. $575.00

APES, William. *A Son of the Forest: The Experience of William Apes.* New York: 1829. Half calf gilt. 12mo. First edition. Near fine. $625.00

ARIOSTO, Ludovico. *Orlando Furioso.* Milan: 1866. Mid-twentieth century full navy calf. Small quarto. Illustrated with hundreds of full-page engravings by Gustave Dore. Housed in a custom slipcase. Near fine. $1,500.00

ARISTOTLE. *The Works.* Oxford: The Clarendon Press, 1930. Twelve volumes. Three-quarter red calf. Gilt decorated spines. Near fine. $975.00

ARMSTRONG, Sir Walter. *Gainsborough His Place in English Art.* London: Wm. Heineman, 1898. Three-quarter green morocco. Gilt decorated spine. Illustrated. Near fine. $275.00

ARMSTRONG, Sir Walter. *Turner.* London: Thomas Agnew & Sons, 1902. Three-quarter green morocco. Gilt decorated spine. Thick folio. Illustrated. Near fine. $275.00

ARNOLD, Matthew. *Selected Poems.* London: MacMillan & Co., 1910. Full burgundy morocco by Ramage. Raised bands, gilt covers. Near fine. $280.00

ARIOSTO, Ludovico. *The Orlando Furioso.* **London: Henry G. Bohn, 1864. Two volumes. Full tree calf by Riviere. Highly gilt spine with marbled edges. Steel engravings. 7" tall. Near fine. $475.00**

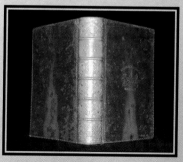

ARNOLD, Matthew. *Poetical Works of Matthew Arnold.* **London: MacMillan and Co., 1819. Full tree calf by Oxford. Prize binding with marbled edges. 7" tall. Near fine. $225.00**

ARNOLD, Matthew. *The Poetical Works of Matthew Arnold*. London: MacMillan & Co., 1890. Full butterscotch calf. All edges gilt. 7½" tall. Near fine. $175.00

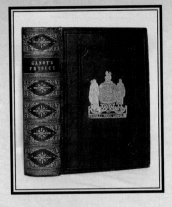

ATKINSON, E. *Elementary Physics*. London: Longmans, Green & Co., 1879. Full black calf. Prize binding. Ninth edition. Fine. $260.00

ASHTON, John. *Modern Street Ballads*. London: 1896. Three-quarter blue calf. Octavo. Illustrated with 56 wood-engravings. First trade edition. Near fine. $250.00

AUDEN, W.H. and ISHERWOOD, Christopher. *Journey to a War*. London: Faber & Faber Limited, 1939. Full calf. Illustrated with frontispiece illustration, folding map, and numerous photographs by Auden. Near fine. $225.00

AUDUBON, John James and BACHMAN, John. *The Quadrupeds of North America*. New York: 1849 – 54. Three volumes. Royal octavo. Original full black morocco gilt. First octavo edition, illustrated with 155 hand-colored lithographic plates. Near fine. $17,800.00

AUDUBON, John James and BACHMAN, John. *The Quadrupeds of North America*. New York: Published by V.G. Audubon, 1851 – 54. Three royal octavo volumes. Original publisher's morocco. All edges gilt, raised bands and marbled boards. Illustrated with 155 hand-colored plates. Near fine. $13,500.00

AUDUBON, John James. *The Birds of America from Drawings Made in the United States and Their Territories*. New York: Published by V.G. Audubon, 1856. Seven royal octavo volumes. Full brown morocco gilt. Raised bands, gilt edges. Illustrated with 500 hand-colored plates. Second edition. Fine. $42,000.00

AUGUSTINE. *The Confessions of Saint Augustine*. London: 1921. Full red morocco gilt by Riviere & Son. Octavo. Illustrated with eleven color plates by Maxwell Armfield. Housed in a custom slipcase. Near fine. $350.00

AULDJO, John. *Journal of a Visit to Constantinople, and Some of the Greek Islands, In the Spring and Summer of 1833*. London: Longman, Rees, Orme, Brown, Green, & Longman, 1835. Quarter green calf over marbled paper boards. Flat spines. Illustrated by George Cruikshank. First edition. Near fine. $430.00

AURELIUS ANTONINUS, Marcus. *Meditations*. London: 1908. Small square quarto. Contemporary full blue crushed morocco gilt. Near fine. $160.00

ARNOLD, Thomas. *History of Rome and The History of the Later Roman Commonwealth*. London: T. Fellows, F. and J. Rivington, 1857. Five volumes. Full tan calf. Marbled edges. Prized binding. 9" tall. Very good. $450.00

AUSTEN, Jane. *The Novels of Jane Austen*. Edinburgh: John Grant, 1911. 12 volumes. Three-quarter black morocco, bound by Zaehnsdorf. Winchester edition. Fine. $6,800.00

AUSTEN, Jane. *The Selected Works of Jane Austen.* **Leipzig: Bernhard Tauchnitz, 1870. Four volumes. Three-quarter red morocco. Top edges gilt. 6" tall. Near fine. $475.00**

AUSTEN, Jane. *Austen's Novels.* London: Richard Bentley & Son, 1879 – 1882. Six octavo volumes. Contemporary full tan calf gilt by Simpson & Renshaw. Gilt decorated spines, raised bands with green and red morocco labels. Engraved frontispiece in each volume. Near fine. $3,100.00

AUSTEN, Jane. *Emma: A Novel in Three Volumes.* London: Printed for John Murray, 1816. Three volumes. Contemporary half calf. 12mo. First edition, one of only 2,000 copies. Near fine. $9,100.00

AUSTEN, Jane. *Mansfield Park: A Novel.* London: Printed for T. Egerton, 1814. Three volumes. Full red crushed morocco gilt by Sangorski & Sutcliffe. Raised bands with spine compartments gilt with centerpiece scrolls and fleuron. Marbled endpapers, all edges gilt. First edition. Fine. $11,500.00

AUSTEN, Jane. *The Novels and Letters.* New York and Philadelphia: Frank S. Holby, 1906. Twelve octavo volumes. Contemporary three-quarter red calf gilt. Red silk boards, marbled endpapers. "Winchester Edition," one of only 1,250 copies. Illustrated with plates by C.E. and H.M. Brock. Edited by R. Brimley Johnson. Near fine. $8,800.00

AUSTEN, Jane. *The Novels of Jane Austen.* Boston: Little, Brown and Co., 1901 – 02. Twelve small octavo volumes. Contemporary three-quarter green morocco gilt. Gilt decorated spines, raised bands, and marbled endpapers. "Roberts Brothers Edition." Tissue-guarded frontispieces in each volume. Near fine. $2,500.00

AUSTEN, Jane. *The Novels of Jane Austen.* Boston: Little, Brown and Co., 1905 – 1906. Twelve small octavo volumes. Contemporary three-quarter tan calf, gilt decorated spines, raised bands, marbled boards, and endpapers. Near fine. $2,100.00

AUSTEN, Jane. *The Novels.* Edinburgh: John Grant, 1911. Twelve octavo volumes. Three-quarter brown morocco gilt. Gilt decorated spines with raised bands. "Winchester Edition." Frontispiece portrait in Volume 1. Near fine. $6,800.00

AUSTEN, Jane. *The Novels.* London: Richard Bentley, 1833. Five octavo volumes. Three-quarter red morocco gilt. Raised bands, marbled boards, and endpapers. Near fine. $3,400.00

AUSTEN, Jane. *The Works.* London: MacMillan & Co., 1899. Five volumes. Three-quarter calf. Ribbed spines gilt decorated. Illustrated by C.E. Brock. Near fine. $2,700.00

AUSTEN, Jane. *Works.* Boston: Little, Brown and Company, 1901 – 03. Twelve small octavo volumes. Modern half green morocco gilt. Gilt decorated spines. Near fine. $2,500.00

AUSTEN, Jane. *Works.* London: 1953. Five volumes. Small octavo, contemporary half crushed green morocco gilt. Near fine. $775.00

AUSTEN, Jane. *Works.* London: J.M. Dent & Co., 1892. Ten volumes. One of only 100 "Large Paper Editions." Full red morocco gilt. Near fine. $5,600.00

AUSTEN, Jane. *Works.* London: J.M. Dent Co., 1893. Ten volumes. Three-quarter green calf gilt. Ribbed spines gilt decorated. Edited by Reginald B. Johnson. Near fine. $5,400.00

AYTOUN, William Edmondstoune. *Lays of the Scottish Cavaliers.* **Edinburgh and London: William Blackwood & Sons, 1863. Full red morocco. All edges gilt. Gold gilt embossed cover. Illustrated by Paton. 9½" tall. Fine. $550.00**

BACHELLER, Irving. *A Man of the Ages.* Indianapolis: The Bobbs-Merrill Co., 1919. Full red morocco. Flat signed signature and letter on fly leaf from author. Top edges gilt. First edition. 8" tall. Near fine. $575.00

BACK, George. *Narrative of the Arctic Land Expedition.* London: 1836. Thick quarto. Nineteenth century three-quarter red morocco gilt. First edition. Large-paper edition with large folding map. Near fine. $3,100.00

BACON, Francis. *Letters.* London: Printed for Benjamin Tooke, 1702. Contemporary blind paneled calf gilt. Raised bands, spine gilt, floral ornaments, and scrolling on corners. First edition. Near fine. $275.00

BACON, Francis. *The Works.* London: A. Millar, 1765. Five volumes in full tan contemporary calf, gilt panels. Quarto. Near fine. $1,200.00

BACON, Francis. *The Works.* London: C & J Rivington, 1826. Ten volumes in full tan polished calf, red and green labels, gilt toolings on spine. Near fine. $1,175.00

BAKER, Sir Richard. *A Chronicle of the Kings of England.* London: 1733. Folio, early full speckled calf. Folio edition of Baker's famous history of the English Kings. Near fine. $975.00

BACON, Francis. *The Works of Francis Bacon.* New York: Hurd and Houghton, 1878. Two volumes. Three-quarter maroon morocco. Marbled edges. Illustrated. 7½" tall. Near fine. $150.00

BALDWIN, Henry. *The Orchids of New England.* New York: 1884. Three-quarter navy calf. Slim octavo. Illustrated with numerous full-page engravings by the author. First edition. Fine. $650.00

BALDWIN, William. *African Hunting From Natal To The Zambesi. Including Lake Nagami & The Kalahari Desert.* London: Richards Bentley, 1863. Full brown morocco. Raised bands with gilt decorated spine and covers. Illustrated. First edition. Near fine. $625.00

BALZAC, Honore de. *The Works.* New York: 1899. Thirty-two octavo volumes. Contemporary half brown morocco gilt. Illustrated with numerous photogravures. Edition Royale, one of only 1,000 sets. Near fine. $3,200.00

BALZAC, Honore. *Works.* London: J.M. Dent & Co., 1896. Forty volumes. Three-quarter red morocco. Gilt decorated spines. Illustrated. Near fine. $5,000.00

BADEAU, Adam. *Grant in Peace.* Hartford: S.S. Scranton & Co., 1887. Three-quarter chocolate calf by Launder and MacDonald. Top edges gilt. Illustrated. First edition. 9" tall. Near fine. $450.00

BACHELLER, Irving. *The Master.* New York: Doubleday, Page & Co., 1909. Full navy morocco. Top edges gilt. Inlaid red morocco doublures and silk moiré endpapers. Signed by the author. First edition. 8" tall. Fine. $575.00

BADEAU, Adam. *Military History of Ulysses S. Grant.* New York: D. Appleton & Co., 1868. Three volumes. Three-quarter dark brown calf by Launder and MacDonald. Top edges gilt. Illustrated with pull-out maps. First edition. Near fine. $950.00

BANCROFT, George. *History of the United States.* New York: D. Appleton & Co., 1891. Twelve volumes. Contemporary full navy morocco. Quarto. Raised bands, red morocco doublures with floral designs. Large paper edition, one of only 100 copies. Illustrated with over 250 prints. Near fine. $3,200.00

BANNERMAN, Helen. *The Story of Little Black Sambo.* New York: Frederick A. Stokes Company, circa 1900. Original quarter tan buckram over tan pictorial boards. 12mo. Illustrated with 27 full-page color illustrations by the author. Near fine. $1,650.00

BARRIE, J. M. *The Works.* New York, 1929. Fourteen volumes. Tall octavo. Contemporary three-quarter blue morocco gilt. Gilt decorated spines. Limited "Peter Pan" edition, one of only 1,030 sets. Near fine. $3,400.00

BARRIE, J.M. *The Works.* London, New York: Toronto: Hodder and Stoughton, 1913. Ten tall octavo volumes. Contemporary three-quarter dark green morocco. "The Limited Kirriemuir Edition of Barrie's Works," one of only 1,000 sets produced. Near fine. $2,600.00

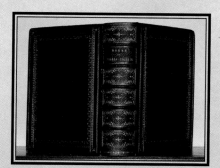

BAILLIE, Joanna. *The Dramatic and Poetical Works of Joanna Baillie.* London: Longman, Brown, Green and Longmans, 1853. Full black calf. All edges gilt. 8" tall. Near fine. $150.00

BALL, Eliza Craufurd. *The Christian Armour.* New York: Charles Scribner & Co., 1866. Full brown calf with deep set and highly gilt embossed cover. All edges gilt. Bennett pg. 8 states: "One of the most elaborate books of its type," illuminated." 11" tall. Near fine. $1,400.00

BALL, Robert Stawell. *Star-Land.* London: Cassell and Co., 1900. Full tree calf. Prize binding with marbled edges. 94 illustrations. 7½" tall. Near fine. $190.00

BALZAC. *Droll Stories.* London: John Camden Hotten, 1865. Three-quarter tan calf. Highly gilt spine with top edges gilt. 425 illustrations by Dore. 8" tall. Near fine. $320.00

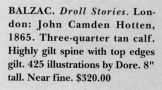

BANCROFT, George. *History of the American Revolution.* London: Richard Bentley, 1852. Three volumes. Full tan calf with marbled edges. 8" tall. Near fine. $625.00

BANCROFT, George. *History of the Colonization of the United States.* Boston: Little Brown & Co., 1872. Ten volumes. Three-quarter butterscotch calf. 9" tall. Near fine. $1,600.00

BANCROFT, George. *The History of the United States of America.* New York: D. Appleton, 1886. Six volumes. Three-quarter butterscotch calf. Marbled edges. 8½" tall. Near fine. $950.00

BANCROFT, Hubert Howe. *The Native Races of the Pacific States of North America.* New York: D. Appleton and Co., 1875. Five volumes. Three-quarter calf with marbled edges. Illustrated with pull-out maps. 9" tall. Near fine. $2,100.00

BARROW, John. *Travels in China.* London: T. Cadell and W. Davies, 1804. Full contemporary mottled calf with black morocco label. Quarto. Illustrated with hand-colored frontispiece and seven engraved plates. First edition. Near fine. $925.00

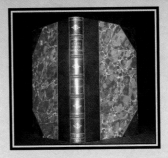

BARBIERE, Joe. *Scraps From the Prison Table.* Doylestown: W.W.H. Davis, 1868. Three-quarter brown calf by Launder and Macdonald. Top edges gilt. Illustrated. First edition. 8½" tall. Near fine. $440.00

BARTH, Henry. *Travels and Discoveries in North and Central Africa.* London: Ward, Lock & Co., 1890. Two volumes. Full tree calf. Illustrated. Near fine. $470.00

BARTLETT, John. *Familiar Quotations.* Boston: Little Brown & Co., 1899. Three-quarter blue morocco gilt. Ribbed gilt decorated spine. Thick 8vo. Near fine. $125.00

BARTLETT, William Henry. *The Scenery and Antiquities of Ireland.* London: circa 1842. Two volumes bound in one. Quarto. Full calf, gilt-stamped. Early edition. Illustrated with over 100 steel engravings. Near fine. $625.00

BARTON, William P. C. *A Flora of North America.* Philadelphia: M. Carey & Sons, 1821 – 23. Three thick quarto volumes bound in one. Three-quarter blue morocco with marbled boards. Illustrated with 106 hand-colored plates. First edition. Near fine. $3,600.00

BAUDIER, Dominique. *Amores.* 1638. Nineteenth century green morocco. Raised bands with decorative spine, all edges gilt. First edition. Full-page engraved portrait. Near fine. $975.00

BECKER, W.A. *Gallus or Roman Scenes of the time of Augustus.* London: Longmans, Green & Co., 1876. Full tree calf. Near fine. $225.00

BEHN, Aphra. *The Plays, Histories, and Novels of the Ingenious Mrs. Aphra Behn. With Life and Memories.* London: John Pearson, 1871. Six octavo volumes. Contemporary three-quarter brown morocco. Raised bands, gilt decorated spines. Marbled boards and endpapers. Large paper edition. Near fine. $760.00

BEHN, Aphra. *The Works of Aphra Behn.* London: William Heinemann, 1915. Six octavo volumes. Three-quarter navy morocco. Raised bands with top edges gilt. One of only 750 copies. Near fine. $875.00

BARNUM, P.T. *Life of B.T. Barnum.* New York: Redfield, 1855. Three-quarter brown calf with marbled edges. Flat signed by P.T. Barnum. First edition. 6" tall. Near fine. $675.00

BELCHER, Edward, Sir. *Narrative of a Voyage Round The World, Performed In Her Majesty's Ship Sulphur, During the Years 1836 – 1842.* London: Henry Colburn, 1843. Two volumes. Half calf over marbled paper boards. Flat spine with red morocco labels. Illustrated with engraved plates and three folding maps. First edition. Near fine. $980.00

BELL, Currer. *Jane Eyre: An Autobiography.* London: Smith, Elder, and Co., 1847. Three octavo volumes. Full green morocco gilt. Raised bands, gilt decorated spines, top edges gilt. First edition of Charlotte Bronte's classic published under pseudonym. Near fine. $9,500.00

BERKELEY, Grantley F. *The English Sportsman in the Western Prairies.* London: 1861. Three-quarter brown calf. Thick octavo. Illustrated with numerous wood engravings. First edition. Near fine. $475.00

BERRYMAN, John. *Poems.* Norfolk: New Directions, 1942. Full calf. Front cover titled in black. First edition, one of only 2,000 copies. Near fine. $225.00

BARRIE, J.M. *The Works of J.M. Barrie.* London, New York, Toronto: 1913. Ten volumes. Full green morocco by Morrell. Top edges gilt. Illustrated with sanguine plates. Bound with Celia's Doves by Dorat. The Kirriemuir edition, one of 650. Near fine. $1,400.00

BARTLETT, W.H. *The History of the United States of North America from the Discovery of the Western World to the Present Day.* London, New York: George Virtue, 1886. Three volumes. Three-quarter black calf. Illustrated with hand-colored pull-out maps. First edition. 10" tall. Near fine. $680.00

BATES, Samuel P. *The Battle of Chancellorsville.* Meadville: Edward T. Bates, 1882. Three-quarter chocolate calf. Highly gilt cover with all edges gilt. Illustrated with maps. First edition. 9" tall. Near fine. $425.00

BEATTIE, William. *Switzerland Illustrated, in a series of Views taken on the spot and expressly for this work.* London: George Virtue, 1836. Two volumes. Full black morocco. Highly gilt spines and covers with all edges gilt. Illustrated with engravings by H. Bartlett. 11" tall. Fine. $1,400.00

BEVERIDGE, Albert J. *Abraham Lincoln.* Boston and New York: Houghton Mifflin Co., 1928. Two volumes. Three-quarter brown morocco gilt. First edition. Near fine. $750.00

BENNET, Thomas. *A Confutation of Quakerism*. Cambridge: University Press, 1709. Full tan calf. Second edition. Replaced spine. 7½" tall. Very good. $225.00

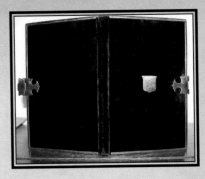

BERNIER, Madame. *Woman's Mission*. London: J.W. Parker, 1841. Full blue velvet. All edges gilt. Velvet and silk moiré doublures and end papers, brass board edges, clasp and shield with leather slip case. 6½" tall. Near fine. $650.00

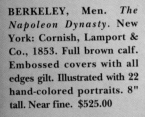

BERKELEY, Men. *The Napoleon Dynasty*. New York: Cornish, Lamport & Co., 1853. Full brown calf. Embossed covers with all edges gilt. Illustrated with 22 hand-colored portraits. 8" tall. Near fine. $525.00

BIBLE. In Arabic. Rome: 1581. Eighteenth century English red morocco backed marbled boards. Raised bands, spine gilt in compartments. Scrolled centerpiece and spray cornerpieces. Illustrated with 67 large woodcuts and 149 illustrations in the text. Near fine. $5,500.00

BEVERIDGE, Albert J. *Abraham Lincoln: 1809 – 1858*. Boston and New York: 1928. Two volumes. Large octavo. Three-quarter burgundy morocco gilt. Illustrated with numerous portraits and illustrations. First trade edition. Near fine. $750.00

BIBLE. London: Printed by C. Baldwin, 1812 – 14. Six volumes. Contemporary dark purple morocco gilt. Covers paneled with gilt outer frame. Flat spines gilt with elaborate scrolling. Silk endpapers, all edges gilt. Near fine. $3,400.00

BEVERIDGE, Albert J. *Abraham Lincoln: 1809 – 1858*. Boston and New York: Houghton Mifflin Company; The Riverside Press Cambridge, 1928. Two large octavo volumes. Three-quarter blue morocco gilt. Raised bands, marbled endpapers, and blue watered silk boards. Illustrated with numerous portraits. Near fine. $950.00

BESANT, Walter. *Captain Cook*. London: Macmillan and Co., 1890. Full red morocco. Prize binding with marbled edges. 7½" tall. Near fine. $275.00

BEVERIDGE, Albert J. *Abraham Lincoln: 1809 – 1858*. Boston and New York: 1928. Four octavo volumes. Full calf. "Manuscript Edition," one of only 1,000 copies. Illustrated with frontispiece engraving of Lincoln and numerous other portraits. Near fine. $1,250.00

BEWICK, Thomas. *A History of British Birds*. Newcastle: Printed by Edward Walker, 1826. Two volumes. Contemporary dark green calf. Raised bands, gilt compartments with floral designs, marbled endpapers and edges. Numerous text illustrations of birds engraved in wood by Thomas Bewick. First edition. Near fine. $650.00

BESANT, Walter. *Jerusalem, The City of Herod and Saladin*. London: Richard Bentley, 1888. Full green morocco by Bickers. Prize binding with highly gilt spine and marbled edges. Illustrated. 8" tall. Near fine. $325.00

BIBLE. Holy Bible. London: G.E. Eyre, circa 1863. Full black calf. All edges gilt. Gauffered edges, inscription in rear (poem). 4½" tall. Very good. $330.00

BIBLE. London: Published for John Reeves, 1802. Nine volumes. Dark blue morocco gilt. Raised bands, spines gilt with floral design, all edges gilt. Written in English. Near fine. $2,400.00

BIBLE. New Testament. London: Longman, Green, Longman, Roberts, and Green, 1865. Full red morocco gilt. Raised bands, gilt spine compartments with floral design. Silk doublures and endpapers, all edges gilt. Illustrated with numerous full page engravings. Near fine. $610.00

BIBLE. Psalms. With: *A New Version of the Psalms of David Fitted to the Tunes Used in Churches.* Cambridge: 1748. Contemporary red morocco gilt. Raised bands, spine compartments gilt. Marbled endpapers with all edges gilt. Near fine. $375.00

BIBLE. The Bishop's Bible. London: By the Deputies of Christopher Barker, 1591. Mottled calf. Raised bands, gilt rules. Woodcut head and tailpieces. Housed in a custom folding cloth box. Illustrated with a full-page woodcut of Adam and Eve in the Garden of Eden. Near fine. $4,600.00

BIBLE. The Family Devotional Bible; Old and New Testament. London: The London Printing and Publishing Co., circa 1830. Two volumes in full black calf. Folio. Illustrated with steel engravings. Near fine. $875.00

BIBLE. The History of the Bible. London: John McGowan, circa 1858. Full black morocco. All edges gilt. Double fore-edge of two views of Canterbury. Illustrated. 11" tall. Near fine. $1,700.00

BIBLE. The Holy Bible. London: Charles Barker, 1675. Printed by J. Bill and Charles Barker. Full black calf with inlaid covers. All edges gilt. Red lined borders on pages. Contemporary binding. 8" tall. Near fine. $1,400.00

BIBLE. The Holy Bible, Containing the Old and New Testaments. Bound with: *The Book of Common Prayer.* Bound with: *The Whole Book of Psalms.* London: 1730. Thick quarto, eighteenth century full paneled brown calf, blind-stamped with ornate centerpieces and with brass clasps and catches. Near fine. $1,500.00

BIBLE. The Holy Bible, Containing the Old and New Testaments. Cambridge: 1768. Two volumes. Tall quarto. Full red calf gilt. Cambridge King James Bible, illustrated with copper-engraved frontispieces by Francis Hayman. Near fine. $2,600.00

BIBLE. The Holy Bible, Containing the Old and New Testaments. Cambridge: 1768. Thick quarto. Contemporary full burgundy calf. Gilt decorated spine, gilt borders on cover with decorative corner pieces. Includes the Apocrypha. Steel-engraved frontispiece by Francis Hayman. Near fine. $2,600.00

BIBLE. The Holy Bible. London: George E. Eyre, 1848. Full black calf. Highly gilt cover, all edges gilt. Inlaid blue and red morocco gilt angels on covers. 6" tall. Very good. $550.00

BIBLE. *The Holy Bible.* London: S.A. Oddy, 1813. Full tree calf. Copper plate illustrations and maps. 17½" tall. Very good. $650.00

BIBLE. *The Holy Bible, Containing the Old and New Testaments.* Oxford: 1682. Thick folio. Contemporary full red morocco gilt. Oxford edition of the King James Bible. Near fine. $6,500.00

BIBLE. *The Holy Bible, Containing The Old Testament and The New....* Oxford: 1715. With: *The Book of Common Prayer....* Oxford: 1720. With: *The Whole Book of Psalms....* London: 1715. Large thick quarto. Contemporary full black morocco gilt. King James Bible. Near fine. $1,800.00

BIBLE. *The Holy Bible. Old and New Testament.* New York: Edward Dinigan, 1844. Quarto. Full tan morocco, all edge gilt. Near fine. $450.00

BIBLE. *The Holy Bible.* Oxford: 1685. Large thick folio. Contemporary full black morocco gilt. Gilt decorated spine with engraved silver corner pieces and centerpieces. King James Bible with clasps. Near fine. $4,300.00

BIBLE. *The King James Bible.* Oxford: Printed by the University Printers, 1699. Contemporary dark calf paneled boards. Four metal corner plates. Raised bands on spine with floral sidepieces. Marbled endpapers. Near fine. $1,150.00

BILLINGS, Robert W. *Antiquities of Scotland.* Edinburgh: circa 1890. Two volumes. Three-quarter green morocco. Raised bands, gilt panels. Illustrated. Large quarto. Near fine. $1,250.00

BINION, Samuel Augustus. *Ancient Egypt or Mizraim.* New York: 1887. Two large folio volumes. Three-quarter brown morocco gilt over pebbled cloth boards. Illustrated. First edition, one of only 800 copies. Near fine. $4,100.00

BIRCH, Samuel. *History of Ancient Pottery, Egyptian, Assyrian, Greek, Etruscan, and Roman....* London: 1873. Full green morocco gilt. Octavo. Gilt decorated spine and covers. Illustrated with color plates and in-text wood engravings. Near fine. $450.00

BIGELOW, John. *Life of Franklin.* **Philadelphia: J.B. Lippincott & Co., 1803. Three volumes. Three-quarter calf. Marbled edges. Near fine. $500.00**

BIGELOW, John. *The Autobiography of Benjamin Franklin.* **New York and London: G.P. Putnams Sons, 1912. Three-quarter butterscotch calf by Putnams. Top edges gilt. 8½" tall. Near fine. $275.00**

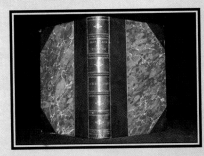

BILLINGS, John. *Hardtack and Coffee.* **Boston: George M. Smith and Co., 1888. Three-quarter brown calf by Launder and MacDonald, 1888. Illustrated. First edition. 8½" tall. Near fine. $450.00**

BINGHAM, Captain D. *The Bastille*. London: Chapman & Hall, 1888. Two volumes. Three-quarter blue morocco. Top edges gilt. Illustrated. Near fine. $500.00

BLAIKIE, Rev. William G. *David, King of Israel*. London: James Nisbet and Co., 1861. Full tan calf by Seton and Mackenzie. Prize binding with marbled edges. 7" tall. Near fine. $225.00

BISSET, Robert. *The History of the Reign of George III*. London: Longman and Rees, 1803. Six volumes. Full tree calf. Near fine. $750.00

BLACKSTONE, William. *Commentaries on the Laws of England*. London: 1825. Four volumes. Octavo. Contemporary full polished tan calf. Near fine. $1,100.00

BLACKSTONE, William. *Commentaries on the Laws of England*. London: Strahan and Woodfall for T. Cadell, 1803. Four octavo volumes. Contemporary full tree calf with red morocco labels. Fourteenth edition. Engraved frontispiece portrait of Blackstone. Near fine. $1,500.00

BLACKSTONE, William. *Commentaries on the Laws of England*. Oxford: Printed at the Clarendon Press, 1766 – 69. Four quarto volumes. Contemporary full tan calf gilt. Raised bands with green and red morocco labels. Near fine. $3,200.00

BLACKSTONE, William. *The Great Charter and Charter of the Forest*. Oxford: Clarendon Press, 1759. Contemporary full calf. Small folio. First edition. Near fine. $3,600.00

BLACKSTONE, William. *The Great Charter and Charter of the Forest*. Oxford: Clarendon Press, 1759. Contemporary full calf. Folio. Large paper copy. First edition. Near fine. $3,200.00

BLAKE, William. *Songs of Innocence and of Experience, Showing the Two Contrary States of the Human Soul....* London: W. Pickering and W. Newbery, 1839. Original three-quarter purple morocco. Slim octavo. First edition. Near fine. $2,600.00

BOCCACCIO, Giovanni. *The Modell of Wit, Mirth, Eloquence, and Conversation....* With: *The Decameron*. London: Isaac Jaggard for Matthew Lownes, 1625. Two volumes bound in one. Full contemporary calf. Folio. First English translation. Near fine. $3,200.00

BONAPARTE, Charles Louis Napoleon. *The Political and Historical Works of Louis Napoleon Bonaparte, President of the French Republic*. London: Illustrated London Library, 1852. Two octavo volumes. Contemporary full navy blue polished calf gilt. Raised bands, marbled endpapers. Housed in a slipcase. Second edition. Illustrated with full-page engraved plates. Near fine. $675.00

BLACKMANTLE, Bernard. *The English Spy*. London: Sherwood, Jones and Co., 1825 – 1826. Two volumes. Full maroon morocco by Tout. Highly gilt spine and covers, all edges gilt. Leather and red silk doublures and silk moiré endpapers. Illustrated with hand-colored plates by Cruikshank. First edition. 9½" tall. Near fine. $2,200.00

BLAKE, W.O. *The History of Slavery and the Slave Trade*. Columbus: H. Miller, 1859. Full black calf with marbled edges. Illustrated. Light foxing. 9½" tall. Very good. $900.00

BLANC, Charles. *The Masterpieces of Italian Art.* Philadelphia: Gebbie & Co., n.d., circa 1870. Two volumes. Full black crushed levant morocco. Highly gilt cover with all edges gilt. Red silk moiré doublures and silk endpapers. Elephant folio. Grand Deluxe Remarque Edition, only 200 copies, this is #59. Edited by J.E. Reed. 18" tall. Near fine. $2,100.00

BOCCACCIO, ROUSEAU, MONTESEQIEU, RABELAIS, d'ANGOULEME. *The Bibliophilists Library.* Philadelphia: George Barrie, n.d., circa 1895. Ten volumes. Full teal morocco by Whitman. Highly gilt spine and covers with top edges gilt. One of 1,000 sets made. Printed on Japanese vellum paper. Illustrated. 9" tall. Fine. $1,200.00

BOSWELL, James. *The Life of Samuel Johnson, LL.D.* London: 1791. Two volumes. Quarto. Full brown calf. First edition. Near fine. $5,900.00

BOSWELL, James. *The Life of Samuel Johnson.* With: *The Principal Corrections and Additions to the First Edition of Mr. Boswell's Life of Dr. Johnson.* London: Henry Baldwin, 1791 – 93. Two volumes. Contemporary calf. Spines gilt in compartments. Illustrated with engraved frontispiece portrait. Near fine. $5,500.00

BOSWELL, James. *The Life of Samuel Johnson...New Addition with Numerous Additions and Notes.* London: John Murray, 1839. Ten small octavo volumes. Nineteenth century red calf gilt by Zaehnsdorf. Raised bands with red morocco labels and marbled endpapers. Illustrated. Near fine. $1,250.00

BOSWELL, James. *Boswell's Life of Johnson.* London: Henry Frowde, 1904. Two volumes. Full tree calf by Oxford. Reprint of 1749 edition. 7" tall. Near fine. $340.00

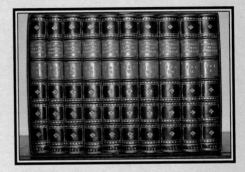

BOSWELL, James. *The Life of Samuel Johnson.* London: John Murray, 1839. Ten volumes. Full navy morocco by Sangorski & Sutcliffe. All edges gilt. Fifty engraved illustrations, with custom clamshell box. 6½" tall. Fine. $2,200.00

BOWDLER, Mrs. *Practical Observations on the Revelation of St. John.* Bath: G.G. & J. Robinson, 1800. Full tree calf. 7½" tall. Near fine. $175.00

BOWMAN, S.M. and IRWIN, R.B. *Sherman and His Campaigns.* New York: Charles B. Richardson, 1865. Three-quarter tan calf. Marbled edges. Illustrated first edition. 9" tall. Very good. $275.00

BOYNTON, Charles B. *The History of the Navy During the Rebellion.* New York: D. Appleton & Co., 1867. Two volumes. Three-quarter brown calf. Illustrated. First edition. 9¾" tall. Near fine. $550.00

BOURRIENNE, M. de. *Memoirs of Napoleon Bonaparte.* London: Richard Bentley, 1836. Four volumes. With: JUNOT, Laura, *Duchess D'Arbantes. Memoirs of Napoleon, His Court and Family.* London: Richard Bentley, 1836. Two volumes. Six volumes together. Full red polished calf. Octavo. Raised bands, gilt decorated spines with Napoleonic emblems, green morocco labels. Illustrated. Near fine. $1,150.00

BOYER, Abel. *The Royal Dictionary Abridged in Two Parts: French and English. English and French.* London: 1755. Contemporary full polished brown calf. Thick octavo. Illustrated with engraved frontispiece portraits of English and French literati. Near fine. $300.00

BOYLE, Robert. *Of Absolute Rest in Bodies.* London: 1669. Modern half brown calf. Slim octavo. First edition. Near fine. $675.00

BRADLEY, Glenn D. *The Story of the Pony Express.* Chicago: 1913. Three-quarter blue calf. 12mo. Illustrated. First edition. Near fine. $375.00

BOYNTON, Charles. *The History of the Navy During the Rebellion.* New York: D. Appleton, 1867. Two volumes. Three-quarter brown calf by Launder and MacDonald. Top edges gilt. Illustrated. First edition. 9½" tall. Near fine. $600.00

BRADLY, A.C. *Shakespearean Tragedy.* London: MacMillan and Co., 1924. Full tree calf by Bickers. Highly gilt spine and cover. Prize binding with marbled edges. 8" tall. Near fine. $245.00

BRANAGAN, Thomas. *A Preliminary Essay, on the Oppression of the Exiled Sons of Africa.* Philadelphia: 1804. Contemporary full brown sheep. Thick 12mo. Illustrated with woodcut frontispiece. First edition. Near fine. $460.00

BRINKLEY, Captain F. *A History of the Japanese People from the Earliest Times to the End of Meyi Era.* London: The Encyclopedia Brittannica Co., 1914. Full green morocco gilt by Asprey. Illustrated by various Japanese artists. Near fine. $210.00

BRINKLEY, Captain F. *Japan and China. Its History, Arts and Literature.* London: T.C. & E.C. Jack, 1903. Twelve volumes. One-quarter tan morocco gilt. Illustrated. Limited edition, one of only 500 copies. Near fine. $1,250.00

BRONTE, Charlotte, Emily, and Anne. *Life and Works of Charlotte Bronte and Her Sisters.* London: Elder & Co., 1899. Seven octavo volumes. Three-quarter green morocco gilt by Riviere. Raised bands, marbled endpapers. "Hawthorn Edition." Includes poems by Currer, Ellis, and Acton Bell. Near fine. $2,800.00

BRITTAIN, Alfred. *The History of North America.* Philadelphia: George Barrie & Sons, 1903. Twenty volumes. Three-quarter navy morocco with all edges gilt. Hand-colored frontispiece in each volume. First edition, set #18 of 1,000 sets printed on Japanese vellum. 8½" tall. Near fine. $2,300.00

BROCKETT, L.P. *Men of Our Day.* Philadelphia: Ziegler & McCurdy, 1872. Full black calf. Hand-tooled covers. Illustrated with 42 portraits. First edition. 9" tall. Near fine. $225.00

BRONTE, Charlotte. *Jane Eyre.* New York and London: J.M. Dent and E. P. Dutton, 1905. Three-quarter maroon morocco. All edges gilt. Six color illustrations by Edmund Dulac. 6½" tall. Near fine. $275.00

BROCKETT, L.P., M.D. *Women's Work in the Civil War.* Philadelphia: Zeigler, McCurdy & Co., 1867. Full tan calf. Illustrated. First edition. Headband, tail band and covers repaired. 9" tall. Very good. $175.00

BRONTE, Charlotte. *The Works of Bronte.* Philadelphia: Porter & Coates, nd, circa 1890. Five volumes. Three-quarter butterscotch calf. Top edges gilt. Illustrated. 7" tall. Near fine. $1,100.00

BRONTE, Charlotte, Emily, and Anne. *Novels of the Sisters Bronte.* Edited by Temple Scott. Edinburgh: John Grant, 1907. Twelve octavo volumes. Three-quarter contemporary olive green morocco gilt. Gilt decorated spines and marbled endpapers. Thornton edition. Illustrated. Near fine. $2,600.00

BRONTE, Charlotte, Emily, and Anne. *Novels of the Sisters Bronte.* Edited by Temple Scott. Edinburgh: John Grant, 1905. Twelve octavo volumes. Contemporary three-quarter red morocco gilt by Bennett. Raised bands, gilt decorated spines, marbled boards and endpapers. Thornton edition. Illustrated with frontispiece portraits of the authors. Near fine. $2,600.00

BRONTE, Charlotte, Emily, and Anne. *The Novels.* London: Smith, Elder, & Co., 1888 – 95. Seven octavo volumes. Three-quarter green morocco. Raised bands, marbled boards and endpapers. Includes *Life of Charlotte Bronte* by Elizabeth Gaskell. Near fine. $2,000.00

BRONTE, Charlotte, Emily, and Anne. *The Works.* London: Smith, Elder and Co., 1857 – 60. Six small octavo volumes. Contemporary three-quarter green morocco gilt. Marbled boards. Near fine. $3,500.00

BRONTE, Charlotte. *Jane Eyre.* London, Bombay, and Sydney: George F. Harrap & Co. 1927. One volume. Bound in full red calf by Riviere. Gilt with raised bands. Color illustrations by Monro S. Orr. Near fine. $280.00

BRONTE, Charlotte. *The Life and Works of Charlotte Bronte and Her Sisters.* London: Smith, Elder, & Co., 1877 – 88. Nine octavo volumes. Contemporary three-quarter brown calf. Raised bands, gilt decorated spines, marbled boards, endpapers, and edges. Illustrated with over 80 steel engravings. Near fine. $2,100.00

BRONTE. *The Works of The Sisters Bronte.* London: Robert Riviere & Son, Ltd., no date. Six volumes. Half blue calf, gilt decorated spines. Small 8vo. Color illustrations by Edmund Dulac. Near fine. $1,250.00

BRONTE. *Wuthering Heights and Agnes Gray.* London: Smith, Elder & Co., 1851. Three-quarter vellum. Ornate spine. Near fine. $520.00

BRONTE, Charlotte. *Bronte's Works.* London: Robert Riviere and Son, circa 1895. Six volumes. Three-quarter red morocco by Riviere. Top edges gilt. 7" tall. Near fine. $800.00

BRONTES, The. *The Works of The Sisters Bronte.* London: Smith, Elder & Co., 1877. Seven volumes. Contemporary half red morocco. 8vo. Illustrated. Near fine. $2,100.00

BRONTE Sisters. *Life and Works of the Sisters Bronte.* New York and London: Harper & Brothers, 1899. Seven volumes. Half recent red morocco with top edges gilt. Illustrated Thornfield edition. 8½" tall. Near fine. $1,300.00

BROTHERS GRIMM. *Little Brother & Little Sister and Other Tales.* London: 1917. Contemporary full green morocco. Octavo. Illustrated by Arthur Rackham. First trade edition. Near fine. $875.00

BROWN, Samuel R. *Views of the Campaigns of the North-Western Army.* Philadelphia: 1815. Half brown morocco. 12mo. Illustrated with engraved frontispiece scene of Perry's victory at Lake Erie. Near fine. $400.00

BROWNING, Elizabeth Barrett. *Poetical Works.* New York: Dodd, Mead, 1899. Five small octavo volumes. Contemporary full green morocco gilt. Raised bands. Illustrated with frontispiece portrait. Near fine. $900.00

BROWNING, Elizabeth Barrett. *Sonnets from the Portuguese.* Portland: 1897. Tall 12mo. Contemporary three-quarter green morocco, gilt spine. First Mosher edition, one of 925 copies on Van Gelder paper. Near fine. $525.00

BROOKE, Stopford A. *Poems of Shelley.* London: MacMillan & Co., 1900. Full red morocco, crushed levant by Ramage. Multi-inlaid morocco spine and covers. Leather inlaid doublures with inset white silk moiré and hearts with 12 stars in all four corners of both inside covers, silk moiré endpapers. 6" tall. Fine. $950.00

BROOKS, Noah. *The Story of Marco Polo.* London: John Murray, 1898. Full blue morocco by Bickers. Prize binding with all edges gilt. Illustrated. 8" tall. Near fine. $275.00

BROWNING, Elizabeth Barrett. *The Poetical Works.* London: 1932. Full crimson crushed morocco. Octavo. "Oxford University Press" edition. Near fine. $175.00

BROWNING, Elizabeth Barrett. *The Poetical Works.* London: Smith, Elder & Co. 1889. Six volumes. Three-quarter blue morocco by Riviere, gilt panels. Near fine. $850.00

BROWNING, Elizabeth Barrett. *The Poetical Works.* London: Smith, Elder & Co. 1890. Six volumes. Three-quarters wine morocco gilt. Marbled boards. Near fine. $750.00

BROWNING, Elizabeth Barrett. *The Poetical Works.* London: Henry Frowde, 1904. Full navy morocco. Raised bands, gilt spine. Octavo. Frontispiece portrait. Near fine. $225.00

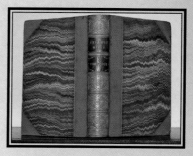

BROWNE, Charles F. *The Complete Works of Charles F. Browne* (Artemus Ward). London: John Camden Hotten, circa 1870. Three-quarter tan calf. Marbled edges. 7½" tall. Near fine. $150.00

BROWNE, J. Ross. *Adventures in the Apache Country.* New York: Harper & Brothers, 1868. Three-quarter black calf. First edition. Twentieth century binding. 7½" tall. Near fine. $650.00

BROWNELL, Charle de Wolf. *The Indian Races of North and South America.* New York: American Subscription House, 1856. Full black calf. Highly gilt spine with marbled edges. Hand-colored illustrations. 9" tall. Very good. $675.00

BROWNING, Elizabeth Barrett. *The Works of Elizabeth Barrett Browning.* New York: Worthington Co., 1889. Seven volumes. Three-quarter butterscotch calf. Marbled edges. From the London edition. Very good. $875.00

BROWNELL, Henry Howard. *The Discoveries, Pioneers and Settlers of North and South America.* Boston: Horace Wentworth, 1853. Three-quarter brown calf. Hand-colored illustrations. 9" tall. Near fine. $525.00

BROWNING, Robert. *The Complete Poetic and Dramatic Works of Robert Browning.* Boston and New York: Houghton Mifflin & Co., 1895. Full tree calf. All edges gilt. Cambridge edition. 7½" tall. Near fine. $230.00

BROWNING, Robert. *Men and Women.* London: Chapman and Hall, 1855. Two volumes. Full navy morocco gilt by Riviere. Raised bands, silk endpapers, and top edges gilt. Gilt floral design on covers and spines. First edition. Near fine. $875.00

BROWNING, Elizabeth Barrett. *Aurora Leigh.* Leipzig: Bernhard Tauchnitz, 1872. Full calf. Brass studs in all corners of both covers. Copyright edition. 6" tall. Near fine. $425.00

BROWNING, Robert. *The Poetic and Dramatic Works.* Boston and New York: 1899. Six octavo volumes. Contemporary three-quarter red morocco gilt. "Riverside Edition." Near fine. $575.00

BROWNING, Robert. *The Poetical Works.* London: 1868. Six volumes. Octavo. Nineteenth century full green morocco. First edition. Near fine. $2,900.00

BROWNING, Elizabeth Barrett. *The Complete Poetical Works of Elizabeth Barrett Browning.* Boston and New York: Houghton, Mifflin and Co., 1900. Full tree calf with all edges gilt. Cambridge edition, The Riverside Press. 8" tall. Near fine. $275.00

BROWNING, Robert. *Works.* Boston and New York: Houghton Mufflin & Co., 1899. Six volumes. Three-quarter wine morocco, gilt panels. Riverside edition. Near fine. $590.00

BROWNING, Robert. *Works.* Boston: Houghton Mufflin & Co., 1886. Seven volumes. Three-quarter tan calf, red and green labels, gilt panels. Near fine. $600.00

BROWNING, Robert. *Dramatis Personae; & Dramatic Romances & Lyrics.* London: 1909. Quarto. Contemporary full crushed tan morocco. Art deco gilt panel. Limited edition, one of only 260 copies, illustrated. Near fine. $875.00

BRUGALLA, Emilio. *The Song of Songs.* London: The Golden Cockerel Press, 1936. Full blue crushed levant morocco. Elaborate gilt on covers and spine. Illustrated. Limited edition, one of only 204 copies. Near fine. $6,500.00

BROWNING, Robert. *The Works of Robert Browning.* Boston and New York: Houghlin, Mifflin and Co., 1899. Six volumes. Three-quarter blue morocco. Highly gilt spine with top edges gilt. Autographed letter of Browning tipped in. Riverside Press. 8" tall. Near fine. $1,200.00

BROWNLOW, W.G. *Sketches of the Rise, Progress and Decline of Secession.* Philadelphia: George Childs, 1862. Three-quarter brown calf. Top edges gilt. Illustrated. First edition. 7½" tall. Near fine. $320.00

BRYAN, Michael. *Dictionary of Painters and Engravers, Biographical and Critical.* London: George Bell & Sons, 1886. Two volumes. Three-quarter tan calf gilt. Large 4to. Near fine. $275.00

BRYANT, William Cullen, and GAY, Sydney Howard. *The Popular History of the United States.* New York: 1884. Four large octavo volumes. Contemporary three-quarter black morocco gilt. Illustrated with numerous steel-engraved and wood-engraved plates. Near fine. $475.00

BRYANT, William Cullen. *Picturesque America; Or, The Land We Live In.* New York: D Appleton and Company, 1827 – 74. Two volumes. Publisher's original full deluxe brown morocco gilt. Thick folio. Raised bands, marbled endpapers. Illustrated with 49 full-page tissue guarded steel-engraved early American views. Near fine. $1,300.00

BRYANT, William Cullen. *A Forest Hymn.* New York: W.A. Townsend & Co., 1860. Full green morocco. All edges gilt. Illustrated by John A. Nums. First edition. 9" tall. Near fine. $325.00

BRYANT, William Cullen. *Picturesque America.* New York: D. Appleton & Co., 1872. Two volumes. Full brown calf. Embossed and highly gilt covers, all edges gilt. Illustrated. First edition. 13" tall. Near fine. $1,300.00

BRYCE, James. *The American Commonwealth.* London and New York: 1888. Three octavo volumes. Three-quarter red morocco gilt by Riviere & Son. First edition. Near fine. $1,300.00

BRYCE, James. *The American Commonwealth.* London and New York: MacMillan and Co., 1888. Two octavo volumes. Three-quarter blue calf. Second edition. Near fine. $1,100.00

BRYCE, James. *The American Commonwealth.* London and New York: MacMillan and Co., 1889. Three octavo volumes. Three-quarter tan morocco gilt with raised bands. First edition. Near fine. $690.00

BUCKINGHAM, J.S. Esq. *The Eastern and Western States of America.* London: Fisher, Son & Co., circa 1830. Three volumes. Full tan polished calf. Raised bands, ornate spines with red and green labels. Illustrated. Near fine. $650.00

BRYCE, James. *The American Commonwealth.* London and New York: MacMillan and Co., 1889. Two volumes. Three-quarter tan calf. Top edges gilt. Pull-out map. 8" tall. Near fine. $350.00

BRYCE, James. *The American Commonwealth*. London: MacMillan and Co., 1893. Two volumes. Three-quarter butterscotch calf by Frost. 7½" tall. Near fine. $450.00

BUDGE, E.A. Wallis. *Some Account of the Collection of Egyptian Antiquities in the Possession of Lady Meux at Theobald's Park*. London: 1896. Three-quarter black morocco gilt. Folio. Illustrated with a folding frontispiece and numerous full-page photographs. Limited second edition, one of only 500 copies. Near fine. $475.00

BUFFON, Count de. *Natural History, General and Particular*. With: *Occasion Notes and Observations By William Smellie*. London: W. Strahan and T. Cadell, 1791. Nine octavo volumes. Full contemporary mottled calf. Gilt spine with olive morocco labels. Illustrated with 300 copper-engraved plates. Near fine. $1,350.00

BULLOCK, William. *Six Months' Residence and Travels in Mexico*. London: 1824. Three-quarter brown calf. Octavo. Illustrated with folding maps and geographical tables. First edition. Near fine. $1,050.00

BUNYAN, John. *The Pilgrim's Progress*. London: 1880. Twentieth century three-quarter tan crushed morocco gilt. Large quarto. Limited edition, one of only 500 copies printed on handmade paper. Illustrated by Frederick Barnard. Near fine. $475.00

BUNYAN, John. *The Pilgrim's Progress*. New York: American Tract Society, n.d., circa 1860. Full black calf. Highly gilt spine and covers, top edges gilt. Illustrated. Light foxing. 8" tall. Very good. $350.00

BURDER, Samuel. *Oriental Customs: Or, and Illustration of the Sacred Scriptures...Two volumes*. Bound with: *Oriental Literature*. London: 1822. Two volumes. Four octavo volumes in total. Full polished calf gilt. Gilt decorated spines. Near fine. $575.00

BURK, John. *The History of Virginia, From Its First Settlement to the Present Day*. Petersburg, Virginia: Dickson & Pescud, 1804 – 05. Four octavo volumes. Full calf gilt by Zaehnsdorf. Green morocco labels, all edges gilt. First edition. Near fine. $1,900.00

BURKE, Edmund. *Works*. London: C. & J. Rivington, 1826. Sixteen volumes. Full brown calf. Gilt decorated spines. Near fine. $1,650.00

BURNET, Jacob. *Notes on the Early Settlement of the North-Western Territory*. Cincinnati: 1847. Modern half brown morocco gilt. Thick octavo. Illustrated. First edition. Near fine. $375.00

BUELL, Augustus. *History of Andrew Jackson*. New York: Charles Scribner, 1904. Two volumes. Full green morocco. Top edges gilt. Silk doublures and endpapers. Embossed floral motif on covers. First edition. Housed in slipcase. Fine. $1,500.00

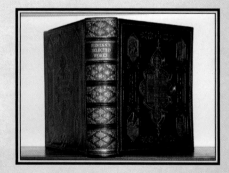

BUNYUN, John. *The Select Works of John Bunyun*. Glasgow, Edinburgh and London: William Collins, Sons and Co., nd, circa 1880. Full black calf. Highly gilt spine with embossed covers. All edges gilt. Hand-colored illustrations. 11½" tall. Near fine. $700.00

BURNEY, Frances (Fanny). *Camilla*. London: T. Payne, 1796. Five volumes. Three-quarter burl morocco by Bayntun. Rebound by Bayntun, highly gilt tree calf. All edges gilt. Fine. $950.00

BURNS, Robert. *The Poetical Works of Robert Burns*. London: Humphrey Milford, 1919. Full tree calf by Morrell. All edges gilt. 7½" tall. Near fine. $190.00

BURNS, Robert. *The Complete Poetical Works of Robert Burns*. London: John Walker & Co., n.d., circa 1870. Black leather spine, sycamore wood. All edges gilt. Mauchline ware cover with floral arrangement transferred onto front cover. 7" tall. Near fine. $425.00

BURNS, Robert. *The Complete Works of Robert Burns*. Philadelphia: Gebbie Publishing Co., 1896. Twelve octavo volumes. Full contemporary navy blue morocco gilt. Gilt decorated spines, red watered silk endpapers. Illustrated with 60 etchings including a frontispiece portrait of the author. Near fine. $2,500.00

BURNS, Robert. *The Complete Works*. Edinburgh: William Patterson, 1883. Six octavo volumes. Contemporary full blue morocco gilt by Zaehnsdorf. Raised bands, marbled endpapers. Frontispiece portrait in Volume 1. Near fine. $1,275.00

BURNS, Robert. *The Complete Works of Robert Burns*. Boston: Phillips, Sampson and Co., 1853. Full purple morocco. Highly gilt spine and inlaid cover with top edges gilt. Light foxing on plates. 10" tall. Very good. $475.00

BURR, Frank A. *Life and Deeds of General U.S. Grant*. Nashville: Southwestern Publishing House, 1885. Three-quarter maroon calf. Illustrated. Memorial edition. First edition. 8½" tall. Near fine. $425.00

BURNS, Robert. *The Life and Works of Robert Burns*. Edinburgh and London: W. & R. Chambers, 1856. Four volumes. Full tree calf with marbled edges. 8½" tall. Near fine. $875.00

BURR, Frank A. and HINTON, Richard J. *The Life of General Philip H. Sheridan*. Providence: Reid, 1888. Three-quarter rust calf. All edges gilt. Illustrated first edition. 9" tall. Very good. $275.00

B

BURROUGHS, John. *Burroughs Works.* Boston: Houghton, Mifflin and Co., 1885. Ten volumes. Three-quarter blue morocco by Little Brown & Co. Top edges gilt. First ten works of Burroughs. Illustrated. Signed first edition. 7" tall. Near fine. $1,500.00

BURROUGHS, John. *The Writings of John Burroughs.* Boston: Houghton Mifflin, 1904 – 1916. Nineteen octavo volumes. Full purple levant morocco with red morocco inlays on the covers and spines. Gilt lettering, brown morocco doublures and silk endpapers. Illustrated. Autographed edition. Near fine. $5,600.00

BURTON, Richard F. *The Book of the Sword.* London: 1884. Three-quarter navy calf. Quarto. Illustrated. First edition. Near fine. $1,200.00

BURTON, Richard F. *The Book of the Thousand Nights and a Night.* Ten volumes. With: *Supplemental Nights to the Book of the Thousand Nights and a Night With Notes Anthropological and Explanatory.* Six volumes. Benares: Printed by the Kamashastra Society for Private Subscribers Only, 1885 – 88. Sixteen volumes in all. Contemporary three-quarter green morocco gilt. Royal octavo. Raised bands with top edges gilt. First edition, one of only 1,000 sets. Near fine. $2,900.00

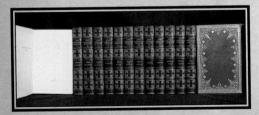

BURROUGHS, John. *The Writings of John Burroughs.* Boston: Houghton, Mifflin & Co., 1904. Fourteen volumes. Full green morocco by Riverside Press. Leather inlaid doublures, silk endpapers. Top edges gilt. Hand-colored illustrations. Autographed edition, signed twice by the author, one of only 750 copies. Near fine. $3,500.00

BURTON, Richard F. *The Book of the Thousand Knights and a Night.* London: The Burton Club, circa 1885. Seventeen volumes (only four shown). Three-quarter red morocco. Highly gilt spine and top edges gilt. Mecca edition, #92 of 1,000 sets, which includes the supplemental *Nights.* Sold for subscribers only. 10" tall. Near fine. $4,250.00

BURTON, Richard F. *The Book of the Thousand Nights and a Night.* London: 1897. Twelve tall octavo volumes. Original three-quarter red morocco gilt. Gilt decorated spines. Library edition. Illustrated with a series of 71 illustrations reproduced from the original oils painted by Albert Letchford. Near fine. $4,500.00

BURTON, Richard F. *The Book of the Thousand Nights and A Night.* With: *Supplemental Nights.* Printed by the Burton Club for Private Subscribers Only, 1905. Seventeen volumes. Contemporary half calf morocco over blue buckram boards. Raised bands, gilt spines, marbled endpapers, top edges gilt. Illustrated with numerous plates. Deluxe edition, one of only 250 copies. Near fine. $3,800.00

BURTON, Richard F. *The Thousand and One Nights.* London: Charles Knight and Co., 1839 – 41. Three volumes. Contemporary pebble grain olive brown morocco gilt. Raised spines gilt in compartments with decorative bands at head and foot. Illustrated with hundreds of drawings by William Harvey. Translated by Edward William Lane. Near fine. $1,250.00

BURTON, Richard F. *Wanderings in West Africa from Liverpool to Fernando Po.* London: 1863. Two octavo volumes. Dark brown calf. Housed in a custom clamshell box. First edition. Near fine. $2,200.00

BURTON, Richard. *Arabian Nights.* Seventeen volumes. Three-quarter green morocco by Bayntun. Top edges gilt, raised bands. "Benares Edition." Near fine. $3,400.00

BURTON. *The Anatomy of Melancholy.* Boston: William Veazie, 1859. Full tan calf with marbled edges. 7½" tall. Three volumes. Near fine. $525.00

BURTON, Richard. *Arabian Nights.* Printed by the Kamashastra Society, 1899. Sixteen volumes. Three-quarter red calf by Bayntun, ornate gilt vignettes on spines. Near fine. $2,900.00

BURTON, Sir R.F. *Arabian Nights.* London: H.S. Nichols. Ltd., 1897. Twelve volumes, illustrated. Three-quarters red morocco, ornate tooling on spines. Near fine. $1,900.00

BURTON, Sir. R. F. *Arabian Nights.* London: H.S. Nichols Ltd., 1897. Twelve volumes. Three-quarter red morocco gilt. Raised bands, ornate spines. "Library Edition." Near fine. $1,900.00

BUSSEY, George M. *History of Napoleon.* London: Joseph Thomas, 1890. Two volumes. Three-quarter tan morocco by Zaehnsdorf. Raised bands, gilt decorated panels. Near fine. $875.00

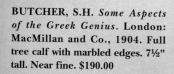

BUTCHER, S.H. *Some Aspects of the Greek Genius.* London: MacMillan and Co., 1904. Full tree calf with marbled edges. 7½" tall. Near fine. $190.00

BUSH, Mrs. Forbes. *Memoirs of the Queens of France.* London: Henry Colburn, 1843. Two volumes. Three-quarter tan calf by Root. Top edges gilt. 8" tall. Near fine. $450.00

BYRON, Lord. *The Poetical Works of Lord Byron.* London: John Murray, 1864. Full green calf. All edges gilt. Illustrated. 9½" tall. Fine. $325.00

BYRON, Lord. *The Poetical Works of Lord Byron.* New York: Leavitt & Allen, 1858. Full tan calf. All edges gilt. Hand-tooled covers. Illustrated. 9½" tall. Near fine. $265.00

BUTLER, Samuel. *Hudibras, a Poem.* London: 1819. Two octavo volumes. Full red morocco gilt by Bayntun. Illustrated by J. Clark. First edition. Near fine. $475.00

BYRON, Lord George Gordon. *The Prisoner of Chillon and Other Poems.* London 1816. Twentieth century full red morocco. Tall thin octavo. First edition, first issue. Near fine. $600.00

BYRON, George Gordon. *The Works.* London: 1832 – 33. Seventeen volumes. Nineteenth century three-quarter blue polished calf gilt by Riviere. 12mo. Illustrated with engraved frontispieces and title page vignettes. Near fine. $2,400.00

BYRON. *Works of Lord Byron.* London: John Murray, 1832. Seventeen volumes. Full sky blue morocco. Marbled edges. Fourteen volumes were done originally, then in 1833 three more were added — all are present. Letters by Thomas Moore. 6½" tall. Fine. $2,400.00

BYRON, George Gordon. *The Works*. London: 1833 – 34. Seventeen volumes. Nineteenth century three-quarter dark green morocco gilt. 12mo. Illustrated with engraved frontispieces and title page vignettes. Near fine. $1,800.00

BYRON, Lord, and ROGERS, Samuel. *Lara, a Tale. Jacqueline, a Tale*. London: 1814. Twentieth century full green morocco gilt by Riviere. Small octavo. First edition. Near fine. $325.00

BYRON, Lord. *Works*. London: John Murray, 1834. Seventeen volumes. Full tan calf by Zaehnsdorf, ornate gilt on spines. Near fine. $2,300.00

CADY, Annie Cole. *The American Continent*. Philadelphia: Gebbie & Co., 1893. Three-quarter green morocco by Boston Book Binding Co. Top edges gilt. Illustrated. Folio. 12" tall. Near fine. $425.00

CAESAR, Julius. *Les Commentaires de Cesar*. Paris: 1650. Large octavo. Contemporary full brown calf gilt. First edition. Near fine. $4,400.00

CALVERT, Charles. *Shakespeare's Tragedy of Anthony and Cleopatra*. Edinburgh: n.d., circa 1880. Printed by Schenck and M. Farlane. Full red morocco. Gilt pyramid embossed on front cover and blind stamped on back cover, all edges gilt. Prime Minister's copy. 8½" tall. Very good. $400.00

CALTHROP, Clayton Dion. *English Costume Painted and Described*. London: Charles Black, 1907. Three-quarter red morocco gilt by Bayntun. Near fine. $225.00

CALVERT, Albert F. *Moorish Remains in Spain*. London: John Lane, 1906. Three-quarter tan morocco. Raised bands, gilt panels and marbled boards. Thick 8vo. Illustrated. Near fine. $425.00

CAMDEN, William. *The Historie of the Life and Reigne of the most Renowned and Victorious Princesse Elizabeth, Late Queene of England*. London: 1630. Contemporary full polished brown calf. Small folio. First edition in English. Near fine. $2,600.00

CAMDEN, William. *The History of the most Renowned and Victorious Princess Elizabeth, Late Queen of England*. London: 1675. Twentieth century three-quarter brown morocco. Quarto. Illustrated with engraved frontispiece portrait of Queen Elizabeth. Third edition in English. Near fine. $1,500.00

CAMP, Walter, and BROOKS, Lilian. *Drives and Puts: A Book of Golf Stories*. Boston: L.C. Page, 1899. Full green morocco by Riviere. Small octavo. First edition. Near fine. $1,300.00

CAMPAN, Madame. *Memoirs of the Private Life of Marie Antoinette*. London: Printed for Henry Colburn, 1824. Two volumes. Full tan calf. Third edition. Very mild spotting. 8½" tall. Fine. $320.00

CAMPBELL, George. *A Dissertation on Miracles*. Edinburgh: Printed for Bell and Bradfute, 1797. Two volumes. Full tan tree calf. Speckled edges. Near fine. $425.00

CAMPBELL, George. *The Four Gospels.* London: William Baynes, 1825. Two volumes. Full tan tree calf. 9" tall. Near fine. $525.00

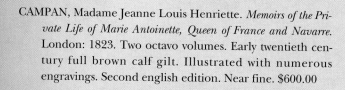

CAMPAN, Madame Jeanne Louis Henriette. *Memoirs of the Private Life of Marie Antoinette, Queen of France and Navarre.* London: 1823. Two octavo volumes. Early twentieth century full brown calf gilt. Illustrated with numerous engravings. Second english edition. Near fine. $600.00

CAMPAN, Madame. *Memoirs of the Private Life of Marie Antoinette.* London: Henry Colburn & Co., 1823. First edition. Two volumes. Full pink calf by Sangorski and Sutcliffe. Near fine. $875.00

CAMPBELL, Dr. J. *Lives of the British Admirals.* London: J. Murray, 1779. Four volumes. Full contemporary calf. Illustrated. Near fine. $1,500.00

CANNING, George. *Poetry of the Anti-Jacobin.* London: 1801. Contemporary full tree calf. Quarto. Fourth edition. Near fine. $425.00

CAMPBELL, Thomas, and ROGERS, Samuel. *The Poetical Works of Campbell and the Poetical Works of Rogers.* (Two separate volumes bound in one.) New York: Leavitt & Allen, n.d., circa 1850. Full black calf. All edges gilt. Highly gilt cover and spine. Gilt raised vines on covers. Heavy gauffed edges, raised gold gilt pastedowns. Illustrated. 9" tall. Fine. $625.00

CAMPBELL, Thomas. *The Poetical Works of Thomas Campbell.* Hartford: Silas Andres and Son, 1850. Full red morocco. All edges gilt. Illustrated with 34 wood cuts. 7" tall. Near fine. $165.00

CAMPBELL, Thomas. *The Poetical Works of Thomas Campbell.* Hartford: Silas, Andrus and Son, 1849. Full black calf. Highly gilt spine and covers. Gilt figures on covers, all edges gilt. Rare American binding. Thirty-four woodcuts. 8" tall. Near fine. $425.00

CAMPBELL, Thomas. *The Poetical Works of Thomas Campbell.* London: Edward Moxon, 1843. Full tan calf. Highly gauffered edges. Illustrated with twenty vignettes by Turner and 37 woodcuts by Harvey. 8" tall. Near fine. $525.00

CAREY, David. *Life in Paris.* London: 1822. Octavo. Full burgundy morocco gilt. Illustrated by George Cruikshank. First edition, large paper issue. Near fine. $750.00

CARLETON, William. *Traits and Stories of the Irish Peasantry.* Dublin: Wm. Curry, Jun., and Co., 1843. Two volumes in one. Three-quarter green morocco. Top edges gilt. Illustrated, plates by Phiz, and bound from numbers with all paper covers bound in at end of volume. First edition. 9" tall. Near fine. $625.00

CARLETON, William. *Traits and Stories of the Irish Peasantry.* Dublin: 1843. Two octavo volumes. Three-quarter brown calf gilt. Gilt decorated spines. Illustrated with engraved frontispieces and full page plates by Phiz. Near fine. $600.00

CARLYLE, Thomas. *Collected Works.* London: Chapman & Hall, 1882. Thirty-four octavo volumes. With: Seven matching volumes of Mrs. Carlyle's letters and Froudes works on Carlyle. Forty-one volumes in all. Three-quarter green morocco gilt. Raised bands and gilt decorated spines. Near fine. $4,100.00

CARLYLE, Thomas. *Collected Works.* London: Chapman and Hall, 1882. Thirty-four volumes. Octavo. Contemporary three-quarters green morocco spines tooled in gilt in compartments. Library edition. Near fine. $3,600.00

CARLYLE, Thomas. *The Complete Works.* London: For Subscribers, 1897. Thirty-three volumes. Three-quarter blue morocco gilt. Gilt decorated spines. "Memorial Edition." Illustrated. Near fine. $3,200.00

CARLYLE, Thomas. *Carlyle's Works.* London: Chapman and Holt, 1831. Thirty-one volumes (only eight shown). Three-quarter red morocco by Bickers. Top edges gilt. 8" tall. Near fine. $3,800.00

CARLYLE, Thomas. *Cromwell.* Boston: circa 1860. Full dark brown morocco levant by The Rose Bindery. Highly gilt spine and cover. Doublures of dark red moiré silk. Extra illustrated with 67 plates and Frank Deering book plate. 8" tall. Near fine. $725.00

CARLYLE, Thomas. *The French Revolution.* London: Chapman and Hall, 1870. Three octavo volumes. Contemporary full tree calf gilt. Marbled endpapers and edges. Near fine. $600.00

CARLYLE, Thomas. *On Heroes and Hero-Worship And the Heroic City.* London: James Fraser, 1841. Full butterscotch calf, marbled edges. First edition. 7½" tall. Near fine. $190.00

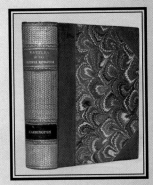

CARRINGTON, Henry. *Battles of the American Revolution.* New York, Chicago and New Orleans: A.S. Barnes, 1876. Three-quarter brown calf. Marbled edges. Illustrated. Signed by the author. Fine. $475.00

CARROLL, Lewis. *Alice's Adventures in Wonderland and Through The Looking-Glass.* London: MacMillan & Co., 1948. Full red calf gilt by Bayntun. Gilt decorated spine with gilt decorations of Rabbit and the Queen on the cover. Near fine. $280.00

CARROLL, Lewis. *Alice's Adventures in Wonderland and Through the Looking Glass and What Alice Found There.* Two volumes. Full maroon morocco by Riviere, 1925. Gold gilt Red Queen and Rabbit on cover. All edges gilt. Illustrated by John Tenniel. 6" tall. Near fine. $875.00

CARROLL, Lewis. *Alice's Adventures in Wonderland.* Full green morocco by Sangorski & Sutcliffe. Embossed gold gilt Alice on front cover. All edges gilt, 1922. Forty-two illustrations by John Tenniel. 7" tall. Near fine. $180.00

CARROLL, Lewis. *Alice's Adventures in Wonderland.* London: MacMillan & Co., 1886. Full red morocco. Early edition with 42 illustrations by John Tenniel. Near fine. $1,250.00

CARROLL, Lewis. *Alice's Adventures in Wonderland.* London: MacMillan and Company, 1872. Octavo. Twentieth century full green morocco gilt. Gilt decorated spines and gold silk endpapers. Kelliegram binding with pictorial leather inlays based on John Tenniel's illustrations. Near fine. $1,850.00

CARROLL, Lewis. *Alice's Adventures in Wonderland.* London: MacMillan and Company, 1876. With: *Through the Looking-Glass, and What Alice Found There.* Together two octavo volumes. Red crushed morocco gilt by Bayntun. Cover gilt-decorated with emblems of the White Rabbit and the Queen. Near fine. $1,600.00

CARROLL, Lewis. *Alice's Adventures in Wonderland.* New York: D. Appleton, 1866. Original red cloth with gilt titling. Octavo. Illustrated by John Tenniel. First American edition. Near fine. $5,500.00

CARROLL, Lewis. *Alice's Adventures in Wonderland.* New York: Limited Editions Club, 1932. With: *Through the Looking Glass and What Alice Found There.* New York: Limited Editions Club, 1935. Two octavo volumes. Original full red (Adventures) and full blue (Looking Glass) morocco gilt. Gilt decorated spines. One of only 1,500 copies. Original illustrations by John Tenniel. Near fine. $975.00

CARROLL, Lewis. *Alice's Adventures in Wonderland.* With: *Through the Looking Glass.* New York: 1935. Two volumes. Full red (Alice) and blue (Looking Glass) morocco gilt. Limited editions, each one of only 1,500 copies. Illustrations by John Tenniel. Near fine. $975.00

CARROLL, Lewis. *Alice's Adventures in Wonderland.* With: *Through The Looking Glass and What Alice Found There.* New York: 1946. Two octavo volumes. Full red morocco gilt. Original illustrations by John Tenniel. Near fine. $450.00

CARROLL, Lewis. *Alice's Adventures in Wonderland.* London: MacMillan and Co., 1927. Full calf by Riviere. All edges gilt. Forty-two illustrations by Tenniel with embossed Alice on front cover in multi-layered morocco. 7½" tall. Fine. $750.00

CARROLL, Lewis. *Through the Looking Glass, And What Alice Found There.* London: MacMillan and Co., 1927. Full tan calf by Riviere. All edges gilt. Fifty illustrations by Tenniel. Special bound with Red Queen and Alice embossed on cover with multicolored layered morocco. With slipcase. 7½" tall. Fine. $750.00

CARTER, William. *The Covenant of God with Abraham.* London: T.C. for John Rothwell, 1654. Full tan calf. 7½" tall. Very good. **$575.00**

CARROLL, Lewis. *Through the Looking Glass and Alice's Adventures in Wonderland.* London: MacMillan & Co., 1953. Two volumes. Full red morocco. Gilt Alice and gilt Red Queen on covers. All edges gilt. Illustrated by Tenniel. 7" tall. Near fine. **$425.00**

CARY, H.F. *The Vision Hell, Purgatory and Paradise of Dante Alighieri.* London: Frederick Warne & Co., 1890. Full brown morocco. Raised bands, gilt panels and covers. Near fine. **$275.00**

CARY, Henry Francis. *The Vision of Dante Alighieri.* London and New York: Frederick Warne & Co., n.d., circa 1900. Full tree calf by Riviere and Son. All edges gilt. 7" tall. Near fine. **$240.00**

CARY, Rev. Henry Francis. *Dante's Inferno.* New York: Cassell, Petter, Galpin & Co., n.d., circa 1880. Full maroon morocco. Embossed and gilt covers, all edges gilt. Illustrated by Gustave Dore. 13½" tall. Near fine. **$550.00**

CARY, Henry Francis. *The Vision; or Hell, Purgatory, And Paradise, of Dante Alighieri.* London: 1819. Three volumes. Octavo. Early twentieth century three-quarter brown morocco gilt. Second edition of Cary's translation. Near fine. **$800.00**

CASANOVA, Jacques. *The Memoirs of Giacomo Casanova di Seingalt.* London: Privately Printed for Subscribers Only, The Casanova Society, 1922. Twelve volumes. Full brown morocco. Silk endpapers. Quarto. Limited edition, one of only 1,000 sets. Illustrated. Near fine. **$3,800.00**

CASANOVA, Jacques. *The Memoirs of Jacques Casanova, An Autobiography.* London and New York: The Venetian Society, 1928. Twelve octavo volumes. Full red morocco gilt. Raised bands and gilt decorated spines. One of only 330 sets published for subscribers only. Near fine. **$2,200.00**

CASANOVA, Jacques. *The Memoirs of Jacques Casanova.* London: 1902. Six octavo volumes. Three-quarter teal morocco gilt. Limited edition. Near fine. **$1,800.00**

CASANOVA, Jacques. *The Memoirs of Jacques Casanova....* London: 1894. Twelve octavo volumes. Contemporary three-quarter red morocco gilt by Blackwell. Limited edition, one of only 1,000 sets. Illustrated with frontispieces. Near fine. **$3,100.00**

CASHIN, Hershel V. *Under Fire with the Tenth U.S. Cavalry. Being a Brief Comprehensive Review of the Negro's Participation in the Wars of the United States.* Chicago: 1902. Full calf binding. Octavo. Illustrated with historic photographs. Near fine. **$800.00**

Cassell's Popular Natural History. London: Cassell, Petter, circa 1900. Two volumes. Three-quarter red morocco. Raised bands, gilt panels. Large octavo. Illustrated. Near fine. **$410.00**

CASH, C.G. *The Life and Voyages of Captain James Cook.* London: Blackie & Son, circa 1891. Full calf by Allman. All edges gilt. Prize binding. Mild foxing. Very good. **$190.00**

CATLIN, George. *Illustration of the Manners, Customs and Condition of the North American Indians.* London: Henry G. Bohn, 1848. Two volumes. Three-quarter red morocco with marbled edges. 360 engravings. Seventh edition. 10" tall. Near fine. $1,500.00

CATLIN, George. *Illustrations of the Manners, Customs & Condition of the North American Indians....* London: 1876. Two large octavo volumes. Original cloth covers bound in the rear of the book. Illustrated with 360 color engravings. First edition. Near fine. $3,600.00

CATLIN, George. *Letters and Notes on the Manners, Customs, and Condition of the North American Indians.* London: 1841. Two volumes. Octavo. Contemporary full green morocco with gilt decorated spines. Second edition. Illustrated with maps and numerous plates. Near fine. $2,000.00

CATLIN, George. *Letters and Notes on the Manners, Customs, and Condition of the North American Indians.* London: 1841. Two octavo volumes. Three-quarter tan calf gilt. Gilt decorated spines with red morocco labels and raised bands. Illustrated with over 300 plates and a folding map. Near fine. $2,000.00

CATLIN. *Letters and Notes on the Manners, Customs & Conditions of the North American Indian.* Philadelphia: J.W. Bradley, 1859. Two volumes in one. Full black calf. Original publishers binding with embossed covers. 150 illustrations on steel and wood. Many of them are hand colored. Light foxing on a few plates. 10" tall. Very good. $1,550.00

CAVE, William. *Primitive Christianity.* London: J.G. for R. Chiswell. Full brown calf. All original. 7" tall. Very good. $1,200.00

CATLIN, George. *North American Indians: Being Letters and Notes on the Manners, Customs and Conditions, Written During Eight Years' Travel Amongst the Wildest Tribes of Indians in North America.* Edinburgh: John Grant, 1926. Two large octavo volumes. Three-quarter calf. Illustrated with 180 color plates. Near fine. $800.00

CATLIN, George. *North American Indians: Being Letters and Notes on the Manners, Customs and Conditions, Written During Eight Years' Travel Amongst the Wildest Tribes of Indians in North America, 1832 – 1839.* Philadelphia: Leary, Stuart and Company, 1913. Two large octavo volumes. Three-quarter red morocco. Illustrated with over 300 color illustrations and folding maps. Near fine. $975.00

CAVALCASELLE, and Crawe. *History of Painting in Italy.* London: John Murray, 1912. Nine volumes. Three-quarter blue morocco by Riviere. Ornate spines with raised bands. Illustrated. Near fine. $1,200.00

CERVANTES, M. *The Life and Adventures of Don Quixote.* London: Hurst, Robertson & Co., 1820. Four volumes. Full red morocco gilt. Contains engravings by Richard Westall. Near fine. $1,100.00

CERVANTES, Miguel. *Don Quixote de la Mancha.* London: J. J. Dubochet & Co., 1837 – 39. Three tall octavo volumes. Nineteenth century full navy polished calf gilt. Raised bands, red and green morocco labels. First edition. Illustrated by Tony Johannot. Translated by Charles Jarvis. Near fine. $1,250.00

CERVANTES, Miguel. *Don Quixote de la Mancha.* London: Joseph Thomas, 1840. Three tall octavo volumes. Three-quarter tan calf by Zaehnsdorf. Gilt decorated spines. Illustrations by Tony Johannot. Near fine. $975.00

CERVANTES. *Don Quixote.* Edinburgh: William Patterson, 1879. Four volumes. Green morocco gilt. Illustrated. Near fine. $900.00

CHAILLU, Paul B. *The Viking Age*. New York: Charles Scribners Sons, 1889. Two volumes. Three-quarter butterscotch calf. Marbled edges, 1,366 illustrations and map. 9" tall. Near fine. $265.00

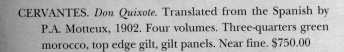

CERVANTES. *Don Quixote*. Translated from the Spanish by P.A. Motteux, 1902. Four volumes. Three-quarters green morocco, top edge gilt, gilt panels. Near fine. $750.00

CERVANTES. *The Life and Exploits of Don Quixote*. London: W. Wilson, 1821. Four volumes. Full red morocco gilt. Small 8vo. Raised bands with gilt panels and covers. Translated by Charles Jarvis. Near fine. $1,300.00

CHAMBERS, Robert. *Domestic Annals of Scotland*. Edinburgh: 1859. Three volumes. Full tan calf, marbled edges, red and green labels. Near fine. $600.00

CHAMBERS, Talbot. *The Bible Gallery*. London: Cassell, Petter, Galpin & Co., 1880. Full brown calf. Highly gilt cover with all edges gilt. Illustrated by Gustave Dore. 13" tall. Fine. $850.00

CHAMBERS, W. *France Its History and Revolutions*. Edinburgh and London: W & R. Chambers, 1875. Full navy morocco. Prize binding, marbled edges. 7" tall. Near fine. $180.00

CHAPIN, L.N. *The Crown Book of the Beautiful, The Wonderful and the Wise*. Philadelphia: John Winston & Co., 1887. Full brown calf with embossed covers. All edges gilt. Illustrated. 9" tall. Near fine. $350.00

CHAMPNEY, Elizabeth W. *Romance of Roman Villas (The Renaissance)*. G.P. Putnam's Sons, 1909. Three-quarter brown morocco. Gilt decorated spine. Near fine. $225.00

CHAPMAN, Abel. *On Safari Big Game Hunting in British East Africa....* New York: Longmans, Green & Co., 1908. Full green morocco gilt. Raised bands, ornate panels. Illustrated. Near fine. $480.00

CHAPTAL, M.I.A. *Elements of Chemistry*. London: J&J Robinson, 1791. Three volumes. Full contemporary calf. Gilt panels with red labels. Translated from French by W. Nicholson. First edition in English. Near fine. $975.00

CHARLOTTE, Catherine. *The Court of France in the Sixteenth Century*. London: John C. Nimmo, 1899. Two volumes. Full tan calf. Illustrated. 8½" tall. Near fine. $300.00

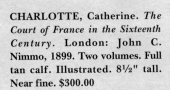

CHASE, D.P. *The Ethics of Aristotle*. London: Arthur L. Humphreys, 1902. Two volumes. Three-quarter red morocco by Stikman. Raised bands and marbled boards. Near fine. $1,250.00

CHAUCER, Geoffrey. *Canterbury Tales*. Oxford: The Clarendon Press, 1798. Two volumes. Three-quarter tan morocco gilt. Quarto. Near fine. $1,200.00

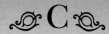

CHAUCER, Geoffrey. *The Poetical Works of Geoffrey Chaucer*. Edinburgh: Apollo, 1782. Fourteen volumes. Full tan calf. Bell's edition. 5" tall. Near fine. $1,700.00

CHAUCER, Geoffrey. *The Canterbury Tales*. Boston: Hale Cushman & Flint, and London: Jonathan Cape & The Medici Society, 1928. Full blue morocco gilt. Raised bands, gilt decorated spines and covers. Illustrated by W. Russell Flint. Near fine. $400.00

CHAUCER, Geoffrey. *The Canterbury Tales*. London: Jonathan Cape The Medici Society, 1928. Full tan morocco by Riviere, ornate gilt on spines and cover. Illustrated. Near fine. $850.00

CHAUCER, Geoffrey. *The Poetical Works*. London: William Pickering, 1845. Six volumes. Full wine morocco, gilt. Small 8vo. Near fine. $1,800.00

CHAUCER, Geoffrey. *The Works of Our Ancient Learned & Excellent English Poet, Jeffrey Chaucer....* London: 1687. Folio, period-style full speckled and paneled calf gilt. Near fine. $3,400.00

CHAUCER, Geoffrey. *The Poetical Works of Geoffrey Chaucer*. London: William Pickering, 1845. Six volumes. Full green morocco. All edges gilt. Urn decoration on spines. First edition. Near fine. $1,800.00

CHESNEY, Charles Cornwallis. *A Military View of Recent Campaigns in Virginia and Maryland*. London: Smith, Elder and Co., 1863 – 65. Two octavo volumes. Three-quarter red polished calf gilt. Gilt decorated spines with marbled boards and endpapers. First editions. Near fine. $700.00

CHESTERFIELD, Earl of. *Letters Written by the Earl of Chesterfield to His Son*. London: 1774. Two volumes. Quarto, twentieth century three-quarter red morocco gilt. First edition. Near fine. $800.00

CHESTERFIELD, Lord. *Letters to His Son*. New York: Dingwall Rock, 1925. Two volumes. Three-quarter tan morocco. Raised bands, gilt panels. Near fine. $275.00

CHESTERFIELD, Lord. *Letters Written by the Late Right Honourable Philip Dormer Stanhope, Earl of Chesterfield, to his Son, Philip Stanhope, Esq.* London: Printed for J. Dodsley, 1774. Two quarto volumes. Full diced calf gilt. Raised bands with red morocco labels. Marbled endpapers and edges. First edition. Fine. $1,100.00

CHESTERFIELD, Philip Dormer Stanhope, Earl of. *Letters to His Son*. London: J. Dodsley, 1774. Two volumes. Contemporary speckled calf gilt. Raised bands with gilt compartments and red and green morocco labels. Marbled endpapers. First edition. Engraved frontispiece portrait. Near fine. $900.00

CHESTERFIELD, Philip Dormer Stanhope, Earl of. *Miscellaneous Works*. London: Edward and Charles Dilly, 1777. Two volumes. Full brown calf gilt. Raised bands with red morocco labels. Engraved armorial headpiece on dedication page. Illustrated with tissue guarded portraits. Near fine. $650.00

CHEEVER, George B. *The Poets of America*. Hartford: Silas Andrus and Son, 1850. Full black calf. Highly gilt spine and covers, all edges gilt. Illustrated. 8" tall. Near fine. $440.00

CHETWOOD, William. *The Voyages, Dangerous Adventures and Imminent Escapes of Captain Richard Falconer*. London: 1720. Full paneled calf. Octavo. Illustrated with engraved frontispiece. First edition. Near fine. $975.00

CHURCHILL, Randolph S. *Winston S. Churchill*. London: 1966 – 88. Eight volumes. Octavo. Modern three-quarter dark blue morocco gilt. First edition of the official biography of Winston Churchill, the first two volumes written by his son. Near fine. $2,600.00

CHILD, Francis James. *English and Scottish Ballads.* Boston: Little Brown and Co., 1857. Eight volumes. Three-quarter butterscotch calf with marbled edges. 6½" tall. Near fine. $750.00

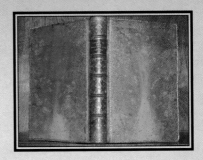

CHURCH, Alfred J. *The Story of the Persian War.* London: Seeley, Jackson & Halliday, 1882. Full tree calf, prize binding. Marbled edges. Illustrated with 16 color plates. First edition. 8" tall. Very good. $160.00

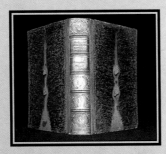

CHILD, Helen, and KITTREDGE, George. *English and Scottish Popular Ballads.* Boston and New York: Houghton Mifflin and Co., 1904. Full tree calf with all edges gilt. Cambridge edition, The Riverside Press. 8" tall. Near fine. $225.00

CHURCHILL, Sir. W. *Marlborough, His Life and Times.* London: George G. Harrap & Co., 1933. Four volumes. Three-quarter red morocco gilt. Raised bands with gilt panels. First edition. Near fine. $1,600.00

CHURCHILL, Sir. W. *The Second World War.* London: Cassell & Co., 1948. Six volumes. Full navy morocco gilt. Raised bands with gilt panels. First edition. Near fine. $2,100.00

CHURCHILL, Sir. W. *The War Speeches.* London: Cassel & Co., Ltd., 1941. Seven volumes. Three-quarter blue morocco gilt. Raised bands with gilt panels. First edition. Near fine. $1,350.00

CHURCHILL, Winston S. *Collection of World War II Speeches.* London: 1941 – 46. Seven volumes. Full dark blue morocco gilt. First edition. Near fine. $2,100.00

CHURCHILL, Winston S. *Marlborough: His Life and Times.* London: 1933 – 38. Four volumes. Octavo. Modern full dark blue morocco gilt. First trade editions, with numerous maps, plates, and document facsimiles. Near fine. $1,600.00

CHURCHILL, Winston S. *The Second World War.* London: 1948 – 54. Six volumes. Thick octavo. Modern full dark green morocco gilt. Near fine. $1,900.00

CHURCHILL, Winston S. *The Second World War.* London: 1948 – 54. Six volumes. Thick octavo. Full red morocco gilt. First edition of Churchill's masterpiece. Near fine. $1,900.00

CHURCH, Alfred J. *Stories from Virgil.* London: Seeley and Co., 1902. Full red morocco. Marbled edges. Prize binding. Twenty-four illustrations from Pinelli's design. 8" tall. Near fine. $150.00

CHURCH, Rev. Alfred L. *Stories from Levy.* London: Seeley and Co., 1895. Full light green morocco. Prize binding with marbled edges. Colored plates from designs by Pinelli. 7" tall. Near fine. $140.00

CHURCH, Thomas. *The History of the Great Indian War of 1675 and 1676, Commonly Called Philip's War.* New York: H. Dayton, n.d., circa 1840. Three-quarter brown calf with top edges gilt. Hand-colored frontis. Twentieth century binding. 9" tall. Near fine. $575.00

CHURCHILL, Winston. *A History of English Speaking Peoples.* London: Cassell and Company, 1956 – 58. Four octavo volumes. Full red morocco. Raised bands, all edges gilt. Illustrated. First edition. Near fine. $1,100.00

CHURCHILL, Winston. *The Second World War: The Gathering Storm; Their Finest Hour; The Grand Alliance; The Hinge of Fate; Closing the Ring; Triumph and Tragedy.* London: Cassell & Co., Ltd. 1948 – 1954. Six octavo volumes. Three-quarter red morocco gilt. Raised bands, top edges gilt. Illustrated. First edition. Near fine. $1,900.00

CHURCHILL, Winston. *The World Crisis.* London: 1923 – 31. Six volumes. Octavo. Modern full navy morocco gilt. First editions of Churchill's important history of World War I. Near fine. $2,100.00

CICERO, Marcus Tullius. *Tully's Three Books of Offices.* London: Sam Buckley, 1699. Contemporary sprinkled calf. Raised bands with engraved title page. Near fine. $950.00

CIVIL WAR. *Campaigns of the Civil War.* New York: Charles Scribner's Sons, 1881. Thirteen volumes. Three-quarter brown calf with top edges gilt. Illustrated with maps. First edition. 7½" tall. Near fine. $1,750.00

CLARK, Mary Cowden. *World-Noted Women.* New York: D. Appleton & Co., 1858. Full red morocco. Raised gilt covers. All edges gilt. Illustrated. 11" tall. Near fine. $575.00

CLARKE, Adam. *The Holy Bible and Commentary.* New York: Carlton & Porter, 1856. Six volumes (only two shown). Full black calf. All edges gilt. 10½" tall. Near fine. $575.00

CLEMENT, Clara Erskine. *Handbook of Legendary Art.* New York: Hurd and Houghton, 1875. Full tree calf. All edges gilt. Illustrated. 7½" tall. Near fine. $150.00

CLEMENT, Clara Erskine. *Painters, Architects, Engravers and Their Works.* New York: Hurd and Houghton, 1875. Full tree calf. All edges gilt. Illustrated. 7½" tall. Near fine. $150.00

CLOUGH, Arthur Hugh. *The Poems and Prose Remains of Arthur Hugh Clough.* London: MacMillan & Co., 1869. Two volumes. Three-quarter green morocco by Leary Young & Sons. Top edges gilt. First edition. 7½" tall. Near fine. $350.00

CLEVELAND, Horace William Shaler. *Landscape Architecture, as Applied to the Wants of the West.* Chicago: 1873. Three-quarter calf. Tall 12mo. First edition. Near fine. $275.00

CODY, William F. *The Life of Hon. William F. Cody Known as Buffalo Bill, the Famous Hunter, Scout and Guide. An Autobiography.* Hartford: 1879. Three-quarter calf. Octavo. Illustrated with sixteen full-page wood-engravings and a steel-engraved frontispiece portrait. First edition. Near fine. $775.00

COFFIN, Charles Carleton. *Four Years of Fighting.* Boston: Ticknor & Fields, 1866. Full tan calf. Illustrated. First edition. Very good. $350.00

COFFIN, Charles. *Four Years of Fighting.* Boston: Ticknor & Fields, 1866. Three-quarter black calf with marbled edges. Owned by John Motley, imminent American historian and author, inscribed from author to Motley. 8½" tall. Very good. $625.00

COLEMAN. *A Collection of the Facts, Documents, Relative to the Death of Major General Alexander Hamilton.* New York: Hopkins and Seymour, 1804. Full tan calf. Binding has inlaid calf borders. First edition. 8" tall. Near fine. $700.00

COLERIDGE, Samuel Taylor. *The Poetical Works of Samuel Taylor Coleridge.* London: Ward, Lock & Co., circa 1880. Full tree calf. Prize binding. Vignette illustrations. 7" tall. Near fine. $175.00

COLBY, Charles. *The Diamond Atlas.* New York: Samuel N. Gaston, 1857. Full red morocco gilt. Covers and spine heavily gilt. Illustrated with color illustrations and 56 hand-colored maps. Near fine. $750.00

COLERIDGE, Samuel T. *The Rime of the Ancient Mariner.* London: George Harrap, 1910. Full green morocco by Sangorski & Sutcliffe. Ornate covers and spine. Quarto. Illustrated by Willy Pogany. Near fine. $1,600.00

COLLINS, Wilkie. *The Moonstone.* London: 1868. Three octavo volumes. Three-quarter brown morocco. First edition. Near fine. $2,100.00

COLLINS, Rev. W. Lucas. *Ancient Classics for English Readers.* Edinburgh and London: William Blackwood and Sons, 1878. Fourteen volumes. Three-quarter butterscotch calf with marbled edges. 7" tall. Near fine. $1,600.00

COLTON, Calvin. *The Life and Times of Henry Clay.* New York: A.S. Barnes & Co., 1846. Two volumes. Full tan calf with marbled edges. 9" tall. Very good. $625.00

COMBE, William. *The History of Johnny Quae Genus.* London: 1822. Contemporary full burgundy morocco gilt. Octavo. Illustrated with hand-colored engravings by Thomas Rowlandson. First edition. Near fine. $425.00

COMBE, William. *The Tour of Doctor Syntax, in Search of the Picturesque.* With: *The Second Tour of Doctor Syntax in Search of Consolation.* With: *The Third Tour of Doctor Syntax, in Search of a Wife.* London: 1855. Three octavo volumes. Nineteenth century three-quarter polished brown calf. Illustrated with hand-colored engravings by Thomas Rowlandson. Late edition. Near fine. $1,100.00

COMBE. *The Tours of Dr. Syntax.* London: R. Ackerman, 1812 – 1821. Three volumes. Full red morocco gilt by Root. Raised bands, gilt panels. Illustrated. First edition. Near fine. $2,800.00

CONGREVE, W. *Plays In Two Volumes.* London: J. Tonson, 1735. Two volumes. Full tan calf. Raised bands, gilt panels with brown morocco labels. Near fine. $460.00

CONGREVE, William. *The Works.* Birmingham: Printed by John Baskerville, 1761. Three volumes. Marbled calf by Morrell. Gilt spines with red and black morocco labels. Marbled endpapers, all edges gilt. Illustrated with six engraved plates. Near fine. $580.00

CONRAD, Joseph. *Collected Works.* Garden City: 1925 – 26. Twenty-three octavo volumes. Three-quarter green morocco gilt. Memorial edition, one of only 99 sets signed by the author. Near fine. $7,600.00

CONRAD, Joseph. *The Works.* Garden City, New York: 1920 – 26. Twenty-two volumes. With: *Life and Letters.* Two volumes. Garden City: 1928. Twenty-four octavo volumes in all. Three-quarter green morocco gilt. "Sun-Dial Edition," one of only 735 sets. Illustrated with a frontispiece portrait in Volume 1. Near fine. $7,400.00

CONRAD, Joseph. *The Works.* London: 1921 – 27. Twenty volumes. Octavo. Contemporary full navy morocco gilt. Signed limited edition, one of only 780 sets signed by Conrad. Near fine. $8,000.00

CONRAD, Joseph. *Works.* New York: Doubleday & Co. 1925. Twenty-three volumes. Memorial Edition, one of only 499 sets. Three-quarter blue morocco gilt. Near fine. $4,600.00

CONRAD, Joseph. *Works.* Garden City, New York: Doubleday, 1925. Twenty-three volumes. Three-quarter green morocco. Raised bands, gilt panels and edges. Near fine. $4,600.00

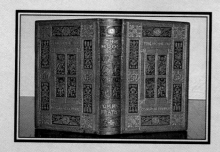

COMMON PRAYER. The Book of Common Prayer. London: Bickers and Bush, 1863. Full tan calf by Leightonson & Hodge. Highly gilt spine and highly gilt and embossed covers. All edges gilt. Each page is illustrated where the illustrations are comprised within a border. 7" tall. Near fine. $675.00

COMMON PRAYER. The Book of Common Prayer. London: Longman, Hurst, Rees, Orme and Brown, 1815. Full red morocco by Armstrong. All edges gilt, highly gilt and embossed covers and spine. Copper plate engravings, two silver buckles. 4" tall. Fine. $450.00

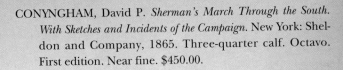

CONYBEARE, Rev. W.J. *The Life and Epistles of St. Paul.* New York and Bombay: Longmans, Green and Co., 1901. Full tree calf prize binding. All edges gilt. 7½" tall. Near fine. $190.00

CONYNGHAM, David P. *Sherman's March Through the South. With Sketches and Incidents of the Campaign.* New York: Sheldon and Company, 1865. Three-quarter calf. Octavo. First edition. Near fine. $450.00

COOPER, James Fenimore. *Novels.* London: George Routledge and Sons, 1866 – 67. Fourteen volumes. Three-quarter dark green morocco. 12mo. Raised bands with gilt spines and marbled boards. Frontispiece illustrations in each volume. Near fine. $1,800.00

COOPER, James Fenimore. *The History of the Navy of the United States of America.* Philadelphia: Lea & Blanchard, 1839. Two octavo volumes. Three-quarter calf. First edition. Near fine. $525.00

COOKE, John Esten. *Stonewall Jackson A Military Biography.* New York: D. Appleton & Co., 1876. Three-quarter dark brown calf by Launder and MacDonald. Top edges gilt. Illustrated. Near fine. $675.00

COOPER, James Fenimore. *The Last of the Mohicans.* London: Colburn and Bentley, 1831. Three-quarter green calf gilt. Small 8vo. Raised bands with green and red labels. First English edition. Near fine. $850.00

COOPER, James Fenimore. *Works.* G.P. Putnam's Sons, 1896. Thirty-two volumes. Three-quarter tan calf gilt. Raised bands, gilt panels with red and green morocco labels. "Mohawk Edition." Near fine. $4,100.00

COOKE, John Esten. *Stonewall Jackson, A Military Biography.* New York: D. Appleton, 1876. Three-quarter chocolate morocco. Marbled edges. Illustrated with steel engravings and maps. Bookseller's stamp. Near fine. $575.00

COOPER, J.F. *The Prairie.* London: Henry Colburn and Richard Bentley, 1832. One-quarter green morocco. First edition with new introduction. 6" tall. Near fine. $265.00

COOKE, John Esten. *The Life of General Robert E. Lee.* New York: D. Appleton & Co., 1871. Three-quarter tan calf. Illustrated. First edition. 9¼" tall. Near fine. $1,050.00

COOPER, James Fenimore. *The Last of the Mohicans.* New York: W.A. Townsend, 1859. Full green morocco. Highly gilt spine and covers with red edges. First illustrated edition. Drawings by Darley and original pencil drawing is tipped in. 8½" tall. Near fine. $1,250.00

COOPER, James Fenimore. *Works*. New York: W.A. Townsend & Co., 1860. Thirty-two volumes. Three-quarter green morocco gilt. Ribbed gilt decorated spines. Illustrated by T.O.C. Darley. Near fine. $4,200.00

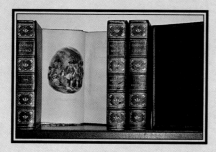

COOPER, James Fenimore. *The Works of James Fennimore Cooper*. New York and London: D. Appleton & Co., n.d., circa 1885. Thirty-two volumes. Full navy crushed levant morocco. Top edges gilt. Illustrated with hand-colored frontispieces. Grand Format edition, one of 50 sets. Section of manuscript from Wish Ton Wish. 8½" tall. Near fine. $4,800.00

COOPER, James Fenimore. *The Works*. New York: G.P. Putnam & Sons, circa 1890. Sixteen volumes. Quarter red morocco. The Pathfinder edition, one of 1,000 copies. Fine. $2,200.00

COOPER, Rev. Wm. M. *Flagellation and the Flagellants — A History of the Rod*. London: John Camden Hotten, 1869. Three-quarter tan calf. Marbled edges. Illustrated. 7" tall. Near fine. $225.00

COOPER, Susan Fenimore. *Pages and Pictures from the Writings of James Fenimore Cooper*. New York: W.A. Townsend & Co., 1861. Full black calf. Highly gilt spine and cover, all edges gilt. Illustrated. First edition. 11" tall. Near fine. $450.00

COPPEE, Henry. *A Gallery of English and American Women*. Philadelphia: J.M. Stoddart & Co., 1875. Full dark brown calf. Illustrated with 100 steel engravings. First edition. Fine. $280.00

COPPEE, Henry. *Grant and His Campaigns*. New York: Charles B. Richardson, 1866. Three-quarter tan calf. Marbled edges. Illustrated first edition. 9" tall. Near fine. $350.00

CORNWALL, Barry. *Dramatic Scenes*. London: Chapman and Hall, 1857. Full green morocco. Highly gilt spine and covers. Gilt urn on covers with all edges gilt. Illustrated first edition. Wood engravings by Dalziel from drawings by Foster, Weir, and Tenniel. 8" tall. Near fine. $425.00

CORRELLI, Marie. *The Works of Marie Correlli.* London: 1897 – 1912. Eighteen volumes. Full morocco by Bumpus. Various colors. All bindings are specially made and are likely each one of a kind. All edges gilt. Five first editions; *Ziska, Holy Orders, Delicia, The Life Everlasting,* and *Temporal Power.* All eighteen volumes are signed by Marie Correlli and dated 1912. Fine. $5,500.00

COSTELLO, Louisa Steward. *The Rose Garden of Persia.* London: Longman, Brown, Green, and Longmans, 1845. Full light green morocco by Sangorski & Sutcliffe. Highly gilt covers with red morocco inlaid floral covers. All edges gilt. Pages with colored borders. Illuminated illustrations. Doheny bookplate. First edition. 7½" tall. Near fine. $975.00

COWPER, William. *Poems.* London: J. Johnson, 1812. Two volumes. Full tree calf. Marbled edges. 6½" tall. Very good. $375.00

COWPER, William. *The Poetical Works of William Cowper.* New York: Leavitt & Allen, circa 1870. Two volumes in one. Full red morocco. Highly gilt spine and covers, all edges gilt. Illustrated. 9½" tall. Near fine. $385.00

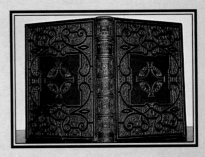

COXE, Rev. A. Cleveland. *Christian Ballads.* New York: D. Appleton & Co., 1865. Full green morocco. Highly gilt spine and embossed covers. All edges gilt. Illustrations by L.A. Howes. 8¼" tall. Near fine. $425.00

COXE, William. *Travels into Poland, Russia, Sweden, and Denmark.* London: 1784. Two volumes. Three-quarter brown calf. Large quarto. Illustrated. First edition. Near fine. $750.00

CRAIK & MacFARLANE. *The Pictorial History of England.* London: Charles Knight & Co., 1846. Eight volumes. Full tan calf. Gilt decorated spines with green morocco labels. Thick 8vo. Near fine. $1,250.00

CRANE, Stephen. *The Monster and Other Stories.* New York and London: 1899. Three-quarter red morocco. Octavo. Illustrated. First edition. Near fine. $825.00

CREVIER, Mr. *The History of the Roman Emperors from Augustus to Constantine* (translated from the French). London: J. and P. Knapton, 1755 – 1761. Ten volumes. Full tan contemporary calf. Illustrated with maps and other copper plates. Near fine. $1,850.00

CRAFTS, W.A. *The Southern Rebellion: Being a History of the U.S.* Boston: Samuel Walker, 1862. Two volumes. Three-quarter black calf. Marbled edges. Illustrated. First edition. 11" tall. Near fine. $875.00

CROMEK, R.H. *The Reliques of Robert Burns.* London: J.M. McCreery, 1817. Full mottled calf by Bayntun. All edges gilt. Fourth edition. Bound with Robert Burns's works. Near fine. $250.00

CROSS, J.W. *George Eliot's Life as related in her Letters and Journals.* Edinburgh: William Blackwood & Sons, 1885. Three volumes. Full green morocco. Gilt decorated spines. Near fine. $250.00

CRAFTS, William A. *Pioneers in the Settlement of America.* Boston: Samuel Walker and Co., 1876. Two volumes. Three-quarter brown calf. All edges gilt. Illustrated by Darley, Shepard, and Perkins. First edition. 11½" tall. Near fine. $900.00

CRAIK, Dinah. *John Halifax Gentleman.* London: Hurst and Blackett, 1856. Three volumes. Full red morocco by Bayntun. Highly gilt spine, with all edges gilt. First edition, with slipcase. 8½" tall. Fine. $1,100.00

CROWE & CAVAL, Caselle. *Titian: His Life and Times with Some Account of His Family.* London: John Murray, 1877. Two volumes. Three-quarter blue morocco by Zaehnsdorf. Gilt decorated spines. Illustrated. Near fine. $225.00

CUMMING, Roualeyn Gordon. *Five Years of a Hunter's Life in the Far Interior of South Africa.* London: John Murray, 1850. Two volumes. Three-quarter green morocco. Second edition. Near fine. $575.00

CRUNDER, Romesh. *History of India.* London: The Grolier Society, 1906. Nine volumes. Three-quarter red morocco. Top edges gilt. Hand-colored frontis. Nationale edition, one of 1,000 copies. First edition. 10" tall. Near fine. $1,100.00

CUNDALL, Joseph. *The Great Works of Raphael Sanzio of Urbino.* London: 1870. Full red morocco. Gilt tooled spine and covers. Quarto. Illustrated with 30 full page photographic plates. Near fine. $380.00

CURTIS, Charles Henry. *Orchids: Their Description and Cultivation.* London. Quarto, original full green crushed morocco gilt. Limited edition, one of only 125 copies. Thirty full-color plates. Near fine. $825.00

CUNNINGHAM, A. *Anecdotes of Napoleon Bonaparte.* London: Charles Daly, 1839. Three-quarter brown calf by Larkins. All edges gilt. Illustrated. 4¼" tall. Near fine. $280.00

CUNNINGHAM, Allan. *The Complete Works of Robert Burns.* London: George Virtue, 1848. Full black calf. Highly gilt cover. All edges gilt. Illustrated with steel engravings. 10" tall. Near fine. $425.00

D'ANUIS, Countess. *Fairy Tales.* London: Walker & Edwards, 1817. Two volumes. Full brown calf. 5⅛" tall. Near fine. $500.00

CURRIE, James. *The Works of Robert Burns.* London: T. Cadell, 1820. Four volumes. Full mottled calf by Bayntun. All edges gilt. Plates by Stothard. (This set bound with a volume 5 *Reliques of Robert Burns*) Near fine. $1,100.00

D'AUBIGNE, J.H. Merle. *History of the Reformation in the 16th Century.* London: Whittaker and Co., n.d., circa 1860. Full tan calf. All edges gilt. 9" tall. Very good. $90.00

CURTIS, George Ticknor. *Life of Daniel Webster.* New York: D. Appleton and Company, 1870. Four octavo volumes. Contemporary full brown levant morocco gilt. Raised bands and silk endpapers. Illustrated with fine engravings. Near fine. $1,100.00

CURTIUS RUFUS, Quintus. *The Historie of Quintus Curtius.* London: Roger Warde, 1584. Half polished tan calf. Gilt decorated spine. Small 8vo. Translated into English by John Brende. Near fine. $3,600.00

CUSTER, George A. *My Life on the Plains, Or, Personal Experiences with Indians.* New York: 1874. Full morocco. Illustrated. First edition. Near fine. $1,700.00

D'ARBLAY. *Diary and Letters.* London: Swan Sonnenschein & Co., 1900. Eight volumes. Full red morocco gilt. Raised bands, gilt spines. Illustrated. Near fine. $1,600.00

DA VINCI, Leonardo. *A Treatise of Painting...adorned with a great Number of Cuts.* London: 1721. Contemporary full paneled calf. Octavo. Illustrated. First edition. Near fine. $2,100.00

DABNEY, R.L. *Life and Campaigns of Lieut.-Gen. Thomas J. Jackson (Stonewall Jackson).* New York: 1866. Octavo. Original half brown calf gilt. Illustrated with a steel-engraved frontispiece portrait of Jackson and maps. First American edition. Near fine. $675.00

DALTON, Michael. *The Country Justice: Containing the Practice of the Justices of the Peace out of their Sessions.* London: 1635. Contemporary full calf. Small folio. Near fine. $675.00

D'ANDILLY, Arnauld. *The Works of Josephus.* London: H. Herringman, 1683. Full tan calf. Marbled edges. Nineteenth century binding, copper plate illustrations. 14½" tall. Very good. $1,200.00

DABNEY, Prof. R.L. *Life and Campaigns of Lieut. Gen. Thomas J. Jackson (Stonewall Jackson).* New York: Blelock & Co., 1866. Three-quarter tan calf. Marbled edges. Illustrated. First edition. 8½" tall. Very good. $650.00

DAHLGREN, Madeleine Vinton. *Memoir of John Dahlgren.* **Boston: James Osgood, 1882. Full brown calf by Launder and MacDonald. Top edges gilt. Illustrated. First edition. 9" tall. Near fine. $350.00**

DALTON, J. *The Gentleman in Black.* **London: 1840. Full cobalt morocco by Riviere. Top edges gilt. Illustrated by George Cruikshank. Printed for Chas. Daly. Fine. $300.00**

DAMPIER, Captain William. *A New Voyage Round the World.* With: *Voyages and Descriptions in Three Parts.* With: *A Voyage to New-Holland.* Bound with: *A Continuation of a Voyage to New-Holland.* London: Printed for James Knapton, 1703 – 1709. Four thick octavo volumes in all. Half calf. Illustrated with numerous plates and maps. Near fine. $3,600.00

DANA, Charles A. *The Life of Ulysses S. Grant.* **Cincinnati: Gurdon Bill & Co., 1868. Full brown calf with marbled edges. Illustrated. First edition. 8" tall. Near fine. $375.00**

DANA, Charles A. *The Life of Ulysses S. Grant.* Springfield, Massachusetts: Gurdon Bill & Co., 1868. Octavo. Contemporary full black blind-stamped morocco. First edition. Near fine. $375.00

DANIEL, William B. *Rural Sports.* Bunny and Gold, 1801. Two volumes. Full tree calf levant, ornate gilt on spines. Illustrated. Near fine. $375.00

DARLEY, F.O.C. *A Selection of War Lyrics.* **New York: Hurd and Houghtons, 1866. Full brown calf with all edges gilt. Illustrated. 9" tall. Very good. $210.00**

DANTE. *The Divine Comedy.* Boston, 1897 – 99. Three volumes. Octavo. Contemporary full brown polished calf gilt. "Riverside" edition of Longfellow's translation of Dante's *Divine Comedy.* Near fine. $380.00

DARBY, William. *The Emigrant's Guide to the Western and Southwestern States and Territories....* New York: Kirk & Mercein, 1818. Half black calf over paper covered boards. Octavo. Illustrated with a hand-colored folding map and full page chart. First edition. Near fine. $1,400.00

DARWIN, Charles. *The Descent of Man, and Selection in Relation to Sex.* London: John Murray, 1871. Two octavo volumes. Three-quarter blue calf with gilt lettered spines. First edition. Near fine. $1,250.00

DARWIN, Charles. *The Descent of Man, and Selection in Relation to Sex.* London: John Murray, 1871. Two octavo volumes. Full green morocco gilt. First edition, first issue. Near fine. $1,350.00

DARTON, J.M. *Brave Boys Who Have Become Illustrious Men of our Time.* **London: Swan Sonnenschein & Co., n.d., circa 1900. Full tree calf. Prize binding with marbled edges. 7" tall. Near fine. $240.00**

DARWIN, Charles. *Darwin's Works.* New York: D. Appleton & Co., 1883. Thirteen volumes. Three-quarter butterscotch calf. Marbled edges. Illustrated with pull-outs. 7½" tall. Near fine. $4,200.00

DARWIN, Charles. *The Life and Letter* (including an autobiographical chapter edited by his son, Francis Darwin). London: John Murray. 1888. Three volumes. Three-quarter wine morocco by Zaehnsdorf. Ornate gilt on spines. Near fine. $375.00

DARWIN, Charles. *Works.* London: John Murray, 1872 – 77. Ten volumes. With: Muller, Fritz. *Facts and Arguments for Darwin.* London: John Murray, 1869. Eleven octavo volumes all together. Three-quarter green calf gilt. Near fine. $4,200.00

DARWIN, Charles. *Works.* New York: 1897. Fifteen volumes. Octavo. Early twentieth century three-quarter burgundy morocco. Near fine. $4,600.00

DARWIN, Charles. *Works.* New York: 1897 – 98. Fifteen octavo volumes. Three-quarter tan crushed morocco gilt. Illustrated. Near fine. $4,600.00

DAUDET, Alphonse. *Sapho: Parisian Customs.* Philadelphia: 1897. Contemporary three-quarter brown morocco gilt. Octavo. Illustrated. Limited edition, one of only 1,000 copies. Near fine. $275.00

DAVIS, Jefferson. *The Rise and Fall of the Confederate Government.* New York: 1881. Two thick octavo volumes. Contemporary three-quarter brown morocco gilt. Marbled boards and endpapers. First edition. Illustrated with engraved portraits of Davis and his presidential staff. Also includes numerous maps and plates. Near fine. $1,350.00

DAVIS, Varina. *Jefferson Davis Ex-President of the Confederate States of America. A Memoir by His Wife.* New York: 1890. Two thick octavo volumes. Three-quarter calf. First edition. Illustrated with numerous plates and two folding maps. Near fine. $875.00

DAVIS, Jefferson. *The Rise and Fall of the Confederate Government.* New York: D. Appleton, 1881. Two volumes. Three-quarter brown calf by Launder and MacDonald. Illustrated with all pull-out maps. First edition. 9½" tall. Near fine. $1,300.00

DAWSON, William Leon. *The Birds of California. A Complete and Popular Account of the 580 Species and Subspecies of Birds Found in the State.* San Diego: South Moulton Company, 1923. Four volumes. Original three-quarter tan morocco gilt. Tall thick quarto. Limited edition. Illustrated with full-color plates and photogravures. Near fine. $1,800.00

DE BOURRIENNE, M. *Memoirs of Napoleon Bonaparte. An Account of Important Events of the Hundred Days of Napoleon's Surrender to The English, And of His Residence And Death....* London: Richard Bentley, 1836. Four octavo volumes. Three-quarter brown morocco gilt. Gilt decorated spines, marbled endpapers, all edges gilt. Illustrated with numerous plates and a map. Near fine. $800.00

DAWSON, Henry. *Battles of the United States by Sea and Land.* New York: Johnson, Fry and Co., 1858. Two volumes. Three-quarter black calf. Thirty-nine steel engravings and six hand-colored illustrations. First edition. 11½" tall. Near fine. $950.00

DE BOURRIENNE, Louis Antoine Fauvelet. *Memoirs of Napoleon Bonaparte.* New York: Thomas Y. Crowell & Co., circa 1910. Four volumes bound in two volumes. Three-quarter tan calf. Top edges gilt. Illustrated. 8" tall. Near fine. $325.00

DE BOURRIENNE, Louis Antoine. *Memoirs of Napoleon Bonaparte.* New York: Thomas Crowell & Co., n.d., circa 1850. Four volumes. Three-quarter tan calf. Highly gilt spine with marbled edges. Illustrated. 8" tall. Near fine. $475.00

DE BOURRIENNE, M. *Private Memoirs of Napoleon Bonaparte.* London: Henry Colburn, 1830. Four volumes. Full tan calf. Illustrated with hand-colored frontispieces and 20 extra plates. 9" tall. Very good. $650.00

DE BOURRIENNE, Louis. *Napoleon.* New York: The Grolier Society, n.d., circa 1900. Sixteen volumes (only two shown). Three-quarter red morocco. Top edges gilt, moiré center boards. All volumes with hand-colored frontispiece. One of only 425 sets. 9" tall. Fine. $2,200.00

DE FOE, Daniel. *The Life and Adventures of Robinson Crusoe.* London: Routledge, Warne, and Routeledge, 1864. Full brown calf. Illustrated, gauffered edges. 9" tall. Near fine. $380.00

DE BOURRIENNE, M. *Memoirs of Napoleon Bonaparte.* London: Richard Bentley, 1836. Eight volumes (only three shown). Full red morocco by G.P. Putnam. French crushed levant with highly gilt covers. Top edges gilt. Four volumes bound into eight. Extra illustrated. Red and green morocco doublures, green silk moiré endpapers. Covers inlaid with blue morocco tulips and gold crowns in all corners. Reinforced covers. 8" tall. Very good. $1,300.00

DE FOE, Daniel. *Mere Nature Delineated: Or, A Body Without a Soul.* London: T. Warner, 1726. Three-quarter calf. Raised bands, marbled endpapers. First edition. Near fine. $875.00

DE FOE, Daniel. *The Life and Adventures of Robinson Crusoe.* London, 1852. Octavo. Late nineteenth century full tan polished calf, elaborately gilt-decorated spine. Illustrated by H.K. Browne. Near fine. $375.00

DE FOE, Daniel. *The Life and Adventures of Robinson Crusoe.* London: J.C. Nimmo & Bain, 1882. Two volumes. Three-quarter green morocco gilt. Ribbed spines. Contains illustrative notes and etchings. Near fine. $275.00

DE FOE, Daniel. *The Life and Times of Robinson Crusoe.* London: Cadell and Davies, 1820. Two volumes. Full polished blue calf, gilt. Engravings by Thomas Stothard. Near fine. $800.00

DE FOE, Daniel. *The Novels and Miscellaneous Works of Daniel De Foe.* London: George Bell and Sons, 1887. Seven volumes. Three-quarter green morocco with marbled edges. 7" tall. Near fine. $725.00

DE FOE, Daniel. *The Novels and Miscellaneous Works of Daniel DeFoe.* Oxford: D.A. Talboys, 1840. Twenty volumes (only four shown). Three-quarter black morocco. 6" tall. Near fine. $5,500.00

DE MAINTERON, Madame. *The Secret Correspondence.* London: George B. Whittaker, 1827. Three volumes. Three-quarter burgundy morocco. Raised bands with top edges gilt. Near fine. $375.00

DE MAUPASSANT, Guy. *Works.* St. Dunston Society, 1903. Seventeen volumes. Three quarter red morocco gilt with ribbed gilt decorated spines. Near fine. $2,250.00

DE NOLHAC, Pierre. *Marie Antoinette, The Dauphine.* London and Paris: Goupil and Co., 1896. Two volumes. Three-quarter crushed navy levant morocco. Top edges gilt. #17 of 800 copies. Illustrated with hand-colored frontispieces. 13" tall. Near fine. $2,100.00

DE MUSSET, Alfred. *The Confession of a Child of the Century.* Philadelphia: 1899. Contemporary three-quarter morocco gilt. Octavo. Illustrated with frontispiece and numerous etchings. Limited edition, one of only 1,000 copies. Near fine. $185.00

DE PARIS, Comte. *History of the Civil War In America.* Philadelphia: Proctor and Co., 1875. Four volumes. Three-quarter dark brown calf by Launder and MacDonald. Top edges gilt. Illustrated with pullout maps. First edition. Near fine. $1,250.00

DE PEZAY, Marquis. *Delia Bathing.* London: Vizetelly Teo, n.d., Full maroon morocco by Bayntun. Marbled edges. Near fine. $325.00

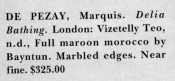

DE KOCK, Charles Paul. *The Masterpieces of Charles Paul De Rock.* Philadelphia: George Barrie & Son, 1903. Twenty volumes (only three shown). Full blue morocco. Top edges gilt. Illustrated with hand-colored frontispieces. Printed on Japanese vellum, inlaid multicolored leather doublures and silk moiré endpapers. One of only 1,000 copies. 9" tall. Fine. $2,100.00

DE QUINCEY, Thomas. *The Works.* Edinburgh: circa 1880. Sixteen octavo volumes. Contemporary full burgundy morocco gilt by Birdsall & Son. Illustrated with numerous frontispiece portraits. Near fine. $1,650.00

DE TOCQUEVILLE, Alexis. *Democracy in America.* Cambridge: Sever and Francis, 1863. Two volumes. Three-quarter black calf. Marbled edges. Fine. $750.00

DELLENBAUGH, Frederick S. *The North-Americans of Yesterday.* New York and London: G.P. Putnam, 1900. Three-quarter blue morocco. Top edges gilt. 350 illustrations. Fine. $450.00

DE TROBRIAND, Regis. *Four Years With the Army of the Potomac.* Boston: Ticknor and Co., 1889. Three-quarter dark brown calf by Launder and MacDonald. Top edges gilt. Illustrated with maps. First edition. $425.00

DENNISTOUN, James Dennistoun of. *Memoirs of the Duke of Unbino.* New York: John Lane the Bodley Head, 1909. Three volumes. Three-quarter green morocco. Gilt decorated spine. Illustrated. Near fine. $260.00

DENT, C.T. *Mountaineering.* London: Longmans, Green & Co., 1892. Full blue morocco gilt. 4to. Illustrated. Limited edition, one of only 250 copies. Near fine. $350.00

DE SPINOZA, Benedict. *Ethic.* Oxford: University Press, 1910. Full tan calf by Bayntun. Gilt decorated spine with green and red labels. Near fine. $160.00

DIBDIN, Thomas Frognall. *The Bibliomania or Book Madness, History, Symptoms and Cure of This Fatal Disease.* Boston: The Bibliophile Society, 1903. Four volumes. Full green morocco by Harcourt. Gilt decorated spines and covers, brown morocco doublures. Illustrated. Limited edition, one of only 483 copies. Near fine. $750.00

DE TOCQUEVILLE, Alexis. *Democracy in America.* London: Longman, Green, 1862. Two volumes. Full blue morocco gilt. Ribbed gilt decorated spines by Bayntun. Translated by Henry Reeve. Near fine. $750.00

DICKENS, Charles. *A Christmas Carol. In Prose. Being A Ghost Story of Christmas.* London: Chapman and Hall, 1843. Three-quarter calf. Gilt stamped spine and front board. all edges gilt. 12 mo. First edition. Illustrated by John Leech's hand colored illustrations. Near fine. $5,500.00

DECLE, Lionel. *Three Years in Savage Africa.* London: Methuen & Co., 1900. Full green morocco. Raised bands, gilt decorated panels. Top edges gilt. Numerous illustrations and maps. Near fine. $425.00

DICKENS, Charles. *David Copperfield.* London: Bradbury & Evans, 1850. Full tan polished calf by Morrell. Raised boards, red and green labels. Illustrated by H.K. Browne. Near fine. $1,100.00

DELL, E.M. *The Way of An Eagle.* New York: A.L. Burt Co., 1911. Full red morocco. Gilt vines and inlaid flowers on covers and spine. Top edges gilt. 7½" tall. Near fine. $575.00

DICKENS, Charles. *Bleak House.* London: Bradbury and Evans, 1853. Full butterscotch calf by Riviere. Highly gilt spine with all edges gilt. Illustrated by H.K. Brown with vignette title page. Includes the 10 dark plates. First edition. 8½" tall. Near fine. $800.00

DICKENS, Charles. *Dombey and Son*. London: Bradbury & Evans, 1848. Three-quarter maroon morocco. Marbled edges. Illustrated by H.K. Browne. First edition in book form. 8½" tall. Very good. $625.00

DICKENS, Charles. *Master Humphrey's Clock*. London: Chapman and Hall, 1840. Three volumes. Full brown calf. First edition in book form. Illustrations by George Cattermole and Hablot Brown. 10" tall. Near fine. $850.00

DICKENS, Charles. *Oliver Twist*. London: Richard Bentley, 1838. Three volumes. Three-quarter brown calf. Marbled edges. Illustrated. First edition. 7½" tall. Very good. $1,100.00

DICKENS, Charles. *Our Mutual Friend*. London: Chapman and Hall, 1865. Two volumes. Three-quarter red morocco. Marbled edges. Illustrated by Marcus Stone. First book edition. 8½" tall. Near fine. $675.00

DICKENS, Charles. *Dombey and Son*. London: 1848. Three-quarter green morocco gilt. Octavo. First edition. Illustrated by Hablot Knight Browne. Near fine. $850.00

DICKENS, Charles. *The Chimes*. New York and London: Putnam's Sons, 1911. Three-quarter blue morocco with top edges gilt. First design edition. Color and black and white plates, illustrated by Coburn. 7½" tall. Near fine. $210.00

DICKENS, Charles. *Dombey and Son*. London: Bradbury & Evans, 1848. One quarter brown morocco, ribbed gilt decorated spine. First edition. Illustrated with numerous plates by H.K. Browne. Near fine. $580.00

DICKENS, Charles. *Master Humphrey's Clock*. London: Chapman and Hall, 1840 – 41. Three large octavo volumes. Three-quarter calf. First edition. Illustrated by H.K. "Phiz" Browne and George Cattermole. Near fine. $850.00

DICKENS, Charles. *Memoirs of Joseph Grimaldi*. London: 1838. Two volumes. Octavo. Mid-twentieth century Cosway style binding. Full red morocco gilt with portrait of Dickens set into the front cover. First edition, first issue. Illustrated by George Cruikshank. Near fine. $4,600.00

DICKENS, Charles. *Oliver Twist*. London: Richard Bentley, 1838. Three octavo volumes. Three-quarter calf, blind stamped. Custom cloth and calf-backed slipcase. First edition. Near fine. $1,300.00

DICKENS, Charles. *Oliver Twist; on the Parish Boy's Progress*. London: Chapman & Hall, 1841. Three volumes. Three-quarter tan calf gilt. Raised bands, ornate spines with green and red labels. Near fine. $850.00

DICKENS, Charles. *Our Mutual Friend*. London: 1865. Two volumes. Thick octavo. Early twentieth century full polished green calf gilt. First edition. Illustrated by Marcus Stone and the Dalziel Brothers. Near fine. $675.00

DICKENS, Charles. *Our Mutual Friend*. London: Chapman and Hall, 1865. Two volumes. Full red morocco gilt. Ribbed gilt decorated spines, gilt dentelles. First edition. Illustrated by Marcus Stone. Near fine. $725.00

DICKENS, Charles. *The Life and Adventures of Nicholas Nickleby*. London: Chapman and Hall, 1839. Three-quarter rust morocco. Illustrations by "Phiz" Brown. First edition, first state, in book form with "visitor" for sister on page 123. 8½" tall. Near fine. $650.00

DICKENS, Charles. *Our Mutual Friend*. London: Chapman and Hall, 1865. Two volumes bound in one. Contemporary three-quarter green morocco gilt. Octavo. Raised bands, gilt decorated spine with marbled boards and endpapers. First edition. Two frontispieces by Marcus Stone. Near fine. $725.00

DICKENS, Charles. *Our Mutual Friend*. London: Chapman and Hall, 1865. Two volumes bound in one. Full tan calf gilt with ribbed gilt decorated spine. First edition. Illustrations by Marcus Stone. Near fine. $725.00

DICKENS, Charles. *Pickwick Papers*. London: Chapman & Hall, 1837. First edition. Full tan polished calf by Bayntun. Forty-three illustrations by R. Seymour and Phiz. Near fine. $925.00

DICKENS, Charles. *The Christmas Books*. London: Chapman and Hall, 1846. Five volumes. Full red morocco gilt by Sangorski & Sutcliffe. Raised bands and gilt panels. Illustrated. Near fine. $2,950.00

DICKENS, Charles. *The Mystery of Edwin Drood*. London: Chapman and Hall, 1870. Contemporary three-quarter red calf with raised bands, marbled boards, brown morocco label. First edition. Near fine. $550.00

DICKENS, Charles. *The Personal History of David Copperfield*. London: 1850. Octavo. Contemporary three-quarter green morocco. First edition. Near fine. $1,600.00

DICKENS, Charles. *The Personal History of David Copperfield*. London: 1850. Octavo. Modern full blue crushed morocco gilt. First edition. Illustrated by Phiz. Near fine. $1,100.00

DICKENS, Charles. *The Personal History of David Copperfield*. London: Bradbury and Evans, 1850. Half tan calf gilt with gilt decorated spines by Bayntun. First edition. Illustrated by H.K. Browne. Near fine. $1,100.00

DICKENS, Charles. *The Personal History of David Copperfield*. London: Bradbury & Evans, 1850. Nineteenth century full red morocco gilt. Octavo. Gilt decorated spine. First edition. Numerous steel-engraved plates by Halbot Knight Browne. Near fine. $1,100.00

DICKENS, Charles. *The Personal History of David Copperfield*. London: Bradbury & Evans, 1850. Three-quarter black polished calf gilt. Octavo. First edition. Forty steel-engraved plates by Hablot Knight Browne. Near fine. $1,100.00

DICKENS, Charles. *The Works of Charles Dickens*. London: 1881 – 82. Thirty volumes. Large thick quarto. Three-quarter burgundy morocco gilt. "Edition de Luxe," one of only 1,000 copies. Illustrated with almost 800 mounted engravings on India paper. Near fine. $5,600.00

DICKENS, Charles. *The Works of Charles Dickens*. New York: Bigelow, Brown and Co., circa 1925. Forty octavo volumes bound in 20. Three-quarter blue morocco, raised bands, gilt-decorated spines. "National Library Edition" illustrated by "Phiz" Browne and Cruikshank. Near fine. $2,500.00

DICKENS, Charles. *The Mystery of Edwin Drood*. London: Chapman and Hall, 1870. Three-quarter brown calf. Marbled edges. Twelve illustrations by S.L. Fildes. First edition in book form. 8¾" tall. Near fine. $550.00

DICKENS, Charles. *The Personal History of David Copperfield*. London: Bradbury and Evans, 1850. Three-quarter maroon morocco by Hawes. Marbled edges. Illustrated by H.K. Browne with fireside plate, Boz on title page. First edition. 8½" tall. Very good. $1,300.00

DICKENS, Charles. *The Pickwick Papers*. London: Chapman and Hall, 1837. Full tan calf by Henry Young. Top edges gilt. Forty-three illustrations by R. Seymour and Phiz Browne. Front hinge reinforced. First state of text, second issue of first four plates. Contains the two suppressed buss plates. First edition bound from parts. 8¾" tall. Very good. $675.00

DICKENS, Charles. *The Works*. London: Chapman & Hall Ltd., circa 1900. Twenty-five volumes. Three-quarter tan calf gilt. Illustrated. Near fine. $2,800.00

DICKENS, Charles. *The Works*. London: Chapman & Hall, 1897. Thirty-six volumes. Three-quarter brown morocco gilt. Raised bands, gilt tooled panels. Introduction by Andrew Lang. Illustrated. Near fine. $5,200.00

DICKENS, Charles. *Works*. Boston: 1871 – 75. Twenty-nine volumes. Octavo. Three-quarter brown morocco gilt. Library edition of Dickens's works including all major and minor works. Near fine. $4,100.00

DICKENS, Charles. *Works*. Boston: Dana Estes & Co., circa 1890. Thirty volumes. Three-quarter blue morocco by MacDonald. Ribbed floral gilt decorated spines. Illustrated cabinet edition. Near fine. $4,000.00

DICKENS, Charles. *Works*. Boston: Dana Estes Co., circa 1890. Thirty volumes. Three-quarter green morocco, ribbed gilt floral decorated spines. Top edge gilt. Illustrated cabinet edition. Near fine. $4,000.00

DICKENS, Charles. *Works*. London: 1867. Fifteen volumes. Small octavo. Three-quarter straight grain red calf gilt. Engraved frontispieces. Near fine. $1,900.00

DICKENS, Charles. *Works*. London and Philadelphia: 1873 – 1876. Thirty octavo volumes. Contemporary three-quarter olive morocco gilt. Illustrated by Cruikshank, Phiz, Leech, and other artists. Near fine. $4,300.00

DICKENS, Charles. *Works of Charles Dickens*. Boston: Chapman & Hall, 1868. Thirty volumes (only seven shown). Three-quarter butterscotch calf. Top edges gilt. Illustrated. 8" tall. Near fine. $4,300.00

DICKENS, Charles. *Works*. London: Chapman & Hall, circa 1885. Thirty volumes. Three-quarter green morocco. Gilt panels, raised bands and marbled edges. "Illustrated Library Edition." Near fine. $4,000.00

DICKENS, Charles. *Works*. London: Chapman & Hall, circa 1890. Twenty-two volumes. Three-quarter calf gilt, ribbed gilt decorated spines. Illustrated. Near fine. $2,800.00

DICKENS, Charles. *Works*. London: Chapman and Hall, 1906 – 1908. Forty octavo volumes. Contemporary three-quarter red morocco gilt, raised bands, decorated spines. "National Edition," one of only 750 copies. Includes Forster's *Life of Charles Dickens*. Near fine. $4,800.00

DICKENS, Charles. *Works*. London: Chapman and Hall, circa 1875. Thirty octavo volumes. Three-quarter tan calf gilt. "Illustrated Library" edition with hundreds of illustrations by Cruikshank, Phiz Browne, Leech, and others. Near fine. $4,200.00

DICKENS, Charles. *Works*. London: Chapman and Hall, Ltd., 1906. Forty volumes. Full turquoise morocco gilt. Raised bands, ornate spines and covers. Illustrated by George Cruikshank and H.K. Browne. Near fine. $5,000.00

DICKENS, Charles. *Works*. London: Edinburgh Press, circa 1900. Nineteen octavo volumes. Three-quarter green morocco gilt. Raised bands, gilt decorated spine with rose emblems. "Memorial Edition," one of only 480 copies. Numerous tissue-guarded plates and hand-colored frontispieces. Near fine. $2,600.00

DICKENS, Charles. *Works*. New York and Boston: Houghton Mifflin & Co., 1894. "Large Paper Edition." Thirty-two volumes. Three-quarter red morocco gilt. Illustrated by Browne. Near fine. $4,300.00

DICKINSON, Emily. *Bolts of Melody*. New York and London: Harper and Brothers, 1945. Three-quarter brown calf. Top edges gilt. First edition. 8½" tall. Near fine. $425.00

DISRAELI, Benjamin, Earl of Beaconsfield. *The Works of Benjamin Disraeli*. London and New York: M. Walter Dunne, 1904. Twenty volumes (only three shown). Full maroon morocco. Floral gilt spine and gilt and painted covers. #9 of 100, hand gilt and painted chapter titles. Illustrated with various hand-colored illustrations. Purple velvet doublures and purple silk moiré endpapers. Top edges gilt. 9½" tall. Near fine. $5,500.00

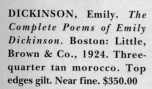

DICKINSON, Emily. *The Complete Poems of Emily Dickinson*. Boston: Little, Brown & Co., 1924. Three-quarter tan morocco. Top edges gilt. Near fine. $350.00

DISRAELI, Benjamin. *Works*. New York and London: 1904. Twenty octavo volumes. Twentieth century full green crushed morocco. Gilt decorated spines and boards. "Crown Edition," one of only 1,000 sets. Illustrated with numerous plates, some hand colored. Near fine. $4,200.00

DICKENS, Charles. *Works*. New York: Charles Scribner's Sons, 1898 – 1900. Thirty-six octavo volumes. Three-quarter dark green morocco. Raised bands, floral decorated gilt spines, marbled boards and endpapers. "Gadshill Edition," illustrated by Cruikshank, Browne, and others. Also contains John Forster's *Life of Dickens*. Near fine. $4,400.00

DISRAELI, Benjamin. *Works*. New York: M. Walter Dunne, 1904. Twenty volumes. Three-quarter green morocco gilt. "Earls Edition," one of only 1,200 sets. Near fine. $2,800.00

DICKENS, Charles. *Works*. Philadelphia: J.B. Lippincott. London: Chapman & Hall, circa 1910. Thirty octavo volumes. Contemporary three-quarter brown morocco gilt. Raised bands, marbled endpapers, and gilt decorated spines. Illustrated by George Cruikshank, H.K. Browne, and others. Near fine. $3,400.00

DIXON, Charles. *Annals of Bird Life*. London: Chapman and Hall, 1890. Full tan calf by Bickers. Prize binding with marbled edges. Illustrated. 7" tall. Near fine. $245.00

DICKINSON, Emily. *A Collection of First Editions: Poems*. With: *Poems. Second Series*. With: *Poems. Third Series*. Boston: Roberts Brothers, 1890 – 1896. Three volumes all together. Modern blue morocco gilt. Top edges gilt. 12mo. Near fine. $6,000.00

DILLMANN, Dr. A. *Genesis Critically and Exegetically Expounded*. Edinburgh: T. & T. Clark, 1897. Two volumes. Full tan calf. Prize binding with marbled edges. 8¾" tall. Fine. $675.00

DIXON, William Hepworth. *Robert Blake, Admiral and General at Sea*. London: Bickers & Sons, 1919. Full tree calf by Bickers. Prize binding with marbled edges. Illustrated with photogravures. 7½" tall. Near fine. $240.00

DIXON, William Hepworth. *The Holy Land*. London: Chapman and Hall, 1865. Two volumes. Full tan calf with marbled edges. First edition. 8½" tall. Very good. $315.00

DODGE, Richard Irving. *The Hunting Grounds of the Great West*. London: Chatto and Windus, 1878. Full navy morocco prize binding. Marbled edges. Illustrated second edition. 8" tall. Near fine. $425.00

DIXON, George. *A Voyage Round the World; But More Particularly to the North-West Coast of America....* London: Geo. Goulding, 1789. Contemporary full calf. Large quarto. Illustrated. First edition, first issue. Near fine. $3,200.00

DIXON, H. William. *New America*. London: Hurst and Blackett, 1867. Two volumes. Three-quarter tan calf. Raised bands, marbled boards. Illustrated. Near fine. $275.00

DODDRIDGE, Joseph. *Notes, On the Settlement and Indians Wars, Of The Western Parts Of Virginia & Pennsylvania, From the Year 1763 Until The Year 1783 Inclusive. Together With A View, Of The State Of Society And Manners Of The First Settlers Of The Western Country*. Wellsburgh, Virginia: 1824. Original sheepskin. Near fine. $825.00

DODGSON, Charles Lutwidge. *The Collected Verse of Lewis Carroll*. London: MacMillan & Co., 1932. Three-quarter teal morocco by Sangorski & Sutcliffe. Top edges gilt. Illustrated by John Tenniel. 8" tall. Near fine. $275.00

DORAN, Dr. *Habits and Men*. London: Richard Bentley, 1854. Full butterscotch calf. Top edges gilt. 8" tall. Near fine. $165.00

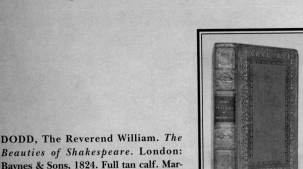

DODD, The Reverend William. *The Beauties of Shakespeare*. London: Baynes & Sons, 1824. Full tan calf. Marbled edges. Highly gilt cover. 5" tall. Near fine. $235.00

DORAN, Dr. *The Book of the Princes of Wales*. London: Richard Bentley, 1860. Full butterscotch calf. Top edges gilt. 8" tall. Near fine. $210.00

DODGE, Col. Richard Irving. *Our Wild Indians*. Hartford: A.D. Worthington and Co., 1882. Three-quarter brown calf. Illustrated with several chromolithographic plates. 9" tall. Near fine. $1,100.00

DODSLEY, Robert. *A Collection of Poems*. London: 1782. Six volumes. Contemporary brown calf. Flat spines, gilt compartments with scrolled corner pieces. Green and red morocco labels. Engraved vignette title page. Two engraved plates. Near fine. $850.00

DOMENECH, Abbe Emmanuel. *Seven Years' Residence in the Great Deserts of North America.* London: 1860. Two octavo volumes. Three-quarter calf. Illustrated with numerous plates by Joliet and a hand-colored folding map of North America. Near fine. $750.00

DONNE, John. *Poems.* With Elegies on the Author's Death. London: 1669. Contemporary full brown calf. Octavo. Raised bands and calf spine label. Fifth edition. Near fine. $3,800.00

DOSTOYEVSKY, Feodor. *Crime and Punishment.* New York: 1886. Full blue morocco by Bayntun. Octavo. First edition in English. Near fine. $2,200.00

DOW, Lorenzo. *The Life and Travels of Lorenzo Dow.* Hartford: 1804. Contemporary full brown calf. 12mo. First edition. Near fine. $275.00

DOUCE, Francis. *Illustration of Shakespeare and of Ancient Manners with Dissertations.* London: Longman, Hurst, Rees and Orme, 1807. Two volumes. Full tree calf with marbled edges. First edition. Twentieth century binding. 9½" tall. Near fine. $750.00

DOWLING, William. *Poets and Statesmen, Their Homes and Memorials.* London: E.P. Williams, 1857. Full green morocco. Highly gilt spine and covers, gilt image on front cover, marbled edges. Illustrated. 9" tall. Near fine. $325.00

DOYLE, Arthur Conan. *My Friend The Murderer.* New York: Hurst and Co., circa 1900. Three-quarter brown calf. Top edges gilt. Front hinge broken and pages are brittle. 7" tall. Good. $80.00

DOYLE, Arthur Conan. *The Green Flag.* New York: McClure, Phillips & Co., 1900. Three-quarter brown calf. Top edges gilt. 7" tall. Very good. $235.00

DOYLE, Arthur Conan. *The Hound of the Baskervilles.* London: George Newnes, Ltd., 1902. Three-quarter red morocco. Octavo. First edition, first issue. Illustrated by Sidney Paget. Near fine. $1,900.00

DOYLE, Arthur Conan. *The Hound of the Baskervilles.* London: George Newnes. 1902. Full blue morocco by Bayntun, gilt. Near fine. $850.00

DOYLE, Arthur Conan. *Works.* Garden City, New York: 1930. Twenty-four octavo volumes. Three-quarter blue morocco gilt. "Crowborough Edition," one of only 760 sets signed by the author. Near fine. $9,600.00

DOYLE, Arthur Conan. *The Works of Arthur Conan Doyle.* New York: D. Appleton & Co., 1902. Thirteen volumes. Three-quarter tan calf. Top edges gilt. Hand-colored illustrations. The author's edition, limited to 250 sets. With tipped in signature of Arthur Conan Doyle. 8½" tall. Near fine. $6,250.00

D

DOYLE, Arthur Conan. *Works*. London: 1903. Twelve volumes. Author's edition, one of only 1,000 sets. Octavo. Full red crushed morocco gilt. Near fine. $6,100.00

DOYLE, Arthur Conan. *Works*. London: John Murray, 1903. Twelve octavo volumes. Three-quarter red morocco. Raised bands, gilt decorated spines. "Author's Edition," one of only 1,000 sets signed by the author. Illustrated. Near fine. $6,900.00

DRAKE, Edward Cavendish. *New Universal Collection of Authentic and Entertaining Voyages and Travels....* London: J. Cooke, 1770. Full speckled calf. Raised bands, gilt decorated spine with black morocco label. Folio. Illustrated with map and numerous full page engraved plates. Second edition. Near fine. $950.00

DRAKE, Samuel G. *History of the Early Discovery of America and Landing of the Pilgrims*. Boston: Higgins and Beadley, 1854. Full tan calf. Illustrated. 9½" tall. Near fine. $380.00

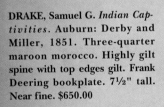

DRAKE, Samuel G. *Indian Captivities*. Auburn: Derby and Miller, 1851. Three-quarter maroon morocco. Highly gilt spine with top edges gilt. Frank Deering bookplate. 7½" tall. Near fine. $650.00

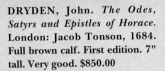

DRYDEN, John. *The Odes, Satyrs and Epistles of Horace*. London: Jacob Tonson, 1684. Full brown calf. First edition. 7" tall. Very good. $850.00

DRYDEN, John. *The Poetical Works of John Dryden*. Boston: Houghton Mifflin Co., 1908. Full tree calf. All edges gilt. Cambridge edition. 8½" tall. Near fine. $230.00

DREISER, Theodore. *An American Tragedy*. New York: 1925. Two octavo volumes. Three-quarter calf. Signed limited edition, one of only 795 copies signed by author. Near fine. $675.00

DRYDEN, John. *Fables Ancient and Modern...With Original Poems*. London: Jacob Tonson, 1700. Contemporary tree calf gilt. Raised bands, gilt tooled spine with red morocco label. First edition. Near fine. $650.00

DULAC, Edmund. *A Fairy Garland, Being Fairy Tales from the Old French*. London: Cassell & Co., New York: Charles Scribner's Sons, 1928. Half vellum and blue cloth. Quarto. First edition. One of only 1,000 copies signed by Dulac. Illustrated with full-page color plates. Near fine. $1,100.00

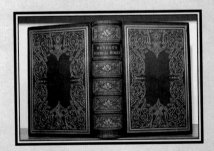

DRYDEN, John. *The Poetical Works of John Dryden*. New York: Leavitt & Allen, n.d., circa 1870. Full green morocco. Highly gilt spine and covers, all edges gilt. Illustrated by John Franklin. 9½" tall. Near fine. $385.00

DRAKE, Samuel. *The Aboriginal Races of North America*. Philadelphia: Charles DeSilver, 1860. Full black calf. Marbled edges. Hand-colored plates. Fifteenth edition. Very good. $460.00

DRYDEN, Mr. *The Works of Virgil.* London: James Swan, 1806. Three volumes. Full maroon morocco. Copper plate illustrations by Bartolozzi, new spines with original boards. 8¾" tall. Very good. $325.00

DULAC, Edmund, and Housman, Laurence. *Stories from the Arabian Nights.* London: Hodder and Stoughton, 1907. Full red morocco gilt. Gilt spine and covers, marbled endpapers. Illustrated by Dulac with numerous color plates. Limited edition. Near fine. $2,600.00

DULAC, Edmund. *Sinbad the Sailor and Other Stories from the Arabian Nights.* London: Hodder and Stoughton, 1914. Full blue morocco gilt. Raised bands, gilt decorated spine. Illustrated. Limited edition, one of only 500 copies signed by the author. Near fine. $4,100.00

DULAC, Edmund. *Stories from Hans Anderson.* London: Hodder & Stoughton, 1911. Three-quarter red morocco. Gilt decorated spines, marbled endpapers. Illustrated with 28 full page tissue-guarded color plates. Limited edition. Near fine. $1,150.00

DULAC, Edmund. *Stories from the Arabian Nights. Retold by Laurence Housman.* London: 1907. Thick quarto. Full paneled red morocco gilt. First trade edition with 50 of Dulac's illustrations. Near fine. $2,700.00

DUFRESNOY, Abbe Lenglet. *Chronological Tables of Universal History from the Creation of the World to the Year 1743.* London: Printed for A. Millar J. Newbery, 1762. Two volumes. Full tree calf with all edges gilt. 8½" tall. Fine. $625.00

DUKE, Basil. *History of Morgan's Cavalry.* Cincinnati: Miami Printing, 1867. Three-quarter brown calf by Launder and MacDonald. Top edges gilt. First edition. 9" tall. Near fine. $400.00

DUMAS, Alexandre. *Celebrated Crimes.* London: H.S. Nichols, 1895. Eight volumes. Three-quarter green morocco. Ornate spines and marbled boards. Illustrated with photogravures. Near fine. $1,100.00

DUMAS, Alexandre. *The Count of Monte Cristo.* London and New York: George Routledge and Sons, 1888. Five volumes. Full crushed brown levant morocco. Gilt decorated spines with fleur de lis onlays. Illustrated. Near fine. $2,600.00

DUMAS, Alexandre. *The Count of Monte Cristo.* London: 1846. Two volumes. Octavo. Nineteenth century calf gilt. First English edition. Illustrated by M. Valentin. Near fine. $3,600.00

DUMAS, Alexander. *The Three Musketeers.* London: George Routledge and Sons, 1894. Two volumes. Three-quarter black calf. Top edges gilt. 250 illustrations by Maurice Leloir. Engraved on wood by J. Huxot. Edition Deluxe, #91 of 750 copies made. 12" tall. Near fine. $1,250.00

DUMAS, Alexandre. *The Romances of Alexandre Dumas.* Little, Brown, and Company, 1894. Forty-five octavo volumes. Three-quarter burgundy morocco, raised bands, top edge gilt. "Navarre Edition," one of only 1,000 copies on Japanese paper. Illustrated with full-page engravings and hand-colored frontispieces. Near fine. $6,500.00

DUMAS, Alexandre. *The Works of Alexandre Dumas.* Boston: Little, Brown & Co., 1901. Thirty-six volumes (only five shown). Three-quarter red morocco. Highly gilt spine with top edges gilt. Valois edition. 7½" tall. Near fine. $5,500.00

DUMAS, Alexandre. *Works. Includes; The Three Musketeers, The Count of Monte Cristo etc.* Thirty five octavo volumes. "International Limited Edition," one of only 1,000 numbered copies. Twentieth century half red levant morocco. Decorative spines with two raised bands and marbled endpapers. Near fine. $2,600.00

DUNTON, John. *Athenian Sport: Or, Two Thousand Paradoxes Merrily Argued, To Amuse and Divert The Age.* London: B. Bragg, 1707. Contemporary Cambridge calf. Raised bands, gilt spines with ornate floral design, and red morocco label. Near fine. $375.00

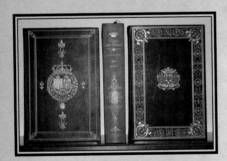

DUNNE, Walter. *Memoirs and Secret Chronicles of Courts of Europe.* London: Walter Dunn, 1901. Eleven volumes (only three shown). Full morocco with coat of arms on each cover. Hand-colored frontispieces. Near fine. $625.00

DUPPA, R. *The Life and Literary Works of Michel Angelo Buonarroti.* London: John Murray, 1806. Three-quarter brown morocco. Raised bands, marbled covers and endpapers. Folio. Illustrated with frontispiece portrait, a large folding plate of the Sistine Chapel, and 26 full-page drawings by Romanelli. First large paper edition. Near fine. $975.00

DURAND. *Anecdotes of The Court and Family of Napoleon Bonaparte.* London: Henry Colburn, 1818. Three-quarter red morocco. Gilt decorated spines. Second edition. Near fine. $225.00

DURANT, Will. *The Story of Philosophy/The Mansions of Philosophy.* New York: Simon and Schuster, 1927 – 1929. Two volumes. Three-quarter red morocco by Bayntun. Top edges gilt. Mansions book, first edition with slipcase. 9½" tall. Near fine. $600.00

DURUY, Victor. *History of Rome and The Roman People.* London: Kegan Paul, 1883. Six volumes. Three-quarter red morocco gilt. Thick quarto. Illustrated with 2,500 engravings and 100 colored maps. Near fine. $1,100.00

DUTT, Romesh C. *History of India. From the Earliest Times to the 6th Century B.C.* London: Grolier Society, 1906. Nine volumes. Three-quarter green morocco gilt with ribbed gilt spines with floral decoration. 4to. Limited edition, one of only 50 sets. Near fine. $1,850.00

DUYCKINCK, Evert A. *National History of the War for the Union, Civil, Military and Naval.* New York: Johnson, Fry and Company, 1861 – 65. Three quarto volumes. Three-quarters publisher's black morocco. Raised bands. First edition. Illustrated. Near fine. $1,100.00

DYER, Thomas Henry. *Ancient Athens: Its History, Topography, And Remains.* London: Bell and Daldy, 1873. Contemporary full calf gilt. Tall octavo. Raised bands with black and red morocco labels and marbled endpapers. Illustrated. First edition. Near fine. $375.00

DUYCKINCK, E.A. *History of the War For the Union.* New York: Johnson, Fry and Co., 1862. Three volumes. Three-quarter black calf. Marbled edges. Illustrated by Alonzo Chappel. First edition. 11" tall. Near fine. $1,250.00

DUYCKINCK, E.A. *Portrait Gallery of Eminent Men and Women of Europe and America.* New York: Johnson, Wilson & Co., 1873. Two volumes. Full black calf. All edges gilt. First edition. Steel engraved illustrations. 11" tall. Near fine. $850.00

EBERS, G. *Egypt: Descriptive, Historical and Picturesque.* Cassell, Peter, Galpin & Co., circa 1800. Two volumes. Three-quarter maroon morocco. Gilt decorated spines and marbled edges. First edition. Near fine. $750.00

EDGEWORTH, Maria. *The Novels of Maria Edgeworth.* London: J.M. Dent & Co., 1893. Twelve octavo volumes. Three-quarter brown morocco gilt by Root. Raised bands, marbled boards and endpapers. Limited edition, one of only 250 sets. Near fine. $2,400.00

EDGAR, John G. *The Heroes of England.* London: Bickers & Son, 1919. Full tree calf. Highly gilt spine and cover. Prize binding with marbled edges. Illustrated. 7½" tall. Fine. $240.00

EDGEWORTH, Maria. *Tales and Novels.* London: Balwin and Cradock, 1832. Nineteen volumes. Full tan calf. Eighteen volumes (only three shown). This set has the novel *Hellen* which was added later. 6½" tall. Near fine. $1,600.00

EDMONDS, Clement. *The Commentaries of C. Julius Caesar, Of his Wars in Gallia; And the Civil Wars betwixt him and Pompey. Translated into English....* In the Savoy, 1676 – 1677. Contemporary full brown calf. Small folio. Illustrated with numerous full-page and double-page plates. Near fine. $1,200.00

EGAN, Pierce. *Life in London.* London: 1821. Octavo. Early twentieth century full tan morocco gilt. First edition, second issue. Illustrated by Robert and George Cruikshank. Near fine. $750.00

EDMONDS, S. Emma. *Nurse and Spy in the Union Army.* Hartford: W.S. Williams & Co., 1866. Full maroon calf. Fifty illustrations by Tenniel. 8½" tall. Near fine. $195.00

EDWARD, Earl of Clarendon. *The History of the Rebellion and Civil Wars in England.* Oxford: Clarendon Press, 1826. Eight volumes. Full tan calf. Marbled edges. 9" tall. Near fine. $950.00

EDWARD, Earl of Derby. *The Iliad of Homer.* London: John Murray, 1864. Two volumes. Full tan calf. Marbled edges. 7" tall. Very good. $225.00

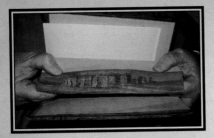

EDWARDS, J. Fore-edge Painting. London: Bodani, 1741. Full tan calf by J. Edwards. Original Edwards Etruscan binding with marbled edges. Edwards edition of the *Castle of Otranto*, with an original Edwards of Halifax fore-edge painting of Stonehenge. 9" tall. Very good. $5,500.00

EDWARDS, John N. *Shelby and His Men: Or, The War in The West*. Cincinnati: Miami Printing and Publishing Co., 1867. Three-quarter dark brown calf by Launder and MacDonald. Top edges gilt. First edition. Near fine. $450.00

EDWARDS, Jonathan. *The Life and Character of Jonathan Edwards*. Northhampton, 1804. Printed by Andrew Wright. Full brown tree calf. 7" tall. Very good. $380.00

EICKMEYER, Carl. *Over the Great Navajo Trail*. New York: 1900. Three-quarter calf. Illustrated with frontispiece portrait and numerous full-page photographs. First edition, inscribed by author. Near fine. $460.00

ELDRIDGE, Elleanor, and GREEN, Francis Harriet. *Memoirs of Elleanor Eldridge*. Providence: 1842. Contemporary half calf. 16mo. Illustrated with frontispiece portrait of the author. Early edition. Near fine. $375.00

EGAN, Pierce. *The Finish to the Adventures of Tom And Jerry and Logic, In Their Pursuits Through Life In and Out of London*. London: Reeves & Turner, 1889. Full red morocco with top edges gilt. Hand-colored illustrations by Cruikshank. Reinforced covers. 10" tall. Very good. $1,100.00

ELGOOD, George S. *Italian Gardens*. London: 1907. Folio, full crushed morocco gilt. First edition. Illustrated with drawings by the author. Near fine. $975.00

ELIOT, George. *Daniel Deronda*. Edinburgh and London: 1876. First edition. Eight parts bound in four. Full mottled calf gilt. Near fine. $2,100.00

ELIOT, George. *The Works*. London: William Blackwood & Sons, 1900. Twenty-four volumes. Three-quarter green morocco gilt. Small 8vo. Cabinet edition. Near fine. $2,600.00

ELIOT, George. *The Works*. Edinburgh and London: William Blackwood & Sons, 1900. Twenty-one volumes. Three-quarter green morocco gilt. Standard edition. Near fine. $2,500.00

ELIOT, George. *The Works*. Edinburgh and London: William Blackwood and Sons. Twenty-four octavo volumes. Three-quarter burgundy morocco gilt. "Cabinet Edition" illustrated with portraits and facsimilies. Near fine. $2,900.00

ELIOT, George. *Essays and Leaves from a Notebook*. Edinburgh and London: William Blackwood and Son, 1884. Full tree calf. All edges gilt with tree calf slip case, rebound. First edition. 7½" tall. Near fine. $575.00

ELIOT, George. *The Works of George Eliot*. Boston: Dana Estes & Co., 1907. Twenty-four volumes (only four shown). Three-quarter red morocco by Launder. Top edges gilt. #310 of 500 copies made, University Press, Holly Lodge edition. Illustrated. 8" tall. Near fine. $3,600.00

ELIOT, George. *The Writings*. Boston and New York: Houghton Mifflin Co., 1908. Twenty-five volumes. Octavo. Contemporary three-quarter red morocco gilt. Raised bands, marbled endpapers and boards. Limited edition, one of only 750 sets. Near fine. $3,200.00

ELIOT, George. *Works*. Boston and New York: 1907 – 08. Twenty-five volumes. Octavo. Three-quarter red morocco gilt. Illustrated with over 150 fine plates. Near fine. $3,200.00

ELIOT, George. *Works*. Edinburgh and London: William Blackwood and Sons, circa 1900. Twenty-four small octavo volumes. Contemporary three-quarter turquoise morocco gilt. Spines are heavily gilt decorated, marbled boards and endpapers. "Cabinet Edition." Near fine. $2,900.00

ELIZABETH, Charlotte. *Chapters on Flowers*. London: Seeleys, 1853. Full black calf. Gauffered edge, all edges gilt. Illustrated. 6" tall. Near fine. $260.00

ELLARD, Harry. *Ranch Tales of the Rockies*. Canon City, Colorado: 1899. Three-quarter red morocco. Octavo. Illustrated with frontispiece portrait and numerous full page illustrations. First edition. Near fine. $350.00

ELIZABETH, Charlotte. *Judah's Lion*. London: Seeleys, 1849. Full maroon morocco. Gauffered edge. Fourth edition. 6¾" tall. Fine. $425.00

ELLET, Mrs. *Queens of American Society*. New York: Charles Scribners, 1867. Full black calf. Highly gilt spine and covers with all edges gilt. Illustrated. 9" tall. Near fine. $425.00

ELLSWORTH, Erastus W. *Poems*. Hartford: F.A. Brown, 1855. Full navy morocco, heavily gilt cover. All edges gilt. First edition. 7" tall. Near fine. $380.00

ELLIS, Edward S. *Bill Biddon, Trapper; Or, Life in the Northwest*. New York: 1860. Twentieth century three-quarter tan calf gilt by Bayntun. Illustrated. First edition. Near fine. $500.00

EMERSON, Ralph Waldo. *The Complete Works*. Boston: Houghton, Mifflin and Co., 1892. Eleven volumes. Riverside Press. Three-quarter calf. Highly gilt spine with top edges gilt. 7" tall. Near fine. $2,750.00

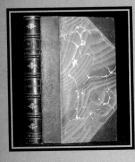

ESTUAN, B. *War Pictures From the South.* New York: D. Appleton, 1863. Three-quarter brown calf by Launder and MacDonald. Top edges gilt. First edition. 8" tall. Near fine. $300.00

EMBURY, Emma. *American Wild Flowers in their Native Haunts.* New York: D. Appleton & Co., 1845. Original full black morocco gilt. Quarto. Illustrated with twenty hand-colored plates. First edition. Near fine. $1,500.00

EMERSON, Ralph Waldo. *Complete Works.* Boston and New York: 1903 – 04. Twelve octavo volumes. Three-quarter brown morocco gilt by MacDonald. "Centenary Edition" of Emerson's works. Illustrated with frontispiece portraits. Near fine. $2,500.00

EMERSON, Ralph Waldo. *The Complete Works.* Boston and New York: 1902. Twelve small octavo volumes. Contemporary three-quarter red morocco gilt. "Centenary Edition." Near fine. $2,500.00

EMERSON, Ralph Waldo. *The Complete Works.* Cambridge: 1903 – 04. Twelve volumes. Octavo. Three-quarter green morocco gilt. Near fine. $2,500.00

EMERSON, Ralph Waldo. *The Works.* Boston and New York: Houghton, Mifflin & Co., 1903. Twelve volumes. Three-quarter wine morocco gilt. Illustrated. Concord edition. Near fine. $2,250.00

EVELYN, John. *Diary and Correspondence of John Evelyn.* London: Henry Colburn, 1854. Four volumes. Three-quarter navy morocco by Sangorski & Sutcliffe. Top edges gilt. Fine. Sold by Gardenside Book Shop. $825.00

EMERSON, Ralph Waldo. *Works of Ralph Waldo Emerson.* London: MacMillan and Co., 1888 – 1896. Six small octavo volumes. Contemporary three-quarter blue morocco gilt by Sotheran. Raised bands with marbled boards and endpapers. Near fine. $950.00

EMERSON, Ralph Waldo. *Works.* Boston and New York: 1929. Six volumes. Octavo. Modern three-quarter brown morocco gilt. Near fine. $950.00

EVANS, C.S. *The Sleeping Beauty.* London: William Heinemann, 1920. Full red morocco gilt by Bayntun. Illustrated by Arthur Rackham. First English edition. Near fine. $1,300.00

EVANS, Charles Seddon. *Cinderella.* London: William Heinemann, and Philadelphia: J.B. Lippincott Co., 1919. Original vellum-backed white Japan vellum boards pictorially stamped in gilt. Illustrated by Arthur Rackham. Limited edition. Near fine. $1,850.00

EVERETT, Edward. *The Life of George Washington.* New York: 1860. Two volumes, 12mo. Early twentieth century full red straight grain morocco gilt. First edition, illustrated with 76 portraits and 31 scenes. Near fine. $1,100.00

EVANS, Charles H. *Kings Without Crowns or Lives of American Presidents.* Edinburgh: W.P. Nimmo, 1887. Three-quarter red morocco with marbled edges. 7½" tall. Very good. $140.00

EVERETT, Edward. *The Life of George Washington.* New York: Sheldon and Co., 1860. Full green morocco. Highly gilt spine and covers with all edges gilt. Illustrated. First edition. 8½" tall. Near fine. $525.00

FALCONER and BLAIR. *Poetical Works of Thomas Falconer and Blair.* London: Thomas Nelson and Sons, 1871. Black calf spine with Mauchline fern binding. All edges gilt. Illustrated. 6½" tall. Near fine. $450.00

FALKLAND, The Viscountess. *Chow-Chow; Being selections From a Journal Kept in India, Egypt, and Syria.* London: Hurst and Blackett, 1857. Two volumes. Three-quarter tan calf. Gilt decorated spines and marbled edges. Illustrated. Near fine. $375.00

FARRAR, Frederic W. *The Life of Christ.* London, Paris and New York: Cassell, Petter Galpin & Co., circa 1890. Quarto. Full burgundy morocco gilt. Raised bands, ornate tooling on covers and spine. Near fine. $375.00

FERGUSON, Adam. *The History of the Progress and Termination of the Roman Republic.* Edinburgh: 1799. Five octavo volumes. Contemporary full marbled calf. Second edition. Near fine. $890.00

FERGUSSON, James. *A History of Architecture in All Countries, From the Earliest Time to the Present Day.* London: John Murray, 1874 – 76. Four thick octavo volumes. Three-quarter green morocco. Gilt decorated spines. Illustrated with over 1,700 in-text and full-page illustrations. Second edition. Near fine. $800.00

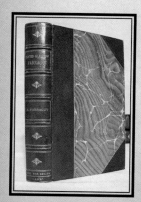

FARRAGUT, L. *The Life of David Glascow Farragut, First Admiral of the United States Navy.* New York: D. Appleton & Co., 1882. Three-quarter dark brown calf by Launder and MacDonald. Top edges gilt. Illustrated. Near fine. $375.00

FARRAR, Frederick W. *The Life of Christ.* London: Cassell and Co., 1907. Full tan calf. Prize binding with red edges. Illustrated with sixteen illustrations. 8" tall. Near fine. $210.00

FERRERO, G. *The Greatness and Decline of Rome.* New York: G.P. Putnam's & Sons, circa 1900. Five volumes. Three-quarter brown morocco. Raised bands, top edges gilt. Near fine. $475.00

FIELDING, Henry. *The History of Tom Jones, A Foundling.* London: 1749. Six volumes, full brown polished calf, custom clamshell box. First edition, first issue, one of a first printing of only 2,000 copies. Fine. $11,500.00

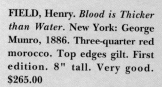

FIELD, Henry. *Blood is Thicker than Water.* New York: George Munro, 1886. Three-quarter red morocco. Top edges gilt. First edition. 8" tall. Very good. $265.00

FIELDING, Henry. *A Journey from This World to the Next.* London: J. Hales, 1798. Full tan tree calf. Illustrated with copper plates. Cooke's edition. 5¾" tall. Near fine. $425.00

FINLAY, George. *A History of Greece from its Conquest by the Romans to the Present Time.* Oxford: Clarendon Press, 1877. Seven volumes. Three-quarter wine morocco gilt. Near fine. $1,050.00

FIELDING, Henry. *The Works of Henry Fielding.* London: W. Strahan, 1771. Eight volumes. Full tan calf. 1771 edition with Alexander Hamilton bookplates. 9" tall. Very good. Value unknown.

FINDEN. *Gallery of the Graces.* London: Charles Tilt, 1834. Full red morocco. All edges gilt. Illustrated with 36 steel engravings. Book plate of Thomas Philip Earl de Grey. 9½" tall. Near fine. $300.00

FIQUIER, Louis. *The Human Race.* New York: D. Appleton, 1872. Three-quarter tan calf by Hogg. Marbled edges. Illustrated with color frontis. 8" tall. Near fine. $240.00

FISHER, Alexander. *Journal of A Voyage of Discovery, To The Arctic Regions...In His Majesty's Ship Alexander, Wm. Edw. Parry, Esq. Lieut. And Commander.* London: Richard Phillips, 1819. Contemporary half calf over marbled boards. Raised bands, gilt ruled with brown morocco label. Illustrated with engraved plates and folding maps. First edition. Near fine. $425.00

FISKE, John. *The Critical Period of American History, 1783 – 1789. The Beginnings of New England. The American Revolution (2 vol.). The Discovery of America (2 vol.). Old Virginia and Her Neighbors (2 vol.). Dutch and Quaker Colonies (2 vol.). New France and England.* Boston and New York: Houghton, Mifflin and Company, 1888 – 1902. Eleven octavo volumes. Three-quarter blue morocco gilt. Raised bands with marbled boards and endpapers. First edition. Illustrated with maps and portraits. Near fine. $1,600.00

FISHER, P. *The Anglers Souvenir.* London: Charles Tilt, 1835. Three-quarter green crushed levant morocco. Top edges gilt. Illustrated by Beckwith and Topham. Illustrations in the form of borders on every page. First edition. 7" tall. Near fine. $365.00

FISHER, Sydney Geo. *Men, Women & Manners in Colonial Times.* Philadelphia and London: J.B. Lippincott, 1878. Two volumes. Three-quarter gold morocco. Highly gilt spine with top edges gilt. First edition. 7" tall. Fine. $525.00

FISKE, John. *The Discovery of America. With Some Account of Ancient America and the Spanish Conquest.* Cambridge: Riverside Press, 1892. Two volumes bound in four. Thick royal octavo. Contemporary blue levant morocco gilt. Raised bands and marbled endpapers. First edition, one of only 250 large-paper copies produced. Illustrated with full page engraved color plates and folding maps. Near fine. $2,100.00

FISKE, Arnold. *The Works of John Fiske*. Boston and New York: Houghton, Mifflin & Co., 1892. Twelve volumes. Three-quarter red morocco. Top edges gilt. Pull-out maps. 8" tall. Near fine. $2,100.00

FISKE, John. *The Works*. Cambridge: 1888 – 1904. Thirteen volumes. Large octavo, modern three-quarter red morocco gilt. Limited edition, one of only 250 sets. Illustrated with portraits and maps. Near fine. $2,400.00

FISKE, John. *The Works*. Cambridge: Printed at the Riverside Press, 1892 – 1904. Thirteen octavo volumes. Modern three-quarter blue morocco gilt by Sangorski and Sutcliffe. Raised bands. Large paper edition, one of only 250 sets. Near fine. $2,400.00

FISKE, John. *The Works*. Cambridge: Riverside Press, 1902. Twenty-four volumes. With: *The Life and Letters of John Fiske*. Boston and New York: Houghton Mifflin Co., 1917. Twenty six volumes in all. Contemporary three-quarter wine morocco gilt. Marbled boards and endpapers. Limited edition, one of only 1,000 copies. Illustrated with full-page maps and plates, some in color. Near fine. $3,100.00

FISKE, John. *The Works*. With: *The Life and Letters*. Cambridge: 1902. Twenty-six volumes. Three-quarter morocco gilt. Limited edition, one of only 1,000 copies. Illustrated. Near fine. $3,200.00

FISKE, John. *Works*. Boston: Houghton Mifflin, 1920. Twenty-four volumes. Three-quarter maroon morocco gilt. Decorated spines. Deluxe edition. Near fine. $1,600.00

FISKE, John. *The Mississippi Valley in the War*. Boston: Houghton, Mifflin and Co., 1900. Three-quarter red morocco. Top edges gilt. Illustrated with maps, the Riverside Press. 8" tall. Near fine. $175.00

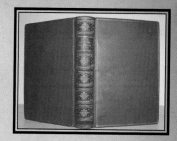

FITCHETT, W.H. *Deeds That Won the Empire*. London: Smith, Elder & Co., 1907. Full red morocco. Prize binding with marbled edges. Illustrated. 7" tall. Near fine. $150.00

FITZGERALD, Edward. *Rubaiyat of Omar Khayyam*. London: MacMillian and Co., 1898. Two volumes. Three-quarter green morocco gilt. Near fine. $475.00

FITZGERALD, Edward. *Rubaiyat of Omar Khayyam*. The First and Fourth Renderings in English. London: George G. Harrap & Co., 1930. Quarto. Contemporary full blue crushed morocco gilt. Illustrations by Willy Pogany. Limited edition signed by the artist, one of only 750 copies. Near fine. $375.00

FITZGERALD, Edward. *The Rubaiyat of Omar Khayyam*. London: George G. Harrap & Co., Ltd., circa 1900. Full blue calf gilt by Riviere. Gilt decorated spine and covers. Illustrated by Willy Pogany. Near fine. $575.00

FITZGERALD, Edward. *Works*. London: MacMilliam & Co., 1902. Seven volumes. Full red morocco. Raised bands, ornate floral gilt design on spines and covers. Green leather and silk doublures. Near fine. $2,200.00

FITZGERALD, F. Scott. *The Great Gatsby*. New York: 1925. Octavo, Full blue morocco. First edition. Near fine. $2,700.00

FITZGERALD, Edward. *The Rubaiyat of Omar Khayyam*. London and Glasgow: Collins Clear-Type Press, n.d., circa 1920. Full brown morocco. Gold gilt snake and chalice embossed in front cover. All edges gilt. Illustrated with color plates by Charles Robinson. Translated by Edward Fitzgerald. 11" tall. Fine. $1,350.00

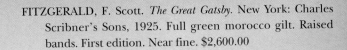

FITZGERALD, F. Scott. *The Great Gatsby*. New York: Charles Scribner's Sons, 1925. Full green morocco gilt. Raised bands. First edition. Near fine. $2,600.00

FITZGERALD, Scott. *The Great Gatsby*. New York: Charles Scribner's Sons, 1925. Full black morocco gilt. Raised bands. First edition. Near fine. $1,700.00

FLAUBERT, Gustave. *Madame Bovary. Moeurs de Province*. Paris: Michel Levy Freres, 1857. Two small octavo volumes in one. Full navy morocco gilt. Raised bands, blue marbled endpapers and gilt dentelles. First edition. Near fine. $6,100.00

FLAUBERT, Gustave. *Madame Bovary*. Philadelphia: George Barrie & Son, circa 1900. Two volumes. Three-quarter blue morocco gilt. Raised bands, gilt panels. Near fine. $750.00

FLAUBERT, Gustave. *The Complete Works of Gustave Flaubert. Embracing Romances, Travels, Comedies, Sketches and Correspondence*. New York and London: 1904. Ten octavo volumes. Contemporary full dark red morocco gilt. Blue and red morocco gilt doublures. Illustrated. Sainte Beuve edition. Near fine. $3,100.00

FLAUBERT, Gustave. *The Complete Works*. New York: M. Walter Dunne, 1904. Ten volumes. Saint Beuve edition, one of only 100 sets. Full brown morocco gilt. Silk and leather doublures. Near fine. $1,650.00

FLAUBERT, Gustave. *The Complete Works*. New York: Walter Dunne, 1904. Ten volumes. Three-quarter red morocco gilt with decorated spines. Near fine. $1,650.00

FITZGERALD, Edward. *The Rubaiyat of Omar Khayyam.* **London: Bernard Quaritch, 1859. Full morocco by Riviere. Inside covers and endpapers are hand-tooled leather with geometric floral patterns. Endpapers are tooled leather with inscriptions. Top edges gilt. Jeweled binding, front cover has eleven bunches of grapes with 14 amethyst in each grouping. Includes a raised, carved chalice with nine semi-precious stones encircled by inlaid snake with a ruby eye. Total of 164 stones. Rear cover has raised carved skull with ten ivory teeth. Housed in a custom full-leather, silk-lined case. 8¼" tall. Fine. $75,000.00**

FLEETWOOD, Rev. John. *The Life of Christ.* **Glasgow: William Collins Sons and Co., 1870. Full brown calf. Gold embossed medallions on covers, all edges gilt. Full chromo plates and numerous wood cuts. 11" tall. Very good. $575.00**

FLEETWOOD, Rev. John. *The Life of Our Lord and Savior Jesus Christ.* Philadelphia: Leary & Getz, 1858. Full red morocco. All edges gilt. Illustrated with hand-colored plates. Very good. $350.00

FLORA, British. *The Romance of Wild Flowers.* London: Frederick Warne & Co., 1901. Full navy morocco by Relfe Brothers. Prize binding with highly gilt spine and marbled edges. Illustrated. 7½" tall. Near fine. $290.00

FLEETWOOD, Rev. John. *The Light in the East.* New York: The National Publishing Co., 1870. Full brown calf. Highly gilt spine and embossed cover, all edges gilt. Two hundred illustrations. First edition. 9" tall. Near fine. $325.00

FORD, W.C. *George Washington.* New York: Charles Scribner, 1900. Two volumes. Full sky blue morocco. Illustrated with hand-colored frontis. Edition De Luxe, #149 of 200 printed. Includes a duplicate set of all full-page illustrations in sepia tint. Near fine. $900.00

FLINT, W. Russell. *Le Morte D'Arthur.* London: 1920 – 21. Four volumes. Quarto. Original full vellum gilt. Limited first edition illustrated by Flint, one of only 500 copies. Housed in a cloth-covered slipcase. Near fine. $1,400.00

FORESTER, Frank. *Mr. Sponge's Sporting Tour.* New York: Stringer & Townsend, 1856. Full red morocco. Raised bands, top edge gilt. Illustrations by John Leech. Near fine. $375.00

FORSTER, E.M. *A Room with A View.* London: Edward Arnold, 1908. Full red morocco by Bayntun. Ribbed gilt decorated spine and covers. First edition. Near fine. $825.00

FORSTER, Edward. *The Arabian Nights.* London: William Miller, 1802. Five octavo volumes. Contemporary full tree calf. Raised bands, gilt spines with tan and red morocco labels. Illustrated. First edition. Near fine. $1,000.00

FORSTER, John. *The Life of Charles Dickens.* London: Chapman and Hall, 1872 – 74. Three octavo volumes. Full red morocco gilt. Raised bands and marbled endpapers. First edition illustrated with full paper engravings. Near fine. $875.00

FOURNIER, August. *Napoleon I.* London: Longmans, Green and Co., 1911. Two octavo volumes. Full green morocco gilt. First English edition. Illustrated with frontispiece portraits. Housed in a custom cloth slipcase. Near fine. $475.00

FOX, John. *An Universal History of Christian Martyrdom.* London: 1807. Thick octavo. Contemporary full straight-grain black morocco gilt. Illustrated edition with 16 engravings depicting the suffering of martyrs. Near fine. $625.00

France Illustrated. London: Fisher & Co., circa 1890. Two volumes. Full navy calf gilt. Raised bands, gilt decorated spines and covers. Quarto. Illustrations by Thomas Allon. Near fine. $575.00

FRANCE, Anatole. *The Works.* New York: Gabriel Wells, 1924. Thirty volumes. Full blue morocco. Raised bands, gilt decorated spines and covers. "Autograph Edition" signed by the author. Near fine. $4,100.00

FORREST, Mary. *Women of the South*. New York: Derby & Jackson, 1861. Full brown calf. Embossed and gilt covers with all edges gilt. Illustrated. 9½" tall. Near fine. $585.00

FORSTER, John. *The Life and Adventures of Oliver Goldsmith*. London: Bradbury & Evans, 1848. Full tan calf. Illustrated first edition. 8½" tall. Near fine. $325.00

FORSTER, John. *The Life of Charles Dickens*. London: Chapman and Hall, 1872. Three volumes. Three-quarter butterscotch calf. Highly gilt spine with marbled edges. First edition. Front gutter on volume one is cracked. 8" tall. Very good. $725.00

FOSTER, John. *Essays in a Series of Letters*. New York: Robert Carter, 1852. Full rust and tan morocco. Highly gilt spine and cover with all edges gilt. 7½" tall. Near fine. $325.00

FOX, John. *A Universal History of Christian Martyrdom*. London: Sherwood, Jones and Co., 1824. Three-quarter black calf. Illustrated. 9" tall. Very good. $235.00

FRANKLIN, Benjamin. *Experiments and Observations on Electricity...with; Letters and Papers on Philosophical Subjects*. London: David Henry, 1769. Three-quarter mottled calf. Quarto. Illustrated with engraved plates. Complete first edition. Near fine. $3,400.00

FRANKLIN, Benjamin. *Political, Miscellaneous, and Philosophical Pieces*. London: 1779. Octavo. Modern full crushed brown morocco. First edition, with engraved frontispiece portrait. Near fine. $2,700.00

FRANKLIN, Benjamin. *Political, Miscellaneous, and Philosophical Pieces....* London: Johnson, 1779. Contemporary tan calf. Raised bands with red morocco label. Octavo. First edition. Near fine. $2,500.00

FRANKLIN, Benjamin. *The Works of Benjamin Franklin, Including the Private as well as the Official and Scientific Correspondence Together with the Unmutilated and Correct Version of the Autobiography*. New York: G.P. Putnam's Sons, 1904. Twelve large octavo volumes. Three-quarter red morocco gilt. Raised bands. Connoisseur's Federal edition, one of only 400 sets. Near fine. $1,900.00

FOXE, John. *Foxe's Book of Martyrs*. London: Company of Stationers, 1641. Three volumes (only one shown). Full brown calf. Red edges. Illustrated throughout with copper plate illustrations. Nineteenth century, re-backed spines. 14" tall. Very good. $5,500.00

F

FROST, John. *The American Generals*. Hartford: Case, Lockwood & Co., 1860. Full black calf with embossed covers. Illustrated. 10½" tall. Very good. $350.00

FRANKLIN, Benjamin. *The Works of Benjamin Franklin*. New York: G.P. Putnam's Sons, The Knickerbocker Press, 1904. Compiled and edited by John Bigelow. Twelve large octavo volumes. Full brown morocco gilt. Federal edition, one of only 1,000 sets. Photogravure frontispieces. Near fine. $1,900.00

FRANKLIN, Benjamin. *The Works*. New York and London: G.P. Putnam's Sons. Twelve volumes. Limited to 400 copies. Three-quarter blue morocco gilt. Federal edition. Near fine. $1,900.00

FRANKLIN, Benjamin. *The Works*. Boston: 1856. Ten octavo volumes. Contemporary half brown calf. Illustrated with frontispiece portraits and engraved plates. Sparks' edition. Near fine. $1,600.00

FRANKLIN, Benjamin. *The Works*. Philadelphia: circa 1858. Ten volumes. Octavo. Contemporary three-quarter green calf gilt. Illustrated with 22 engraved plates. Near fine. $1,500.00

FRANKLIN, Benjamin. *Works*. New York and London: Putnam's Sons, 1904. Twelve volumes. Three-quarter red morocco gilt, 8vo. Federal edition, one of only 400 sets. Illustrated frontispiece. Near fine. $1,900.00

FROST, John. *Thrilling Adventures Among the Indians*. Boston: L.P. Crown & Co., 1849. Full black calf. Marbled edges. Light foxing. Illustrated first edition. Hand-colored frontispiece. Very good. $675.00

FROST, John. *Thrilling Adventures Among the Indians*. Philadelphia: J.W. Bradley, 1850. Half red morocco. Marbled edges. Illustrated with hand-colored frontis. Mild foxing. Rebound, first edition. Near fine. $550.00

FRANKLIN, John. *Narrative of a Journey to the Shores of the Polar Sea, In the Years 1819 – 1822*. London: John Murray, 1823. With: *Narrative of a Second Expedition to the Shores of the Polar Sea, in the Years 1825 – 1827*. London: John Murray, 1828. Two volumes together. Nineteenth century full brown paneled calf. Quarto. Raised bands, gilt decorated spines, and marbled endpapers. Near fine. $2,300.00

FREEMAN, Douglas S. *Lee's Lieutenants*. New York: Charles Scribner's Sons, 1946. Three volumes. Three-quarter green morocco gilt. Raised bands and gilt panels. Near fine. $475.00

FREEMAN, Douglas Southall. *R.E. Lee: A Biography*. New York and London: 1935. Four volumes. Octavo. Contemporary three-quarter navy calf gilt by Sangorski & Sutcliffe. First edition. Near fine. $1,250.00

FREER, Martha W. *English and French Courts*. London: Hurst & Blackett, 1858. Fifteen volumes. Full green calf by Zaehnsdorf. Raised bands, gilt decorated spines with red labels. Near fine. $2,200.00

FRITH, Frances. *Egypt and Palestine Photographed and Described*. London: James S. Virtue, 1858 – 1859. Two volumes. Folio. Full brown paneled morocco gilt. First edition. Illustrated with numerous photographic prints of Egyptian and Palestinian antiquities. Near fine. $14,000.00

FROISSART. *Froissarts Chronicles: England, France, Spain, Portugal, Scotland, etc.* Oxford: The Shakespeare Head Press, 1827. Eight volumes. Full red morocco. Gilt spines. Translated from French by Lord Berners. Near fine. $1,200.00

FROUDE, James A. *A History of England*. London: Longmans, Green & Co., 1870. Twelve volumes. Full tree calf levant, red and green labels. Near fine. $2,200.00

FROUDE, James Anthony. *Caesar*. New York, Bombay, and Calcutta: 1912. Full tree calf. Prize binding with marbled edges. 7½" tall. Near fine. $250.00

FULLER, Thomas. *The Holy State*. With: *The Profane State*. Cambridge: R.D. for John Williams, 1648. Full tan calf. Hand-tooled cover boards. Original spine laid down, original boards. Illustrated. 11" tall. Very good. $1,200.00

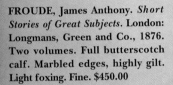

FROUDE, James Anthony. *Short Stories of Great Subjects*. London: Longmans, Green and Co., 1876. Two volumes. Full butterscotch calf. Marbled edges, highly gilt. Light foxing. Fine. $450.00

FULLER, Thomas. *A Pisgah-Sight of Palestine*. London: by J. F. for John Williams, 1650. Contemporary full brown calf. Folio. Illustrated with numerous maps and plates. First edition. Near fine. $3,200.00

FURTWANGLER, Adolph. *Masterpieces of Greek Sculpture*. London: William Heinemann, 1895. Three-quarter blue morocco by Zaehnsdorf. Raised bands, gilt spine, and marbled boards. Illustrated. First edition. Near fine. $600.00

FROUDE, James Anthony. *Short Stories on Great Subjects*. London: Longmans, Green and Co., 1868. Two volumes. Full sky blue morocco by Bickers. Highly gilt spine with marbled edges. 8½" tall. Near fine. $550.00

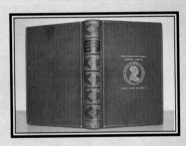

FURNEAUX, W. *Butterflies and Moths (British)*. London: Longmans Green and Co., 1897. Full red morocco with marbled edges. Illustrated with twelve colored plates. 8" tall. Near fine. $625.00

FROUDE, James Anthony. *The Spanish Story of the Armada*. London: Longmans Green and Co., 1898. Full tree calf with marbled edges. 8" tall. Near fine. $270.00

GARDINER, S.R. *Oliver Cromwell*. New York: Goupil & Co. 1899. Limited to 350 copies. Full blue morocco by Zaehnsdorf. Near fine. $975.00

FROUDE, James A. *A History of England*. London: Longmans, Green & Co., 1910. Twelve volumes. Full red polished calf gilt, ornate tooling on covers and spines. Near fine. $1,400.00

GARNETT, Thomas. *Observations on a Tour Through the Highlands and Parts of the Western Isles of Scotland*. London: 1800. Two volumes. Full mottled brown calf. Quarto. Illustrated with numerous plates by William Green. First edition. Near fine. $825.00

GABLE, G.W. *Famous Adventures and Prison Escapes of the Civil War*. New York: The Century Co., 1911. Three-quarter green calf. Spine faded to brown by the sun. Top edges gilt. J.P. Morgan Jr. copy, spine is stamped "Steamer J.P. Morgan." Illustrated. 8" tall. Very good. $425.00

GARDINER, Samuel Rawson. *Oliver Cromwell*. London, Paris and New York: Goubil & Co., 1899. Full red morocco by Adams. Highly gilt spine and covers. Marbled edges, silk moiré endpapers. Multicolored inlaid inside covers, carved insets in all corners. Illustrated. Folio, 13" tall. Near fine. $900.00

GARDINER, Samuel. *History of the Great Civil War*. New York and Bombay: Longmans, Green, and Co., 1901. Four volumes. Full tan calf by Brighton. Highly gilt spine with marbled edges. Prize binding. Illustrated with hand-colored pull-out maps. 7½" tall. Near fine. $600.00

GASKELL, Elizabeth. *Cranford*. London: 1935. Octavo. Contemporary full red morocco gilt. Illustrated by Hugh Thomson. Near fine. $375.00

GASKELL, Mrs. *Cranford with a Preface by Anne Thackerary Ritchie*. London: MacMillan & Co., 1900. Full brown morocco by Kelly and Sons. Raised bands, gilt decorated panels and covers. Fore-edge painting. Illustrated by Hugh Thomson. Near fine. $975.00

GASKELL, Mrs. *Novels and Tales*. London: Smith, Elder & Co., 1886. Seven volumes. Three-quarter green morocco gilt. Near fine. $1,150.00

GASKELL, Mrs. *Cranford*. London: MacMillan and Co., 1907. Full blue morocco. Highly gilt spine with all edges gilt. Hand-colored plates by Hugh Thompson. 8" tall. Fine. $580.00

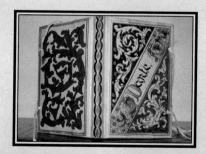

GARDNER, Edmund. *Dante*. London: J.M. Dent, 1905. Full white vellum. Hand-painted spine and covers, top edges gilt, gauffered edges, and suede cover ties. 6" tall. Near fine. $550.00

GASKELL, Mrs. *The Life of Charlotte Bronte*. London: Smith, Elder & Co., 1879. Three-quarter tan calf. Marbled edges. 7¾" tall. Near fine. $120.00

GAUTIER, Theophile. *A Night of Cleopatra.* Paris: Societe Des Beaux Arts, circa 1880. Full maroon morocco. Green and white inlaid flowers and gilt vine work to covers. Top edges gilt. Salon edition, #58 of 550. Illustrated, hand-colored frontis, written in English. 10" tall. Fine. $900.00

GAY, John. *Fables with a Memoir by Austin Dobson.* London: Kegan Paul, 1882. Full red morocco. Raised bands, gilt decorated spine and covers. Housed in a full blue morocco slipcase. One of only 50 copies. Near fine. $750.00

GAY, John. *Fables.* London: John Stockdale, 1793. Two volumes. Full red morocco gilt. Illustrated with 70 plates, 12 by William Blake. Near fine. $1,150.00

GERSHWIN, George. *Porgy and Bess. An Opera in Three Acts.* New York: 1935. Folio. Original full red morocco, original slipcase. Limited edition of the piano-vocal score of *Porgy and Bess*, one of only 250 copies signed by George Gershwin, Ira Gershwin, DuBose Heyward, and Rouben Mamoulian. Near fine. $7,500.00

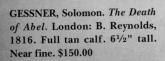

GAY, John. *Fables.* London: G.C. and J. Robinson, 1801. Three-quarter brown calf. Copper plate illustrations by John Bewick. 6" tall. Near fine. $425.00

GESSNER, Solomon. *The Death of Abel.* London: B. Reynolds, 1816. Full tan calf. 6½" tall. Near fine. $150.00

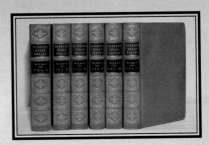

GIBBON, Edward. *The History of the Decline and Fall of the Roman Empire.* London: John Murray, 1846. Six volumes. Full butterscotch calf. Hand-colored pull-out maps. Notes by H.H. Milman. Second edition. Fine. $1,200.00

GIBBON, Edward. *An Essay On The Study of Literature.* London: T. Becket and P.A. DeHondt, 1764. Quarter calf over marbled paper boards. Flat spine with red and green morocco labels. First English edition. Near fine. $475.00

GIBBON, Edward. *Decline and Fall of the Roman Empire.* London: Methuen & Co., 1909. Seven volumes. Full blue calf gilt. With 20 illustrations and maps. Near fine. $1,150.00

GIBBON, Edward. *The History of the Decline & Fall of the Roman Empire.* London: W. Allason, 1819. Twelve volumes. Full navy morocco, ribbed gilt decorated spines and covers. Near fine. $1,750.00

GIBBON, Edward. *The History of the Decline and Fall of the Roman Empire.* London: John Murray, 1854. Eight volumes. Three-quarter tan calf gilt. Near fine. $1,200.00

GIBBON, Edward. *The History of the Decline and Fall of the Roman Empire.* London: 1788. Six volumes. Thick quarto. Contemporary full brown calf. First edition. Near fine. $4,500.00

GIBBON, Edward. *The History of The Decline and Fall of the Roman Empire.* London: T. Cadell, 1838. Eight volumes. Full tan calf gilt. Illustrated with maps and plates. Near fine. $1,250.00

GIBBON, Edward. *The History of the Decline and Fall of the Roman Empire.* London: 1862. Eight octavo volumes. Twentieth century three-quarter polished tan calf gilt. Illustrated with a frontispiece portrait of Gibbon and twelve large folding hand-colored maps. Near fine. $1,150.00

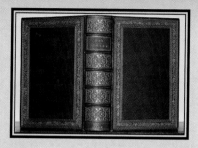

GIFFORD, William. *The Works of Ben Johnson.* London: Edward Moxon, 1846. Full maroon morocco. All edges gilt. 9½" tall. Near fine. $230.00

GILBERT, Henry. *King Arthur's Knights.* Edinburgh and London: T.C. and E.C. Jack, 1911. Full red morocco. Highly gilt spine and covers, all edges gilt. Sixteen color illustrations by Walter Crane. 9" tall. Fine. $800.00

GILFILLAN. *Robert Burns.* New York: The Anglo American Authors Association, n.d., circa 1880. Two volumes. Full green morocco. Hand-painted title page, extra illustrated. Top edges gilt. Red morocco doublures, silk moiré endpapers. From The British Poets Collection. Spines faded to tan. 9" tall. Near fine. $450.00

GIFFORD, E. *Memoirs of the Life and Campaigns of Napoleon Bunoparte in France, Italy, Germany, Egypt, Etc.* J & J Cundee, circa 1800. Two volumes. Full brown calf. Gilt decorated spines. Illustrated with numerous plates and maps. Near fine. $560.00

GIFFORD, John. *A History of the Political Life of the Right Honourable William Pitt.* London: 1809. Six octavo volumes. Three-quarter burgundy morocco gilt. Gilt decorated spines. Frontispiece portraits. First edition. Near fine. $780.00

GILMAN, Arthur. *Rome.* London and New York: T. Fisher Unwin, 1891. Full tree calf. Top edges gilt. Illustrated with pull-out map. 7½" tall. Near fine. $240.00

GLAZIER, Captain Willard. *Down the Great River.* Philadelphia: Hubbard Brothers, 1888. Full black morocco. Marbled edges. Illustrated embossed cover, highly gilt spine. First edition. Fine. $325.00

GLAZIER, Captain Willard. *Heroes of Three Wars.* Philadelphia: Hubbard, 1884. Full brown morocco. All edges gilt. Illustrated. Fine. $250.00

GOETHE. *Faust.* Boston: Dana Estes & Co., n.d., Full green morocco. Top edges gilt. Silk endpapers and inlaid doublures. Illustrated by William Pogany. First deluxe edition, one of only 500 copies. Very good. $900.00

GOETHE. *Faust*. London: Hutchinson & Co., n.d., Full red morocco. Highly gilt spine and covers, all edges gilt. Illustrated by William Pogany. 10" tall. Fine. $1,200.00

GOETHE, J. W. Von. *Goethe's Works*. Illustrated by the Best German Artists. Philadelphia: George Barrie, 1885. Five large quarto volumes. Contemporary three-quarter brown morocco gilt. Marbled boards and endpapers, raised bands and gilt decorated spines. Illustrated with mounted steel engravings and full-page and in-text wood engravings. Near fine. $1,200.00

GOETHE, J.W. *The Works*. Boston: For Subscribers, 1905. Twenty-four volumes. Octavo. Contemporary three-quarter blue morocco gilt. Limited edition, one of only 500 copies. Illustrated. Near fine. $3,600.00

GOLDSMITH, Lewis. *The Secret History of the Cabinet of Bonaparte*. London: Printed for J.M. Richardson & J. Hatchard, 1810. Three-quarter green morocco. Marbled edges. Fine. $375.00

GOLDSMITH, Oliver. *A History of Earth and Animated Nature*. Glasgow: Blackie and Son, 1853. Two volumes. Full tan calf. Embossed covers and marbled edges. Two hundred illustrations, many hand colored. 9½" tall. Near fine. $600.00

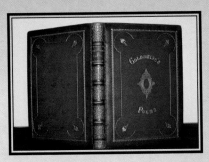

GOLDSMITH, Oliver. *The Poems of Oliver Goldsmith*. London: George Routledge, 1877. Full blue morocco by R. Ingalton Drake. Edited by Robert Aris Willmont. Highly gilt cover with top edges gilt. Illustrated with color plates. 9" tall. Near fine. $245.00

GOLDSMITH, Oliver. *The Vicar of Wakefield*. London: John C. Nimmo, 1889. Blue crushed morocco by Bayntun. Raised bands, gilt spine compartments, marbled endpapers, all edges gilt. Housed in a linen slipcase. Near fine. $650.00

GOLDSMITH, Oliver. *Works of Oliver Goldsmith*. New York: G. P. Putnam's Sons, 1908. Ten octavo volumes. Full navy morocco gilt. Gilt decorated spines and marbled endpapers. "Turk's Head" edition, one of only 1,000 sets signed by the publisher. Illustrated by Frederick S. Coburn. Near fine. $1,800.00

GOLDSTON, Will. *Modern Card Tricks Without Apparatus*. London: 1915. Three-quarter calf. Small octavo. First edition. Near fine. $325.00

GOODRICH, Frank B. *The Tribute Book*. New York: Derby & Miller, 1865. Full purple morocco. Top edges gilt. Illustrated. 11" tall. Near fine. $425.00

GOODRICH, Frank. *Man Upon the Sea*. Philadelphia: J.P. Lippincott & Co., 1856. Full brown calf. Gold gilt embossed ship on cover. Illustrated. First edition. 9" tall. Near fine. $475.00

GOODRICH, S.G. *A History of All Nations.* Cincinnati: Derby & Miller, 1853. Two volumes. Full black morocco. Marbled edges. Illustrated with 70 stylographic maps and 700 engravings. 11" tall. Very good. $350.00

GOODRICH, S.G. *The Manners, Customs, and Antiquities of the Indians of North and South American.* Boston: George C. Rand, 1852. Full tan calf. Illustrated. Cabinet Library. 6" tall. Near fine. $350.00

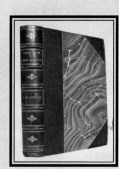

GORDON, G.H. *Brook Farm to Cedar Mountain.* Boston: James R. Osgood and Co., 1883. Three-quarter dark brown calf by Launder and MacDonald. Top edges gilt. First edition. Very good. $400.00

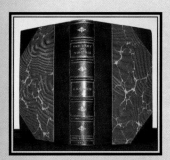

GORDON, George H. *The History of the Campaign of the Army of Virginia.* Boston: Houghton Osgood & Co., 1880. Three-quarter brown calf by Launder and MacDonald. Top edges gilt. Illustrated with large pull-out map and a series of smaller pull-out maps. 9½" tall. Near fine. $475.00

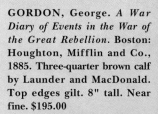

GORDON, George. *A War Diary of Events in the War of the Great Rebellion.* Boston: Houghton, Mifflin and Co., 1885. Three-quarter brown calf by Launder and MacDonald. Top edges gilt. 8" tall. Near fine. $195.00

GOSS, Warren Lee. *The Soldier's Story.* Boston: I.M. Richardson, 1872. Three-quarter brown calf. Marbled edges. Illustrated. 8½" tall. Very good. $175.00

GOSSIP, Robert. *Turkey and Russia, The Races, History and Wars.* Edinburgh: Thomas C. Jack, 1879. Three-quarter green morocco. Raised bands, gilt spines. Large 4to. Illustrated. Near fine. $675.00

GOUGH, John B. *Sunlight and Shadow.* Hartford: 1881. Full red morocco. Octavo. Illustrated with frontispiece portrait and numerous full page engravings. First edition. Near fine. $175.00

GOWER, Lord Ronald Sutherland. *Sir Thomas Lawrence.* London: Goupil and Co., 1900. Full green morocco. Highly gilt spine and covers, with top edges gilt. Hand-colored frontis, illustrated with many fine folio size engravings. Red morocco doublures and red silk moiré endpapers. #146 of 200 copies printed. 16" tall. Near fine. $875.00

GRACIUS, J. *The Birds of Australia*. Melbourne: 1890 – 1891. Six volumes. Three-quarter dark brown morocco gilt. Folio. Illustrated with numerous chromolithographic plates. First edition. Near fine. $5,600.00

GRACIAN, Balthasar. *The Art of Worldly Wisdom*. **London: MacMillan and Co., 1924. Full tan calf by Riviere. All edges gilt. 6" tall. Near fine. $150.00**

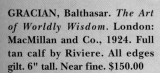

GRAHAM, C.R. *Under Both Flags*. **Philadelphia: Peoples Publishing Co., 1896. Full maroon morocco. Highly gilt cover. 250 illustrations. Original spine laid down, reinforced inner covers. First edition. 11½" tall. Very good. $410.00**

GRAHAM, Thomas John. *Sure Methods of Improving Health and Prolonging Life*. London: 1828. Three-quarter brown calf gilt. Tall 12mo. Third edition. Near fine. $175.00

GRANT, Anne. *Memoirs of an American Lady: with Sketches of Manners and Scenery in America, as they existed previous to the Revolution*. London: Longman, 1808. Two octavo volumes. Full red morocco. First edition. Near fine. $875.00

GRANT, George Monro. *Picturesque Canada*. **Toronto: Belden Bros., 1882. Two volumes. Full brown calf with embossed covers. All edges gilt. Illustrated with over 500 engravings on wood. First edition. 13" tall. Near fine. $800.00**

GRANT, James. *History of India*. **London, Paris and New York: Cassell Petter & Galpin, 1876. Two volumes. Three-quarter olive calf. Marbled edges. Illustrated. 10½" tall. Very good. $350.00**

GRANT, James. *History of India*. London: Cassell & Co., 1900. Two volumes. Three-quarter green calf gilt. Illustrated. Near fine. $375.00

GRANT, Ulysses S. *Personal Memoirs of U.S. Grant*. New York: 1885 – 86. Two volumes. Octavo. Original three-quarter dark brown morocco gilt. First edition. Near fine. $850.00

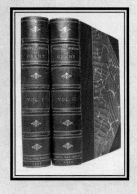

GRANT, U.S. *Personal Memoirs of U.S. Grant*. **New York: Charles L. Webster & Co., 1885. Two volumes. Three-quarter dark brown calf by Launder and MacDonald. Top edges gilt. Illustrated. First edition. Near fine. $850.00**

GRANT, U.S. *Personal Memoirs of U.S. Grant*. **New York: Charles L. Webster, 1885. Two volumes. Three-quarter black calf. Gold gilt medallion on covers. Marbled edges. Illustrated with maps and Lee's surrender letter. First edition. 9" tall. Near fine. $1,000.00**

GRANT, Ulysses S. *Personal Memoirs of U.S. Grant.* New York: 1885 – 1886. Two octavo volumes. Full brown morocco gilt. First edition, illustrated with steel engravings, facsimiles and numerous maps. Published by Mark Twain. Near fine. $1,100.00

GRANT, Ulysses S. *Personal Memoirs of U.S. Grant.* New York: Charles L. Webster & Co., 1885 – 86. Two octavo volumes. Full black morocco gilt. First edition illustrated with steel engravings with tissue guards and numerous maps. Near fine. $1,100.00

GRAVES, Robert. *I Claudius and Claudius The God.* London: Arthur Barker, 1934. Two volumes. Full brown morocco. Raised bands with ornate inlays on covers. First edition. Near fine. $875.00

GRAY, Henry. *Anatomy, Descriptive and Surgical.* Philadelphia: Blanchard and Lea, 1870. Contemporary full sheep with black morocco label. Illustrated. Near fine. $425.00

GRAY, Thomas. *Elegy in a Country Churchyard.* London: circa 1920. Tall, slim octavo. Full crushed green morocco. Illuminated edition of Gray's most famous poem. Binding by Sangorski & Sutcliffe. Near fine. $460.00

GRAY, Thomas. *The Works of Thomas Gray.* London: Harding, Triphook and Lepard. Two volumes. Full brown morocco with marbled edges. 7" tall. Very good. $250.00

GREASY, Sir Edward. *The Fifteen Decisive Battles of the World.* London: Richard Bentley, 1871. Full tan calf. Marbled edges. 7" tall. Near fine. $175.00

GRAY, Thomas. *Poems by Thomas Gray.* London: Eton College Press, 1902. Full tan calf. All edges gilt. Prize binding. Illustrated. 10½" tall. Near fine. $275.00

GREELEY, Horace. *The American Conflict.* Chicago: O.D. Case & Co., 1864. Two volumes. Three-quarter tan calf. Marbled edges. With large hand-colored map and signed letter from Greeley on Chicago Tribune letterhead. Illustrated. First edition. 9½" tall. Near fine. $1,400.00

GRAY, Thomas. *The Poems of Gray.* Philadelphia: Henry Carey Baird, 1851. Full black calf. Highly gilt spine and cover by American Binders. All edges gilt. Illustrated. 8" tall. Near fine. $240.00

GREELEY, Horace. *The American Conflict.* Hartford: O.D. Case & Co., 1864. Two volumes. Three-quarter dark brown calf by Launder and MacDonald. Top edges gilt. Illustrated. First edition. Near fine. $850.00

GREEN, Mary Anne E. *Lives of the Princesses of England.* London: Henry Colburn, 1849. Six volumes. Three-quarter green morocco by Riviere. Near fine. $975.00

GREGORY, Sir Richard. *Discovery.* London: MacMillan and Co., 1921. Full navy morocco. Highly gilt spine and cover with marbled edges. Illustrated. 7" tall. Near fine. $150.00

GREEN, Mary Anne Everett. *Lives of the Princesses of England.* London: Henry Colburn, 1850. Six volumes. Full butterscotch calf with marbled edges. 7½" tall. Near fine. $775.00

GRIMM, Herman. *Life of Michael Angelo.* Boston: Little, Brown & Co., 1870. Two volumes. Three-quarter calf. Fifth edition. Near fine. $375.00

GRIMM, Brothers. *Fair Tales.* London: Constable & Co., 1909. Full vellum. Illustrated and signed by Arthur Rackham. Limited edition, one of only 750 copies. Near fine. $3,200.00

GRIMM, Herman. *Life of Michael Angelo.* Boston: Little Brown & Co., 1896. Two volumes. Three-quarter red morocco gilt, ribbed spines. Near fine. $275.00

GREGG, David. *Makers of the American Republic.* New York: E.B. Treat, 1896. Full brown calf. Top edges gilt. First edition, signed by the author. 8" tall. Near fine. $235.00

GRIMM, Herman. *Life of Michael Angelo.* Boston: Little Brown & Co., 1896. Two volumes. Three-quarter brown morocco gilt. Ribbed gilt decorated spines. Illustrated. Near fine. $275.00

GREGO, Joseph. *Reminiscences of Captain Gronow.* London: John C. Nimmo, 1889. Two volumes. Full red morroco by Riviere. Gold embossed front and rear covers. Top edges gilt. One of 870 copies. Plates in two states, colored and uncolored. With slipcase, original cloth covers and spine bound in rear. 10½" tall. Near fine. $1,100.00

GRISWOLD, Rufus W. *Scenes in the Life of the Savior.* Philadelphia: Lindsay and Blakiston, 1845. Full black calf, highly gilt spine and covers. All edges gilt. Rare American binding, illustrated with steel engravings. First edition. 9½" tall. Near fine. $450.00

GRISWOLD, Rufus Wilmot. *The Republican Court.* New York: D. Appleton, 1855. Full purple morocco. Highly gilt spine and cover with all edges gilt. Illustrated with steel engravings. 11" tall. Near fine. $460.00

GROSE, Frances. *The Antiquities of England, Wales, Scotland and Military.* London: Hooper and Wigstead, circa 1820. Twelve volumes. Full blue morocco gilt. Raised bands, gilt decorated spines and covers. Quarto. Illustrated. Near fine. $2,600.00

GROTE, George. *History of Greece.* London: John Murray, 1854. Twelve volumes. Full polished tan calf, gilt decorated spines. Fourth edition. Near fine. $1,650.00

GROTE, George. *History of Greece.* London: John Murray, 1869. Twelve volumes. Full tree calf levant. Raised bands and ornate gilt on spines. Illustrated with portraits and maps. Near fine. $2,400.00

GROTE, George. *Plato and the Other Companions of Socrates.* London: John Murray, 1865. Three volumes. Full tan calf gilt. Raised bands, gilt decorated spines with green and red labels. Near fine. $450.00

GROVE. *Grove's Dictionary of Music and Musicians.* London: MacMillan & Co., 1904. Five volumes. Three-quarter blue morocco. Gilt decorated spines. Near fine. $425.00

GROTE, George. *A History of Greece.* London: John Murray, 1862. Eight volumes. Full tan calf. Marbled edges. Pull-out maps. 9¾" tall. Near fine. $1,100.00

GUERNSEY, Alfred H., and ALDEN, Henry M. *Harper's Pictorial History of the Great Rebellion.* New York: Harper Brothers, 1866. Two volumes. Three-quarter green morocco. Top edges gilt. Illustrations on every page. First edition. 17" tall. Very good. $875.00

GUIZOT, F. *Works.* London: Richard Bently, 1858. Fifteen volumes. Three-quarter red morocco. Raised bands, gilt decorated. Near fine. $1,500.00

GUIZOT, M. *A Popular History of France from the Earliest Times.* Boston: Estes and Lauriat, n.d., circa 1878. Six volumes. Three-quarter butterscotch calf. Marbled edges. Illustrated. 10¾" tall. Near fine. $575.00

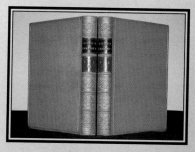

GUIZOT, M. *History of Charles the First and the English Revolution.* London: Richard Bentley, 1854. Two volumes. Full butterscotch calf. Highly gilt spine with marbled edges. Lord Cheylesmore bookplate. 8" tall. Fine. $425.00

GUIZOT, M. *Works*. Boston: Dana Estes and Charles E. Lauriat, 1876. Ten volumes. Contains A Popular History of England and History of France. Three-quarter tan calf, gilt panels. 4to. Illustrated. Near fine. $1,100.00

GULLIVER, Lemuel. *Gulliver's Travels*. London: MacMillan & Co., 1922. Full green morocco by Bayntun. Highly gilt spine and covers. One hundred illustrations by Charles Brock. 7" tall. Near fine. $420.00

GUTCH, John Matthew. *Robin Hood, the Lytell Geste*. London: Longman, 1847. Two volumes. Full butterscotch calf. All edges gilt. Illustrated by Fairholt. Near fine. $580.00

GUTTENBERG BIBLE. *Guttenberg Facsimile*. Patterson, N.J.: Pageant Books, 1961. Two volumes. Full red morocco with all edges gilt. This is the first facsimile ever printed in the U.S.A. and second in the world. Over 100 illuminated pages on 100% rag paper. Limited to 996 copies. Elephant folio. 19" tall. Fine. $2,200.00

HAGGARD, H. Rider. *Heart of the World*. New York and Bombay: Longmans, Green and Co., 1899. Full navy morocco. Prize binding. Marbled edges. Illustrated. 7" tall. Near fine. $175.00

HALL, Basil. *Fragments of Voyages and Travels*. London: 1856. Contemporary full brown calf gilt. Royal octavo. Illustrated with folding chart. Late edition. Near fine. $225.00

HALL, Basil. *Travels in North America, in the Years 1827 – 1828*. Edinburgh: Cadell & Co., 1829. Three volumes. Three-quarter calf. Large 12mo. First edition. Housed in a custom slipcase. Illustrated. Near fine. $860.00

HALL, S.C. *The Book of Gems*. London: Saunders and Otley, 1836, 1837 & 1839. Three volumes. Full pebbled calf. Marbled edges. Illustrated. 9" tall. Near fine. $450.00

HALL, James Norman, and NORDHOFF, Charles, editors. *The Lafayette Flying Corps*. Boston and New York: Houghton Mifflin Co., 1920. Two octavo volumes. Three-quarter calf. Illustrated with numerous photographs and line drawings. First editions. Near fine. $1,200.00

HALL, Thornton. *Love Intrigues of Royal Courts*. London: T. Werner Laurie, 1890. Full red morocco by Bayntun gilt. Illustrated with 54 portraits. Near fine. $575.00

HALLAM, Henry. *Hallam's Works*. New York: Hurd and Houghton, 1864. Ten volumes (only three shown). Three-quarter tan calf. Marbled edges. 8" tall. Very good. $750.00

HAMILTON, Alexander. *Works*. New York and London: G.P. Putnams & Sons, 1885. Nine volumes. Three-quarter maroon morocco by Bentley. Top edges gilt. Edited by Henry Cabot Lodge. Printed for Sale by the Letter Press edition, one of only 500 sets. Fine. $1,350.00

HALLAM, Henry. *View of the State of Europe During the Middle Ages*. London: John Murray, 1878. Three volumes. Full tan calf. Prize binding with marbled edges. 7" tall. Near fine. $525.00

HAMILTON, Count A. *Memoirs of Count Grammont*. London: Longman, Hurst, Rees and Orme, 1809. Three volumes. Full mottled morocco by Bayntun. All edges gilt. Illustrated with 40 fine portraits. Second edition. Fine. $600.00

HALLAM, Henry. *View of the State of Europe During the Middle Ages*. With: *The Constitutional History of England*. With: *Introduction to the Literature of Europe*. Boston: 1853 – 54. Nine octavo volumes. Contemporary full brown polished calf gilt. Gilt decorated spines with red and black morocco labels. Near fine. $1,250.00

HANNAY, James. *The History of Acadia*. St. John N.B.: MacMillan, 1879. Three-quarter tan calf. Illustrated. First edition. 8½" tall. Near fine. $375.00

HARDIN, John Wesley. *The Life of John Wesley Hardin from the Original Manuscript*. Seguin, Texas: 1896. Full calf. Octavo. First edition. Near fine. $450.00

HARDY, Thomas. *Collected Poems*. London: 1928. Octavo. Three-quarter calf. Early edition. Illustrated with frontispiece portrait of the author. Near fine. $1,250.00

HAMILTON and MADISON. *The Federalist*. Hallowell: Grazier & Co., 1826. Full burl calf. Marbled edges. Light foxing. First edition. Very good. $675.00

HARDY, Thomas. *Novels*. London: 1893. Eight octavo volumes. Three-quarter brown morocco by Sotheran. "Half-Crown" edition. Near fine. $2,600.00

HARDY, Thomas. *The Works of Thomas Hardy*. New York and London: Harper & Brothers, 1905. Twenty volumes (only four shown). Three-quarter red morocco with top edges gilt. 8½" tall. Near fine. $3,200.00

HARDY, Thomas. *The Works. In Prose and Verse with Prefaces and Notes*. London: MacMillian & Co., Ltd., 1912 – 1926. Twenty-four volumes. Full green calf gilt by Sotherans. Raised bands with red labels. Wessex edition. Near fine. $7,500.00

HARDY, Thomas. *The Works*. London: MacMillian & Co., 1919 – 1920. Thirty-seven volumes. 8vo. Half blue morocco gilt. Box design on spines with raised bands. Near fine. $11,000.00

HARDY, Thomas. *The Writings in Prose and Verse, With Prefaces and Notes*. New York and London: 1893 – 1904. Twenty octavo volumes. Three-quarter green morocco by Brentano. Illustrated "Autograph Edition," one of only 153 sets. Each volume is illustrated with a frontispiece. Near fine. $12,000.00

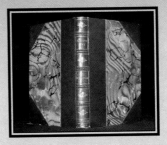

HARRISON, Walter. *Pickett's Men*. New York: D. Van Nostrand, 1870. Three-quarter brown calf by Launder and MacDonald. Top edges gilt. First edition. 7½" tall. Near fine. $400.00

HARDY, Thomas. *The Writings of Thomas Hardy in Prose and Verse, With Prefaces and Notes*. New York and London: Harper & Brothers, 1920. Twenty-one octavo volumes. Three-quarter burgundy morocco gilt. Raised bands, marbled endpapers. Illustrated in each volume with a frontispiece. Volume 1 contains a double-page map of "The Wessex of the Novels." "Anniversary Edition," one of only 1,250 sets made. Near fine. $9,500.00

HARDY, Thomas. *Writings in Prose and Verse*. New York and London: Harper & Bros., 1893. Twenty-one volumes. Three-quarter blue morocco gilt by Bayntun. Anniversary edition. Near fine. $9,800.00

HARTE, Bret. *Her Letter His Answer and Her Last Letter*. Boston and New York: Houghton Mifflin & Co., 1905. Full olive morocco by MacDonald. Crushed levant, white and red inlaid floral pattern on boards and spine. All edges gilt. Color illustrations by Arthur Keller. White silk moiré doublures and endpapers. 9" tall. Fine. $750.00

HARRISON, Constance Cary. *Fads and Fancies*. New York: Topics Publishing, 1905. Full green morocco by MacDonald. Highly gilt spine and covers with all edges gilt. Printed on Japanese vellum paper, each page illustrated. Green silk moiré doublures and endpapers. Signed by the publisher and housed in a special oak wood case, felt lined with latches. 16" tall. First edition. Portraits of over 80 of the early twentieth century most notable American men. Near fine. $3,500.00

HARTE, Bret. *The Poetical Works of Bret Harte*. Boston and New York: Houghton, Mifflin and Co., 1882. Full tree calf. All edges gilt. Illustrated. 8" tall. Near fine. $225.00

HARTE, Bret. *The Writings of Bret Harte*. Boston: Houghton, Mifflin & Co., 1902. Nineteen volumes. Three-quarter blue morocco. Riverside edition. Near fine. $2,800.00

HAWTHORNE, Nathaniel. *Our Old Home*. Boston: Ticknor and Fields, 1863. Three-quarter brown calf. Red edges. First edition. 7" tall. Very good. $325.00

HAWTHORNE, Nathaniel. *Complete Writings*. Boston and New York: 1900. Twenty-two volumes. Three-quarter brown morocco gilt. Old Manse edition. Near fine. $2,100.00

HAWTHORNE, Nathaniel. *Tanglewood Tales*. London: 1918. Contemporary full green morocco gilt. Large quarto. Illustrated by Edmund Dulac. Limited edition, one of only 500 copies signed by the illustrator. Near fine. $875.00

HAULTAIN. *Hints for Lovers*. London: Constable & Co., 1909. Full green morocco. Marbled edges, silk doublures and endpapers. First edition. Fine. $450.00

HAWTHORNE, Nathaniel. *The Scarlet Letter*. London: Methuen & Co., 1920. Full red morocco gilt by Stikeman. Tan morocco doublures and silk endpapers. Illustrated. 4to. First trade edition. Near fine. $1,200.00

HARPER, Ida Husted. *The Life and Work of Susan B. Anthony*. Indianapolis and Kansas City: Bowen-Merrill Co., 1898 – 1899. Two octavo volumes. Three-quarter tan calf. Raised bands with green and red morocco labels, marbled boards. First edition. Near fine. $950.00

HAWTHORNE, Nathaniel. *The Scarlet Letter*. New York: 1904. Quarto. Contemporary full red morocco gilt, silk endpapers. Limited edition, one of only 125 copies on Japanese vellum. Near fine. $975.00

HAWKESWORTH, John. *An Account of the Voyages Undertaken by the Order of His Present Majesty for making Discoveries in the Southern Hemisphere, and Successfully Performed by Commodore Byron, Captain Wallis, Captain Carteret, And Captain Cook*. Three volumes. With: COOK, James. *A Voyage Towards the South Pole, and Round the World....* Three volumes (two of text, one of plates). With: COOK, James, and KING, James. *A Voyage to the Pacific Ocean, Undertaken, by the Command of His Majesty, for Making Discoveries in the Northern Hemisphere*. Four volumes (three volumes plus atlas). London: W. Strahan and T. Cadell, 1773 – 1784. Ten volumes in total. Three-quarter brown calf. Marbled boards and endpapers. Illustrated with numerous plates, charts and maps. First editions. Fine. $15,000.00

HAWTHORNE, Nathaniel. *The Snow Image, and Other Twice-Told Tales*. Boston: 1852. Three-quarter calf. First edition. Near fine. $675.00

HAWTHORNE, Nathaniel. *The Works*. Boston: circa 1900. Fifteen volumes. Octavo. Contemporary full red morocco gilt. Standard library edition, with 33 full-page engravings. Near fine. $2,100.00

HAWTHORNE, Nathaniel. *A Wonder Book*. London and New York: Hodder and Stoughton, 1922. Full blue morocco by Bayntun. Quarto. Illustrated and signed by Arthur Rackham. Near fine. $1,600.00

HAWTHORNE, Nathaniel. *Scarlet Letter*. London: Walter Scott, n.d., Full cobalt morocco by Riviere. All edges gilt. Limited edition. Fine. $365.00

HAWTHORNE, Nathaniel. *The Works of Nathaniel Hawthorne.* Boston and New York: Houghlin Mifflin & Co., 1884. Fifteen volumes. Three-quarter tan calf. Top edges gilt. Illustrated. 8" tall. Near fine. $1,850.00

HAWTHORNE, Nathaniel. *The Writings.* Boston and New York: Houghton, Mifflin and Company, 1900. Twenty-two large octavo volumes. Contemporary three-quarter brown morocco gilt. Large paper edition, one of only 500 sets. Illustrated with portraits and over 100 plates. Near fine. $2,800.00

HAYDN, Joseph. *Haydn's Celebrated Overture...Adapted for the Piano Forte, with an Accompaniment for a Violin & Violoncello. No. 1.* With: *Nos. 2 – 6.* Edinburgh: circa 1796. Modern half brown morocco. Folio. Engraved. Near fine. $1,900.00

HAYNES, F. Jay. *Yellowstone National Park. Photo-Gravures From Nature.* Fargo and New York: Photo-Gravure Co., 1887. Full calf. Oblong quarto. Illustrated. First edition. Near fine. $1,650.00

HAYWARD, Sir John. *The Lives of the III Normans, Kings of England.* London: 1613. Contemporary full limp vellum. Square octavo. First edition. Near fine. $1,450.00

HAZLITT, William. *The Life of Napoleon.* London: Office of the Illustrated London Library, 1852. Four octavo volumes. Three-quarter brown calf gilt. Gilt decorated spines with green and black morocco labels. Second edition. Illustrated with engraved frontispiece portraits. Near fine. $625.00

HAZLITT, William. *Wit and Humor.* London: Gay and Bird, 1901. Full blue morocco by Zaehnsdorf. Top edges gilt. Illustrated. One of only 60 copies. 5" tall. Near fine. $275.00

HAZLITT, William. *The Life of Napoleon.* London: The Grolier Society, n.d., Six volumes. Three-quarter green morocco gilt. Gilt spines are decorated with Napoleonic symbols. "Edition Connoisseur Astrale," limited to 75 copies. Near fine. $675.00

HAZLITT, William. *The Life of Napoleon.* London: The Grolier Society, circa 1910. Six octavo volumes. Contemporary three-quarter red morocco gilt. "Edition de Luxe," one of only 1,000 sets. Illustrated with battle scenes and numerous black and white portraits. Near fine. $775.00

HAZLITT, William. *The Life of Napoleon.* New York: Anglo-American Publishing Co., circa 1900. Seventeen volumes. Three-quarter red morocco gilt. Ribbed gilt decorated spines. Near fine. $2,800.00

HEADLEY, J.T. *Farragut and Our Naval Commanders.* New York: E.B. Treat & Co., 1867. Three-quarter tan calf with marbled edges. Illustrated. First edition. Near fine. $380.00

HAZELTON, Captain Joseph Powers. *Scouts, Spies, and Heroes of the Great Civil War.* Jersey City: Star, 1892. Three-quarter maroon morocco. Marbled edges. First edition, illustrated. 9" tall. Near fine. $375.00

HEADLEY, J.T. *The Great Rebellion.* Hartford: Hurlburt, Williams & Co., 1863. Two volumes. Full maroon morocco. Highly gilt spine with all edges gilt. Illustrated. First edition. Cover hinge broken on volume 1. 9½" tall. Good. $280.00

HEADLEY, J.T. *The Sacred Mountains*. New York: Baker and Scribner, 1848. Full black calf. All edges gilt. Illustrated. Light foxing on frontis and title page only. Fine. $245.00

HEINE, Heinrich. *The Prose and Poetical Works of Heinrich Heine*. New York: Groscup and Sterling, 1892 – 1905. Twenty octavo volumes. Translated with introductions by Charles G. Leland. Three-quarter navy morocco gilt. Raised bands, gilt decorated spine with red morocco inlays. "Dusseldorf Edition," one of only 250 sets. Illustrations and hand-colored frontispieces. Near fine. $2,800.00

HEINE, Heinrich. *The Prose and Poetical Works of Heinrich Heine*. New York: Croscup & Sterling Co., n.d., circa 1898. Twenty volumes (only two shown). Three-quarter blue morocco by Croscup. Top edges gilt. Embossed flower with red morocco insets. Extra illustrated, handmade paper, hand-colored frontis in each volume. Dusseldorf edition, one of 250 copies. 8½" tall. Near fine. $2,900.00

HELPER, Hinton Rowan. *The Impending Crisis of the South*. New York: Burdick Bros., 1857. Three-quarter brown calf with top edges gilt. First edition. 7½" tall. Near fine. $310.00

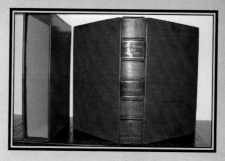

HEMINGWAY, Ernest. *For Whom the Bell Tolls*. New York: Scribner, 1940. Full brown morocco Nigerian goat leather. First trade edition. Recently rebound, with slipcase. 8½" tall. Near fine. $1,200.00

HEMINGWAY, Ernest. *For Whom the Bell Tolls*. New York: Charles Scribner's Sons, 1940. First edition. Full red morocco gilt. Near fine. $1,200.00

HEMINGWAY, Ernest. *For Whom The Bell Tolls*. New York: Charles Scribner's Sons, 1940. Octavo. Three-quarter calf. First edition. Near fine. $1,200.00

HENDERSON, George. *Stonewall Jackson and the Civil War*. London: Longmans, 1898. Two octavo volumes. Twentieth century three-quarter red morocco gilt. First edition illustrated with portraits of Jackson, maps, and plans. Four of the maps are foldouts. Near fine. $1,100.00

HENDERSON, Lieut. Col. G.J.R. *Stonewall Jackson and the American Civil War*. London: Longmans, Green & Co., 1900. Two volumes. Full maroon calf. Raised bands, gilt decorated and marbled edges. Illustrated. Near fine. $550.00

HENDERSON, G.E.R. Lieutenant Colonel. *Stonewall Jackson and The American Civil War*. London, New York, Bombay: Longmans, Green and Co., 1902. Two volumes. Full tree calf. Highly gilt spine with all edges gilt. Illustrated with portraits, maps, and plans. 8" tall. Near fine. $1,200.00

HENRY, M.S. *This is of Aucassin and Nicolette.* Edinburgh: Turnbull and Spears, 1902. Full blue morocco by Otto Schulze. Fleur de lis emblems on cover. One of 25 copies numbered on Japanese vellum, illustrated number 17 of 25. Versified by Edward Thomson. 11½" tall. Fine. $850.00

HENRY IV. *A Caveat for France, Upon the Present Evils that It Now Suffereth. Together with the Remedies Necessarie for the Same.* London: 1588. Small quarto, Cosway binding, full red morocco, elaborate gilt decorated covers and spine. Portrait of Henry IV set into the front cover. First edition. Near fine. $9,600.00

HENRY, O. *Works.* Garden City, New York: 1917. Twelve octavo volumes. Contemporary three-quarter brown morocco gilt. Near fine. $975.00

HERBERT, Edward Lord of Cherbury. *The Life and Reign of King Henry the Eighth.* London: Thomas Whitaker, 1649. Full calf. Raised bands with red morocco label. Small folio. Illustrated with frontispiece portrait of Henry VII. First edition. Near fine. $975.00

HERBERT, George. *The Remains of the Sweet Singer of the Temple George Herbert.* London: Pickering, 1836. Two volumes. Full red morocco by W. Strong. Highly gilt spine and cover. All edges gilt. Gauffered edges. 6½" tall. Fine. $600.00

HERBERT, Edward, Lord of Cherbury. *The Life and Reign of King Henry the Eighth.* London: 1683. Contemporary full calf. Folio. Illustrated with frontispiece portrait of Henry VIII. Sixth edition. Near fine. $875.00

HERBERT, George. *Poetical Works.* London: 1870. Contemporary full vellum gilt. 12mo. Illustrated. Near fine. $150.00

HERRICK. *The Fables of Aesop.* New York: Hurd and Houghton, 1865. Full green morocco. All edges gilt. Illustrated with 111 engravings. 7½" tall. Near fine. $265.00

HERODOTUS. *The History. A New English Version.* London: John Murray, 1880. Four volumes. Three-quarter tan calf gilt. Raised bands, gilt decorated spines with green and red morocco labels. Fourth edition of Rawlinson's translation. Near fine. $890.00

HEWLETT, Henry G. *The Heroes of Europe.* London: Bickers and Bush, 1860. Full tan calf. Prize binding with marbled edges. Illustrated. 6" tall. Near fine. $145.00

HIGGINS, Godfrey. *The Celtic Druids.* London: 1829. Contemporary full brown calf. Quarto. Illustrated with numerous plates and maps. First edition. Near fine. $650.00

HILL, W. Henry, Arthur F., and Alfred E. *Antonio Stradavari: His Life and Work (1644 – 1737).* London: 1902. Full green morocco. Illustrated with color plates and in-text illustrations. First edition, one of 100 copies. Near fine. $2,400.00

HOFFMAN, Heinrich. *The English Struwwelpeter.* London: 1890. Three-quarter calf. Slim quarto. Illustrated. Later edition. Near fine. $375.00

HOGARTH, George. *Memoirs of the Musical Drama.* London: Richard Bentley, 1838. Two volumes. Three-quarter green morocco. Gilt decorated spines. First edition. Near fine. $450.00

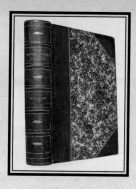

HOFLAND, T.C. *The British Anglers Manual or the Art of Angling.* London: How & Parsons, 1841. Three-quarter green morocco. Top edges gilt. Illustrated with steel and wood engravings. Very good. $275.00

HOGARTH, William. *The Works.* Including the *Analysis of Beauty and Five Days Peregrination.* Philadelphia: George Barrie, 1900. Ten volumes. Three-quarter red morocco. Raised bands, ornate spines. Royal 8vo. Illustrated with engraved plates. Near fine. $2,100.00

HOGG, Robert, and MOORE, Thomas. *The Florist and Pomologist.* London: 1863 – 66. Four volumes. Contemporary three-quarter green calf gilt. First edition with hand-colored lithographic plates of fruits and flowers. Near fine. $2,100.00

HOLLYER, Samuel. *Old New York.* New York: 1911. Two volumes. Large quarto. Full gilt paneled crushed blue morocco, gilt decorated spines. One hundred etchings of New York landmarks. Near fine. $3,600.00

HOLLAND, J.G. *Christ and the Twelve.* Springfield: Bill Nichols & Co., 1869. Full black calf. Highly gilt spine and covers, all edges gilt. Illustrated. 10½" tall. Near fine. $375.00

HOLLAND, J.G. *The Life of Abraham Lincoln.* Springfield, Massachusetts: Bill Gurdon, 1866. Full maroon morocco. Illustrated with steel engravings. Marbled edges. First edition. Near fine. $425.00

HOLMES, Oliver Wendell. *The Complete Poetical Works of Oliver Wendell Holmes.* Boston: Houghton Mifflin Co., 1895. Full tree calf. All edges gilt. Cambridge edition, Riverside Press. 8¼" tall. Near fine. $240.00

HOLME, Charles. *The Gardens of England.* London, Paris, and New York: The Studio, 1907 – 1908. Three-quarter green morocco by Zaehnsdorf. Raised bands with gilt spine. Thick quarto. Illustrated. Near fine. $450.00

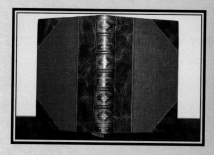

HOLMES, Oliver Wendell. *The Guardian Angel.* Boston: Ticknor and Fields, 1867. Modern three-quarter morocco, flame stitch blue. First edition. Tipped in note from Oliver Wendell Holmes. 7" tall. Near fine. $550.00

HOLMES, Oliver Wendell. *The Works of Oliver Wendell Holmes.* Boston and New York: Houghton, Mifflin and Co., 1899. Fourteen volumes (only six shown). Three-quarter butterscotch calf. Top edges gilt. Highly gilt spine. 8" tall. Near fine. $2,100.00

HOLMES, Richard R. *Queen Victoria*. London: Boussod, Valadon & Co., 1897. Full maroon morocco. Royal family coat of arms in gilt on covers. Watercolor hand-painted frontis, illustrations throughout. White silk moiré doublures and endpapers. Top edges gilt. 13" tall. Near fine. $1,400.00

HOLMES, F.M. *Firemen and Their Exploits: With Some Account of the Rise and Development of Fire-Brigades*. London: 1899. Full calf. Octavo. Illustrated with full-page illustrations. First edition. Near fine. $450.00

HOLMES, Oliver W. *The Works*. Boston and New York: Houghton, Mifflin & Co., 1900. Fifteen volumes. Three-quarter brown morocco gilt. Raised bands and gilt panels. Illustrated and photogravures. Near fine. $1,800.00

HOLMES, Richard R. *Queen Victoria*. London and Paris: Boussod, Valadon & Co., 1897. Full red morocco by Zaehnsdorf. Folio. Illustrated. Near fine. $900.00

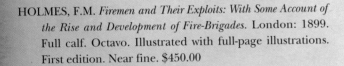

HOOD, J.B. *Advance and Retreat*. New Orleans: Hood Orphan Memorial Fund, 1880. Three-quarter brown calf by Launder and Mac-Donald. Top edges gilt. Illustrated with maps. First edition. 9" tall. Near fine. $390.00

HOOD, Thomas. *Hood's Own*. London: E. Moxon, Son & Co., 1873. Two volumes. Full butterscotch calf. Marbled edges. Highly gilt. Illustrated. Near fine. $295.00

HOOD, Thomas. *The Works of Thomas Hood*. London: E. Moxon Son & Co., 1869. Ten volumes. Three-quarter red morocco. Marbled edges. Illustrated. 7" tall. Near fine. $1,250.00

HOMER. *The Iliad and The Odyssey*. London: 1931. Two volumes. Octavo. Original full morocco. Illustrated by Fritz Kredel. *The Iliad* is one of only 1,450 copies. *The Odyssey* is one of only 1,300 copies. Near fine. $1,300.00

HOMER. *The Iliad of Homer. Translated by Mr. Pope*. London: Printed by W. Bowyer for Bernard Lintot, 1715 – 1720. Six volumes. Contemporary full calf, small folio. First edition. Illustrated with engraved frontispiece portrait by Vertue. Near fine. $6,700.00

HOOKE, N. Esq. *The Roman History from the Building of Rome to the Ruin of the Commonwealth*. London: F.C. and J. Rivington, 1818. Eleven volumes. Full tan calf. Raised bands, gilt panels and edges. Illustrated. Near fine. $1,700.00

HOPE, Laurence. *The Garden of Kama and other Love Lyrics from India*. London: William Heinemann, 1919 – 1920. Three volumes. Full green morocco gilt. Raised bands, gilt panels. Near fine. $575.00

HOPLEY, Catherine C. *Rambles and Adventures In The Wilds Of The West*. London: The Religious Tract Society, circa 1870. Three-quarter green calf. Illustrated. Near fine. $125.00

HORNE, Alistair. *The Price of Glory, Verdun 1916*. New York: St. Martin's Press, 1963. Full navy morocco by Bayntun. All edges gilt. Illustrated, Marceau book plate. 8" tall. Fine. $140.00

HORNE, Charles. *The Great Events of the Great War.* National Alumni, 1920. Seven volumes. Full black calf. Highly gilt cover. Top edges gilt. Leather inlaid inner covers and doublures, silk moiré endpapers. Registered edition. Illustrated. 9½" tall. Fine. $650.00

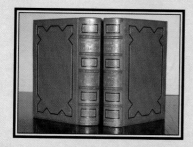

HORNE, R.H. *The New Spirit of the Age.* London: Smith, Elder & Co., 1844. Two volumes. Full tan calf by Bayntun. Highly gilt spine and covers, all edges gilt. Extra illustrated with 62 extra plates, 20 of which are in color. Tan silk moiré doublures and endpapers. 8" tall. Fine. $1,100.00

HORNE, R. H. *The History of Napoleon.* London: Robert Tyas, 1841. Two large octavo volumes. Contemporary full polished brown calf gilt. Raised bands with black morocco labels, marbled boards. First edition. Illustrated with full page illustrations. Near fine. $375.00

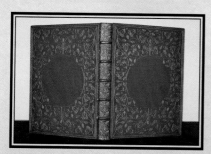

HOUSMAN, Laurence. *All Fellows.* London: Kegan Paul, 1896. Full maroon morocco. Highly gilt spine and covers with gold embossed flowers on covers and spine. All edges gilt. Illustrated. First edition signed by the author. 7½" tall. Near fine. $650.00

HOUGHTON, Walter R. *Kings of Fortune or the Triumphs and Achievements of Noble, Self-made Men.* Chicago: 1888. Modern calf. Thick octavo. Illustrated with numerous wood-engraved plates. $150.00

HOW, W.W. *Hanibal.* London: Seeley & Co., 1899. Full red morocco by Relfe Brothers. Marbled edges. Near fine. $175.00

HOWE, Henry. *Adventures and Achievements of Americans.* New York: George F. Tuttle, 1858. Full black calf. Marbled edges. Illustrated with hand-colored frontis and pull-out map. First edition. 9½" tall. Near fine. $295.00

HOWE, Henry. *The Great West.* Cincinnati: Henry Howe, 1852. Full maroon calf hand-tooled binding. Marbled edges. Illustrated with hand-colored frontis. Light foxing. 9" tall. Very good. $575.00

HOWE, Henry. *The Great West.* New York: George F. Tuttle, 1859. Full black calf. Hand-tooled binding. Marbled edges. Hand-colored plates. 9" tall. Very good. $475.00

HOWE, Henry. *The Travels and Adventures of Celebrated Travelers in the Principal Countries of the Globe.* New York: George F. Tuttle, 1860. Full black morocco. Hand-tooled binding. Marbled edges. Illustrations hand-colored in oil colors, mezzotint engravings and wood cuts. Light foxing. 9" tall. Near fine. $450.00

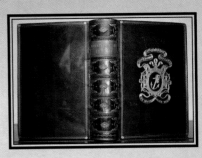

HOWSON, Rev. J.S., and CONYBEARE, Rev. W.J. *The Life and Epistles of St. Paul.* London: Longmans, Green, and Co., 1875. Full navy morocco. Highly gilt spine and covers, marbled edges. 7" tall. Near fine. $225.00

HOWELL, James. *The Familiar Letters of James Howell.* Boston and New York: Houghton, Mifflin and Co., 1907. Three volumes. Full multi-layered morocco inset inner covers. Silk moiré endpapers with top edges gilt. 7½" tall. Near fine. $1,250.00

HUC, M. *The Chinese Empire.* London: Longman, Brown, Green & Longman's, 1855. Two volumes. Three-quarter black morocco by Zaehnsdorf. Illustrated with pull-out colored maps. Second edition. Near fine. $450.00

HOWELLS, W.D. *A Little Swiss Sojourn.* New York: Harper & Brothers, 1893. Full green morocco with all edges gilt. Illustrated. With slipcase. 5¼" tall. Fine. $375.00

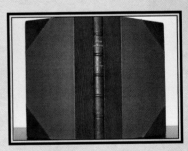

HUDSON, W. H. *Green Mansions, A Romance of the Tropical Forest.* New York: The Limited editions Club, 1935. Three-quarter green morocco by Sangorski & Sutcliffe. Top edges gilt. Illustrated. First edition. With slipcase. 11" tall. Near fine. $450.00

HOWIE, James. *The Scots Worthies: Their Lives and Testimonies.* London, Glasgow and Edinburgh: Blackie & Son, 1876. Three-quarter green calf. Marbled edges. Illustrated with steel engravings, sepia-tone engravings and hand-colored engravings. Fine. $475.00

HUGHES, Thomas. *Alfred the Great.* London: MacMillan and Co., 1881. Full navy morocco with marbled edges. Illustrated. 7" tall. Near fine. $265.00

HUGHES, Thomas. *David Livingstone.* London: MacMillan and Co., 1908. Full tree calf by Lawrence. Marbled edges. Illustrated with pull-out map. 7" tall. Near fine. $225.00

HUGO, Victor. *Les Miserables.* **New York: Carleton, 1842. Three-quarter black calf. Marbled edges. Two volumes bound as one volume. New endpapers, mildly foxed. First American edition. 9" tall. Very good. $425.00**

HUGO, Victor. *Les Miserables.* Bruxelles: 1862. Ten volumes bound in five. Thick octavo. Contemporary three-quarter blue calf gilt. First edition. Near fine. $2,800.00

HUGO, Victor. *Les Miserables.* London: Hurst and Blackett, 1862. Three octavo volumes. Three-quarter tan calf. Raised bands and leather labels. Near fine. $1,800.00

HUGO, Victor. *Les Miserables.* New York: Carleton, 1862. Five octavo volumes. Three-quarter calf. Translated from French by Charles E. Wilbour. Near fine. $1,700.00

HUGO, Victor. *Les Miserables.* Paris: Emile Testard, 1890. Five volumes. Three-quarter red morocco gilt. Large quarto. "Edition Nationale." Near fine. $1,400.00

HUGO, Victor. *Les Miserables.* **New York: Thomas Y. Crowell & Co., 1887. Five volumes. Three-quarter butterscotch calf. Top edges gilt. Illustrated edition. 7½" tall. Near fine. $950.00**

HUGO, Victor. *Novels Complete and Unabridged.* Edinburgh: John Grant, 1903. Fourteen volumes. Three-quarter burgundy morocco gilt. Ribbed gilt decorative spines. Near fine. $1,650.00

HUGO, Victor. *Novels Dramas and Selected Poems.* Philadelphia: George Barrie & Son, 1893. Forty-one volumes. Full brown morocco gilt. Green leather doublures, raised bands, gilt on panels. Near fine. $4,500.00

HUGO, Victor. *The Novels Complete and Unabridged.* New York and Boston: E.B. Hall & Co., 1893. Twenty volumes. Three-quarter wine morocco gilt, floral gilt on spines. Illustrated with etchings. The Buckner Library edition. Near fine. $3,000.00

HUGO, Victor. *The Novels Complete and Unabridged.* Philadelphia: George Barrie, 1892. Forty-one volumes. Three-quarter red morocco. Gilt decorated spines with raised bands. Illustrated. Edition de Bibliophile, one of only 250 sets. Near fine. $3,400.00

HUGO, Victor. *The Works.* Boston: circa 1900. Thirty octavo volumes. Three-quarter blue morocco gilt. Illustrated with over 200 frontispieces and full page illustrations. "International Limited Edition," one of only 1,000 sets. Near fine. $3,300.00

HUGO, Victor. *The Works.* Philadelphia: G. Barrie, 1892 – 97. Twenty-one volumes (consisting of 14 in fiction, five in drama, and selected poems in two volumes). Original red morocco gilt. Small folio. Raised bands, gilt dentelles, and marbled endpapers. Illustrated with over 100 full-page engravings. Near fine. $3,900.00

HUGO, Victor. *Victor Hugo's Works.* **Philadelphia and New York: John Wanamaker, n.d., circa 1870. Ten volumes. Three-quarter tan calf. Top edges gilt. Illustrated. 7½" tall. Near fine. $1,100.00**

HUME, Martin A.S. *Sir Walter Raleigh*. London: T. Fisher Unwin, 1903. Full red morocco. Prize binding with marbled edges. Illustrated with pull-out map. 7½" tall. Near fine. $175.00

HUMPHREYS, Henry Noel. *The Miracles of our Lord*. London: Longman & Co., 1848. Black calf spine, with high relief papier maché covers. Illuminated. All edges gilt. 6½" tall. Near fine. $850.00

HULME, Frederick Edward. *Familiar Wild Flowers*. London: Cassell and Company, 1894. Five octavo volumes. Three-quarter green calf. Each volume has a hand-painted floral centerpiece. Illustrated with hundreds of full-page color lithographs. Near fine. $1,500.00

HUME & SMOLLETT. *History of England*. London: T & J Allman, 1825. Thirteen volumes. Full tan polished calf gilt. Raised bands and ornate gilt spines. Near fine. $1,600.00

HUMPHREYS, Henry Noel. *The Parables of Our Lord*. London: Longman and Co., 1847. Black gutta percha binding. All edges gilt. Illuminated. First edition. 6½" tall. Near fine. $1,200.00

HUMPHREYS, Henry Noel. *Sentiments and Similes of William Shakespeare*. London: Longman, Green, Longman, Roberts & Green, n.d., circa 1855. Black calf spine, papier mache binding. All edges gilt. Terra cotta insets on front and back covers, gold gilt border pages, chromo frontis. 7½" tall. Near fine. $1,200.00

HUMPHREYS, Noel. *The Book of Ruth, from the Holy Scriptures*. London: Longman, Brown, Green and Longmans, 1850. Hand-carved raised spine and covers, relievo binding with detailed flowers and vines. Illuminated. Illustrated by Owen Jones. 6½" tall. Near fine. $1,100.00

HUMPHREYS, Henry Noel. *Sentiments and Similes of William Shakespeare*. London: Longman, Brown, Green and Longmans, 1851. Black calf spine, papier maché binding. All edges gilt, terra cotta insets on front and back cover, gold gilt border pages, chromo frontis. 8" tall. First edition. Near fine. $1,450.00

HUMPHREYS, Noel. *The Origin and Progress of the Art of Writing.* London: David Bogue, 1854. Gutta percha binding. Illuminated. 17" tall. Near fine. $1,250.00

HUMPHREYS, Henry Noel. *Sentiments and Similes of William Shakespeare. A Classified Selection of Similes, Definitions, Descriptions, and Other Remarkable Passages in the Plays and Poems of Shakespeare.* London: 1857. Small quarto. Black papier mache boards with terra cotta cameos and crimson paper underlays, with all gilt edges. Second edition. Near fine. $1,300.00

HUNTER, W.W. *The Indian Empire: Its History People and Products.* London: Trubner & Co., 1882. Contemporary half calf gilt. Raised bands, red leather labels. 8vo. Illustrated. First edition. Near fine. $275.00

HUNTER, William S. *Hunter's Ottawa Scenery.* Ottawa City: 1855. Modern calf. Thin folio. Illustrated with many views of Ottawa and a large folding map. First edition. Near fine. $1,100.00

HUTCHINSON, Francis. *An Historical Essay Concerning Witchcraft.* London: 1718. Octavo. Contemporary full paneled brown calf. First edition. Near fine. $1,900.00

HUTCHINSON, Horace G. *Golf.* London: Longmans, Green & Co., 1890. Full blue morocco gilt. Illustrated by Thomas Hodge and Harry Furniss. Near fine. $625.00

HUTCHINSON, Horace, editor. *Big Game Shooting.* London and New York: 1905. Two volumes. Octavo. Three-quarter green morocco gilt. First edition, with 100 photographic plates. Near fine. $600.00

HYDE, Mabel. *Jingles from Japan.* San Francisco: 1901. Three-quarter calf. Octavo. Illustrated by Helen Hyde in the Japanese style. First edition. Near fine. $375.00

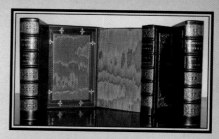

INGERSOLL, Robert G. *The Works of Robert Ingersoll.* New York: The Dresden Publishing Co., 1901. Thirteen volumes (only four shown). Full blue morocco by The Monastery Hill Bindery. Highly gilt spine and cover with top edges gilt. Blue silk moiré doublures and endpapers. 9" tall. Near fine. $1,850.00

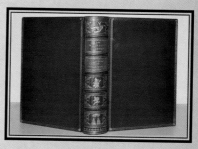

INGOLDSBY, Thomas. *The Ingoldsby Legends.* London: J.M. Dent & Sons, 1930. Full blue crushed levant morocco by Riviere. All edges gilt. Illustrated by Arthur Rackham. 7" tall. Fine. $600.00

INGOLDSBY, Thomas. *The Ingoldsby Legends.* London: Richard Bentley, 1877. Full maroon morocco. All edges gilt. Illustrated by George Cruikshank, John Leech and John Tenniel. Near fine. $475.00

IBSEN, Henrik. *Works.* New York: 1911 – 1912. Sixteen octavo volumes. Three-quarter blue morocco by Stikeman. Illustrated with frontispiece in each volume. Near fine. $2,200.00

IRELAND, William H. *Life of Napoleon Bonaparte.* London: 1828. Four volumes. Octavo. Twentieth century full navy morocco gilt by Bumpus. Illustrated with 27 folded engravings hand colored by George Cruikshank. Near fine. $2,100.00

INMAN, John. *The History of the World*. New York: Henry Bill, 1860. Two volumes. Full black calf with marbled edges. Thirty-four hand-colored plates. First edition. 9½" tall. Near fine. $650.00

IRELAND, William H. *Life of Napoleon Bonaparte*. London: 1828. Four octavo volumes. Nineteenth century full red morocco gilt by Riviere & Son. First edition, first issue. Illustrated by George Cruikshank. Near fine. $2,100.00

IRVING, Washington. *A History of New York, From the Beginning of the World to the End of the Dutch Dynasty*. Philadelphia: 1819. Two small octavo volumes. Contemporary full brown calf gilt. Third edition. Near fine. $500.00

IRVING, Washington. *Astoria, or Anecdotes of an Enterprise Beyond the Rocky Mountains*. Philadelphia: Carey, Lea & Blanchard, 1836. Two octavo volumes. Three-quarter calf. Illustrated. First edition. Near fine. $575.00

IRVING, Washington. *Life of George Washington*. New York: 1855 – 1859. Five octavo volumes. Three-quarter green morocco gilt. First edition. Illustrated with numerous portraits, maps, and battle plans. Near fine. $1,250.00

IRVING, Washington. *Old Christmas*. London: MacMillan and Co., 1876. Full navy crushed levant morocco by Riviere. Highly gilt spine and covers. First Caldecott edition, illustrated by Caldecott. Rust colored silk doublures and endpapers, original covers and spine bound in. All edges gilt. 7" tall. Fine. $750.00

IRVING, Washington. *Life of George Washington*. With Extra Illustrations. New York: 1859. Five volumes expanded to ten. Large octavo. Three-quarter green morocco gilt. First edition. Illustrated with over 400 engraved portraits, maps, and battle plans (some double-page). Near fine. $2,100.00

IRVING, Washington. *Rip Van Winkle and The Legend of the Sleepy Hollow*. London: MacMillan and Co., 1907. Full tree calf by Riviere. Marbled edges. Illustrated with 53 illustrations by Boughton. 7½" tall. Near fine. $350.00

IRVING, Washington. *A History of the Life and Voyages of Christopher Columbus*. London: John Murray, 1828. Four volumes. Full red morocco by Frost & Co. All edges gilt. Illustrated with pull-out folding maps in each volume. First edition, precedes first American edition. With slipcase. 8½" tall. Near fine. $1,250.00

IRVING, Washington. *Rip Van Winkle and the Legend of the Sleepy Hollow*. London: MacMillan & Co., 1910. Full purple morocco by Bickers. All edges gilt. Illustrated with 53 engravings by Boughton. 7½" tall. Near fine. $475.00

IRVING, Washington. *The Land of Sleepy Hollow and The Home of Washington Irving.* New York and London: G.P. Putnam, 1887. Full green morocco, all edges gilt, folio. White silk doublures and white silk moiré endpapers. #583 of 600 copies. First edition. The Letter Press edition. 14" tall. Near fine. $1,200.00

IRVING, Washington. *The Sketch Book of Geoffrey Crayon.* New York and London: G.P. Putnam, 1895. Two volumes. Full green morocco. Highly gilt spines and covers. VanTassel edition, Knickerbocker Press. Illustrated, each page boxed with colored vine borders. Top edges gilt. Near fine. $1,250.00

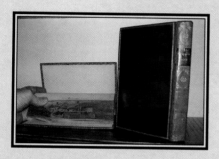

IRVING, Washington. *The Sketch Book of Geoffrey Crayon.* London: John Murray, 1822. Two volumes. Full brown calf. Fore-edge painting on each volume, one of Westminster Abbey and one of Ann Hathaway's cottage. Housed in slipcase. 8¾" tall. Near fine. $1,850.00

IRVING, Washington. *The Works of Washington Irving.* London: Henry G. Bohn, 1859. Ten volumes. Full sky blue calf. Marbled edges. Highly gilt. 7¼" tall. Fine. $2,600.00

IRVING, Washington. *The Works of Washington Irving.* With: *Life of George Washington.* London: George Bell and Sons, 1868 – 1877. Fourteen octavo volumes. Contemporary full tan calf gilt. Raised bands with green and red morocco labels. Engraved frontispieces in each volume. Near fine. $1,600.00

IRVING, Washington. *The Works.* New York and Philadelphia: 1864 – 1874. Thirteen octavo volumes. Three-quarter green calf gilt. "Knickerbocker Edition," illustrated with engraved frontispiece and full-page illustrations. Near fine. $1,500.00

IRVING, Washington. *The Works.* Philadelphia: J.B. Lippincott & Co., New York: G.P. Putnam and Sons, 1868 – 70. Twenty-six small octavo volumes. Three-quarter tan calf gilt. Gilt decorated spines, red and green morocco labels. "Riverside Edition," illustrated with engraved frontispiece in each volume. Near fine. $1,900.00

IRVING, Washington. *The Works of Washington Irving.* New York: G.P. Putnam's Sons, n.d., circa 1865. Twenty-eight volumes (only five shown). Three-quarter butterscotch calf. Marbled edges. 7½" tall. Near fine. $2,200.00

IRVING, Washington. *Works.* Philadelphia: J.B. Lippincott & Co., 1872. Twenty-six volumes. Three-quarter red calf gilt. Ribbed gilt decorated spines. Near fine. $1,300.00

IVES, Jospeh C. *Report upon the Colorado River of the West.* Washington: 1861. Full black morocco gilt. Quarto. Illustrated with maps and full-page engravings and lithographs. First edition. Near fine. $1,200.00

JACKSON, William. *The Christian's Legacy.* Philadelphia: William Jackson, 1852. Full red morocco. Highly gilt spine and covers, all edges gilt. 7" tall. Near fine. $285.00

JAMES, George Wharton. *The Indians of the Painted Desert Region.* Boston: Little, Brown & Co., 1904. Three-quarter tan calf. All edges gilt. Illustrated from photographs. 8¼" tall. Near fine. $475.00

JAMES, G.P.R. *The Life and Times of Louis the Fourteenth.* London: Richard Bentley, 1838. Four volumes. Full butterscotch calf. Marbled edges. Illustrated. Second edition. 8½" tall. Near fine. $525.00

JAMES, Henry. *Washington Square.* Leipzig: Bernhard Tauchnitz, 1881. Two volumes in one. Three-quarter blue morocco. First European edition. 6" tall. Very good. $125.00

JACKSON, A. V. William. *History of India.* London: The Grolier Society, 1906. Nine volumes. Full green morocco gilt, doublures in crimson levant. Designs in white morocco and gilt. Printed on Japanese vellum paper. Limited edition of 50 sets. Illustrated. Near fine. $5,100.00

JACKSON, Lady Charlotte. *The French Court and Society.* London: Richards Bently & Co., 1881. Ten volumes. Full navy morocco gilt by Baytun. Raised bands, gilt panels. Illustrated. Near fine. $1,800.00

JACOB, Giles. *An Historical Account of the Lives and Writings of Our Most Considerable English Poets.* London: E. Curll, 1720. Contemporary blind paneled calf. Raised bands with red morocco label. Near fine. $175.00

JAMES, Henry. *The Novels and Tales of Henry James.* New York: Charles Scribner's Sons. 1907 – 18. Twenty-six octavo volumes bound in 25. Three-quarter green morocco gilt over green cloth boards. Each volume has a frontispiece illustration by Alvin L. Coburn. First collected edition, limited issue. Near fine. $9,700.00

JAMES, Marquis. *Andrew Jackson, The Border Captain.* Indianapolis: The Bobbs - Merrill Co., 1933. Two volumes. Three-quarter red morocco. Top edges gilt. Illustrated. First edition. 9" tall. Near fine. $575.00

JAMESON, Mrs. *Jameson's Works.* London: Longman, Green, Longman, Roberts & Green, 1865. Six volumes. Full tree calf by Riviere. Highly gilt spine with all edges gilt. Illustrated. Second edition. 9" tall. Near fine. $1,100.00

JAMES, Henry. *The Two Magics. The Turn of the Screw. Covering End.* London: 1898. Full red morocco by Riviere. Octavo. First edition, early issue. Near fine. $1,100.00

JAMES, Henry. *Works.* New York: Charles Scribner's Sons, 1922. Twenty-six volumes. Full maroon calf. Gilt decorated spines in a floral pattern. New York edition. Near fine. $6,800.00

JEFFERIES, Richard. *The Life of the Fields.* London: Chatto & Windus, 1892. Full butterscotch calf by Relfe Brother. Marbled edges. Prize binding. 7" tall. Near fine. $150.00

JAMESON, Mrs. *Shakespeare's Heroines. Characteristics of Women, Moral, Poetical and Historical.* London: George Bell and Sons, York Street, Covent Garden, 1891. Full blue calf. Prize binding with marbled edges, signed by Relfe Brothers. 7" tall. Near fine. $180.00

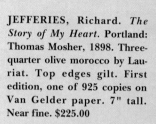

JEFFERIES, Richard. *The Story of My Heart.* Portland: Thomas Mosher, 1898. Three-quarter olive morocco by Lauriat. Top edges gilt. First edition, one of 925 copies on Van Gelder paper. 7" tall. Near fine. $225.00

JASPER, Theodore. *The Birds of North America.* Columbus: Jacob Studer, 1878. Three-quarter black calf. 119 color plates and 700 different species and varieties of North American birds by Theodore Jasper. With: *Ornithology, or the Science of Birds,* from the Text of Dr. Brehn. With 212 illustrations by Theodore Jasper. Two volumes complete. All edges gilt. Near fine. Folio size. $1,400.00

JEAFFRESON, John C. *A Book About Lawyers.* London: Hurst and Blackett, 1867. Four volumes. Full brown morocco gilt. Illustrated with over 200 engravings. Near fine. $800.00

JEFFERSON, Thomas. *Memoir Correspondence and Miscellanies.* Boston: Gray & Bowen, 1830. Four volumes. Full blue morocco gilt. Raised bands, gilt panels. Second edition. Near fine. $1,700.00

JEFFERSON, Thomas. *Memoirs, Correspondence, and Private Papers of Thomas Jefferson.* London: 1829. Four octavo volumes. Late nineteenth century three-quarter brown morocco. Illustrated with frontispiece in each volume and numerous plates by Stikeman. First English edition. Near fine. $2,000.00

JEFFERSON, Thomas. *Notes of the State of Virginia.* With an Appendix. Boston: 1802. Three-quarter calf. Thick 12mo. Illustrated with frontispiece portraits and folding map and charts. Early Boston edition. Near fine. $975.00

JEFFERSON, Thomas. *Notes on the State of Virginia. With an Appendix.* New York: 1801. Octavo. Contemporary full tree calf rebacked with original black morocco spine label laid down. Early American edition with folding maps and charts. Near fine. $1,400.00

JEFFERSON, Thomas. *The Works of Thomas Jefferson.* New York: G.P. Putnam's Sons, 1904. Twelve octavo volumes. Modern half dark brown morocco gilt. Red morocco spine labels and raised bands. "Collector's Federal Edition," one of only 600 sets. Collected and edited by Paul Leicester Ford. Frontispiece portraits and title pages printed on Japanese vellum paper. Near fine. $2,300.00

JERROLD, Douglas. *A Man Made of Money*. London: Punch Office, 1849. Full green morocco. First edition in book form. Illustrated by Leech. 7½" tall. Near fine. $325.00

JERDEN, William. *National Portrait Gallery of Illustrious and Eminent Personages of the 19th Century*. London: 1830. Five volumes. Full blue morocco gilt. Near fine. $975.00

JERROLD, Blanchard. *Life of Gustave Doré*. London: W.H. Allen & Co., 1885 – 1891. Two volumes. Three-quarter red morocco. Gilt decorated spines. Includes 138 illustrations by Doré. Near fine. $450.00

JERROLD, Blanchard. *The Life of George Crukshank*. London: Chatto & Windus, 1883. Full wine morocco by Kelligram. Raised bands, gilt decorated covers and silk doublures. Near fine. $950.00

JESSE, J. Heneage. *Literary and Historical Memorials of London*. London: Richard Bentley, 1847. With: *London and Its Celebrities. A Second Series of Literary and Historical Memorials of London*. London: Richard Bentley, 1850. Four octavo volumes all together. Full red morocco gilt. Gilt decorated spines, dentelles and marbled endpapers. Illustrated. First editions. Near fine. $700.00

JESSE, John H. *Memoirs of the Court of England from the Revolution in 1688 to the Death of George II*. London: Richard Bentley, 1843. Three volumes. Full polished tan calf. Raised bands, ornate spines with red and brown labels. First edition. Near fine. $475.00

JOHNES, Thomas. *Sir John Froissarts Chronicles*. London: Longman, Hurst, Rees, Orme, 1808. Full tan calf by Riviere. Twelve volumes (only three shown). Yellow edges. 9" tall. Very good. $850.00

JOHNES, Thomas. *The Chronicles of Enguerrand de Monstrelet*. London: Longman, Hurst, Rees, Orme and Brown, 1810. Twelve volumes (only three shown). Full tan calf by Riviere. Yellow edges. 9" tall. Very good. $800.00

JEVONS, W. Stanley. *Pure Logic or the Logic of Quality Apart from Quantity*. London: Edward Stanford, 1864. Three-quarter calf. Small octavo. First edition. Near fine. $1,800.00

JOHNSON and BUEL. *Battles and Leaders of the Civil War*. New York: The Century Co., 1887. Four volumes. Three-quarter brown calf. Illustrated. First edition. 11" tall. Near fine. $950.00

JOHNSON, Fletcher. *The Life of Sitting Bull & The History of the Indian War*. Edgewood, 1891. Half maroon morocco. All edges gilt. Illustrated. Near fine. $325.00

JOHNSON, Henry F. *Johnson's Household Book of Nature — Mammalia*. New York: Henry J. Johnson, 1880. Full black calf. Highly gilt cover. All edges gilt. Many chromolithographic illustrations. First edition. 9½" tall. Near fine. $485.00

JOHNSON, Rossiter. *A Short History of The War of Secession.* Boston: Ticknor and Co., 1888. Three-quarter brown calf. Illustrated. First edition. 9½" tall. Near fine. $375.00

JOHNSON, Samuel. *Political Tracts.* London: 1776. Half brown calf. Octavo. First edition. Near fine. $675.00

JOHNSON, Susannah. *A Narrative of the Captivity of Mrs. Johnson. Containing an Account of Her Sufferings, during the Four Years with the Indians and French.* Walpole, New Hampshire: 1796. Contemporary full tan calf with brown morocco spine label. 12mo. First edition. Near fine. $3,800.00

JOHNSON, Russiter. *Campfire and Battlefield.* New York: Bryan, Taylor & Co., 1894. Full red morocco. Highly gilt cover. Gold gilt soldier on front cover, embossed leather, all edges gilt. Profusely illustrated. First edition. 13½" tall. Near fine. $550.00

JOHNSTON, William Preston. *The Life of General Sidney Albert Johnston.* New York: D. Appleton & Co., 1880. Three-quarter dark brown calf by Launder and MacDonald. Top edges gilt. Illustrated. Near fine. $300.00

JOHNSON, Robert Underwood, and BUEL, Clarence Clough. *Battles and Leaders of the Civil War.* New York: 1887 – 88. Four volumes. Quarto, mid twentieth century three quarter brown morocco gilt. First edition. Numerous illustrations, maps, and war plans. Near fine. $1,100.00

JOHNSTON, William. *The History of Inventions and Discoveries.* London: Longman, Hurst, Rees, Orme and Brown, 1817. Four volumes. Full tan calf. Two volumes have cracked hinges. 8½" tall. Very good. $390.00

JOHNSON, Samuel. *A Dictionary of the English Language.* London: J. Johnson, 1799. Replica speckled calf by Sean Richards. Eleventh edition. Near fine. $425.00

JOHNSON, Samuel. *A Dictionary of the English Language.* London: W. Strahan, 1775. Two thick folio volumes. Three-quarter polished calf. Raised bands and marbled boards. First edition. Near fine. $8,500.00

JOMINI, Baron. *Life of Napoleon.* New York: D. Van Nostrand, 1864. Five volumes. Three-quarter brown morocco. Gilt decorated spines. Translated from French by HW Halleck. Near fine. $675.00

JOHNSON, W. Fletcher. *Life of Wm. Tecumseh Sherman.* Edgewood Publishing, 1891. Three-quarter red morocco. All edges gilt. Illustrated. First edition. 8" tall. Very good. $160.00

JONES, J. William. *Personal Reminiscences, Anecdotes, and Letters of General Robert E. Lee.* New York: D. Appleton and Co., 1876. Three-quarter dark brown calf by Launder and MacDonald. Top edges gilt. Illustrated. Near fine. $950.00

JONES, Owen. *The Preacher.* **London: Longman & Co., 1849. Hand-carved wooden covers. All edges gilt. Eighteen chromolithographic illustrations in gold, red, blue, and green. Illustrations by Owen Jones. First edition. 11½" tall. Near fine. $2,500.00**

JONES, George M. *Travels in Norway, Sweden, Finland, Russia and Turkey; also on the coasts of The Sea of Azor and of The Black Sea.* London: John Murray, 1827. Two volumes. Three-quarter calf. Raised bands and gilt decorated. Illustrated with maps. Near fine. $275.00

JONES, Rev. J. William. *Personal Reminiscences, Anecdotes and Letters of General Robert E. Lee.* **New York: D. Appleton & Co., 1874. Full dark brown calf. All edges gilt. Illustrated. First edition. 9" tall. Near fine. $950.00**

JONES, Rev. J. Wm. *Christ in the Camp or Religion in Lee's Army.* **Richmond: B.F. Johnson & Co., 1888. Three-quarter red morocco. All edges gilt. Illustrated. Contains letter from author. 8½" tall. Very good. $550.00**

JOSEPHUS, Flavius. *Famous and Memorable Works of Josephus. A Man of Much Honour and Learning Among the Jews.* London: Humphrey Lownes, 1609. Translated from Latin and French by Theodore Lodge. Full polished tree calf with raised bands. Second edition in English. Near fine. $2,800.00

JORDAN, Thomas, and PRYOR, J.P. *The Campaigns of Lieutenant-General N.B. Forest.* **New Orleans, Memphis and New York: Blelock & Co., 1868. Three-quarter brown calf by Launder and MacDonald. Top edges gilt. Illustrated. First edition. 8" tall. Near fine. $350.00**

JOSEPHUS, Flavius. *The Whole Genuine and Complete Works of Flavius Josephus, the Learned and Authentic Jewish Historian.* With: *A Continuation of the History of the Jews, from Josephus down to the Present Time. Written by G.H. Maynard.* London: C. Cooke, circa 1785. Contemporary full tree calf with raised bands. Illustrated with copper-engraved plates. Maynard's translation of Josephus. Near fine. $1,200.00

JOSEPHUS, Flavius. *The Whole Works.* London: 1785. Contemporary full tree calf gilt, re-backed with the original spine. First Clarke edition. Folio. Illustrated with frontispiece portrait and full-page copper engravings. Near fine. $975.00

JOYCE, James. *Finnegans Wake.* London: 1939. Three-quarter calf. First edition, one of only 425 large paper copies signed by the author. Near fine. $6,500.00

JOYCE, James. *Ulysses.* Paris: 1922. Quarto. Mid 20th century full blue morocco gilt, custom slipcase. First edition, one of only 750 copies. Near fine. $8,800.00

JOYCE, James. *Ulysses.* Paris: Shakespeare & Co., 1927. Three-quarter blue morocco. Raised bands, gilt panels. Near fine. $675.00

JUDSON, Ephraim. *Sermons on Important Subjects; Collected from a Number of Ministers.* Hartford: 1797. Contemporary full brown calf. Octavo. First edition. Near fine. $225.00

JUNOT, Madame. *Memoirs of the Emperor Napoleon.* London: M. Walter Dunne, 1901. Three volumes. Three-quarter green morocco. Ribbed gilt decorated spines. Illustrated with full-page portraits and photogravures printed on Japanese vellum. Near fine. $380.00

KANE, Elisha Kent. *Arctic Explorations: The Second Grinnell Expedition in Search of Sir John Franklin.* Philadelphia: Childs & Peterson, 1856. Two octavo volumes. Contemporary three-quarter brown calf gilt. Raised bands with black and red morocco labels. First edition. Illustrated with the author's sketches. Near fine. $850.00

KAVANAGH, Julia. *Woman in France During the 18th Century. And French Women of Letters. With Portraits.* London: Smith, Elder & Co., 1850 – 1862. Four volumes. Three-quarter wine morocco. Raised bands, gilt panels. Near fine. $850.00

KANE, Elisha Kent. *Arctic Explorations: The Second Grinnell Expedition.* Philadelphia: Childs & Peterson, 1856. Two volumes. Three-quarter green morocco by Frost. Purple and red spine labels, top edges gilt. Upwards of 300 engravings and pull-out maps. 8½" tall. Near fine. $850.00

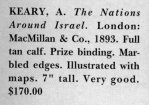

KEARY, A. *The Nations Around Israel.* London: MacMillan & Co., 1893. Full tan calf. Prize binding. Marbled edges. Illustrated with maps. 7" tall. Very good. $170.00

KEATS, John. *The Complete Poetical Works and Letters.* Boston and New York: Houghton, Mifflin & Co., 1899. One volume. Three-quarter tan calf gilt with marbled boards. Cambridge edition. Near fine. $160.00

KEATS, John. *The Poetical Work.* London: Oxford University Press. 1925. Full blue calf by Riviere. Near fine. $180.00

KEATS, John. *The Poetical Works.* London: Oxford University Press, 1921. Full dark blue crushed morocco gilt by Riviere. Small octavo. Raised bands and marbled endpapers. Illustrated with frontispiece portrait. Near fine. $220.00

KEATS, John. *The Eve of St. Agnes.* Boston: Estes & Lauriat, 1887. Full brown relievo binding. Heavily embossed front cover with image. All edges gilt. Limited to 280 copies of which this is #147. Illustrated by Edmund Garrett. Foxed. 12½" tall. Very good. $550.00

KEATS, John. *The Poetical Works of Keats.* London: George Bell, 1876. Full red morocco. All edges gilt. Edited by Lord Houghton. The Alpine edition. Very good. $180.00

KEENE, J. Harrington. *Fly-Fishing and Fly-Making for Trout, Bass, Salmon, Etc.* New York: Forest and Stream, 1891. Small octavo. Three-quarter calf. Second edition. Illustrated with various materials for making flies. Near fine. $425.00

KELLOGG, Robert. *Life and Death in Rebel Prisons.* Hartford: L. Stebbins, 1865. Three-quarter black calf. Illustrated. First edition. Light foxing. 7" tall. Very good. $240.00

KELTIE, John S. *History of the Scottish Highlands.* London: William Mackenzie, circa 1900. Two volumes. Three-quarter red morocco gilt. Quarto. Illustrated. Near fine. $425.00

KELTIE, John S. *History of the Scottish Highlands.* London: William Mackenzie, circa 1900. Two volumes. Three-quarter blue morocco gilt. Quarto. Raised bands, gilt panels, and marbled boards. Illustrated. Near fine. $450.00

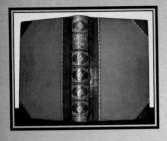

KELTIE, John S. *The Works of Daniel De Foe.* Edinburgh: William P. Nimmo, 1880. Three-quarter blue morocco with marbled edges. 9½" tall. Near fine. $150.00

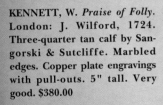

KENNETT, W. *Praise of Folly.* London: J. Wilford, 1724. Three-quarter tan calf by Sangorski & Sutcliffe. Marbled edges. Copper plate engravings with pull-outs. 5" tall. Very good. $380.00

KENNET, Basil. *The Lives and Characters of the Ancient Grecian Poets.* London: Abel Swall, 1697. Contemporary paneled calf. Original red morocco label. Illustrated with numerous illustrations and three engraved plates. Near fine. $450.00

KHAYYAM, Omar. *The Rubaiyat of Omar Khayyam.* London: Robert Riviere & Son, Ltd., 1928. Octavo. Full polished red calf gilt. Raised bands and marbled endpapers. Cover is decorated with gilt arabesques. Full page illustrations by Gilbert James. Hand-colored frontispiece. Near fine. $680.00

KILLIGREW, Thomas. *Comedies and Tragedies.* London: 1664. Folio. Early twentieth century full black morocco gilt. First edition with the scarce engraved frontispiece portrait. Near fine. $2,100.00

KENT, Charles. *The Poetical Works of Thomas Moore.* London: George Routledge and Son, n.d., circa 1890. Full tan calf. Prize binding. Marbled edges. 8" tall. Near fine. $310.00

KINGSLEY, Charles. *Kingsley's Works.* London and New York: MacMillan and Co., 1893. Thirteen volumes (only four shown). Full tan calf by Zaehnsdorf. All edges gilt. Eversley edition. 7" tall. Fine. $1,400.00

KINGSLEY, Charles. *The Novels, Poems and Life of Charles Kingsley.* New York: J.F. Taylor and Company, 1898. Fourteen octavo volumes. Full blue crushed levant morocco gilt. Raised bands, gilt decorated spines. Red and white morocco gilt rose inlays on spines and covers. Illustrated with original watercolors and hand-colored frontispiece plates. Autograph edition, one of only 26 sets. Near fine. $4,800.00

KINGSLEY, Charles. *The Water Babies.* London: circa 1890. Octavo. Three-quarter blue levant morocco gilt. Later illustrated edition with 17 plates by Arthur Dixon. Near fine. $400.00

KINGSTON, W.H.G. *In the Wilds of Florida.* London: T. Nelson and Sons, 1882. Full navy morocco. Prize binding with marbled edges. Illustrated. 7" tall. Near fine. $240.00

KINGSTON, William, and RATHBONE, Charles. *Great African Travelers.* London: George Routledge and Sons, 1890. Full green morocco. Prize binding with highly gilt spine and cover, marbled edges. One hundred illustrations. First edition. 8" tall. Near fine. $425.00

KIPLING, Rudyard. *Collection of Works.* London: MacMillan & Co., 1904 – 1937. Thirty-three octavo and small octavo volumes. Three-quarter red morocco gilt over red cloth boards by Dangorski & Sutcliffe. First editions of *Traffics and Discoveries, A Diversity of Creatures, The Years Between, Letter of Travel, A Book of Words, Limits and Renewals, Something of Myself.* Remainder are later editions. Near fine. $4,400.00

KIPLING, Rudyard. *The Collected Works of Rudyard Kipling.* Doubleday, Doran & Co., 1941. Twenty-eight volumes (only five shown). Three-quarter blue morocco. Top edges gilt. One of 1,010 sets signed by Kipling. Burwash edition. Spines lightly faded. First American edition. 9" tall. Near fine. $8,000.00

KIPLING, Rudyard. *The Collected Works of Rudyard Kipling.* Twenty-eight volumes. New York: Doubleday, Doran & Co., 1941. Octavo. Original red cloth gilt. The Burwash edition, one of 1,000 sets signed by Kipling. Near fine. $6,400.00

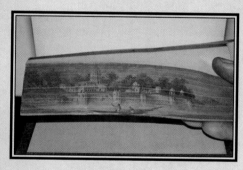

KIPLING, Rudyard. *From Sea to Sea.* London: MacMillan and Co., 1924. Full maroon morocco by Riviere. Highly gilt cover with all edges gilt. Fore-edge painting by Miss Currie three different views: Surseya, Ghaut, and Cawnpore. The endpaper is signed by Currie and has this fore-edge number "8." 7" tall. Near fine. $7,500.00

KIPLING, Rudyard. *The Jungle Book and the Second Jungle Book.* London: MacMillian & Co., 1895. Two volumes. First edition. Full blue morocco by Bayntun. Near fine. $3,200.00

KIPLING, Rudyard. *The Jungle Book and The Second Jungle Book.* London: MacMillan & Co., 1894 – 95. Two volumes. First editions. Illustrated. Full blue morocco gilt by Sangorski & Sutcliffe. Front cover of volume one is decorated with three gilt elephants. Volume two is decorated with a gilt snake. Near fine. $3,600.00

KIPLING, Rudyard. *Just So Stories for Little Children.* London: 1902. Three-quarter navy calf. Royal octavo. Illustrated. First edition, first issue. Near fine. $850.00

KIPLING, Rudyard. *The Jungle Book and The Second Jungle Book.* London: MacMillan & Co., 1894 – 95. Two volumes. Octavo. Full dark blue morocco gilt by Riviere. Watered silk doublures and endpapers. Housed in a blue cloth and marbled paper cardboard slipcase. First editions, illustrated by Kipling's father, J. Lockwood Kipling. Near fine. $4,300.00

KIPLING, Rudyard. *The Jungle Book and, The Second Jungle Book.* London: MacMillan & Co. 1894 – 95. Two volumes. First editions. Illustrated. Full blue morocco, floral gilt decorated spines by Sangorski & Sutcliffe. Near fine. $3,200.00

KIPLING, Rudyard. *The Bombay Edition of the Works of Rudyard Kipling.* Twenty-six volumes. London: MacMillan & Co., 1913 – 27. Octavo. Contemporary full navy crushed morocco gilt by Riviere & Son. Gilt decorated spines with red morocco onlays. One of only 1,050 sets. Signed by Kipling in Volume 1. Near fine. $11,000.00

KIPLING, Rudyard. *The Jungle Book.* With: *The Second Jungle Book.* London: MacMillan & Company, 1894, 1895. Two volumes. Octavo. Full blue morocco, all edges gilt. First editions. Illustrated by Kipling's father. Near fine. $3,200.00

KIPLING, Rudyard. *The Jungle Book and the Second Jungle Book.* **London: MacMillan & Co., 1894 – 1895. Two volumes. Full tan calf. All edges gilt. With illustrations by J.L. Kipling. First edition. 7½" tall. Near fine. $2,750.00**

KIPLING, Rudyard. *The Jungle Book.* With: *The Second Jungle Book.* London: 1894 – 95. Two volumes. First editions. Full morocco by Riviere. Pictorial inlays. Near fine. $3,600.00

KIPLING, Rudyard. *The Jungle Book.* With: *The Second Jungle Book.* London: MacMillan & Co., 1894 – 95. Two volumes. Octavo. Original blue cloth gilt. Gilt pictorial cover and spine. Fine half-morocco slipcase. First editions, illustrated by his father. Near fine. $2,900.00

KIPLING, Rudyard. *The Jungle Book.* With: *The Second Jungle Book.* London: 1894 – 95. Two volumes. Octavo. Full tree calf. Custom three-quarter morocco gilt clamshell box. First editions. Illustrated by Kipling's father. Near fine. $3,100.00

KIPLING, Rudyard. *The Jungle Books.* London: MacMillan & Co., 1894. Two volumes. Three-quarter blue morocco gilt by Bayntun, gilt vignettes on spine. Illustrated by J.L. Kipling. Near fine. $1,800.00

KIPLING, Rudyard. *The Works of Rudyard Kipling.* Garden City: Doubleday, Page & Co., 1925. Thirteen volumes. Octavo. Contemporary three-quarter blue morocco gilt. Gilt decorated spines, marbled endpapers. Mandalay edition. Near fine. $2,600.00

KIPLING, Rudyard. *Works.* London: MacMillan & Co., 1913. Twenty-six volumes. Full red morocco gilt. Includes all of Kipling's major titles. Near fine. $3,300.00

KIPLING, Rudyard. *Works.* London: 1902 – 19. Twenty-four volumes. Octavo. Early Twentieth century three-quarter red calf gilt. Contains all of Kipling's major works, including *Kim, The Jungle Book, Just So Stories.* With first editions of *The Five Nations, Traffics and Discoveries,* and *Verse: Inclusive Edition 1885 – 1918.* Near fine. $4,200.00

KNIGHT, Charles. *A History of England.* London: Brodbury, Evans & Co., 1820. Eight volumes. Three-quarter red morocco gilt, marbled boards and raised bands. Near fine. $800.00

KNIGHT, Charles. *Half Hours with the Best Authors.* **London: Frederick Warne and Co., n.d., circa 1860. Two volumes. Full tan calf. Marbled edges. 8½" tall. Near fine. $350.00**

KNIGHT, Charles. *Old England, A Pictorial Museum.* **London: James Sangster, n.d., circa 1860. Two volumes. Full green morocco. 15" tall. Very good. $1,100.00**

KIPLING, Rudyard. *The Writings in Prose and Verse of Rudyard Kipling.* **New York: Charles Scribner, 1899. Thirty-two volumes. Three-quarter maroon morocco by Altier. Top edges gilt. Near fine. $4,500.00**

KNIGHT, Charles. *The Pictorial Edition of the Works of Shakespeare.* **London: Charles Knight, 1839. Eight volumes. Full sky blue morocco by M. Dent. Top edges gilt. Extra illustrated with 200 plates. Near fine. $1,750.00**

KNIGHT, Charles. *The Popular History of England.* London: James Sangster and Co., 1862. Eight volumes. Full tree calf with marbled edges. Illustrated. 10" tall. Near fine. $1,750.00

KNIGHT, E. Cornelia. *Marcus Flaminius.* London: T. Cadell & W. Davies, 1808. Two volumes. Full mottled calf, flame stitched. Marbled edges. Second edition. 7" tall. Fine. $575.00

KOBBE, Gustav. *The Complete Opera Book.* London: Putnam, 1935. Full red morocco by Riviere. Highly gilt spine and cover with all edges gilt. Illustrated. 8½" tall. Fine. $375.00

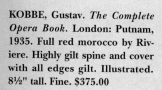

KOENIG, Gustav. *The Life of Luther.* London: Longman, Brown, Green and Longmans, 1855. Full navy morocco. Marbled edges. Illustrated. Housed in slipcase. Fine. $375.00

KNOLLES, Richard. *Historie of the Turkes....* With: *The Lives and Conquests of the Othoman Kings and Emperours unto the yeare 1621.* London: Adam Islip, 1621. Full calf. Raised bands, gilt spine with red morocco label. Illustrated with numerous portraits. Third edition. Near fine. $1,100.00

KNOX, John. *An Answer to a Great Number of Blasphemous Vacillations Written by an Anabaptist and Adversary to God's Eternal Predestination.* London: Thomas Charde, 1591. Dark brown crushed morocco gilt by Riviere & Son. Raised bands, spine gilt with leaf and acorn design. Second edition. Near fine. $2,500.00

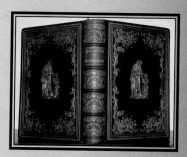

KRUMMACHER, F.A. *The Parables of Frederick Adolphus Krummacher.* Philadelphia: Lindsay & Blakiston, 1854. 8½" tall. Near fine. $380.00

LA BREE, Ben. *The Confederate Soldier in the Civil War.* Louisville: The Courier-Journal Job Printing Co., 1895. Three-quarter black calf. Red edges. Illustrations on every page, spine replaced. Folio. 16" tall. Very good. $1,600.00

LA CROIX, Paul. *Manners, Customs and Dress During the Middle Ages and During the Renaissance Period.* London: 1874. With: *Military and Religious Life in the Middle Ages and at the Period of the Renaissance.* London: 1874. With: *Science and Literature in the Middle Ages and at the Period of the Renaissance.* London: 1878. Three volumes. Royal octavo. Contemporary full green morocco gilt. Gilt decorated spines. Early English translations. Illustrated with over 1,200 in-text wood engravings and 42 hand-finished chromolithographic plates. Bound by Bickers & Son. Near fine. $1,700.00

LA CROIX, Paul. *Military and Religious Life in the Middle Ages and at the Period of the Renaissance.* London: Bickers & Son, circa 1875. Four volumes. Royal octavo. Contemporary three-quarter red morocco gilt, pink endpapers by Morrell. English translations. Illustrated with over 1,000 in-text wood engravings and numerous chromolithographic plates by F. Kellerhoven. Near fine. $475.00

LA CROIX, Paul. *Military and Religious Life in the Middle Ages.* New York: D. Appleton and Co., 1874. **Full blue morocco with all edges gilt. Illustrated with chromo plates and 400 engravings on wood. 10" tall. Near fine. $425.00**

LA CROIX, Paul. *The Arts in the Middle Ages and at the Period of Renaissance.* With: *Manners, Customs, and Dress During the Middle Ages.* With: *Military and Religious Life in the Middle Ages.* With: *Science and Literature in the Middle Ages.* With: *The XVIIIth Century, Its Institutions, Customs and Costumes.* London: 1878. Five royal octavo volumes. Contemporary three-quarter red morocco gilt by Birdsall. Illustrated with numerous chromolithographic plates and thousands of wood-engravings. Near fine. $1,700.00

LA CROIX, Paul. *The Works of Paul LaCroix.* London: Bickers and Son, n.d., circa 1881. Five volumes. Three-quarter red morocco. Highly gilt spine, many chromolithographic illustrations. 10½" tall. Near fine. $1,400.00

LA FAYETTE. *Memoirs of General La Fayette.* Hartford: Barber & Robinson, 1825. Full tan calf with yellow edges. First edition with all three plates. 7" tall. Very good. $375.00

LA FONTAINE, J. de. *Tales and Novels. In Verse.* London: 1896. Two volumes. Royal octavo. Modern full burgundy morocco gilt. Limited illustrated edition, one of only 520 copies. Numerous engravings, some by Eisen. Near fine. $950.00

LA FONTAINE, Jean de. *Fables of La Fontaine.* Illustrated by Gustave Dore. London and New York: circa 1870. Three-quarter green morocco. Thick folio. Early edition. Illustrated with frontispiece portrait of La Fontaine. Near fine. $675.00

LA FONTAINE, Jean de. *Tales and Novels in Verse.* Paris: J. Lemonnyer; New York: E. F. Bonaventure, 1883. Two volumes. Octavo. Full red morocco gilt, raised bands and ornately gilt spines. In custom cloth slipcase. Limited edition by R.W. Smith. Eighty-five steel-engraved plates by Eisen. With frontispiece portraits of LaFontaine and Eisen. Near fine. $380.00

LAING, Malcolm, and JAMIESON, R. *The History of Scotland with Letters from a Gentleman in the North Of Scotland.* London: J. Mawman, 1804 and 1822. Six volumes. Three-quarter tan calf. Top edges gilt. 9" tall. Near fine. $850.00

LAMB, Charles and Mary. *Tales From Shakespeare.* London: Bickers and Sons, 1885. Full green morocco by Bickers. Highly gilt spine with marbled edges. Twelve illustrations in permanent photography from the Boydell Gallery. 9" tall. Near fine. $245.00

LAMB, Charles and Mary. *Tales from Shakespear.* London: Printed for Thomas Hodgkins, at the Juvenile Library, 1807. Two 12mo volumes. Late nineteenth century brown crushed levant morocco gilt by Riviere & Son. In a cloth slipcase. Twenty engraved plates by Wm. Mulready. Near fine. $2,300.00

LAMB, Charles. *English Dramatic Poets.* London: J.M. Dent and Co., 1893. Two volumes. Full maroon morocco by Morley. Highly gilt spine and cover, top edges gilt. Gold gilt stamped floral pattern on covers. Large paper edition. 8" tall. Near fine. $550.00

LAMB, Charles and Mary. *Tales from Shakespeare. Designed for the Use of Young Persons.* London: 1807. Two volumes. Nineteenth century three-quarter dark green morocco gilt. 12mo. First edition, first issue. Twenty copper plates engraved by William Blake. Near fine. $2,400.00

LAMB, Charles and Mary. *Tales from Shakespeare.* London: J.M. Dent, 1909. Quarto. Limited edition, one of only 750 copies signed by Arthur Rackham. Full black morocco by Zaehnsdorf, raised bands, gilt tilting. Near fine. $1,400.00

LAMB, Charles and Mary. *Tales from Shakespeare.* Philadelphia: circa 1900. Octavo. Modern full red calf gilt. Illustrated. Near fine. $275.00

LAMB, Charles. *Tales From Shakespeare.* London: M.J. Godwin and Co., 1816. Two volumes. Full brown speckled calf by Wallis. All edges gilt. Illustrated with 20 plates by Blake. 7" tall. Near fine. $800.00

LAMB, Charles. *The Adventures of Ulysses.* London: Printed by T. Davidson, Whitefriars, 1808. Full red morocco by Riviere & Son. Highly gilt dentelles with top edges gilt. First edition for the Juvenile Library. The text is a skillful adaptation of Chapman's *Homer.* 7½" tall. Near fine. $875.00

LANE, Edward William. *An Account of the Manner and Customs of the Modern Egyptians.* London: John Murray, 1871. Two volumes. Full blue morocco. Prize binding, marbled edges. Illustrated. 7½" tall. Near fine. $575.00

LAMB, Charles. *Beauty and the Beast.* London: Field & Tuer, The Leadenhall Press, circa 1886. Small quarto. Cosway binding. Full light brown crushed levant morocco bound by Riviere & Son. Front and back covers have miniature scenes on ivory under glass by C.B. Currie. Comes with a cloth clamshell case. Near fine. $16,000.00

LAMB, Charles. *Tales from Shakespear, Designed for the Use of Young Persons.* London: 1810. Two volumes. Full tan calf gilt by Zaehnsdorf. Illustrated with 20 engraved plates. Second edition. Near fine. $480.00

LAMB, Charles. *The Life and Works.* New York: circa 1900. Twelve volumes. Limited edition, one of only 130 sets. Full autumn leaf levant. The India House edition. Near fine. $3,100.00

LAMPING, Clemens, and FRANCE, M. de. *French in Algiers. Crusades in Africa and a Five Months Captivity Among the Arabs.* New York: 1848. Three-quarter calf. Small octavo. Early American edition. Near fine. $375.00

LANE, Edward William. *The Thousand and One Knights.* London: Charles Knight and Co., 1839. Three volumes. Full red morocco by Hayday. All edges gilt. Illustrated. First edition of the first English translation. 10" tall. Near fine. $1,900.00

LANFREY, P. *The History of Napoleon First*. London and New York: MacMillan & Co., 1871. Four volumes. Three-quarter red morocco by Sangorski & Sutcliffe. Top edges gilt. Highly gilt. 8¾" tall. Fine. $1,100.00

LANDSEER, Edwin. *The Works*. London: 1879. Contemporary three-quarter brown morocco gilt by Harrison. Folio. Illustrated with 54 engraved plates and numerous in-text woodcuts. Near fine. $800.00

LANE, Edward William. *The Thousand and One Nights*. London: Gibbings & Co. Ltd., and Philadelphia: J.B. Lippincott, 1896. Six volumes. 12mo. Contemporary three-quarter red polished calf gilt by Sangorski & Sutcliffe. Later edition of Lane's translation. Near fine. $800.00

LANFREY, P. *The History of Napoleon the First*. London and New York: MacMillan & Co., 1871. First English edition. Four volumes. Full tan calf by Zaehnsdorf. Red labels, raised bands, ornate gilt on spines. Near fine. $900.00

LANFREY, Pierre. *The History of Napoleon I*. London and New York: MacMillan & Co., 1871 – 1879. Four volumes. Octavo. Three-quarter blue morocco with Napoleonic emblems. Marbled boards and endpapers. First English edition. Near fine. $1,000.00

LANG, Andrew. *The Blue Fairy Book. The Red Fairy Book. The Green Fairy Book. The Yellow Fairy Book. The Pink Fairy Book. The Grey Fairy Book. The Violet Fairy Book. The Crimson Fairy Book. The Brown Fairy Book. The Orange Fairy Book. The Olive Fairy Book. The Lilac Fairy Book*. London: Longmans, Green, and Co., 1889 – 1910. Twelve small octavo volumes. First editions. Illustrated by H.J. Ford, J.P. Jacomb Hood, and Lancelot Speed. Three-quarter harlequin morocco over cloth boards by Sangorski & Sutcliffe. Spines tooled and lettered in gilt. Complete set of *The Fairy Books*. Near fine. $6,750.00

LANG, Andrew. *The Green Fairy Book*. London: Longman's, 1892. Three-quarter green morocco gilt. First edition. Near fine. $350.00

LANG, Andrew. *Books and Bookmen*. New York: George J. Coombes, 1886. Full blue morocco. Heavily gilt floral covers by Fletcher Battershall. Top edges gilt. Highly gilt spine. First edition. 8" tall. Near fine. $850.00

LANG, Andrew. *History of English Literature*. New York, Bombay & Calcutta: Longmans, Green and Co., 1913. Full tree calf by Bickers. 7½" tall. Near fine. $225.00

LANG, Andrew. *The Red Book of Animal Stories*. New York and Bombay: Longmans, Green and Co., 1899. Full navy crushed levant morocco by Bayntun. All edges gilt. Illustrations by H.J. Ford, original cloth binding bound in rear. First edition. 7" tall. Near fine. $450.00

LANGHORNE, John and William. *Plutarch's Lives*. London: C. Dilly, 1792. Six volumes. Full contemporary tan calf with green and red labels. Near fine. $975.00

LANGHORNE, John D. D. and William. *Plutarchs Lives*. London: Printed for C. Dilly, 1792. Six volumes. Full brown calf. 8" tall. Very good. $625.00

LARCOM, Lucy. *The Poetical Works of Lucy Larcom.* Boston and New York: Houghton Mifflin & Co., 1884. Full maroon morocco. All edges gilt. The Riverside Press, illustrated, Household edition. 8" tall. Near fine. $110.00

LAS CASAS, *Count de. Journal of the Private Life and Conversations of the Emperor Napoleon at Saint Helena.* London: Henry Colburn, 1824. Eight volumes bound in four. Octavo. Contemporary full red polished calf gilt. Marbled endpapers and edges. Illustrated with hand-colored plates. Near fine. $890.00

LAS CASAS. *Journal of the Private Life and Conversations of the Emperor Napoleon at Saint Helena.* London: Printed for Henry Colburn & Co., 1823. Eight volumes. Full green morocco. Illustrated with pull-out maps. First edition. 8½" tall. Near fine. $1,200.00

LATILLA, Eugenio. *Cartoons in Outline Illustrations of the Gospels with Illuminated Text.* Florence: 1848. Full brown calf relievo binding. Heavy relief carved covers with figures in all corners and central raised cartouche and eight white porcelain feet. Gauffered edge, hand-painted frontis and illuminated text, light foxing. All edges gilt. 17" tall. Very good. $1,700.00

LATIMER, Hugh. *Twenty-seven Sermons Preached by the Ryght Reverende...Maister Hugh Latimer.* London: 1562. Full brown calf. Small thick octavo. First edition. Near fine. $1,700.00

LAWRENCE, John. *The History and Delineation of the Horse....* Albion Press, 1809. Contemporary calf. Raised bands, gilt decorated spine and covers. Illustrated. Near fine. $975.00

LAWRENCE, T.E. *Revolt in the Desert.* London: 1927. Quarto. Original half brown morocco. First edition, one of only 315 large-paper copies, illustrated by Lawrence. Includes a folding map. Near fine. $1,350.00

LE CLERC, SEBASTIEN. *Practical Geometry: Or, A New and Easy Method of Treating That Art.* London: John Bowles, 1768. Contemporary red morocco. Raised bands with green morocco label. Marbled endpapers. Illustrated with 82 full-page engraved illustrations. Fifth edition. Near fine. $375.00

LE SAGE, Alain Rene. *The Adventures of Gil Blas of Santillane.* London: W. Strahan, 1782. Four volumes. Speckled calf gilt by Brentano's. Raised bands with gilt spine compartments and red and black morocco labels. Marbled endpapers. Illustrated with 33 engraved plates and frontispieces. Translated by Tobias Smollett. Fifth edition. Near fine. $650.00

LE SAGE, Alain Rene. *The Adventures of Gil Blas.* Translated by Martin Smart. London: 1807. Four volumes. 12mo. Full red morocco gilt by Bayntun. Illustrated with hand-colored engravings. Later edition. Near fine. $750.00

LEAKE, Isaac Q. *Memoir of the Life and Times of General John Lamb, an Officer of the Revolution.* Albany: 1850. Three-quarter black morocco gilt. Octavo. Illustrated with numerous engravings and a frontispiece portrait. First edition. Near fine. $550.00

LEE, Fitzhugh. *General Lee.* New York: D. Appleton & Co., 1894. Three-quarter blue morocco. Large paper edition, one of only 1,000 copies. Near fine. $575.00

LECKY, William Edward Hartpole. *Democracy in America.* London and Bombay: Longmans & Green, 1896. Two volumes. Three-quarter red morocco by Frost. Top edges gilt. First edition, signed by author. Fine. $900.00

LEE, Rawdon B. *A History & Description of the Modern Dogs of Great Britain and Ireland*. London: Horace Cox, 1906. Two volumes. Three-quarter red morocco. Marbled edges. Illustrated by Arthur Wardle. 8¾" tall. Near fine. $1,150.00

LESAGE, A.R. *The Adventures of Gil Blas*. London: Richard Phillips, 1807. Four volumes. Full two-tone mottled tree calf by Bayntun. Highly gilt spine and cover with top edges gilt. One hundred copper plate illustrations. 7" tall. Fine. $850.00

LEE, Robert E. *Memoirs of the War in the Southern Department of the U.S.* New York: University Publishing, 1870. Three-quarter calf. Marbled edges. Illustrated. Good. $675.00

LEE, Guy Carleton, and THORPE, Francis Norton. *The History of North America*. Philadelphia: 1907. Twenty volumes. Octavo. Full navy morocco gilt. Near fine. $3,600.00

LEE, Henry, Jr. *Observations on the Writings of Thomas Jefferson*. New York: 1832. Three-quarter calf. Octavo. First edition. Near fine. $450.00

LEIGHTON, John M. *The Lake of Scotland*. Glasgow: Joseph Swan, 1836. Three-quarter green morocco gilt. Raised bands, gilt panels. Illustrated. Near fine. $600.00

LEMERY, Louis. *A Treatise of All Sorts of Foods, Both Animal and Vegetable: Also of Drinkables*. London: T. Osborne, 1745. Original speckled calf. Raised bands with double gilt rules and spine label. Translated from the French by D. Hay, MD. Fourth English edition. Near fine. $650.00

LEVER, Charles. *Roland Cashel*. London: Chapman and Hall, 1855. Two volumes. 8vo. Full red morocco gilt by Zaehnsdorf. Red silk doublures and endpapers. First edition. Illustrated by Phiz. Near fine. $560.00

LIEVRE, Edouard. *Works of Art in the Collections of England*. London: 1873. Contemporary three-quarter calf. Tall folio. Illustrated by the author. Near fine. $800.00

LEIGHTON, Robert. *A Practical Commentary Upon the First Easter of St. Peter*. London: James Duncan, 1835. Full brown calf diced morocco. 8" tall. Near fine. $325.00

LEE, Robert E. *Robert E. Lee in Memoriam*. Louisville: 1879. Octavo. Original full brown morocco, gilt decorated cover with Lee's initial's in medallion. Near fine. $750.00

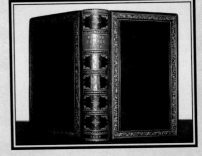

LEVER, Charles. *Roland Cashel*. London: Chapman & Hall, 1850. Full navy morocco with marbled edges. Illustrated by Phiz Browne. First edition. 9" tall. Near fine. $825.00

LEVER, Charles. *The Novels of Charles Lever.* London: Downey & Co., 1872. Thirty-seven volumes (only three shown). Full tan calf by Zaehnsdorf. Blue morocco insets in all corners of the covers and all edges gilt. Three page signed letter from Lever. Autograph alphabet edition. Many hand-colored illustrations. Limited to only 26 volumes, one for each letter of the alphabet. 9" tall. Fine. $5,800.00

LINCOLN, Abraham. *The Complete Works.* Harrogate, Tennessee: 1926. Twelve octavo volumes. Three-quarter red morocco gilt. Illustrated with frontispiece portraits in each volume. Limited "Sponsor's" edition. Near fine. $1,900.00

LINCOLN, Abraham. *The Complete Works.* New York: 1905. Twelve volumes. Octavo. Three-quarter burgundy morocco gilt. Limited edition, one of only 300 sets. Frontispiece portraits in each volume. Gettysburg edition de Grand Luxe. Near fine. $2,100.00

LINCOLN, Abraham. *The Complete Works.* New York: 1905. Twelve volumes. Octavo. Original three-quarter red morocco gilt. Gettysburg Edition de Luxe, one of only 700 sets. Frontispiece portraits in each volume. Near fine. $2,100.00

LINCOLN, Abraham. *The Complete Works.* New York: Francis Tandy Co., circa 1905. Twelve octavo volumes. Full red morocco gilt. Gilt decorated spines and covers. Illustrated. "Biographical Edition." Near fine. $1,250.00

LIVERMORE, Mary A. *My Story of the War: A Woman's Narrative of Four Years Personal Experience.* Hartford: A.D. Worthington and Co., 1889. Three-quarter dark brown calf by Launder and MacDonald. Top edges gilt. Illustrated. Near fine. $275.00

LLOYDS. *Lloyd's Battle History of the Great Rebellion.* New York: H.H. Lloyd & Co., 1866. Full black calf. Highly gilt spine and covers with marbled edges. Illustrated with pull-out maps. Each page is bordered with an illustration. First edition. Hinges have been repaired. 10" tall. Very good. $425.00

LIVINGSTONE, David. *Missionary Travels and Researches in South Africa.* London: 1857. Modern full brown morocco gilt. Thick octavo. Illustrated. First edition. Near fine. $1,100.00

LOCKE, John. *Posthumous Works.* London: A.B. and W.J. Churchill, 1706. Contemporary brown calf gilt. Raised bands, gilt spine compartments and red morocco label. First edition. Near fine. $1,200.00

LOCKE, John. *The Works of John Locke.* London: 1714. Three volumes. Folio. Full paneled brown calf. Near fine. $3,100.00

LOCKE, John. *The Works.* London: 1768. Four volumes. Thick quarto. Contemporary full dark brown calf gilt rebacked and recornered with original spines laid down. Early edition. Near fine. $1,900.00

LOCKHART, Bart. *Memoirs of the Life of Sir Walter Scott.* Edinburgh: Robert Cadell, 1837. Seven volumes. Full tan calf by Lewis. Prize binding. All edges gilt. Tipped in letter from Lockhart. 7" tall. Near fine. $900.00

LOCKHART, J.B. *History of Napoleon*. London: John Murray, 1839. Two volumes. Full purple morocco. Illustrated on steel and wood by Cruikshank. 5¾" tall. Near fine. $475.00

LOCKE, John. *The Works*. London: 1794. Nine octavo volumes. Contemporary full tree calf. Gilt decorated spines. Illustrated with frontispiece portrait. Near fine. $1,400.00

LOCKHART, J.G. *The Life of Napoleon Bonaparte*. London: 1927. Full blue polished calf by Riviere. Illustrated. Near fine. $450.00

LOCKHART, J.G. *The Life of Napoleon Bonaparte*. London: Bickers and Son, Ltd., 1883. Full blue calf with ornate gilt on spine. Illustrated with photography and engravings on wood. Near fine. $550.00

LOCKHART, J.G. *The Life of Napoleon Bonaparte*. London: 1897. Octavo. Contemporary full polished blue calf, gilt-decorated spine. Illustrated. Near fine. $550.00

LOCKWOOD, Luke Vincent. *Colonial Furniture in America*. New York: Charles Scribners, 1913. Two volumes. Three-quarter tan calf. Folio. Illustrated. Near fine. $450.00

LODGE, Edmund. *Portraits of Illustrious Personages of Great Britain*. London: Harding, Mavor and Lepard, 1823 – 34. Twelve volumes. Contemporary full burgundy morocco gilt by Mackenzie. Quarto. Raised bands with all edges gilt. Illustrated. First edition. Near fine. $1,800.00

LOCKHART, J.G. *The Life of Napoleon Bonaparte*. London: Bickers & Sons, 1897. Full maroon morocco. Prize binding with marbled edges. Illustrated with nine photographic plates. 8½" tall. Near fine. $340.00

LOCKHART, John G. *The History of the Ingenious Gentleman Don Quixote of La Mancha*. Boston: Little, Brown & Co., 1870. Four volumes. Three-quarter butterscotch calf. Translated by Motteux. 7" tall. Near fine. $575.00

LOGAN, John A. *The Great Conspiracy, Its Origin and History*. New York: A.R. Hart & Co., 1886. Two volumes. Three-quarter brown calf by Launder and MacDonald. Top edges gilt. Illustrated. 9" tall. Near fine. $525.00

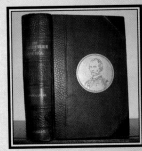

LOGAN, John A. *The Volunteer Soldier*. Chicago and New York: R.S. Peale, 1887. Three-quarter maroon morocco. Gold embossed front cover, marbled edges. Illustrated. First edition. 9½" tall. Near fine. $275.00

LOGAN, John. *The Great Conspiracy*. New York: A.R. Hart & Co., 1886. Full calf. Marbled edges. Maps and illustrations. Near fine. $280.00

LONG, A.L. *Memoirs of Robert E. Lee.* New York, Philadelphia and Washington: J.M. Stoddart & Co., 1886. Full rust calf. All edges gilt. Illustrated with pull-out maps. First edition. 9½" tall. Near fine. $875.00

LONGFELLOW, Henry Wadsworth. *Song of Hiawatha.* Boston: Ticknor and Fields, 1855. Full red morocco. Highly gilt cover, top edges gilt, leather doublures, silk moiré endpapers and slipcase. First edition, first issue with Longfellow signature tipped in. 7" tall. Near fine. $950.00

LONG, A.L. *Memoirs of Robert E. Lee.* New York: J.M. Stoddart and Co., 1887. Three-quarter dark brown calf by Launder and MacDonald. Top edges gilt. Illustrated with pull-out maps. Near fine. $900.00

LONGFELLOW, Henry Wadsworth. *The Complete Poetical Works of Henry Wadsworth Longfellow.* Boston and New York: 1902. Full tree calf with top edges gilt. 270 illustrations. Household edition, Riverside Press. 8" tall. Near fine. $225.00

LONGFELLOW, H. W. *The Works.* Boston and New York: Houghton, Mifflin & Co., 1886. Eleven volumes. Riverside edition. Three-quarter blue morocco gilt. Raised bands and gilt panels. Near fine. $1,400.00

LONGFELLOW, H.W. *The Complete Writings.* Boston and New York: Houghton, Mifflin & Co., 1904. Eleven volumes. Edition DeLuxe. Three-quarter red morocco gilt. Raised bands and gilt panels. Illustrated with portraits and fac-similes. Near fine. $1,800.00

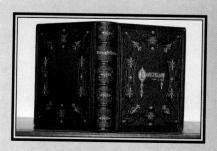

LONGFELLOW, Henry Wadsworth. *The Poetical Works of Henry Wadsworth Longfellow.* London: Frederick Warne & Co., 1879. Full black calf. Embossed and gilt covers, all edges gilt. Illustrated. Has a rare fore-edge painting of Northhampton, Massachusetts, on a English bound book. 8" tall. Fine. $1,200.00

LONGACRE and HERRING. *The National Portrait Gallery of Distinguished Americans.* Philadelphia: Henry Perkins, 1834 – 1839. Four volumes (only one shown). Full red morocco with embossed cover. Illustrated. 11" tall. Near fine. $650.00

LONGFELLOW, Henry Wadsworth. *The Poetical Works of Longfellow.* Boston: Houghton, Mifflin and Co., 1881. Two volumes (only one shown). Full brown calf. Embossed and gilt covers, all edges gilt. Folio. Illustrated. 12" tall. Near fine. $625.00

LONGFELLOW, Henry Wadsworth. *The New England Tragedies.* Boston: Ticknor and Fields, 1868. Full red morocco by Gaz. Multicolored morocco inlays inside covers, silk moiré endpapers, top edges gilt. First edition. 6½" tall. Near fine. $525.00

LONGINUS, Dionysius. *A Treatise of the Loftiness or Elegancy of Speech.* London: John Holford, 1680. Modern polished calf. Flat spine with maroon morocco label. Translated from French. Near fine. $850.00

LOSSING, Benson J. *The Pictorial Field-Book of the Revolution.* New York: Harper & Brothers, 1859. Two volumes. Full black calf. Highly gilt spine and covers with all edges gilt. Deluxe gilt binding. Chromo frontis. 1,100 wood engravings. 10½" tall. Near fine. $1,100.00

LOSSING, Benson J. *Field Book of the War of 1812.* New York: Harper & Brothers, 1868. Three-quarter tan calf. Marbled edges. Illustrated with chromo frontis. First edition. 10" tall. Near fine. $380.00

LOSSING, Benson J. *The Pictorial Field-Book of the Revolution.* New York: Harper & Brothers, 1859. Two volumes. Full black calf. Highly gilt spine and covers with all edges gilt. 10½" tall. Near fine. $1,050.00

LOSSING, Benson J. *Pictorial History of the Civil War in the United States of America.* Philadelphia: George W. Childs, 1866. Three volumes. Three-quarter brown calf. Marbled edges. Illustrated. First edition. 10" tall. Near fine. $725.00

LOSSING, Benson J. *The Pictorial Field-Book of the Revolution.* New York: 1851 – 52. Two volumes. Large octavo. three-quarter contemporary brown calf. First edition, illustrated with 1,100 wood engravings. Near fine. $875.00

LOSSING, Benson J. *Washington and the American Republic.* New York: Virtue and Yorston, 1870. Three volumes. Three-quarter brown morocco gilt. Decorated spines. Illustrated. Near fine. $975.00

LOSSING, Benson J. *Washington and The American Republic.* New York: Virtue & Yorston, 1870. Three volumes. Three-quarter brown calf. All edges gilt. 10" tall. Illustrated. First edition. Near fine. $975.00

LOUDON, Mrs. *Ladies' Flower-Garden of Ornamental Greenhouse Plants.* London: 1848. Contemporary three-quarter green morocco. Quarto. Illustrated with 42 lithographed plates. First edition. Near fine. $3,600.00

LOVER, Samuel. *Legends and Stories of Ireland.* London: Baldwin and Cradock, 1837. Two volumes. Full green calf by Root. Top edges gilt. Prize binding. First and second series. Fourth edition. Fine. $475.00

LOWELL, James Russell. *The Vision of Sir Launfal.* Cambridge: The Riverside Press, 1891. Full purple morocco. Highly gilt spine and covers, original vellum covers and spine bound in. Top edges gilt, silk moiré endpapers, leather inlaid inside covers. Designs by E.H. Garrett, illustrator. One of 100 printed on Japanese paper, with slipcase. 7½" tall. Fine. $675.00

LOVER, Samuel. *Novels and Tales of Samuel Lover.* New York: D. & J. Sadlier & Co., 1881. Five volumes. Three-quarter butterscotch calf with marbled edges. 7½" tall. Near fine. $450.00

LOWELL, James Russell. *The Complete Works of James Russell Lowell.* Cambridge: The Riverside Press. 1904. Sixteen volumes. Edition De Luxe. Limited edition, one of only 1,000 copies. Full deep blue morocco gilt. Matching blue morocco doublures gilt decorated and white silk moiré endpapers. Frontis portrait in volume one. Near fine. $1,900.00

LOWE, E.J. *Beautiful Leaved Plants.* London: Groombridge & Sons, 1861. Half crushed contemporary purple morocco gilt. Near fine. $1,200.00

LOWELL, James Russell. *Heartsease and Rue.* Boston: 1888. Twentieth century full navy morocco gilt by Zaehnsdorf. Octavo. Illustrated with frontispiece portrait of the author. First edition. Near fine. $325.00

LOWELL, James Russell. *The Works of James Russell Lowell.* Boston: Houghton, Mifflin & Co., 1886. Five volumes. Three-quarter butterscotch calf. Marbled edges. 8" tall. Near fine. $550.00

LOWELL, James Russell. *The Complete Poetical Works of James Russell Lowell.* Boston and New York: Houghton Mifflin Co., 1897. Full tree calf with all edges gilt. Cambridge edition, The Riverside Press. 8" tall. Near fine. $225.00

LUBBOCK, Sir John. *Pre-Historic Times.* New York: D. Appleton and Co., 1890. Three-quarter tan calf. Top edges gilt. Illustrated. 9" tall. Very good. $165.00

LUBKE, Dr. Wilhelm. *History of Art.* London: Smith, Elder & Co., 1869. Two volumes. Three-quarter butterscotch calf. Marbled edges. Illustrated. 10" tall. Near fine. $250.00

LUCAS, Joseph. *The Yetholm History of the Gypsies.* Kelso, 1882. Three-quarter calf. Octavo. First edition. Near fine. $275.00

LUCRETIUS CARUS, Titus. *The Epicurean Philosopher, His Six Books De Natura Rerum Done Into English Verse, With Notes.* Oxford: L. Lichfield, 1683. Contemporary calf. Raised bands, blind ruled compartments. Engraved frontispiece. Second edition. Near fine. $750.00

LUDINGTON, Colonel M.I. *Uniform of the Army of the United States From 1774 – 1889.* Washington, D.C.: Quarter Master General, n.d., circa 1890. Three-quarter black calf. Forty-four chromolithographic folio size plates. 17" tall. Very good. $1,500.00

LUDWIG, Emil. *Lincoln.* Boston: Little, Brown & Co., 1930. Full blue morocco. Gilt decorated spine. Illustrated by Alice D. Laughlin. First signed edition. Near fine. $450.00

LUDWIG, Emil. *Napoleon.* London: George Allen & Unwin, 1927. Three-quarter blue morocco. Illustrated. Near fine. $275.00

LYDEKKER, Richard. *The Deer of All Lands.* London: 1898. Quarto. Contemporary three-quarter green morocco gilt. Limited edition, one of only 500 copies. Illustrated with 24 hand-colored plates, photographs, and line drawings. Near fine. $1,800.00

M'KENNEY, Thomas L. *Memoirs, Official Personal with Sketches of Travel Among the Northern and Southern Indians.* New York: Paine and Burgess, 1846. Two volumes bound in one. Three-quarter brown calf. Marbled edges. Illustrated. Light foxing. First edition. 8½" tall. Very good. $425.00

MACAULAY, Lord. *History of England.* London: Longman, Green, 1862. Eight volumes. Tree calf gilt by Riviere. Near fine. $1,500.00

MACAULAY, Lord. *The Works and Life.* London: Longmans, Green & Co., 1898. Ten volumes. Three-quarter blue morocco gilt. Edinburgh edition. Near fine. $1,200.00

MACAULAY, Lord. *The Life and Letters of Lord Macaulay.* London: Longmans, Green, and Co., 1889. Full navy morocco. Prize binding with highly gilt spine and covers, marbled edges. 7" tall. Near fine. $170.00

MACAULAY. *Lord Macaulay's Essays and Lays of Ancient Rome.* London: Longmans, Green and Co., 1888. Full tree calf. Prize binding with marbled edges. Authorized edition. 7½" tall. Near fine. $190.00

MACFALL, Haldane. *A History of Painting.* Boston: D.D. Nickerson & Co., circa 1900. Eight volumes. Three-quarter brown morocco gilt. Raised bands, gilt spines with floral onlays. Quartos. Illustrated with hundreds of color plates. Near fine. $1,800.00

MACKAY, Charles. *Salamandrine*. London: Ingram, Cooke & Co., 1853. Full maroon morocco by Rivingtons. All edges gilt. Inlaid morocco covers. Illustrations drawn by John Gilbert. 11½" tall. Near fine. $1,150.00

MACHIAVELLI, Niccolo. *The Works of the Famous Nicolas Machiavelli.* London: 1675. Contemporary full calf. Folio. First edition in English. Near fine. $5,900.00

MACHIAVELLI, Niccolo. *The Works.* London: Printed for John Starkey, 1675. Folio. Contemporary full calf rebacked. First English edition. Near fine. $4,900.00

MACHIAVELLI, Nicholas. *The Works of the Famous Nicholas Machiavelli.* London: Printed by T.W. for A. Churchill, 1720. Folio. Twentieth century speckled calf gilt. Black leather label with marbled endpapers. Third edition in English. Near fine. $1,800.00

MACKENZIE, Alexander. *Voyages from Montreal, on the River St. Laurence, through the Continent of North America, to the Frozen and Pacific Oceans; In the Years 1789 – 1793.* London: 1801. Quarto. Modern three-quarter olove morocco, original spine label. Near fine. $3,800.00

MACKENZIE, George. *The Lives and Characters of the Most Eminent Writers of the Scots Nation.* Edinburgh: 1708 – 22. Three folio volumes. Contemporary full paneled brown calf. First edition. Near fine. $590.00

MACKENZIE, Henry. *Man of the World.* London: A. Strahan and T. Cadell, 1787. Two volumes. Contemporary flamed calf gilt. Flat spine gilt in compartments with red and blue morocco labels. Fourth edition. Near fine. $475.00

MACKENZIE, William. *The Rustic Bower.* Edinburgh: Oliver & Boyd, 1844. Full green morocco with red, blue, and tan morocco inlays. All edges gilt. First edition. 6½" tall. Near fine. $340.00

MACLEAR, Rev. G.F. *Apostles of Medieval Europe.* London: MacMillan and Co., 1869. Full green morocco prize binding. Marbled edges. Illustrated. 7½" tall. Near fine. $220.00

MACQUOID, Percy. *A History of English Furniture: The Age of Oak; Mahogany; Walnut and Satin Wood.* London: Lawrence & Bullen Ltd., 1904. Four volumes. Three-quarter red morocco. Folio. Illustrated. Near fine. $1,100.00

MACLEOD, Mary. *The Books of King Arthur and His Noble Knights.* London: Wells, Gardner, Darton & Co., n.d., circa 1893. Full tree calf. Price binding with all edges gilt. Illustrated. 8" tall. Near fine. $300.00

MACQUOID, Percy. *A History of English Furniture.* London: Lawrence & Bullen Ltd., 1904. Four volumes. Three-quarter green morocco. Raised bands, gilt spines. Folio. Illustrated. First edition. Near fine. $1,100.00

MACQUOID, Percy. *A History of English Furniture: The Age of Oak, The Age of Walnut, The Age of Mahogany, and The Age of Satinwood.* London and New York: 1904 – 1908. Four volumes. Folio. Contemporary three-quarter brown morocco gilt. First edition of this definitive reference. Hundreds of illustrations. Near fine. $1,100.00

MAETERLINCK, Maurice. *Monna Vanna: A Play in Three Acts.* New York: 1904. Contemporary full green morocco gilt. Illustrated. Early American edition. Near fine. $375.00

MACVEIGH, James. *History of the Highlands and Highland Clans*. London: Jack & Fullarton, 1887. Two volumes. Three-quarter blue morocco. Ninety-four added clan plates. Edited by John Keltie. Fine. $1,200.00

MARCH, Daniel. *Our Father's House*. Cincinnati: P.W. Ziegler & Co., 1878. Full brown calf with embossed covers. Illustrated. 9" tall. Near fine. $280.00

MALORY, Sir Thomas. *Le Morte D'Arthur*. London: MacMillan and Co., 1900. Two volumes. Three-quarter blue morocco. Top edges gilt. 9" tall. Very good. $250.00

MALORY, Thomas. *The Birth, Life and Acts of King Arthur, Of His Noble Knights of the Round Table*. London: 1893 – 1894. Two volumes. Three-quarter calf. Quarto. Illustrated with full-page and double-page illustrations. First edition. Near fine. $2,100.00

MALORY. *Le Morte D'Arthur*. London: Philip Lee Warren, 1920. Two volumes. Full red morocco by Bayntun. Raised bands, ornate covers and spines. Illustrated by Russell Flint. Near fine. $800.00

MARCH, Daniel. *Home Life in the Bible*. Philadelphia: Ziegler & McCurdy, 1873. Full brown calf with embossed covers. All edges gilt. Illustrated First edition. 9" tall. Near fine. $310.00

MARHSALL, John A. *American Bastille*. Philadelphia: Thomas W. Hartley, 1875. Full tan calf with marbled edges. Illustrated. 9" tall. Near fine. $475.00

MARLOWE, Christopher. *The Works....* London: 1850. Three octavo volumes. Contemporary full red morocco gilt. Near fine. $600.00

MARCH, Daniel. *Days of the Son of Man*. Philadelphia: J.C. McCurdy, 1882. Full brown calf with embossed covers. All edges gilt. Illustrated. 9" tall. Near fine. $425.00

MARRYAT, Captain. *The Pirate and the Three Cutters*. London: Clarkson Stanfield, 1836. Three-quarter maroon morocco with marbled edges. Illustrated. 9" tall. Near fine. $275.00

MARSHALL, John. *The Life of George Washington, Commander in Chief of the American Forces.* Philadelphia: C.P. Wayne, 1804 – 07. Five large octavo text volumes and quarto atlas volume. Full contemporary dark brown tree calf; atlas volume in early cloth spine and paper-covered boards. First edition. Atlas volume contains ten folded, double page maps of the American Revolution. $4,500.00

MASEFIELD, John. *Poems.* New York: The MacMillan Co., 1935. Full red morocco by Riviere. Gilt ship on front cover. All edges gilt. 8" tall. Near fine. $375.00

MARSDEN, William. *The Travels of Marco Polo, a Venetian, in the Thirteenth Century.* London: 1818. Full paneled calf gilt. Quarto. Illustrated. First edition. Near fine. $1,700.00

MASON, Emily V. *Popular Life of General Robert Edward Lee.* Baltimore: John Murphy and Co., 1872. Three-quarter brown calf. Illustrated with seventeen designs by Professor Volck. 7½" tall. Very good. $475.00

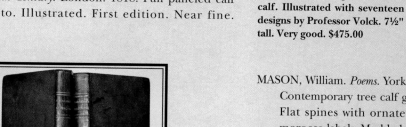

MARSHALL, John. *The Life of George Washington.* Philadelphia: James Crissy, 1838. Two volumes. Full brown calf. 9" tall. Very good. $375.00

MASON, William. *Poems.* York: Printed by W. Blanchard, 1796. Contemporary tree calf gilt by Kalthoeber. Two volumes. Flat spines with ornate gilt compartments and black morocco labels. Marbled endpapers. Near fine. $475.00

MASPERO, G., RAPPOPORT, S., KING, L.W., HALL, H.R. *History of Egypt, Chaldea, Syria, Babylonia and Assyria.* London: The Grolier Society Publishers, 1901. Thirteen large octavo volumes. Three-quarter green morocco. Marbled boards, raised bands, gilt decorated. Connoisseur edition, one of only 200 sets. Near fine. $1,600.00

MASSON, Frederic. *Josephine Empress & Queen.* Paris: Goupil & Co., 1899. Three-quarter green morocco. Gilt decorated spine with raised bands. Illustrated. Near fine. $375.00

MAXIMS. *Napoleon.* London: Arthur L. Humphreys, 1913. Full burgundy morocco gilt. Cosway binding by C.B. Currie. Near fine. $7,500.00

MARTYN, Mrs. S.T. *The Ladies Wreath.* New York: Martin & Ely, 1850. Full brown morocco. Hand-colored botanicals and steel engravings. All edges gilt. Edited by L.T. Martine. 9" tall. Very good. $280.00

MAXIMS. *Napoleon.* London: Arthur L. Humphreys, 1913. Full red morocco by Riviere. Ribbed floral gilt spine and covers. Illustrated by J.H. Stonehouse. Near fine. $7,500.00

MARX, Karl. *Capital: A Critical Analysis of Capitalist Production.* New York: Appleton and Co., London: Swan Sonnenschein, 1889. Three-quarter calf. Thick octavo. First American edition. $975.00

MAXWELL, Marius. *Stalking Big Game with a Camera.* London: The Medici Society, 1924. Full brown morocco. Raised bands, top edges gilt. Folio. Illustrated. Housed in a custom slipcase. Near fine. $1,250.00

MAXWELL, W.H. *Life of Field — Marshall His Grace the Duke of Wellington*. London: A.H. Baily & Co., 1839. Three volumes. Three-quarter wine calf gilt with green labels. Illustrated. Near fine. $800.00

MAXWELL, W.H. *Life of the Duke of Wellington*. Edinburgh: W.P. Nimmo. Full red calf gilt with decorated spine. Near fine. $150.00

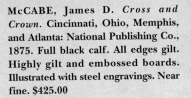

McCABE, James D. *Cross and Crown*. Cincinnati, Ohio, Memphis, and Atlanta: National Publishing Co., 1875. Full black calf. All edges gilt. Highly gilt and embossed boards. Illustrated with steel engravings. Near fine. $425.00

MAXWELL, W.H. *The Life of Wellington*. London: Bickers & Son, 1883. Full purple morocco by Bickers. Highly gilt spine with all edges gilt. Twelve illustrations in permanent photography, numerous others in wood. 8½" tall. Near fine. $375.00.

MCCABE, James D. Jr. *Life and Campaigns of General Robert E. Lee*. Atlanta: National Publishing Co., 1866. Three-quarter tan calf with marbled edges. Illustrated with pull-out maps. 8½" tall. Very good. $875.00

MAXWELL, W. H. *The Victories of Wellington and the British*. London: George Bell & Sons, 1891. Full navy morocco. Prize binding with marbled edges. Illustrated. 6" tall. Near fine. $215.00

MCCARTHY, Justin. *A History of Our Own Times*. London: Chatto and Windus, 1900. Two volumes. Full tree calf by Relfe Brothers. Prize binding with marbled edges. 8" tall. Near fine. $450.00

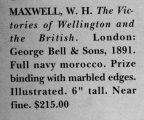

MAXWELL, W.H. *The Life of Wellington*. London: Beckers & Son, 1890. Full tree calf levant with gilt panels. Illustrated including a plan of the battle of Waterloo. Near fine. $350.00

MCCLELLAN, George B. *McClellan's Own Story. The War for the Union, The Soldiers Who Fought It, The Civilians Who Directed It and His Relations to It and to Them*. New York: 1886. Octavo. Three-quarter brown morocco gilt. First edition. Illustrated with frontispiece portrait and numerous plates and maps. Near fine. $450.00

MCCLELLAN, George B. *McClellan's Own Story. The War for the Union, The Soldiers Who Fought It, The Civilians Who Directed It and His Relations to It and to Them*. New York: Charles L. Webster & Company, 1887. Octavo. Three-quarter brown morocco gilt. Red medallion decoration on front cover. First edition. Illustrated with thirteen plates, maps, and facsimiles. Near fine. $450.00

MAYNARD, C.J. *The Butterflies of New England*. Newtonville: C.J. Maynard, 1891. Three-quarter black calf. All edges gilt. Ten hand-colored plates of 106 species. 13½" tall. Near fine. $1,000.00

MCCLELLAN, George B. *McClellan's Own Story*. New York: Charles Webster, 1887. Three-quarter dark brown calf by Launder and MacDonald. Top edges gilt. First edition. Near fine. $475.00

MCCLELLAN, George B. *McClellan's Own Story*. New York: Charles Webster, 1887. Three-quarter black calf. Red and gold gilt medallion on front cover. Marbled edges. Illustrated. First edition. 9" tall. Near fine. $450.00

MCCLELLAN, H.B. *The Life and Campaigns of Major General J.E.B. Stuart*. Boston and New York: Houghton, Mifflin and Co., 1885. Three-quarter dark brown calf by Launder and MacDonald. Top edges gilt. Illustrated with pull-out maps. First edition. Near fine. $475.00

MCELROY, John. *Andersonville*. Toledo: D.R. Locke, 1879. Three-quarter brown calf by Launder and MacDonald. Top edges gilt. Illustrated. First edition. 9" tall. Near fine. $480.00

MCKENNEY, Thomas, and HALL, James. *History of the Indian Tribes of North America, with Biographical Sketches and Anecdotes of the Principal Chiefs....* Philadelphia: 1837 – 44. Three volumes. Folio. Contemporary half black morocco gilt. With 120 hand-colored lithographic plates. Fine. $175,000.00

MCKENNEY, Thomas, and HALL, James. *History of the Indian Tribes of North America....* Philadelphia: Rice, Rutter and Co., 1865. Three royal octavo volumes. Full contemporary publisher's morocco. All edges gilt. Illustrated with 120 hand-colored tissue guarded lithographic plates. Early edition. Near fine. $22,000.00

MCLEAN, John. *The Indians, Their Manners and Customs*. Toronto: William Briggs, 1889. Three-quarter red morocco. Top edges gilt. Eighteen full-page illustrations. 8½" tall. Near fine. $575.00

MEACHAM, A.B. *Wigwam and War-Path*. Boston: John P. Dale, 1875. Three-quarter brown calf. Marbled edges. Illustrated. 9" tall. Near fine. $850.00

MELVILLE, Herman. *Israel Potter*. New York: G.P. Putnam & Co., 1855. Full brown morocco. First edition. Near fine. $550.00

MELVILLE, Herman. *Moby Dick, or, The Whale*. Chicago: The Lakeside Press, 1930. Three volumes. Small folio. Full calf. Original aluminum slipcase. First edition of Rockwell Kent edition. Illustrated by Rockwell Kent with numerous woodcuts. Near fine. $1,400.00

MELVILLE, Herman. *Moby Dick*. New York: Random House, 1930. Full blue morocco gilt. First Kent edition. Illustrated by Rockwell Kent. Near fine. $950.00

MELVILLE, Herman. *Moby Dick.* New York: Random House, 1930. Three-quarter blue morocco. Top edges gilt. The Rockwell Kent illustrated edition, spine faded to green. 7" tall. Near fine. $925.00

MELVILLE, Herman. *Moby Dick.* New York: Random House, 1930. Full black calf by Sangorski and Sutcliffe. Illustrated by Rockwell Kent. First illustrated edition. Near fine. $1,100.00

MELVILLE, Herman. *The Confidence Man.* New York: Dix and Edwards, 1857. Full brown morocco gilt. Raised bands. First edition. Near fine. $350.00

MELVILLE, Herman. *The Piazza Tales.* New York: Dix and Edwards, 1856. Full navy morocco. Raised bands, gilt decorated. First edition. Near fine. $350.00

MELVILLE, Herman. *The Works.* London: Jonathan Cape. 1925. Seven volumes. Full blue morocco gilt. Library edition. Near fine. $2,300.00

MELVILLE, Hermann. *The Works.* London, Bombay, Sydney: Constable & Co., 1922 – 24. Sixteen volumes. Full red morocco gilt by Chelsea Bindery. Raised bands, marbled endpapers and top edges gilt. One of only 750 sets printed. Near fine. $8,300.00

MEMES, John S. *Memoirs of Napoleon Bonaparte.* Edinburgh: for Constable and Co., 1831. Four volumes. Small 8vo. Half black morocco gilt. Near fine. $475.00

MEREJKOWSKI, Dmitri. *The Romance of Leonardo De Vinci.* New York and London: J.P. Putnam's Sons, 1901. Two volumes. Top edges gilt. Three-quarter blue morocco. Illustrated. 8" tall. Near fine. $275.00

MERIDITH, Owen. *Lucile.* Boston and New York: Houghton, Mifflin and Co., 1883. Full tree calf. Cabinet edition with all edges gilt. 6½" tall. Near fine. $190.00

MENDELSSOHN, Moses. *Jerusalem: A Treatise on Ecclesiastical Authority and Judaism.* London: 1838. Two octavo volumes. Three-quarter calf. First American edition. Near fine. $400.00

MERIVALE, Charles. *History of the Romans under the Empire.* London: Longman's Brown, Green, 1852. Second edition. Seven volumes. Full tan calf gilt. Near fine. $750.00

MERIVALE, Charles. *History of the Romans.* London: Longman, Brown, Green and Longmans, 1852. Seven volumes. Full butterscotch calf by W. Nutt. Marbled edges. Illustrated with pull-out maps. 8½" tall. Near fine. $875.00

METEYARD, Eliza. *The Life of Joshua Wedgwood.* London: Hurst & Blackett, 1865. Two volumes. Full blue morocco. Raised bands, gilt decorated spines and covers. First edition. Near fine. $575.00

MICHAUD. *History of the Crusades.* Philadelphia: George Barrie, n.d., circa 1880. Two volumes. Three-quarter brown calf with all edges gilt. Illustrated by Dore. 14" tall. Very good. $1,200.00

MICHENER, James A. *Hawaii*. New York: Random House, 1959. Three-quarter butterscotch calf by Bayntun. Top edges gilt. First edition. 9" tall. Fine. $360.00

MIDDLETON, Conyers. *The Life of M.T. Cicero*. London: J. Cuthell, 1824. Two volumes. Full purple calf gilt. Raised bands with green and red labels. Near fine. $650.00

MILES, Nelson. *Personal Recollections and Observations of General Nelson Miles*. Chicago: The Werner Co., 1876. Three-quarter blue morocco. Marbled edges. Illustrated by Frederick Remington. First edition. Near fine. $375.00

MILL, James. Esq. *The History of British India*. London: Baldwin, Cradock & Joy, 1817. Three volumes. First edition. Three-quarter black calf gilt. Quarto. Illustrated. Near fine. $850.00

MILL, John Stuart. *The Subjection of Women*. London: 1869. Original orange cloth. Octavo. First edition. Near fine. $3,100.00

MILLER, Francis T. *The Photographic History of the Civil War*. New York: Review of Reviews, 1911. Ten volumes. Quarto. Three-quarter brown calf. First edition illustrated with photographs by Matthew Brady. Near fine. $2,800.00

MILLER, Francis Trevelyan. *The Photographic History of the Civil War*. New York: 1911. Ten volumes. Quarto. Original three-quarter navy morocco. First edition. Near fine. $2,800.00

MILLER, Francis Trevelyan. *The Photographic History of the Civil War*. New York: 1911. Ten quarto volumes. Three-quarter brown calf. Illustrated with thousands of photographs. Near fine. $2,800.00

MILMAN, Henry Hart. *History of the Jews, History of Latin Christianity and the History of Christianity*. London: John Murray, 1866 – 1867. Fifteen volumes. Full tree calf with marbled edges. 5" tall. Near fine. $3,200.00

MILNE, A.A. *The Four Pooh Books. When We Were Very Young; Winnie the Pooh; Now We Are Six; The House at Pooh Corner*. London: Methuen & Co., Ltd., 1924 – 28. Four volumes. Small octavo. Full morocco. Illustrated endpapers. In a custom full morocco clamshell box with inlaid leather illustration of Winnie the Pooh. First editions. Near fine. $6,800.00.

MILNE, A.A. *When We Were Very Young*. London: Methuen & Co., 1929. Full wine morocco. Gilt embossed figures on cover. All edges gilt. Illustrated by Ernest H. Shepard. 7¼" tall. Near fine. $410.00

MILNE, A.A. *The Four Pooh Books: When We Were Very Young; Winnie the Pooh; Now We Are Six; The House at Pooh Corner*. London: Methuen & Co., Ltd., 1926 – 1928. Four volumes. Small octavo. Publisher's calf gilt. First editions. Near fine. $6,800.00

MILNE, A.A. *When We Were Very Young; Winnie the Pooh; Now We Are Six; The House at Pooh Corner*. London: Methuen & Co., 1924 – 1928. Four volumes. 8vo. Original publisher's cloth, each book in its distinctive color. With original dust jackets. Illustrated by E. H. Shepard. First editions. Housed in a burgundy cloth solander case with individual gilt lettered morocco spines. Near fine. $9,000.00

MILNE, A.A. *When We Were Very Young; Winnie the Pooh; Now We Are Six; The House at Pooh Corner*. London: Methuen & Co., 1924 – 28. First editions. Small octavo. Full blue, green, red, and salmon morocco by Bayntun-Riviere. Front covers and spines stamped with gilt caricatures. Contained in a cloth slipcase lined with felt. Near fine. $7,100.00

MILNE, A.A. *When We Were Very Young; Winnie the Pooh; Now We are Six; House At Pooh Corner.* London: Mathuen & Co., 1924 – 1928. Four volumes. Full red morocco by Bayntun. Gilt decorated spines and covers. First editions. Near fine. $6,500.00

MILNE, A.A. *Winnie the Pooh.* London: 1926. Small octavo. Full red calf gilt. First edition. Illustrations by Ernest Shepard. Near fine. $2,100.00

MILTON, John. *The Poetical Works of John Milton.* **London: James Nichol, 1853. Two volumes. Full calf. Marbled edges. Edited by George Gilfillan. Mild foxing to prelims. Very good. $250.00**

MILTON, John. *The Poetical Works of John Milton.* **Boston: Phillips, Sampson and Co., 1859. Full tan calf. All edges gilt. Hand-tooled covers. Illustrated. 9½" tall. Near fine. $265.00**

MILTON, John. *A Defence of the People of England, by John Milton: In Answer to Salmasius's Defence of the King.* Amsterdam, 1692. Contemporary full brown calf. Octavo. First edition in English. Near fine. $975.00

MILTON, John. *Paradise Lost, A Poem in Twelve Books.* London: Jacob Tonson, 1688. Twentieth century mottled calf gilt with red morocco label. Illustrated with thirteen engraved plates. Fourth edition. Near fine. $1,200.00

MILTON, John. *Paradise Lost. A Poem in Twelve Books.* London: 1749. Two volumes. With: *Paradise Regain'd.* London: 1752. Together, three volumes. Quarto. Period-style half tan calf. Illustrated edition with 17 copper-engraved scenes after Francis Hayman. Near fine. $1,800.00

MILTON, John. *Paradise Lost.* London, Paris: Cassell & Co., circa 1890. Three-quarter green morocco gilt. Folio. Illustrated by Gustave Doré. Near fine. $850.00

MILTON, John. *Paradise Lost.* London: S. Simmons, 1674. Navy pebble grain morocco gilt. Raised bands, spine compartments ornately gilt. Marbled endpapers with all edges gilt. Near fine. $2,900.00

MILTON, John. *The Poetical Works.* London: 1835. Six small octavo volumes. Contemporary three-quarter green morocco gilt. Illustrated. First edition. Near fine. $1,100.00

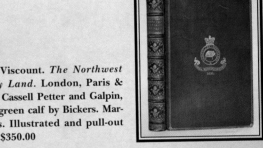

MILTON, Viscount. *The Northwest Passage by Land.* **London, Paris & New York: Cassell Petter and Galpin, 1865. Full green calf by Bickers. Marbled edges. Illustrated and pull-out map. Fine. $350.00**

MILTON, John. *The Poetical Works of John Milton.* **London: Frederick Warne & Co., 1901. Full tan calf. All edges gilt. Prize binding, The Albion edition. 7½" tall. Near fine. $140.00**

MITCHELL, F.A. *Ormsby, MacKnight Mitchell.* **Boston and New York: Houghton, Mifflin and Co., 1887. Three-quarter brown calf by Launder and MacDonald. Top edges gilt. Near fine. $200.00**

MITCHELL, John. *The History of Ireland, Ancient and Modern.* New York: D & J Sadlier & Co., 1861. Full green morocco. All edges gilt. Hand-colored fronits. Illustrated with each page bordered. First edition. 11½" tall. Very good. $625.00

MITCHELL, Lieut. Col. J. *The Fall of Napoleon: A Historical Memoir.* London: G.W. Nickisson, 1845. Three volumes. Three-quarter red morocco gilt. Near fine. $475.00

MITCHELL, Margaret. *Gone with the Wind.* New York: 1936. First edition, first issue. Full blue morocco gilt. Near fine. $2,600.00

MITCHELL, Margaret. *Gone with the Wind.* New York: MacMillian & Co., 1936. Thick octavo. Modern full brown morocco gilt. First edition signed by the author. Near fine. $4,500.00

MITCHELL, Margaret. *Gone with the Wind.* New York: The MacMillan Company, 1936. Thick octavo. Full green calf by Bayntun. First edition. Near fine. $2,900.00

MITCHELL, Margaret. *Gone with the Wind.* New York: The MacMillan Co., 1936. Two volumes. Three-quarter red morocco. Top edges gilt. First edition. 8½" tall. Near fine. $2,800.00

MITFORD, William. *The History of Greece.* London: Printed for T. Cadell, 1822. Ten volumes. Full tan polished calf. Raised bands, ornate spines with red and green labels. Near fine. $1,600.00

MOLIERE. *The Works of Moliere.* London: Printed for D. Browne and A. Millar, 1755. Ten volumes. Full green morocco. All edges gilt. 6½" tall. Near fine. $1,650.00

MITFORD, William. *The History of Greece.* London: T. Cadell, 1838. Eight volumes. Full tan calf. Raised bands, gilt decorated with red and green morocco labels. Near fine. $1,100.00

MOLIERE, J.B.P. *The Works.* Paris: Chez Barrie Freres, Philadelphia: G. Barrie, circa 1900. Twelve volumes. Full green morocco with gray leather and silk doublures. Limited edition, one of only 50 sets. Large quarto. Illustrated by MM Louis Leloir. Near fine. $6,500.00

MOMMSEN, Theodor. *History of Rome.* London: Richard Bentley & Son, 1886. Two volumes. Full tree calf levant. Ornate tooling on spines. Contains eight maps by Professor Kiepert. Near fine. $850.00

MOMMSEN, Theodor. *The History of Rome.* London: Bentley & Son, 1888. Four volumes. Full vellum binding. Red edges. The Popular edition. Near fine. $600.00

MOMMSEN, Theodor. *The History of Rome.* New York: Chas. Scribner's Sons, 1889. Four volumes. Three-quarter blue morocco gilt. Near fine. $475.00

MONTAIGNE, Michel de. *The Works of Michel de Montaigne.* New York: 1910. Ten volumes. Octavo. Contemporary three-quarter purple morocco gilt. Limited Emerson edition, one of only 1,050 sets. Near fine. $2,800.00

MONCRIEFF, A.R. Hope. *Famous Historical Scenes from Three Centuries.* Edinburgh: William P. Nimmo & Co., 1882. Full black calf. Prize binding with all edges gilt. 7" tall. Near fine. $225.00

MONTAIGNE, Michel Eyquem de. *The Essays or Morall, Politike and Millitarie Discourses.* London: 1603. Folio. Period-style full red morocco gilt. First edition in English. Near fine. $6,100.00

MONTAIGNE, Michiel de. *The Essays.* London: George Bell & Sons, 1892. Three volumes. Full tan calf gilt by Riviere. Raised bands with green and red morocco labels. Translated from French by Charles Cotton. Near fine. $275.00

MONTAIGNE. *Essays.* London: Reeves & Turner, 1902. Four volumes. Three-quarter green calf gilt. Illustrations and portraits by Hazlitt. Near fine. $500.00

MONTGOMERY, James. *Poems of James Montgomery.* New York: Routledge Warne & Routledge, 1860. Full green morocco. Highly gilt spine and covers. All edges gilt. Illustrated. 9" tall. Near fine. $320.00

MONTGOMERY, Walter. *American Art and American Art Collections: Essays on Artistic Subjects by The Best Art Works.* Boston: E.W. Walker & Co., 1889. Two volumes. Three-quarter burgundy morocco. Gilt decorated spines. Illustrated. Near fine. $600.00

MOORE, Clement C. *New York Book of Poetry.* New York: George Dearborn, 1837. Full purple morocco. First edition. Near fine. $525.00

MONTGOMERY, James. *The Poetical Works of James Montgomery.* London: Longman, Brown, Green, Longmans & Roberts, 1858. Full navy blue morocco. Highly gilt spine and covers. All edges gilt. Presentation copy to Mrs. Philip Mason. 8" tall. Near fine. $220.00

MOORE, Frank. *American Eloquence: A Collection of Speeches and Addresses by the Most Eminent Orators of America.* New York: D. Appleton & Co., 1857. Two volumes. Three-quarter tan calf. Illustrated. 10" tall. Near fine. $150.00

MOORE, Frank. *The Rebellion Record.* New York: G.P. Putnam, 1861. Twelve volumes (only three shown). Three-quarter red morocco. Top edges gilt. Original paper boards. Illustrated with maps, Colton map in volume 1. First edition. 10" tall. Near fine. $1,250.00

MOORE, Thomas. *The Poetical Works.* London: Longman, Green, 1865. Full green morocco by Ramage. Near fine. $360.00

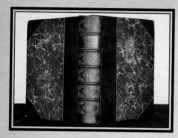

MOORE, Frank. *Women of the War*. Hartford: S.S. Scranton & Co., 1866. Three-quarter brown calf. Top edges gilt. Illustrated. First edition. 9" tall. Very good. $175.00

MOORE, Thomas. *The Poetical Works of Thomas Moore*. London: Henry Frowde, 1910. Full tree calf by Riviere. Edited by A.D. Godley. All edges gilt. 7½" tall. Near fine. $255.00

MOORE, Hannah. *Sacred Dramas*. London: Chiswick Press, 1818. Full tan levant morocco by Whittingham. Marbled edges. New edition, sold by J. Jennings. 5¼" tall. $295.00

MOORE, Thomas. *The Poetical Works of Thomas Moore*. London: Longman & Co., 1854. Ten volumes. Three-quarter green morocco by Larkins. Top edges gilt. Fine. $1,250.00

MOORE, James. *Kilpatrick and Our Cavalry*. New York: W.J. Widdleton, 1865. Three-quarter brown calf by Launder and MacDonald. Top edges gilt. Illustrated. First edition. 8" tall. Near fine. $350.00

MOORE, Joseph West. *Picturesque Washington*. Providence: J.A. and R.A. Reid, 1884. Three-quarter tan calf. Marbled edges. Illustrated. 10" tall. Near fine. $360.00

MOORE, Thomas. *The Poetical Works of Thomas Moore*. New York: D. Appleton, 1846. Full black calf. Highly gilt spine and heavy gold gilt covers with all edges gilt. Illustrated with steel engravings. 8" tall. Near fine. $550.00

MOORE, Thomas. *Irish Melodies*. London: Longman, Brown, Green and Longmans, 1846. Full red morocco. All edges gilt. Each page has an illustrated border and at least every other page has an illustration. 10" tall. Near fine. $475.00

MOORE, Thomas. *The Poets and Poetry of Ireland*. New York: Thomas Farrell & Sons, n.d., circa 1880. Full brown calf. All edges gilt. Illustrated. Colored frontis. 10" tall. Near fine. $575.00

MOORE, Thomas. *The Works of Lord Byron.* London: John Murray, 1833. Seventeen volumes. Three-quarter red morocco. Highly gilt spine, all edges gilt. 6½" tall. Near fine. $1,700.00

MORRIS, Herbert. *Science and the Bible.* Philadelphia: Ziegler & McCurdy, 1873. Full brown calf with embossed covers. Top edges gilt. Illustrated. 9" tall. Near fine. $240.00

MORELL, Sir Charles. *The Tales of the Genii, or the Delightful Lessons of Horan The Son of Asmar.* London: James Wallis, 1805. Two volumes. Full tan morocco gilt. Illustrated. Near fine. $550.00

MORGAN, J. Pierpont. *Pictures in the Collection of J. Pierpont Morgan.* London: Privately printed, 1907. Three-quarter brown morocco gilt with decorated spine. Near fine. $150.00

MORIER, James. *The Adventures of Hajji Baba, of Ispahan.* London: 1824. Three volumes. Three-quarter green calf. 12mo. First edition. Near fine. $625.00

MORRIS, Herbert. *Testimony of the Ages.* Philadelphia: J.C. McCurdy, 1880. Full brown calf. Deep embossed and gilt cover with all edges gilt. Illustrated. First edition. 9" tall. Near fine. $420.00

MORLEY, Henry. *A First Sketch of English Literature.* London: Cassell and Co., 1905. Full navy morocco. Prize binding with highly gilt spine and marbled edges. 7" tall. Near fine. $325.00

MORRIS, Rev. F.O. *History of British Butterflies.* London: Groombridge and Sons, 1865. Full tan calf with marbled edges. Seventy-one hand-colored plates by Fawcett of Driffield. 10" tall. Near fine. $1,150.00

MORRIS, William. *The Roots of the Mountains.* London: 1890. Full calf. Square octavo. "Superior Edition," one of only 250 copies. Near fine. $1,100.00

MORLEY, John. *Rosseau.* London: Chapman and Hall, n.d., circa 1870. Two volumes. Three-quarter maroon morocco by Root. Top edges gilt. 8½" tall. Near fine. $325.00

MORRIS, William O'Connor. *Napoleon Warrior & Ruler and the Military Supremacy of Revolutionary France.* G.P. Putnam's Sons, 1893. Full navy morocco gilt. Near fine. $225.00

MORSE, John T. Jr. *American Statesman.* Boston and New York: Houghton, Mifflin & Co., 1898. Thirty-two volumes (only four shown). Full red morocco by the Book Lovers Bindery. Highly gilt spine and covers with top edges gilt. Red and blue morocco doublures, red silk moiré endpapers. Large paper edition, #37 of 500 copies printed. 9" tall. Fine. $5,500.00

MOSBY, Johns. *Mosby's War Reminiscences*. Boston: George A. Jones & Co., 1887. Three-quarter brown calf by Launder and Mac-Donald. Top edges gilt. First edition. 8" tall. Near fine. $300.00

MOULTRIE, John, and MITFORD, John. *Grays Poetical Works*. London: E.P. Williams, 1853. Full green morocco. All edges gilt. Illustrated. Architecture binding. 9" tall. Near fine. $240.00

MOTLEY, John Lothrop. *Motley's Works*. New York: Harper & Brothers, 1874. Three-quarter butterscotch calf. Marbled edges. Fine. $1,125.00

MOTTELAY, Paul. *Soldier in Our Civil War: A Pictorial History of the Conflict, 1861 – 1865, Illustrating the Valor of the Soldier as Displayed on the Battlefield*. New York: 1886 – 87. Two volumes. Tall folio. Publisher's full leather. Early edition. Illustrated with full and double page wood engravings. Frontispiece portraits of Grant and Lee. Near fine. $1,250.00

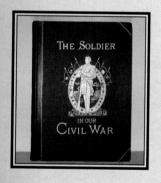

MOTTELAY, Paul F. *The Soldier in Our Civil War*. New York: J.H. Brown, 1884. Two volumes (only one shown). Three-quarter black morocco. Marbled edges. Folio. Illustrations on every page. 16" tall. Near fine. $1,300.00

MUHLBACH, L. *The Works of Muhlbach*. New York: D. Appleton & Co., 1888. Six volumes. Three-quarter butterscotch calf with marbled edges. Illustrated. 9" tall. Near fine. $850.00

MUNNINGS, A. J. *Pictures of Horses and English Life*. London: Eyre and Spottiswoode Ltd., 1927. Limited edition signed by the author. Bound in vellum. Gilt spine and cover. Illustrated. Small folio. Near fine. $1,600.00

MURRAY, Marischal. *Ships and South Africa. A Maritim Chronicle of the Cape*. London: Oxford University Press, 1933. Full blue calf gilt. Raised bands, gilt decorated spine and covers. Near fine. $575.00

MOTTEUX. *The History of the Ingenious Gentleman Don Quixote*. London: Hurst, Robinson and Co., 1822. Five volumes. Three-quarter black calf. 7" tall. Near fine. $650.00

MUTHER, Richard. *The History of Modern Painting*. London: Henry & Co., 1895. Three volumes. Three-quarter wine morocco gilt. Quarto. Illustrated. Near fine. $950.00

MURALTO, Onuphrio. *The Castle of Otranto*. London: Bodoni of Parma, 1791. Full tan calf. All edges gilt. Original Etruscan binding by Edwards of Halifax. Fore-edge painting of Stonehenge. 10" tall. Very good. $5,500.00

MURAT, The Princess Lucien. *The Private Life of Catherine the Great of Russia*. New York, London, Montreal: Louis Carrier & Co., 1828. Full blue morocco by Riviere. Highly gilt spine and all edges gilt. First edition, one of 500 copies. 7½" tall. Near fine. $250.00

NANSEN, Fridtjof. *Farthest North, Being the Record of a Voyage of Exploration of the Ship Fram 1893 – 1896.* Two octavo volumes. Three-quarter calf. Illustrated with frontispiece portrait, color maps, sketches, and photographs. First edition in English. Near fine. $475.00

NAPIER, W.F.P. *History of the War in the Peninsula, and in the South of France, from the Year 1807 to the Year 1814.* London: John Murray, 1828. Six volumes. Three-quarter tan calf. Ornate tooling on spines. First edition. Near fine. $975.00

NAPOLEON, Prince. *Napoleon and His Detractors*. London: W.H. Allen & Co., 1888. Three-quarter red morocco. Gilt decorated spines with raised bands. Illustrated. Near fine. $350.00

NAPOLEON. *The Life of Napoleon Bonaparte.* London: Religious Tract Society, n.d., circa 1860. Two volumes bound in one. Three-quarter green calf. Marbled edges. 5¾" tall. Fine. $240.00

NAPOLEON. *Cruikshank, Life of Napoleon, A Hudibrastic Poem in 15 cantos, by Doctor Syntax.* London: T. Tegg, 1815. Full red morocco gilt by Durrant. First edition. Contains thirty hand-colored engravings by G. Cruikshank. Near fine. $1,900.00

NAPOLEON. *The Court and Camp of Bonaparte*. London: John Murray, 1829. Half brown morocco gilt, decorated spine. Includes fold-out genealogical plates. Near fine. $150.00

NAPOLEON. *The History of the Campaigns in the Years 1796, 1797, 1798 and 1799.* London: T. Gardiner, 1812. Four volumes. Octavo. Late nineteenth century three-quarter polished red calf by Zaehnsdorf. Contains 16 folding maps and plans. Near fine. $600.00

NAUMANN, Emil. *The History of Music*. London: Cassell & Co., circa 1900. Two volumes. Full orange morocco. Raised bands, gilt spines. Illustrated. Near fine. $750.00

NEFF, Jacob K. *The Army and Navy of America*. Philadelphia: John S. Gable, 1845. Octavo. Contemporary full sheepskin with black morocco spine labels. First edition. Contains two folding plates and in-text illustrations. Near fine. $600.00

NEUMANN, Arthur H. *Elephant Hunting in East Equatorial-Africa.* London: Rowland Ward, 1897. Three-quarter brown morocco gilt. Octavo. Illustrated. First edition. Near fine. $1,100.00

NEWTON, Charles Thomas. *Travels and Discoveries in the Levant.* London: 1865. Two tall octavo volumes. Full calf. Illustrated with maps, in-text woodcuts, and scenic plates. First edition. Near fine. $680.00

NEWMAN, George. *Infant Mortality*. London: Methuen & Co., 1906. Full sky blue morocco. Highly gilt cover, all edges gilt. Highly gilt dentelles, silk moiré inlaid inside covers and endpapers. Illustrated. 8½" tall. Fine. $375.00

NIEBUHR, B.G. *Lectures of Ancient History*. London: Taylor, Walton and Maberly, 1852. Three volumes. Full tall calf by Maclehose. Prize binding. Marbled edges. 9" tall. Near fine. $375.00

NICHOLAY, John, and HAY, John. *Abraham Lincoln a History with Abraham Lincoln Complete Works.* New York: Century Co., 1890 – 1894. Twelve volumes. Three-quarter blue morocco gilt. Gilt spines and marbled boards. 8vo. First edition. Near fine. $3,700.00

NICHOLE, John. *English Men of Letters, Byron, Shelley and Keats.* London: MacMillan and Co., 1883. Full tree calf. Prize binding with marbled edges. 7" tall. Near fine. $325.00

NICHOLSON, Peter. *A Treatise on the Construction of Staircases and Handrails.* London: 1820. Contemporary full tree calf gilt. Quarto. Illustrated with numerous copper-engraved plates. First edition. Near fine. $550.00

NICOLAY G. John, and HAY, John. *Abraham Lincoln, A History.* New York: The Century Co., 1914. Ten volumes. Three-quarter tan morocco gilt. Near fine. $1,600.00

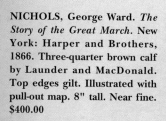

NICHOLS, George Ward. *The Story of the Great March.* New York: Harper and Brothers, 1866. Three-quarter brown calf by Launder and MacDonald. Top edges gilt. Illustrated with pull-out map. 8" tall. Near fine. $400.00

NIMROD. *The Horse and the Hound Their Various Uses and Treatment Including Practical Instructions in Horsemanship and a Treatise on Horse-Dealing.* Adam and Charles Black, 1843. Full tan calf. Raised bands, gilt spine. Illustrations by Alken. Second edition. Near fine. $250.00

NOLHAC, Pierre de. *Louis XV et Madame de Pompadour.* Paris: 1903. Folio. Contemporary full red morocco gilt. Limited edition, one of only 800 copies. Near fine. $975.00

NICHOLS, Rebecca. *Song of the Heart and the Hearth Stone.* Philadelphia: Thomas, Coynperthwait & Co., 1851. Full black calf. Highly gilt spine and cover, all edges gilt. Illustrated. First edition. 8½" tall. Near fine $225.00

NICHOL, John. *Byron.* London: 1880. Full blue morocco gilt with elaborate oak sprays and roses on spine. Cosway binding by Riviere. Housed in a half morocco slipcase. Illustrated. Near fine. $2,700.00

NIMMOS. *Eminent Philanthropists, Patriots, and Reformers.* Edinburgh: W.P. Nimmo, Hay & Mitchell, circa 1875. Full green morocco. Marbled edges. 7" tall. Near fine. $265.00

NORTROP, Henry Davenport. *Indian Horrors*. Chicago: L.P. Miller, circa 1890. Full maroon morocco. Illustrated. Fine. $575.00

NOSTRADAMUS, Michel de. *The True Prophecies or Prognostications*. London: 1672. Contemporary full brown calf. Folio. Gilt decorated spine. Illustrated with an engraved frontispiece portrait. First edition in English. Near fine. $6,800.00

O'CONNOR, Roger. *Chronicles of Eri; Being the History of the Gaal Sciot Iber*. London: Sir Richard Phillips & Co., 1822. Two octavo volumes. Full calf gilt. Raised bands, gilt decorated spines with morocco labels. Illustrated with hand-colored maps. First edition. Near fine. $675.00

O'MEARA, Barry E. *Napoleon in Exile*. London: W. Simpkin, 1822. Two volumes. Three-quarter tan calf. Near fine. $550.00

O'MEARA, Barry E. *Napoleon in Exile; or A Voice from St. Helena*. London: W. Simpken and R. Marhsall, 1822. Two volumes. Three-quarter red calf gilt. Fourth edition. Near fine. $550.00

OKEY, Thomas. *The Old Venetian Palaces and Old Venetian Folk*. New York: E.P. Dutton & Co., 1907. Three-quarter tan morocco. Raised bands with gilt floral decoration. Thick 8vo. Illustrated. Near fine. $275.00

O'REILLY, Rev. Bernard. *Heroic Women of the Bible and the Church*. New York: Fords, Howard & Hurlbert, 1877. Three-quarter brown calf. All edges gilt. Illustrated with 25 chromolithographic plates. First edition. Fine. $550.00

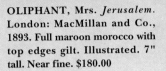

OLIPHANT, Mrs. *Jerusalem*. London: MacMillan and Co., 1893. Full maroon morocco with top edges gilt. Illustrated. 7" tall. Near fine. $180.00

OLIPHANT, Laurence. *Narrative of the Earl of Elgin's Mission to China and Japan in the Years 1857 – 59*. Edinburgh and London: 1859. Two octavo volumes. Modern half black morocco gilt. Illustrated with color lithographs, maps, and numerous engravings. First edition. Near fine. $675.00

OLIPHANT, Mrs. *Makers of Venice*. London: 1891. Full morocco gilt with floral design by Riviere & Son. Octavo. Illustrated with 48 steel-engravings. Near fine. $150.00

OLIPHANT, Mrs. *The Makers of Venice: Doges, Conquerors, Painters and Men of Letters*. London: MacMillan & Co., 1887. Two volumes. Three-quarter brown morocco by Zaehnsdorf. Raised bands, gilt panels, and marbled boards. Illustrated by R.R. Holmes. First edition. Near fine. $625.00

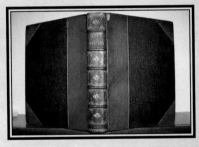

OLLIER, Edmund. *Cassell's Doré Gallery*. New York: Cassell, circa 1870. Three-quarter red morocco. Highly gilt spine, all edges gilt. Two hundred fifty engravings by Dore. 14" tall. Near fine. $675.00

OMAR KHAYYAM. *Rubaiyat of Omar Khayyam*. London: circa 1910. Translated by Edward Fitzgerald. Small quarto. Jeweled binding by Sangorski & Sutcliffe with 68 semi-precious stones. Crimson crushed levant morocco. Red morocco doublures with dark blue morocco strip border decorated in gilt. Near fine. $50,000.00

OMAN, C.W.C. *The Byzantine Empire.* London: T. Fisher Unwin, 1882. Full navy morocco, prize binding. Marbled edges. Illustrated. 7½" tall. Near fine. $180.00

ORANGE, The House of. *The Lives of the Princes of the Illustrious House of Orange.* London: W. Mears, 1734. Contemporary sprinkled calf. Raised bands, gilt spine compartments with red morocco label. Illustrated with numerous portraits and a large folding genealogical table. Near fine. $450.00

ORWELL, George. *Animal Farm. A Fairy Story.* London: Secker & Warburg, 1945. Octavo. Full red morocco. First edition. Near fine. $975.00

OSGOOD, Frances S. *The Poetry of Flowers.* New York: J.C. Riker, 1841. Full black calf. Highly gilt spine with top edges gilt. Illustrated with 12 hand-colored plates. 7" tall. Good. $325.00

PAGE, Thomas Nelson. *The Novels, Stories, Sketches and Poems of Thomas Nelson Page.* New York: Charles Scribner's Sons, 1908. Eighteen volumes (only three shown). Three-quarter brown calf by Stikeman. Top edges gilt. Illustrated. 7½" tall. Very good. $1,500.00

PAGE, Thomas Nelson. *The Works.* New York: 1906 – 1912. Eighteen volumes. Octavo. Contemporary three-quarter dark red morocco gilt. Limited edition, one of only 230 sets. Color illustrations. Near fine. $1,500.00

PAGE, Thomas Nelson. *Tommy Trots Visit to Santa Claus.* New York: Charles Scribner's Sons, 1908. Three-quarter green morocco by Bennett. Highly gilt spine with top edges gilt. Illustrated. First edition. 8" tall. Near fine. $275.00

PAINE, Thomas. *Life and Writings of Thomas Paine.* New York: Vincent Parke and Co., 1908. Ten volumes. Large octavo. Contemporary three-quarter brown morocco gilt. Marbled endpapers, raised bands. Limited "Deluxe Continental Edition," one of only 200 numbered sets. Hand-colored illustrations. Near fine. $2,500.00

PAINE, Thomas. *Life and Writings of Thomas Paine.* New York: Vincent Parke and Company, 1908. Ten octavo volumes. Full brown morocco gilt. Special De Luxe Independence Edition of the Centenary Issue, limited to 500 copies, signed by the editor. Near fine. $3,300.00

PAINE, Thomas. *Rights of a Man.* With: *Rights of Man, Part the Second.* London: 1791 – 1792. Two small octavo volumes. Late nineteenth century three quarter red morocco gilt. Near fine. $675.00

PAINE, Thomas. *The Life and Works.* New Rochelle, New York: 1925. Ten volumes. Octavo. Modern three-quarter dark green morocco gilt. Illustrated with portraits and photographs. Patriot's edition. Near fine. $1,900.00

PAINE, Thomas. *The Writings of Thomas Paine.* New York and London: G.P. Putnam's Sons, 1902 – 08. Four volumes. With: CONWAY, Moncure Daniel. *The Life of Thomas Paine.* New York and London: G.P. Putnam's Sons, 1892. Two volumes. Six volumes in all. Octavo. Contemporary three-quarter dark green morocco gilt by Riviere. Illustrated with two frontispiece portraits. Near fine. $1,600.00

PAINE, Thomas. *The Writings.* Albany: 1791 – 1792. Contemporary full calf. Octavo. First edition. Near fine. $2,600.00

PALGRAVE, Francis. *The Rise and Progress of the English Commonwealth: Anglo Saxon Period.* London: John Murray, 1832. Two volumes. Full tan calf. Large 4to. Near fine. $275.00

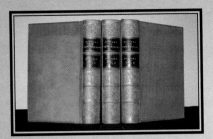

PALFREY, John Gorham. *History of New England.* Boston: Little, Brown and Co., 1865. Three volumes. Full butterscotch calf with marbled edges. Illustrated with maps, very rare in this binding. 9" tall. Fine. $875.00

PARDOE, Julia. *The Court & Reign of Francis the First King of France.* London: Richard Bently & Son, 1887. Three volumes. Full red calf and gilt decorated spine. Near fine. $850.00

PARDOE, Julia. *The Court and Reign of Francis The First, Louis the Fourteenth and Marie De Medicis.* London: Richard Bentley & Son, 1887. Nine volumes. Three-quarter navy morocco gilt. Near fine. $1,800.00

PARDOE, Miss. *Louis XIV and the Court of France in the 17th Century.* New York: Harper & Brothers, 1846. Two volumes. Three-quarter white vellum. Top edges gilt. Illustrated. 8" tall. Near fine. $375.00

PARDOE, Miss. *The Works of Miss Pardoe.* London: Richard Bentley, 1849. Five volumes. Full olive morocco. Highly gilt spine with all edges gilt. Illustrated. Includes *Francis the First & Marie De Medicis.* 9" tall. Near fine. $900.00

PARLEY, Peter. *Heroism of Boyhood.* Edinburgh and London: Gall & Inglis, n.d., circa 1870. Full maroon morocco. Prize binding with marbled edges. Illustrated. 7½" tall. Near fine. $145.00

PARIS, Comte de. *History of the Civil War in America.* Philadelphia: Jos. H. Coates & Co., 1876. Four volumes. Octavo. Contemporary full red morocco, gilt edges, raised bands and marbled endpapers. First edition in English, translated by Louis Tasistro. Illustrated with 17 folding maps in color. Near fine. $1,400.00

PARKMAN, Francis. *Works.* Boston: 1910. Thirteen volumes. Octavo. Three-quarter burgundy calf gilt. Frontispiece in each volume and illustrated with numerous maps. Near fine. $1,800.00

PARKMAN, Francis. *Works.* Boston: Little, Brown & Co., 1884 – 1896. Twelve volumes. Octavo. Three-quarter dark blue morocco gilt, marbled endpapers and boards. Illustrated with maps and portraits. Near fine. $2,200.00

PARTON, James. *The Life and Times of Aaron Burr.* Boston and New York: Houghton, Mifflin & Co., 1900. Two volumes. Octavo. Three-quarter dark blue morocco gilt. Near fine. $325.00

PAYNE, John. *Arabian Nights.* London: Villon Society, 1897. Nine volumes. Full tan morocco gilt by Zaehnsdorf. Limited edition, one of only 500 sets. Near fine. $2,800.00

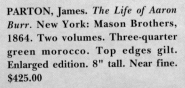

PARTON, James. *The Life of Aaron Burr.* New York: Mason Brothers, 1864. Two volumes. Three-quarter green morocco. Top edges gilt. Enlarged edition. 8" tall. Near fine. $425.00

PEPYS, Samuel. *Everybody's Pepys*. London: R & R Clark, 1932. Full tree calf by Riviere. Highly gilt spine with all edges gilt. Illustrated by Earnest H. Shepard. Reprint of 1832 edition. 7½" tall. Fine. $290.00

PEARY, Robert A. *Northward over the "Great Ice."* London: 1898. Two octavo volumes. Full navy calf. Illustrated with hundreds of illustrations, portraits and maps. First edition. Near fine. $900.00

PEARY, Robert E. *The North Pole*. London: 1920. Large octavo. Contemporary three-quarter blue calf. First English edition. Near fine. $500.00

PEARY, Robert E. *The North Pole*. New York: Frederick A. Stokes Co., 1910. Three-quarter blue morocco. Raised bands, gilt panels. Illustrated. Limited edition, one of only 500 copies. Near fine. $1,100.00

PENN, William. *A Brief Account of the Rise and Progress of the People Called Quakers*. London: Mary Hinde, 1769. Quarter calf over marbled paper boards. Raised bands, paneled spine, and maroon morocco label. Near fine. $375.00

PEPYS, Samuel. *Memoirs of Samuel Pepys*. London: Henry Colburn, 1825. Two large quarto volumes. Early full calf with green morocco labels. Illustrated with numerous engraved portraits and plates. First edition. Near fine. $1,600.00

PERCIVAL, Emily. *The Souvenir Gallery*. Boston: Phillips, Sampson & Co., 1853. Full black calf with all edges gilt. Thirteen steel plates. First edition. 10" tall. Near fine. $475.00

PERRAULT, Claude. *A Treatise of the Five Orders of Columns in Architecture*. London: Printed by Benjamin Motte, 1708. Full speckled calf. Gilt decorated spines. Folio. Illustrated. First edition in English. Near fine. $2,300.00

PETERS, DeWitt C. *The Life and Adventures of Kit Carson*. New York: 1858. Thick octavo contemporary three-quarter brown calf. First edition, illustrated. Near fine. $1,100.00

PHILLIPPS-WOOLEY, Clive. *Big Game Shooting*. London: Longmans, Green & Co., 1894. Two volumes. Three-quarter green morocco gilt. Illustrated. Near fine. $250.00

PHILOSTRATUS, Flavius. *The Two First Books, of Philostratus, Concerning the Life of Apollonius Tyaneus*. London: Nathaniel Thompson, 1680. Nineteenth century contemporary calf. Raised bands with red morocco label and modern endpapers. Translated by Charles Blount. First English edition. Near fine. $675.00

Picturesque America. New York: D. Appleton & Co., 1872. Two volumes. Three-quarter green morocco gilt. Raised bands. Folio. Illustrated by eminent American artists. Near fine. $1,600.00

PIKE, Zebulon. *An Account of Expeditions to the Sources of the Mississippi, and Through the Western Parts of Louisiana, to the Sources of the Arkansaw, Kans, La Platte, and Pierre Juan Rivers. During the Years 1805 – 1807*. Philadelphia: C & A Conrad, 1810. Full brown morocco. Raised bands with red morocco label. Octavo. First edition. Near fine. $6,200.00

PINKERTON, Allan. *The Expressman and the Detective*. Chicago: 1874. Full calf. Octavo. Illustrated. First edition. Near fine. $410.00

PLATO. *The Dialogues of Plato*. Oxford: 1892. Five octavo volumes. Full green polished calf gilt. Gilt decorated spines. Third edition. Near fine. $850.00

PLATO. *The Republic of Plato. In Ten Books*. Glasgow: Robert and Andrew Foulis, 1763. Contemporary full tan calf. Raised bands and red morocco label. Translated from the Greek by H. Spens. First edition in English. Near fine. $2,600.00

POE, Edgar Allan. *Lenore.* Boston: Estes and Lauriat, 1886. Full brown calf. Top edges gilt. Illustrated by Hy Sandham. Heavily carved in relief covers with central carving of a woman. Relievo binding. Near fine. $1,200.00

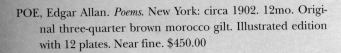

POE, Edgar Allan. *Poems.* New York: circa 1902. 12mo. Original three-quarter brown morocco gilt. Illustrated edition with 12 plates. Near fine. $450.00

POE, Edgar Allan. *Tales and Poems.* London: John C. Nimmo, 1884. Four volumes. Octavo. Full contemporary dark blue calf gilt with tan and red morocco labels. Marbled endpapers. Limited edition, one of only 1,000 sets printed. Near fine. $675.00

POE, Edgar Allan. *The Complete Works of Edgar Allan Poe.* London and New York: G.P. Putnam's Sons, 1902. Ten volumes. Three-quarter butterscotch calf with top edges gilt. Illustrated, The Knickerbocker Press. 8¼" tall. Near fine. $2,100.00

POE, Edgar Allan. *The Complete Works of Edgar Allan Poe.* New York: Fred deFau & Co., 1902. Ten volumes. Three-quarter maroon morocco. Top edges gilt. Hand-colored frontispieces. #725 of 1,000 numbered sets. 8" tall. Near fine. $1,900.00

POE, Edgar Allan. *The Poetical Works of Edgar Allan Poe.* London: J. & C. Brown and Co., n.d., circa 1870. Full green morocco with marbled edges. Illustrated by Wehnert, Godwin, Hulme, Weir, and Anelay. 7½" tall. Near fine. $275.00

POE, Edgar Allan. *Tales and Poems.* New York and Boston: circa 1900. Six octavo volumes. Contemporary three-quarter brown morocco. Illustrated. "Buckner Library Edition." Near fine. $1,100.00

POE, Edgar Allan. *Tales of Mystery & Imagination.* London: George F. Harrap & Co., Ltd., 1935. Quarto. Full original vellum with gilt decorations on the spine and cover. Illustrated by Arthur Rackham. First edition. Limited edition, one of only 460 copies signed by the illustrator. Illustrations include full page color plates and seventeen full-page drawings in black and white. Near fine. $3,000.00

POE, Edgar Allan. *The Bells and other Poems.* London and New York: Hodder & Stoughton, 1900. Full wine morocco, gilt panels and covers. Near fine. $975.00

POE, Edgar Allan. *The Complete Poems.* New York and London: 1908. Octavo. Three-quarter early twentieth century olive morocco gilt. With 12 plates by Coburn. Near fine. $500.00

POE, Edgar Allan. *The Complete Works of Edgar Allan Poe.* New York: G.P. Putnam's Sons, 1902. Ten volumes. Three-quarter tan morocco gilt. One of only 300 sets. Tamerlane edition. Near fine. $3,200.00

POE, Edgar Allan. *The Poetical Works of Edgar Allan Poe.* New York: J.S. Redfield, 1858. Full maroon calf by W. Bone. All edges gilt. Illustrated by Pickersgrill, Tenniel, etc. 9" tall. Near fine. $1,500.00

POE, Edgar Allan. *The Poetical Works of Poe.* New York: J.S. Redfield, 1858. Full chocolate calf with embossed covers. All edges gilt. Illustrated with plates by Tenniel, Foster, and Darley. 9" tall. Near fine. $1,100.00

POE, Edgar Allan. *The Complete Works.* New York: 1902. Ten volumes. Octavo. Contemporary three-quarter dark green morocco gilt. Limited "Book-Lover's Eldorado Edition," One of only 1,050 sets. Sixty-six full page illustrations. Near fine. $2,400.00

POE, Edgar Allan. *The Complete Works.* New York and Chicago: 1902. Seventeen volumes. Octavo. Contemporary three-quarter red morocco gilt. Limited edition, one of 1,000 sets. Illustrated with hand-colored engraved frontispieces in each volume. Near fine. $2,300.00

POE, Edgar Allan. *The Complete Works.* New York and London: 1902. Ten volumes. Octavo. Contemporary three-quarter dark green morocco gilt. Tamerlane edition, one of only 300 copies. Illustrated with full-page photogravures by Frederick Coburn. Near fine. $3,200.00

POE, Edgar Allan. *The Complete Works.* New York: The Lamb Publishing Company, circa 1910. Ten volumes. Octavo. Half red morocco gilt. Hand-decorated endpapers. The Raven edition, one of only 1,000 sets. Illustrated by Frederick Simpson Coburn. Near fine. $1,800.00

POE, Edgar Allan. *The Works.* Boston: Dana Estes & Co., 1884. Six volumes. Octavo. Contemporary three-quarter tan calf gilt. Near fine. $975.00

POE, Edgar Allan. *The Works.* New York: Charles Scribner's Sons, 1894. Ten volumes. Three-quarter blue morocco gilt. Near fine. $2,250.00

POE, Edgar Allan. *Works.* Chicago: 1894 – 1895. Ten volumes. Octavo. Contemporary full vellum decorated with art nouveau floral designs. Limited edition, one of only 250 large paper sets. Near fine. $4,200.00

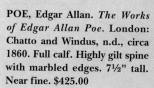 

POE, Edgar Allan. *The Works of Edgar Allan Poe.* London: Chatto and Windus, n.d., circa 1860. Full calf. Highly gilt spine with marbled edges. 7½" tall. Near fine. $425.00

POGANY, Willy. *Rubaiyat of Omar Khayyam.* London: 1930. Quarto. Full turquoise crushed morocco gilt. Limited edition, one of only 1,250 copies. Illustrated with 12 full-page mounted color plates and black and white illustrations. Onlaid leather emblem on front cover. Near fine. $1,100.00

POGANY, Willy. *Rubaiyat.* New York: 1917. Original watered silk. Octavo. Illustrated by Willy Pogany. Near fine. $750.00

POINSETT, Joel Roberts. *Report from the Secretary of War in Compliance with a Resolution of the Senate of the 14th of October, 1837, in Relation to the Protection of the Western Frontier of the United States.* Washington: 1838. Modern half purple morocco. Octavo. Illustrated. First edition. Near fine. $1,100.00

POLIDORI, John William. *The Vampyre; A Tale.* London: 1819. Slim octavo. Full black calf. First edition. Near fine. $2,200.00

POLIDORI, John William. *The Vampyre; A Tale.* London: Printed for Sherwood, Neely and Jones, 1819. Full tan calf. Octavo. First edition. Near fine. $2,200.00

POE, Edgar Allan. *Works of Edgar Allan Poe.* New York and London: GP Putnam's Sons, 1902. Ten volumes. Three-quarter blue morocco by Himebaugh and Browne. Top edges gilt. Ravens embossed on spines. Illustrated with 60 photogravures. Annabel edition. Very good. $1,600.00

POLLARD, E.A. *Southern History of the War*. New York: Charles B. Richardson, 1866. Two volumes bound in one. Three-quarter tan calf. Marbled edges. Illustrated. Light foxing to engraved plates. First edition. 9" tall. Very good. $350.00

POLLARD, Edward A. *The Lost Cause*. New York: E.B. Treat & Co., 1867. Three-quarter brown calf by Launder and MacDonald. Top edges gilt. Illustrated with large pull-out hand-colored map and steel engravings. 9½" tall. Near fine. $525.00

POLLARD, A.F. *Henry VIII*. London, Paris, and New York: Coupil & Co., 1902. Full brown morocco. Raised bands, floral onlays, top edges gilt. Illustrated. Near fine. $900.00

POLLARD, A.F. *Henry VIII*. London: 1902. Folio. Contemporary full red morocco gilt. Limited edition, one of only 1,150 copies printed on fine paper, illustrated with over 30 full-page plates. Near fine. $1,200.00

POLLARD, Alfred W. *The Romance of King Arthur and His Knights of the Round Table*. London: MacMillian & Co., 1917. First trade edition. Three-quarter blue morocco by Sangorski and Sutcliffe. Illustrated by Arthur Rackham. Near fine. $900.00

POLO, Marco. *The Travels of Marco Polo, A Venetian, in the Thirteenth Century: Being a Description, By That Early Traveller, of Remarkable Places and Things in the Eastern Part of the World*. London: 1818. Three-quarter calf gilt by Bayntun. Translated from Italian by William Marsden. Illustrated. Near fine. $375.00

POPE, Alexander. *The Iliad of Homer. The Odyssey of Homer. With Additional Notes, Critical and Illustrative by Gilbert Wakefield*. London: J. Johnson, 1806. Nine volumes. Large octavo. Contemporary full tan calf, red and black leather labels. Engraved frontispiece of Homer. Near fine. $1,200.00

POPE, Alexander. *The Iliad and Odyssey of Homer*. London: Duroverax, 1806. Twelve volumes. Full maroon morocco. Illustrated with copper plates. Bookplates of Sir David Salomons, Bart and John Heroy. Small vo. All edges gilt. Fine. $2,000.00

POPE, Alexander. *The Iliad of Homer*. London: Printed by W. Bowyer, 1715. Six volumes. Full calf. Illustrated. First English edition, sold by Subscription only. 11" tall. Very good. $3,200.00

POPE, Alexander. *The Iliad and The Odyssey*. New York: Leavitt & Allen, circa 1870. Full maroon morocco. Highly gilt spine and covers, all edges gilt. Illustrated. 9½" tall. Near fine. $385.00

POPE, Alexander. *The Iliad of Homer*. Three volumes. With: *The Odyssey of Homer*. Two volumes. London: Vernon and Hood, 1802. Large octavo. Black straight-grain morocco gilt. Raised bands and inner dentelles. Near fine. $950.00

POPE, Alexander. *The Poetical Works of Alexander Pope*. London: William Pickering, 1835. Three volumes. Full green morocco, highly gilt spine and marbled edges. 6½" tall. Near fine. $250.00

PORTER, Admiral. *Incidents and Anecdotes of the Civil War*. New York: D. Appleton, 1885. Three-quarter brown calf by Launder and MacDonald. Top edges gilt. First edition. 9" tall. Near fine. $300.00

POPE, Alexander. *The Works of Alexander Pope*. London: Printed by C. Bathurft, 1788. Six volumes. Full tree calf. Illustrated with copper plates. 7" tall. Near fine. $1,250.00

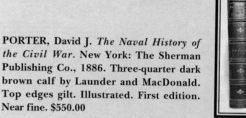

PORTER, David J. *The Naval History of the Civil War*. New York: The Sherman Publishing Co., 1886. Three-quarter dark brown calf by Launder and MacDonald. Top edges gilt. Illustrated. First edition. Near fine. $550.00

POTTER, John. *Antiquities of Greece*. London: A. Wilde, 1764. Two volumes. Full tan calf. Raised bands, gilt spines. Illustrated with copper engraved plates. Near fine. $350.00

POWELL, John Wesley. *Exploration of the Colorado River of the West and Its Tributaries*. Washington: 1875. Contemporary three-quarter brown morocco. Quarto. Illustrated with numerous plates and two large folding maps. First edition. Near fine. $1,750.00

POWER, Tyrone. *Impressions of America; During the Years 1833 – 35*. London: Richard Bentley, 1836. Two octavo volumes. Nineteenth century three-quarter brown calf. Raised bands with red morocco labels. First edition. Near fine. $375.00

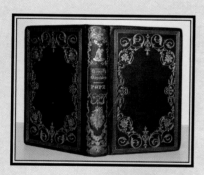

POPE, Alexander. *Translation of the Odyssey of Homer*. Hartford: Silas Andrus and Son, 1851. Full black calf. Highly gilt spine and covers, all edges gilt. 7" tall. Near fine. $310.00

PORTER, Jane. *The Scottish Chiefs*. London: Virtue & Co., circa 1845. Two volumes. Three-quarter red morocco gilt. Raised bands, gilt decorated spines. Illustrated. Near fine. $375.00

PORTER, L.J. Jerusalem. *Bethany and Bethlehem*. London: Thomas Nelson & Sons, 1887. Full navy morocco. Raised bands, gilt panels. 4to. Illustrated. $425.00

PRAED, Winthrop Mackworth. *The Poems of Winthrop Mackworth Praed*. London: Edward Moxon, 1864. Two volumes. Full purple morocco by Hatchard. 8½" tall. Near fine. $450.00

PRESCOTT, William H. *Prescott's Works*. Philadelphia: J.B. Lippincott & Co., 1864. Eleven volumes. Full tan calf. Marbled edges. 8" tall. Near fine. $1,750.00

PRESCOTT, William. *The Works of William Prescott*. London: George Routeledge & Sons, 1867. Eleven volumes (only four shown). Full tree calf. Marbled edges. Illustrated with steel engravings. 9" tall. Near fine. $2,300.00

PRESCOTT, William. *The Works*. London: 1844 – 1864. Fifteen volumes. Three-quarter crimson crushed morocco by Riviere & Son. Near fine. $2,250.00

PRESCOTT, William. *Works*. Philadelphia: J.B. Lippincott, 1880. Fifteen volumes. Three-quarter brown morocco gilt. Near fine. $1,600.00

PRESTON, William. *Illustrations of Masonry*. London: 1804. 12mo. Contemporary full mottled calf. Eleventh edition, originally printed for distribution only to individual lodges. Near fine. $175.00

PRIOR, R.C. Alexander M.D. *Ancient Danish Ballads*. Edinburgh: Williams and Norgate, 1860. Three volumes. Three-quarter green morocco. Top edges gilt. 8" tall. Near fine. $350.00

PUTNAM, G. P. (Various writers). *Homes of American Authors*. New York: G.P. Putnams & Co., 1853. Full green morocco. Highly gilt spine and covers with all edges gilt. Illustrated. 8½" tall. Near fine. $175.00

PUFENDORF, Samuel. *Of the Law of Nature and Nations*. London: 1749. Three-quarter brown calf. Folio. Fifth edition. Near fine. $650.00

PYLE, Howard. *The Story of Sir Launcelot*. New York: Charles Scribner's Sons. Three-quarter tan morocco. Raised bands, gilt panels. First edition. Near fine. $650.00

PYLE, Howard. *The Story of the Champions of the Round Table*. New York: Charles Scribner's Sons, 1905. Three-quarter tan morocco. Raised bands, gilt panels. First edition. Near fine. $600.00

PYLE, Howard. *The Wonder Clock*. New York: Harper & Bros., 1888. Three-quarter brown morocco. Raised bands, gilt panels. First edition. Near fine. $475.00

PYNE, William Henry. *The History of the Royal Residences*. London: A. Dry, 1819. Three large quarto volumes. Full contemporary red morocco gilt. Raised bands, gilt decorated spines. Illustrated with hand-colored plates. First edition. Near fine. $5,500.00

QUINCY, Josiah. *Memoir of the Life of John Quincy Adams*. Boston: Phillips, Sampson & Co., 1858. Full brown calf. All edges gilt. First edition. Near fine. $750.00

RACKHAM, Arthur. *The Allie's Fairy Book.* London: William Heinemann, 1916. Full blue morocco by Bayntun. Highly gilt spine and covers, all edges gilt. Flat signed by Arthur Rackham, #431 of 500 copies. Illustrated by Arthur Rackham with custom slipcase. 9½" tall. Fine. $2,800.00

RACKHAM, Arthur. *Arthur Rackham's Book of Pictures.* London: 1913. Full camel morocco gilt. Limited edition, one of only 1,030 copies signed and illustrated by the author. Near fine. $1,400.00

RACKHAM, Arthur. SHAKESPEARE, William. *A Midsummer-Night's Dream.* London: 1911. Quarto. Mid twentieth century blue morocco gilt with red morocco onlays. Illustrated trade edition. Near fine. $900.00

RACKHAM, Arthur. *Some British Ballads.* London: 1919. Full red morocco by Sangorski & Sutcliffe. Limited edition, one of only 575 copies signed by the author. Near fine. $1,300.00

RACKHAM, Arthur. *The Fairy Tales of the Brothers Grimm.* New York: 1909. Quarto. Modern full brown morocco gilt. Limited edition. Forty full page color illustrations. 55 black and white drawings. Near fine. $2,100.00

RADCLYFFE, C.R.E. *Big Game Shooting in Alaska.* London: 1904. Octavo. Later twentieth century three-quarter black calf. First edition, with 45 photographic illustrations. Near fine. $375.00

RAEBURN, Henry. *The Makers of British Art.* London: The Walker Scott, 1904. Full red morocco gilt by Riviere. Raised bands, floral gilt design on spine and covers. Illustrated. Near fine. $3,100.00

RALEIGH, Walter. *The Historie of the World, in Five Books.* London: 1666. Thick folio. Contemporary full dark brown calf. First published in 1614. Near fine. $2,100.00

RAMBAUD, Alfred. *A Popular History of Russia.* Boston: Dana Estes, 1880. Three volumes. Full tree calf by Estes and Lauriat. All edges gilt. Illustrated. Very good. $375.00

RALEIGH, Walter. *The Historie of the World.* London: 1652. Contemporary full brown calf. Thick folio. Illustrated with engraved maps and plans. Seventh edition. Near fine. $2,400.00

RAMBAUD, A. *A Popular History of Russia from the Earliest Times to 1880.* Boston: Estes & Lauriat, 1880. Three volumes. Three-quarter dark maroon morocco gilt. Gilt decorated spines. Translated by L.B. Lang. Illustrated. Near fine. $450.00

RAMEAU, Jean Philippe. *A Treatise of Musick, Containing the Principles of Composition.* London: 1752. Contemporary half speckled brown calf gilt with marbled boards. Quarto. Second edition in English. Near fine. $650.00

RANDOLPH, John, and MAXWELL, William. *The Case of the Planters of Tobacco in Virginia.* London: 1733. Early twentieth century three-quarter brown calf. Slim octavo. First edition. Near fine. $1,100.00

RANSOME, Stafford. *Japan in Transition, A Comparative Study of the Progress Policy and Methods of the Japanese Since Their War with China.* London: Harper & Bros., 1899. Full blue morocco gilt by Asprey. Illustrated. Near fine. $375.00

RANKE, Leopold. *The Popes of Rome.* London: Blackie and Son, 1846. Two volumes. Full brown crushed levant morocco. Illustrated. 9¾" tall. Near fine. $290.00

RAWLINSON, George M.A. *The History of Herodotus.* New York: D. Appleton & Co., 1859. Four volumes. Three-quarter butterscotch calf. Marbled edges. Illustrated. 9" tall. Near fine. $875.00

RAWLINSON, George. *Ancient Egypt.* London: T. Fisher Unwin, 1895. Full tree calf. Marbled edges. Illustrated with pull-out maps. 8" tall. Near fine. $410.00

RAWLINSON, George. *History of Ancient Egypt.* New York: John W. Lovell Co., 1880. Two volumes. Three-quarter butterscotch calf. Illustrated. 7" tall. Near fine. $475.00

RAYMOND, Henry J. *The Life and Public Services of Abraham Lincoln.* New York: Derby and Miller, 1865. Three-quarter brown calf. All edges gilt. Illustrated. First edition. 9" tall. Near fine. $290.00

READ, Thomas Buchanan. *The Female Poets of America.* Philadelphia: E.H. Butler & Co., 1852. Full red morocco. All edges gilt. Steel engravings. 10" tall. Near fine. $385.00

READE, Charles. *Reade's Works.* Boston: Dana Estes & Co., 1872. Twelve volumes. Three-quarter butterscotch calf. Highly gilt spine. 7½" tall. Near fine. $1,400.00

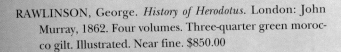

RAWLINSON, George. *History of Herodotus.* London: John Murray, 1862. Four volumes. Three-quarter green morocco gilt. Illustrated. Near fine. $850.00

READE, Charles. *Peg Woffington.* London: 1899. Full red morocco gilt. Small thick octavo. Fine Kelliegram binding. Illustrated by Thomson. First edition. Near fine. $1,500.00

REMINGTON, Frederic. *Crooked Trails.* New York and London: 1898. Octavo. Contemporary full green morocco gilt. First edition with 49 plates by Remington. Near fine. $450.00

REPTON, Humphry. *Observations on the Theory and Practice of Landscape Gardening.* London: 1805. Three-quarter dark green morocco. Folio. Top edge gilt. Illustrated. First edition. Near fine. $7,200.00

REED, Isaac and GILCHRIST, Actavius. *A Select Collection of Old Plays.* London: Septimus Provett, 1825. Thirteen volumes (only four shown). Full tree calf. The thirteenth volume that was added later is included. 8½" tall. Very good. $2,600.00

RESTA, Sebastiano. *The True Effigies of the Most Eminent Painters.* London: 1694. Full paneled brown calf. Folio. Illustrated. First English edition. Near fine. $1,400.00

RICHARDSON, James D. *A Compilation of the Messages and Papers of the Presidents.* New York: 1907. Twenty volumes. Tall octavo. Original black imitation leather. Illustrated. Great Seal on all covers. Near fine. $950.00

RICHARDSON, Albert D. *Personal History of Ulysses S. Grant.* Hartford: American Publishing Co., 1868. Three-quarter tan calf. Marbled edges. Illustrated. First edition. 9" tall. Near fine. $325.00

RICHARDSON, Albert. *The Secret Service, The Field, The Dungeon and The Escape.* Hartford: American Publishing, 1865. Full tan calf. Illustrated first edition. 9" tall. Very good. $250.00

RICHARDSON, James. *A Compilation of the Messages and Papers of the Presidents.* New York: The Bureau of National Literature, 1897. Twenty volumes (only three shown). Full black imitation leather. All edges gilt. Illustrated. 9½" tall. Near fine. $700.00

RICHARDSON, Samuel. *Pamella.* New York: Croscup & Sterling Co., 1901. From the 20 volume set, complete in five. Full red morocco by Stikeman. Top edges gilt. Hand-colored frontis, extra illustrated. Silk endpapers, leather inlaid and silk doublures. Autograph edition, one of 56 numbered sets. Holland handmade paper. Fine. $1,000.00

RICKMAN, Thomas. *An Attempt to Discriminate the Styles of Architecture in England.* London: Longman, Rees, Orme, Green & Longman, 1835. Full blue morocco. Prize binding with marbled edges. Illustrated. 8½" tall. Near fine. $375.00

RIDGEWAY, Henry B. *The Lord's Land.* New York: Nelson & Phillips, 1876. Full black calf with all edges gilt. Rare American binding. Illustrated. First edition. 9¾" tall. Fine. $550.00

RITSON, Joseph. *Robin Hood.* London: J. & G. Todd, 1832. Two volumes. Full red morocco. Printed by William Pickering. Illustrated with Bewick woodcuts. Second edition. 7½" tall. Very good. $800.00

RILEY, W. James. *Works.* All Rights Reserved Copyright, 1913, J.W. Riley. Six volumes. Full wine morocco gilt. Raised bands, green leather, and silk doublures. Ornate gilt spines and covers. Illustrated. Limited edition, one of only 150 sets. Near fine. $1,600.00

RITSON, Joseph. *Robin Hood.* London: John C. Nimmo, 1887. Full green morocco gilt and ribbed decorated spines. Illustrated by A.H. Tourrier and E. Buckman. Near fine. $650.00

ROBERT, Lord of Kandahar. *Forty-one Years in India.* London: MacMillian & Co., 1901. Full red polished calf. Raised bands, gilt spine, and marbled edges. Illustrated. Near fine. $350.00

ROBERTS, David. *The Holy Land, Syria, Idumea, Arabia, Egypt, & Nubia.* London: 1856. Six volumes bound in three. Quarto. Contemporary full tan calf gilt. Illustrated with 250 tinted lithographs of the Holy Land and the Middle East. Near fine. $6,200.00

ROBERTSON, William. *An Historical Disquisition Concerning the Knowledge Which the Ancients Had of India.* London: A. Strahan, 1791. Half calf over marbled paper boards. Raised bands and red morocco label. First edition. Illustrated with two large engraved foldout maps. Near fine. $475.00

ROBERTSON, William. *The History of America.* London: Cadel and Davies, 1808. Four volumes. Full brown pebbled levant morocco. Marbled edges. Illustrated with pull-out maps. 9" tall. Near fine. $575.00

ROBERTSON, William. *The History of America.* London: 1777. Two volumes. Quarto. Contemporary full speckled calf. First edition with folding maps. Near fine. $1,800.00

ROBERTSON, William. *The History of America.* London: A. Strahan and T. Cadell. Edinburgh: J. Balfour, 1788. Three volumes. Contemporary polished calf gilt. Flat spines with gilt compartments and red and dark green morocco labels. Fifth edition. Illustrated with five engraved folding plates. Near fine. $750.00

ROBERTSON, William. *The History of America.* London: W. Strahan, T. Cadell, J. Balfour, 1777 – 1796. Three volumes. Contemporary full calf gilt. Black and green leather labels. First edition. Near fine. $1,100.00

ROBERTSON, William. *The History of the Reign of Emperor Charles V.* London: A. Strahan and T. Cadell, and Edinburgh: J. Balfour, 1787. Four volumes. Contemporary polished calf gilt. Flat spines with red and dark green morocco labels. Sixth edition. Illustrated with four engraved frontispieces. Near fine. $475.00

ROBERTSON, William D.D. *The History of the Reign of the Emperor Charles V.* London: Cadell & Davies, 1806. Four volumes. Full tan early tree calf. 8½" tall. Near fine. $925.00

ROBERTSON, William. *The Works of William Robertson.* London: Longmans, Brown, Green and Longmans, 1852. Full sky blue morocco by Zaehnsdorf. Prize binding with marbled edges. 9" tall. Near fine. $280.00

ROGERS, Samuel. *Human Life*. London: John Murray, 1819. Full calf. All edges gilt. Near fine. $225.00

ROLLIN, M. *The Ancient History*. London: T. Cadell, 1839. Six volumes. Full tan calf. Highly gilt spine, marbled edges. Illustrated with pull-out maps. 8½" tall. Near fine. $1,200.00

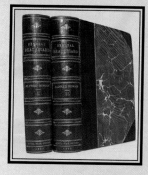

ROGERS, Samuel. *Italy, A Poem*. London: T. Cadell, 1830. Full tan calf. Highly gilt cover with gilt floral vines and flowers. All edges gilt. First edition. Illustrated. Baron Dickinson Webster's copy. 8" tall. Near fine. $475.00

ROMAN, Alfred. *The Military Operations of General Beauregard*. New York: Harper & Brothers, Franklin Square, 1883. Two volumes. Three-quarter dark brown calf by Launder and MacDonald. Top edges gilt. First edition. Near fine. $850.00

ROMAN, Alfred. *The Military Operations of General Beauregard in the War Between the States 1861 – 1865*. New York: Harper & Bros, circa 1885. Two volumes. Thick octavo. Three-quarter dark brown morocco gilt. Raised bands and marbled endpapers. Near fine. $650.00

ROGERS, Samuel. *Poems*. London: T. Cadell, 1834. Full tan calf. Highly gilt cover with gilt floral vines and flowers. All edges gilt. First edition. Illustrated. Baron Dickinson Webster's copy. 8" tall. Near fine. $475.00

ROOSEVELT, Theodore. *African Game Trails*. New York: Charles Scribner's Sons, 1910. Full green morocco gilt. Raised bands, gilt edges. Hundreds of illustrations by Kermit Roosevelt. First edition. Near fine. $675.00

ROOSEVELT, Theodore. *Outdoor Pastimes of an American Hunter*. New York: Charles Scribner's Sons, 1905. Full tan morocco. Raised bands, gilt panels. Illustrated. First edition. Near fine. $600.00

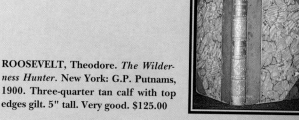

ROLLIN, M. *The Ancient History of the Egyptians, Carthaginians, Assyrians, Babylonians, Medes, Persians, Grecians and Macedonians*. London: G. Griffin, 1847. Six volumes. Three-quarter butterscotch calf. Printed for William Tegg & Co. Illustrated with pull-out maps. Eighteenth edition. Fine. $1,100.00

ROOSEVELT, Theodore. *The Wilderness Hunter*. New York: G.P. Putnams, 1900. Three-quarter tan calf with top edges gilt. 5" tall. Very good. $125.00

ROOSEVELT, Theodore. *The Wilderness Hunter. An Account of the Big Game of the United States and its Chase with Horse, Hound and Rifle.* New York and London: G.P. Putnam's Sons, 1893. Quarto. Full calf. First edition, one of only 200 copies signed by Roosevelt and the publisher. Near fine. $1,800.00

ROOSEVELT, Theodore. *The Winning of the West.* New York and London: G.P. Putnams's Sons, 1900. Four large octavo volumes. Three-quarter green morocco. Raised bands, marbled boards and endpapers. Top edges gilt. Daniel Boone edition, one of only 200 copies. Near fine. $2,600.00

ROOSEVELT, Theodore. *Through the Brazilian Wilderness.* New York: Charles Scribner's Sons, 1914. Full brown morocco gilt. Raised bands, gilt edges. Illustrated by Kermit Roosevelt. First edition. Near fine. $625.00

ROSCO, William. *The Life of Lorenzo De' Medici called the Magnificent.* Liverpool: J.M. Creery, 1795. Two volumes. Three-quarter tan calf. Raised bands, gilt decorated spines. Large 4to. Near fine. $450.00

ROSCOE, Thomas. *The History of Painting in Italy.* London: W. Simpkin, 1828. Six volumes. Full blue calf. Raised bands, gilt panels. Translated from Italian by Lanzi. Near fine. $900.00

ROSCOE, William. *The Life of Lorenzo De Medici, Called the Magnificent.* Liverpool: J. McCreery, 1795. Two quarto volumes. Three-quarter green morocco. Raised bands, gilt panels. Illustrated. Near fine. $450.00

ROSE, John Holland. *The Life of Napoleon I, Including New Materials from the British Official Records.* New York: MacMillan 1913. Two volumes in one. Octavo. Contemporary full green morocco gilt. Contained in a custom cloth slipcase. Illustrated with full page maps. Near fine. $485.00

ROSEN, Lew. *Napoleon's Opera Glass. In Historic Study.* London: Elkin Matthews, 1897. Full green morocco gilt. Illustrated. Near fine. $450.00

ROSS, Alexander. *Pansebeia: Or, A View of All Religions in the World.* London: James Young, 1653. Nineteenth century dark calf. Raised bands, marbled endpapers. Engraved title page and frontispiece portrait. Near fine. $625.00

ROSS, Janet. *Three Generations of English Women Memoirs and Correspondence of Mrs. John Taylor, Mrs. Sarah Austin and Lady Duff Gordon.* London: John Murray, 1888. Two volumes. Three-quarter red morocco. Raised bands, gilt panels. Illustrated. Near fine. $375.00

ROSS, John. *Narrative of a Second Voyage in Search of a North-West Passage, and of a Residence in the Artic Regions.* London: 1835. Large thick quarto. Late nineteenth century full tree calf gilt. First edition with 30 full-page charts and plates. Near fine. $1,500.00

ROSS, John. *Narrative of a Second Voyage in Search of a North-West Passage.* London: A.W. Webster, 1835. Two volumes. Three-quarter red calf. Raised bands, gilt spines, marbled boards and endpapers. Top edges gilt. Illustrated with charts, plates, and a large folding map. First edition. Near fine. $1,500.00

ROSE, John Holland. *The Life of Napoleon I.* London: G. Bell and Sons, 1913. Full tree calf. Top edges gilt. 8" tall. Near fine. $280.00

ROSSETTI, Christina G. *Poems.* London: MacMillan and Co., 1896. Full black calf by Orrock and Son. All edges gilt, highly gilt spine and cover. 7" tall. Near fine. $425.00

ROSSETTI, Dante Gabriel. *The Poems of Dante Gabriel Rossetti.* New York: Brentano's, 1909. Two volumes. Small quarto. Full brown morocco gilt. Cheyene Walk edition. Near fine. $475.00

ROSSETTI, Christina. *Speaking Likenesses*. London: MacMillan & Co., 1874. Full blue morocco. Top edges gilt, inlaid red morocco designs on all four corners of both covers. Leather doublures, silk moiré endpapers. Illustrated by Arthur Hughes. First edition. 7" tall. Near fine. $1,100.00

ROUSSEAU, Jean Jacques. *A Treatise on the Social Compact*. London: 1795. Original full mottled calf. Octavo. Third edition in English. Near fine. $325.00

ROUTLEDGE, George. *Discoveries and Inventions of the Nineteenth Century*. London and New York: George Routledge & Sons, 1898. Full tan calf. Marbled edges. 456 illustrations. 8½" tall. Near fine. $220.00

RUSKIN, John. *Modern Painters*. London: Smith, Elder & Co., 1857. Five volumes. Three-quarter brown morocco gilt by Bumpus. Numerous illustrations. Near fine. $750.00

RUSKIN, John. *Ruskin's Works*. London: George Allen & Sons, 1908. Six volumes. Full tree calf by Bickers. Prize binding. Marbled edges, highly gilt. Illustrated. 7¼" tall. Fine. $1,200.00

RUSKIN, John. *Sesame and Lilies*. London: George Allen, 1901. Hand embroidered silk with gold, blue, and pink on white background. Elaborately embroidered binding, housed in a custom dust jacket and a half Moroccan slipcase. Top edges gilt. Signed letter from Ruskin. 8" tall. Near fine. $2,500.00

RUSKIN, John. *The Stones of Venice*. London: George Allen & Sons, 1911. Three volumes. Full tree calf. Marbled edges. Highly gilt. Illustrated. Prize binding. Fine. $625.00

RUSKIN, John. *The King of the Golden River*. London: 1932. Original limp vellum gilt. Slim octavo. Illustrated by Arthur Rackham. Limited edition, one of only 570 copies signed by the illustrator. Near fine. $875.00

RUSKIN, John. *Works*. New York: John Wiley & Sons, 1886. Twelve volumes. Three-quarter tan calf gilt with ribbed gilt decorated spines. Near fine. $950.00

RUSSELL, M. *History of Ancient and Modern Egypt: Its Temples and Monuments*. London: T. Nelson and Sons, 1853. Full green morocco. Highly gilt spine and cover, all edges gilt. Illustrated. 7" tall. Near fine. $420.00

RUSSELL, William Howard. *My Diary North and South*. Boston: T.O.H.P. Burnham, 1863. Three-quarter brown calf. Top edges gilt. First edition. 7½" tall. Near fine. $310.00

RUSSELL, Patrick. *A Treatise of the Plague.* London: J. Robinson, 1791. Half calf over marbled paper boards. Raised bands with red morocco label. First edition. Near fine. $2,200.00

RUSSELL, William. *The History of America, From Its Discovery by Columbus to the Conclusion of the Late War.* With: *An Account of the Rise and Progress of the Present Unhappy Contest Between Great Britain and her Colonies.* London: 1778. Two quarto volumes. Three-quarter brown morocco gilt. Raised bands and marbled boards. Illustrated with numerous engraved plates and folding maps. First edition. $950.00

RUSSIAN BIBLE, *NEW TESTAMENT.* Evaggelie. Luov, Ukraine: Institut Stravropigiiskii, n.d., circa 1860. Full red velvette. Illustrated with six hand-painted porcelains of Mark, Luke, John, Matthew, Christ, and the nativity scene on back cover. Covers trimmed with brass as are porcelains with double buckles. 18½" tall. Near fine. $3,800.00

RUXTON, *George F. Adventures in Mexico and the Rocky Mountains.* New York: Harper & Brothers, 1848. Three-quarter green morocco. Highly gilt spine with top edges gilt. First American edition. 7½" tall. Near fine. $425.00

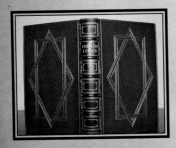

SAINTSBURY, George. *French Lyrics.* London: Kegan Paul, Trench & Co., 1885. Full navy morocco by Bayntun. Covers with gilt geometrical designs. All edges gilt, with slipcase. 6" tall. Near fine. $350.00

SALLUST. *Opera.* Basileae: Per Henricvm Petri, 1564. Seventeenth century speckled English calf gilt by John Fletcher. Raised bands, spine has gilt compartments with floral design. Near fine. $1,900.00

SAND, George. *Amandine Lucille Aurore Dupin, Baroness Dudebant, Works.* Philadelphia: George Barrie & Sons, 1901. Twenty volumes. 8vo. Full rose salmon morocco gilt. Gilt doublures in green and blue with onlaid rose design in red and green. Illustrated by twenty different artists. Near fine. $3,000.00

SAND, George. *Masterpieces of George Sand.* Philadelphia: George Barrie & Son, 1900. Twenty volumes (only three shown). Full rose morocco. Floral gilt design on covers and spine. All edges gilt. Frontispieces in each volume. Illustrated. Astral edition, printed on Japanese vellum paper, one of 150 copies. 8½" tall. Near fine. $4,000.00

SAND, George. *The Devil's Pool.* Philadelphia: 1901. Early twentieth century three-quarter brown morocco. Illustrated with numerous engravings by Rudaux. Limited English edition, one of only 1,000 copies. Near fine. $275.00

SAND, George. *The Masterpieces of George Sand.* Philadelphia: 1901. Twenty volumes. 8vo. Full pink levant gilt with hand-colored frontispieces. Astral edition, one of only 250 sets. Near fine. $3,000.00

SAND, Maurice. *The History of The Harlequinade.* London: Secker, 1915. Two volumes. Three-quarter tan calf. Gilt decorated spine with raised bands. Illustrated. Near fine. $325.00

SANDBURG, Carl. *Abraham Lincoln: The Prairie Years.* Two volumes. With: *The War Years.* Four volumes. New York: 1926 – 1939. Octavo. Three-quarter dark blue morocco gilt. First trade editions. Illustrated with photographic plates, maps, letters, and documents. Near fine. $1,300.00

SANDERS, Daniel C. *A History of the Indians Wars with the First Settlers of the United States, Particularly in New England.* Montpelier, Vermont: 1812. Full red morocco gilt by Bedford. First edition. Near fine. $2,600.00

SARPI, Paolo. *A Treatise of Matters Beneficiary...Wherein is Related...How the Almes of The Faithful Were Distributed in The Primitive Church.* London: Thomas Hodgkin, 1680. Modern gray paper over stiff boards. First edition translated by William Denton. Near fine. $650.00

SARRATT, J. H. *The Works of Damiano, Ruy-Lopez, and Salbio, on the Game of Chess.* London: T. Boosey, 1813. Two volumes. Three-quarter tan calf. Gilt spine with green labels. First edition. Near fine. $750.00

SAVARY, M. *Letters on Egypt Containing a Parallel Between the Manners of the Ancient and Modern Inhabitants its Commerce, Agriculture, Government and Religion....* J & J Robinson, 1737. Two volumes. Full contemporary calf. Gilt spines with green and red morocco labels. Near fine. $750.00

SCHARF, J. Thomas. *History of the Confederate States Navy.* Albany: 1894. Modern half blue morocco gilt. Thick octavo. Illustrated with numerous plates and in-text illustrations. Second edition. Near fine. $700.00

SCHILLER'S. *Works.* Philadelphia: George Barrie, 1883. Four volumes. Full green morocco gilt. Royal quartos. Illustrated by renowned German artists. Near fine. $800.00

SCOTT, Dr. Jonathan. *The Arabian Nights.* London: Pickering and Chatto, 1890. Eight volumes (only three shown). Full red morocco. Highly gilt spine and covers. All edges gilt. The Aldine edition, four volumes bound in eight. Illustrated. Chiswick Press. 6½" tall. Near fine. $1,200.00

SCOTT, Major John. *Partisan Life with Col. John Mosby.* New York: Harper & Brothers, 1867. Three-quarter brown calf by Launder and MacDonald. Top edges gilt. Illustrated with pullout map. First edition. 9½" tall. Near fine. $325.00

SCOTT, Sir Walter. *Historical, Legendary and Romantic Tales.* London: Bickers and Son, 1886. Full tree calf by Bickers. Marbled edges. Illustrated with 12 photogravures. 8½" tall. Near fine. $225.00

SCOTT, Sir Walter. *Ivanhoe.* Boston: Estes and Lauriat, 1893. Two volumes. Full two-tone tan calf with all edges gilt. Illustrated Holiday edition. 7¾" tall. Near fine. $700.00

SCOTT, Sir Walter. *Ivanhoe.* London: McMillan and Co., 1910. Full tree calf by Bickers. Prize binding with marbled edges. Illustrated. 7" tall. Near fine. $240.00

SCOTT, Sir Walter. *Lay of the Last Minstrel.* Edinburgh: Adam and Charles Black, 1856. One-quarter red morocco over sycamore wood. Tartan binding, gauffered edges. All edges gilt. 5" tall. Near fine. $425.00

SCOTT, Sir Walter. *Letters on Demonolgy and Witchcraft.* New York: J & J Harper, 1830. Full navy morocco. Marbled edges. First American edition, Harper's Stereotyped edition. 6" tall. Very good. $310.00

SCOTT, Sir Walter. *Letters on Demonology and Witchcraft.* London: John Murray, 1831. Small 8vo. Engraved frontis. Half maroon calf gilt. Gilt lettered brown and green morocco spine labels. Second edition. Near fine. $180.00

SCOTT, Sir Walter. *Life of Napoleon Bonaparte.* Edinburgh: Adam and Charles Black, 1852. Full tan calf. Highly gilt spine and covers with all edges gilt. Illustrated with steel engravings. 10" tall. Near fine. $525.00

SCOTT, Sir Walter. *Marmion.* Edinburgh: Adam and Charles Black, 1874. Full red morocco. Marbled edges. Prize binding, signed by J.C. Wilbee. 5½" tall. Near fine. $160.00

SCOTT, Sir Walter. *Marmion.* Edinburgh: Adam and Charles Black, 1854. One-quarter red morocco. All edges gilt. Hand-painted wooden cover of a Scottish scene. Mauchline wood rear cover. 5" tall. Near fine. $575.00

SCOTT, Sir Walter. *Scott's Poetical Works.* New York: Oliver S. Felt, circa 1860. Full brown calf. Hand-tooled binding. Illustrated. 9½" tall. Near fine. $240.00

SCOTT, Sir Walter. *Provincial Antiquities and Picturesque Scenery of Scotland.* London: John & Arthur Arch, and Edinburgh: William Blackwood, 1819 – 26. Two volumes. Folio. Contemporary three-quarter dark green morocco gilt. First large paper edition. Illustrated. Near fine. $800.00

SCOTT, Sir Walter. *The Life of Napoleon Bonaparte.* Edinburgh: Ballantyne & Co., 1827. Nine volumes. Full red morocco gilt. First edition. Near fine. $1,600.00

SCOTT, Sir Walter. *The Life of Napoleon Bonaparte, Emperor of the French.* New York: J & J Harper, 1828. Three volumes. Octavo. Contemporary three-quarter brown calf gilt, raised bands, marbled boards and endpapers. Near fine. $500.00

SCOTT, Sir Walter. *The Life of Napoleon Bonaparte, Emperor of the French.* Edinburgh: Ballantyne and Co., 1827. Nine volumes. Octavo. Contemporary three-quarter dark blue calf gilt. First edition. Near fine. $1,100.00

SCOTT, Sir Walter. *The Life of Napoleon Bonaparte.* Edinburgh and London: 1827. Nine volumes. Octavo. Contemporary three-quarter brown calf gilt. First edition. Near fine. $1,100.00

SCOTT, Sir Walter. *The Poetical Works of Sir Walter Scott.* London: George Bell & Sons, 1892. Five volumes. Three-quarter green morocco with marbled edges. Book plate of Horace Porter. Aldine edition. 6½" tall. Fine. $425.00

SCOTT, Sir Walter. *The Waverly Novels and Scotts Poems*. Boston: Estes and Lauriat, 1893. Fifty-four volumes (only three shown). Full tree calf. Top edges gilt. Edition des Amateurs, one of only 24 sets made. All 48 Waverly novels plus six volumes of Scott's poems. Extra illustrated. Very good. $5,500.00

SEARS, John. *The American Navy in the War with Spain*. London: Bickers and Son, 1899. Full tan calf by Bickers. Marbled edges. Prize binding. Over 100 illustrations. Fine. $375.00

SCOTT, Sir Walter. *The Poetical Works of Sir Walter Scott*. Edinburgh: Archibald Constable & Co., 1821. Ten volumes. Octavo. Contemporary full polished red morocco gilt. Raised bands. Near fine. $975.00

SCOTT, Sir Walter. *The Waverly Novels*. Edinburgh: Cadell & Company, 1829 – 33. Forty-eight volumes. Small octavo. Three-quarter red morocco gilt. Raised bands and marbled boards. Illustrated with vignettes on each volume's title page. Near fine. $2,600.00

SCOTT, Sir Walter. *Waverly Novels*. New York: Robert G. Newbegin, 1905. Fifty-one volumes. Quarto. Full polished calf in green, auburn, chestnut gilt. White morocco doublures with gilt centerpieces. Illustrated by H.G. Green. Near fine. $3,100.00

SEARS, Robert. *History of the American Revolution*. New York: Robert Sears, 1845. Three-quarter maroon morocco. Top edges gilt. Illustrated. First edition. Near fine. $425.00

SCOTT, Sir. Walter. *Waverly Novels*. Edinburgh: Robert Cadell, 1843. Thirteen volumes. Full red morocco gilt. Large 8vo. Illustrated. Near fine. $2,400.00

SEARS, Robert. *The Wonders of the World*. New York: Robert Sears, 1848. Full red morocco. Highly gilt spine and covers, all edges gilt. Illustrated, signed by the author. 9" tall. Fine. $650.00

SCOTT, Thomas. *The Pilgrim's Progress*. London: L.B. Seeley, 1801. Full mottled tree calf. All edges gilt. Copper plate illustrations, Marceau copy, twentieth century binding. 9" tall. Fine. $750.00

SCROPE, William. *Days and Nights of Salmon Fishing in The Tweed*. London: John Murray, 1843. Full contemporary red morocco gilt. All edges gilt. Octavo. Illustrated with numerous lithographic plates. First edition. Near fine. $550.00

SECUNDUS, Joannes. *Kisses*. London: J. Bew, 1778. Full white crushed levant morocco with floral design inlaid in rose levant, heightened with gilt leaves and stems. Ivory miniature inlaid front cover by C.B. Currie, wide inner levant borders, gilt, doublures and end-leaves of green watered silk. From designs by J.H. Stonehouse. 7¼" tall. Fine. $12,500.00

SEMMES, Raphael. *Service Afloat; or The Remarkable Career of the Confederate Cruisers Sumter and Alabama During the War Between the States.* Baltimore: The Baltimore Publishing Co., 1887. Three-quarter dark brown calf by Launder and MacDonald. Top edges gilt. Illustrated with chromolithographic plates. First edition. Near fine. $775.00

SETON, Ernest Thompson. *Two Little Savages.* London: Archibald Constable & Co., 1906. Full red morocco. Prize binding. Marbled edges. Over 300 illustrations by Seton. 7" tall. Near fine. $290.00

SEVIGNE, Marchioness de. *Letters to her Daughter the Countess De Srignan.* London: Spurr & Swift, 1927. Five volumes. Three-quarter blue calf. Gilt spines with red morocco labels. Near fine. $375.00

SEWELL, Anna. *Black Beauty.* London: J.M. Dent & Sons, 1920. Three-quarter black morocco by Sangorski & Sutcliffe. Raised bands, gilt panels and edges. Illustrated. Near fine. $675.00

SEWELL, Anna. *Black Beauty.* London: Jarrolds, circa 1900. Full green morocco. Gilt spines with raised bands. 12mo. Illustrated by Cecil Aldini. Near fine. $770.00

SEWELL, Anna. *Black Beauty.* New York: Frederick A. Stokes Co., circa 1930. Three-quarter red morocco gilt. Raised bands, panel with gilt horse's head. Illustrated by Cecil Alden. Near fine. $575.00

SHAKESPEARE, William. *Dramatic Works.* Edinburgh: William Paterson, 1883. Eight volumes. Full tan calf, ribbed gilt spines. Illustrated. Near fine. $900.00

SHAKESPEARE, William. *Songs and Sonnets.* London: Duckworth & Co., n.d., circa 1920. Full red crushed levant morocco by Bayntun-Riviere. Highly gilt spine and cover with all edges gilt. Illustrated by Charles Robinson. 10" tall. Fine. $1,100.00

SHAKESPEARE, William. *The Comedies, Histories, Tragedies and Poems of William Shakespeare.* Boston: Little, Brown, and Co., 1912. Eighteen volumes (only two shown). Three-quarter navy morocco. Top edges gilt. Inlaid red morocco flowers on spine. Each volume has a hand-colored frontis. Old Stratford edition, limited to 124 sets. 9" tall. Near fine. $3,100.00

SHAKESPEARE, William. *The Complete Works of William Shakespeare.* London: Charles Knight, 1839. Eight volumes. Full red morocco. All edges gilt. Woodcut illustrations, highly gilt. Edited by Charles Knight. Near fine. $1,600.00

SHAKESPEARE, William. *The History of King Lear. Acted at the Duke's Theatre. Reviv'd with Alterations. By N. Tate.* London: 1681. Small quarto. Nineteenth century navy blue morocco gilt. First edition. Near fine. $12,000.00

SHAKESPEARE, William. *The Merry Wives of Windsor, a Comedy.* London: George Bell and Sons, 1886. Cosway binding. Octavo. Full burgundy crushed levant morocco by Riviere. Illustrated by C.B. Currie. Near fine. $12,500.00

SHAKESPEARE, William. *The Works of Shakespeare.* London: Virtue and Co., circa 1875. Two volumes in four. Large folio. Three-quarter green morocco gilt. Illustrated. Near fine. $800.00

SHAKESPEARE, William. *The Works of Shakespeare: in Seven Volumes. Collated with the Oldest Copies, and Corrected; with Notes, Explanatory, and Critical: By Mr. Theobald.* London: 1733. Seven octavo volumes. Full brown calf. Illustrated. First edition. Near fine. $6,750.00

SHAKESPEARE, William. *The Dramatic Works of William Shakespeare.* London: Thomas Tegg, 1812. Twelve volumes. Full tan calf straight grain morocco. Marbled edges. Engraved plates in proof state. 9" tall. Near fine. $2,100.00

SHAKESPEARE, William. *The Works of William Shakespeare.* Boston: Phillips, Sampson & Co., 1854. Full red morocco calf. All edges gilt. Illustrated. Light foxing. 9¾" tall. Very good. $375.00

SHAKESPEARE, William. *The Life and Times of William Shakespeare.* London: Swan Sonnenschein, Lowrey & Co., 1888. Full purple morocco by Relfe Brothers. Prize binding with marbled edges. 7" tall. Near fine. $150.00

SHAKESPEARE, William. *The Works of William Shakespeare.* London: H.G. Bohn, 1859. Full green calf. All edges gilt. Illustrated by Harvey. 9½" tall. Fine. $325.00

SHAKESPEARE, William. *The Plays of William Shakespeare.* London: Longman and Co., 1856. Eight volumes. Octavo. Full contemporary tan calf gilt. Red and green morocco spine labels. Marbled endpapers and marbled edges. Near fine. $1,200.00

SHAKESPEARE, William. *The Sonnets.* London: Robert Riviere, 1928. Full brown morocco by Bayntun. Ornate floral tooling on covers and spines. Near fine. $1,400.00

SHAKESPEARE, William. *The Works of William Shakespeare.* New York: Oliver S. Felt, n.d., circa 1870. Full brown calf. Hand-tooled covers. All edges gilt. Illustrated. 9½" tall. Near fine. $285.00

SHAKESPEARE, William. *The Works of Shakespeare.* London: 1873 – 76. Two volumes. Thick folio. Contemporary full red morocco gilt. Imperial edition. Near fine. $2,500.00

SHAKESPEARE, William. *The Works of Shakespeare.* London: 1899. Twelve volumes. Octavo. Contemporary full vellum gilt. One of only 175 sets. Near fine. $6,100.00

SHAKESPEARE, William. *The Works.* London: 1880. Eight volumes. Tall octavo. Contemporary three-quarter green morocco gilt. Illustrated. Near fine. $1,100.00

SHAKESPEARE, William. *The Works of William Shakespeare.* New York: The Knickerbocker Press, n.d., circa 1900. Twenty-four volumes. Full multicolored calf. Miniature boxed set. 3¼" tall. Near fine. $325.00

SHAKESPEARE, William. *The Works.* London: Charles Knight & Co., circa 1900. Eight volumes. Full black morocco gilt. Pictorial edition. Near fine. $1,400.00

SHAKESPEARE, William. *The Works.* London: Chatto & Windus, 1877. Nine volumes. Full tree calf gilt. Third edition. Near fine. $1,800.00

SHAKESPEARE, William. *The Works.* London: Virtue & Co. 1830. Two volumes. Folio. Full red morocco gilt. Imperial edition. Illustrations on steel. Near fine. $1,400.00

SHAKESPEARE, William. *The Works.* London: circa 1900. Ten volumes bound in twenty. Octavo. Contemporary three-quarter blue morocco gilt. Connoisseur edition, one of only 200 sets. Illustrated. Near fine. $2,900.00

SHAKLETON, E.H. *The Heart of the Antarctic Being the Story of the British Antarctic Expedition, 1907 – 1909.* London: William Heinemann, 1909. Two volumes. Three-quarter navy morocco. Raised bands, gilt design on spines. Marbled boards. Illustrated. Near fine. $1,100.00

SHAKLETON, E.H. *The Heart of the Antarctic.* London: 1909. Two large octavo volumes. Three-quarter calf. First trade edition. Near fine. $1,100.00

SHALER, Nathaniel S. *The United States of America.* New York: D. Appleton & Co., 1894. Two volumes. Three-quarter blue morocco gilt. 4to. Illustrated. Near fine. $350.00

SHARSWOOD. *Blackstone's Commentaries.* Philadelphia: George W. Childs, 1857. Two volumes. Full tan calf. Pull outs. 10" tall. Very good. $340.00

SHELDON, George W. *Recent Ideals of American Art.* New York and London: D. Appleton and Co., 1890. Full maroon morocco. Embossed covers, highly gilt spine, all edges gilt. Steel and woodcut engravings throughout. Folio. 16" tall. Near fine. $900.00

SHELLEY, Mary Wollstonecraft. *Frankenstein: Or, The Modern Prometheus. Revised, Corrected, and Illustrated with a New Introduction, by the Author.* With: SCHILLER, Frederick. *The Ghost-Seer.* London: 1831. Two volumes bound in one. Small octavo. Contemporary three-quarter tan calf gilt. Third edition. Near fine. $4,200.00

SHELLEY, Mary Wollstonecraft. *Frankenstein: Or, The Modern Prometheus.* With: SCHILLER, Frederick. *The Ghost-Seer. From the German of Schiller.* London: 1831. Two volumes bound in one. Three-quarter dark blue morocco gilt. Small octavo. Illustrated. Third edition. Near fine. $4,200.00

SHELLEY, Mary. *The Last Man.* London: 1826. Three octavo volumes. Three-quarter brown calf. First edition. Near fine. $6,200.00

SHELLEY, Mary and others. *The Keepsake for 1831.* London: Hurst, Chance and Co., 1831. Full red morocco. Highly gilt spine, covers are profusely gilded with flowers, leaves, and acorns, straight grained morocco. All edges gilt. Red silk moiré doublures and endpapers. Illustrated with steel engravings. 7½" tall. Near fine. $750.00

S

SHELLEY, Percy Bysshe. *The Complete Poetical Works of Shelley.* Boston and New York: Houghton and Mifflin Co., 1901. Full tree calf. All edges gilt. 8" tall. Near fine. $230.00

SHELLEY, Percy Bysshe. *Adonais.* London: 1927. Small quarto. Contemporary full blue levant morocco gilt in the Cosway style bound by Riviere & Son. Portrait of author on front cover. Near fine. $6,800.00

SHELLEY, Percy Bysshe. *The Complete Poetical Works.* Boston and New York: 1901. Octavo. Contemporary three-quarter blue calf gilt. Cambridge edition. Near fine. $350.00

SHERER, Captain Moyle. *Military Memoirs of Field Marshall The Duke of Wellington.* London: Longman, 1832. Two volumes. Full green calf. Cabinet Library. Replaced title page in Volume 1. 6½" tall. Near fine. $340.00

SHERIDAN, P.H. *Personal Memoirs of P.H. Sheridan.* New York: Charles Webster, 1888. Two volumes. Three-quarter dark brown calf by Launder and Mac-Donald. Top edges gilt. First editions. $875.00

SHERIDAN, Philip Henry. *Personal Memoirs of P.H. Sheridan.* New York: 1888. Two volumes. Three-quarter calf. First edition. Illustrated with folding maps and plates. Near fine. $900.00

SHERIDAN, P.H. *Personal Memoirs of P.H. Sheridan.* New York: Charles Webster, 1888. Two volumes. Three-quarter brown calf with marbled edges. Gold gilt picture of Sheridan on horseback on the front cover. Illustrated. First edition. 9" tall. Near fine. $875.00

SHERMAN, John. *John Sherman's Recollections of Forty Years in the House, Senate and Cabinet.* Chicago, New York, London, and Berlin: The Werner Co., 1895. Two volumes. Three-quarter tan calf. Highly gilt spines and covers. Illustrated with portraits. Signed by the author. 10½" tall. Near fine. $675.00

SHERMAN, William T. *Memoirs of General William T. Sherman.* New York: D. Appleton & Co., 1875. Two volumes. Octavo. Three-quarter blue morocco gilt. Raised bands with marbled boards and endpapers. First edition. Near fine. $1,400.00

SHERMAN, William T. *Memoirs of General William T. Sherman.* New York: D. Appleton & Co., 1875. Two volumes. Octavo. Contemporary three-quarter dark blue morocco. First edition. Illustrated with large folding map. Near fine. $1,400.00

SHERMAN, William T. *Memoirs of General William T. Sherman.* New York: D. Appleton and Co., 1887. Two volumes. Three-quarter dark brown calf by Launder and MacDonald. Top edges gilt. Near fine. $575.00

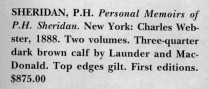

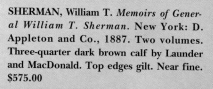

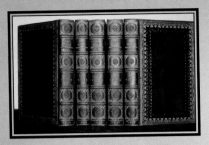

SHOBERL, Frederick (Translator). *The History of the French Revolution.* London: Richard Bentley, 1838. Five volumes. Full black calf. All edges gilt. Fine copy of Theirs French Revolution. Illustrated with steel engravings. First edition. 8½" tall. Near fine. $1,400.00

SHORTT, Adam, and DOUGHTY, Arthur G. (editors). *Canada and Its Provinces.* Toronto: 1913. Twenty-three volumes. Quarto. Publisher's full green levant morocco gilt. One of only 875 sets and illustrated with over 275 plates. Near fine. $3,200.00

SICHEL, Walter. *Emma Lady Hamilton from New and Original Sources and Documents.* London: Archibald Constable, 1905. Three-quarter brown morocco. Gilt spines with raised bands. Illustrated. Near fine. $225.00

SIMMS, Jeptha R. *The Frontiersmen of New York.* Albany: 1882 – 1883. Two octavo volumes. Original full tan sheep. Illustrated. First edition. Near fine. $475.00

SIMONDE DE SISMONDI, Jean Charles Leonard. *Historical View of the Literature of the South of Europe.* London: 1845. Two octavo volumes. Contemporary three-quarter tan calf gilt. Illustrated. Second edition in English. Near fine. $350.00

SKINNER, Charles M. *Myths and Legends of Our Own Land.* Philadelphia and London: J.B. Lippincott Co., 1896. Two volumes. Three-quarter red morocco. Top edges gilt. 7" tall. Near fine. $380.00

SIMPSON, James H. *Report of Explorations Across the Great Basin of the Territory of Utah.* Washington: Government Printing Office, 1876. Three-quarter calf. Quarto. Illustrated with numerous plates, charts and diagrams. First edition. Near fine. $450.00

SKELTON, John. *Charles I.* London, Paris, and Edinburgh: Goupil & Co., 1898. Full red morocco by Riviere. Raised bands, green morocco doublures. Small folio. Limited edition, one of only 500 copies. Near fine. $975.00

SLOANE, William M. *Life of Napoleon Bonaparte.* London: MacMillan & Co., 1896. Four volumes. Small folio. Three-quarter blue morocco gilt. Illustrations in color and black and white. Near fine. $1,600.00

SLOANE, William M. *Life of Napoleon Bonaparte.* New York: The Century Co., 1906. Four volumes. Three-quarter red morocco gilt. Large quarto. Illustrations in black and white and color. Near fine. $1,200.00

SLOANE, William M. *The Life of Napoleon Bonaparte.* New York: Century Co., 1915. Four volumes. Three-quarter green morocco gilt. Near fine. $750.00

SHORTER, Clement. *Charlotte Brontë and Her Circle.* London: Hodder & Stoughton, 1896. Three-quarter olive morocco. Top edges gilt. Illustrated. Second edition. Very good. $105.00

SLOAN, William Milligan. *Life of Napoleon Bonaparte.* New York: The Century Co., 1896. Four volumes. Three-quarter purple morocco. Top edges gilt. First edition. 12" tall. Very good. $1,400.00

SMART, Hawley. *The Works of Hawley Smart.* London: Ward, Lock and Co., circa 1880. Nineteen volumes (only five shown). Three-quarter butterscotch calf. Marbled edges. Signed binding by Bickers. 7" tall. Near fine. $1,750.00

SLOANE, William Milligan. *Life of Napoleon Bonaparte.* New York: The Century Co., 1896. Folio. Publisher's original three-quarter red morocco gilt. Marbled boards and end-papers. Numerous illustrations. Near fine. $1,600.00

SMART, Christopher. *A Poetical Translation of the Fables of Phae-drus.* London: Printed for J. Dodsley, 1765. Full calf. Raised bands with gilt rules and maroon morocco label. Engraved frontispiece. First printing in this translation. Near fine. $475.00

SMILES, Samuel. *Men of Invention and Industry.* London: John Murray, 1884. Full navy morocco by Bickers. Highly gilt spine. Prized binding with marbled edges. Signed. 7" tall. Near fine. $225.00

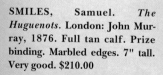

SMILES, Samuel. *The Huguenots.* London: John Murray, 1876. Full tan calf. Prize binding. Marbled edges. 7" tall. Very good. $210.00

SMITH, Adam. *An Inquiry into the Nature and Causes of the Wealth of Nations.* London: 1784. Three volumes. Quarto. Contemporary full tree calf. First octavo edition. Near fine. $5,800.00

SMITH, Adam. *An Inquiry into the Nature and Causes of the Wealth of Nations.* London: William Allason, 1819. Three volumes. Full butterscotch calf. Marbled edges. 8" tall. Near fine. $1,700.00

SMITH, Adam. *An Inquiry into the Nature and Causes of the Wealth of Nations.* London: W. Strahan and T. Cadell, 1776. Two large quarto volumes. Full contemporary calf. Raised bands with green and red morocco labels. First edition. Near fine. $18,500.00

SMITH, Albert. *The Struggles and Adventures of Christopher Tadpole at Home and Abroad.* London: Richard Bentley, 1848. Three-quarter red morocco. Highly gilt spine with marbled edges. Illustrated by Leech. First edition. 8" tall. Near fine. $425.00

SMITH, Gustavus. *Confederate War Papers.* New York: Atlantic Publishing, 1884. Three-quarter brown calf by Launder and MacDonald, 1884. Top edges gilt. 7½" tall. Near fine. $275.00

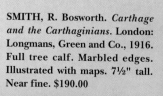

SMITH, R. Bosworth. *Carthage and the Carthaginians.* London: Longmans, Green and Co., 1916. Full tree calf. Marbled edges. Illustrated with maps. 7½" tall. Near fine. $190.00

SMITH, Ronald. *The World's Explorers*. London: Ward, Lock and Tyler, circa 1870. Full maroon morocco. Prize binding. Marbled edges. Illustrated with chromolithographic plates and frontispiece. 7½" tall. Near fine. $275.00

SMITH, Adam. *The Theory of Moral Sentiments*. London: 1797. Two octavo volumes. Contemporary full tree calf gilt. Early edition. Near fine. $1,400.00

SMOLLET, Tobias. *The Exposition of Humphrey Clinker*. London: J. Sibbald, 1793. Two volumes. Full tan calf by Zaehnsdorf. Top edges gilt. Plates by T. Rowland & Son. First edition. 8" tall. Near fine. $650.00

SMOLLETT, T. *The Adventures of Roderick Random*. London: James Cochrane & Co., 1831. Full blue morocco by Bayntun. All edges gilt. Illustrated with five original plates by Cruikshank. Near fine. $225.00

SNOW, Captain William. *Lee and His Generals*. New York: Richardson & Co., 1867. Three-quarter tan calf with marbled edges. Illustrated. 8½" tall. Very good. $625.00

SOLEY, James Russell. *The Navy in the Civil War*. New York: Charles Scribner's Sons, 1885. Three volumes. Three-quarter navy calf. Top edges gilt. Illustrated with maps. Subscription edition. 8" tall. Near fine. $625.00

SONNEBERG, Theodor Brand. *Speaking Picture Book for the Amusement of Children by Image, Verse and Sound*. 1880. Original publisher's carved wooden box with color label. Red-brown boards, gold wooden sides with elaborate decoration. Nine cords pulls that activate a sound corresponding to the animal being pictures. Near fine. $1,400.00

SONNINI, Charles Sigisbert. *Travels in Upper and Lower Egypt*. London: 1800. Half calf. Quarto. Illustrated with frontispiece portrait and numerous engraved plates. Near fine. $975.00

SOUTHEY, Robert. *Joan of Arc*. London: George Routledge & Co., 1853. Full green calf. All edges gilt. Illustrations by John Gilbert. 6¾" tall. Near fine. $325.00

SOUTHEY, Robert. *The Complete Poetical Works of Robert Southey*. New York and Philadelphia: D. Appleton & Co., 1848. Full black morocco. Gilt embossed covers. Highly gilt spine. All edges gilt. Illustrated. 10" tall. Fine. $395.00

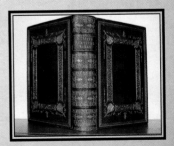

SOUTHEY, Robert. *The Complete Poetical Works of Robert Southey.* New York: D. Appleton & Co., 1851. Full green morocco. All edges gilt. Illustrated. 9" tall. Near fine. $210.00

SPARKS, Jared. *The Writings of George Washington.* New York: Harper & Brothers, 1852. Twelve volumes. Three-quarter brown morocco. Marbled edges. Illustrated with steel engravings and maps. Near fine. $1,300.00

SPARKS, Jared. *The Writings of George Washington.* Boston: American Stationers Co., 1837. Twelve volumes. Full polished calf gilt with brown labels, ribbed spines. Near fine. $1,750.00

SOUTHEY, Robert. *The Life of Horatio Lord Nelson.* New York: J.M. Dent, 1908. Full navy morocco. Prize binding with marbled edges. 6½" tall. Near fine. $130.00

SPARKS, Jared. *Correspondence of the American Revolution: Being Letters of Emiment Men to George Washington, from the Time of His Taking Command of the Army to the End of His Presidency.* Boston: 1853. Four volumes. Octavo. Contemporary three-quarter brown calf. First edition. Near fine. $850.00

SPARKS, Jared. *Memoirs of Life and Travels of John Ledyard.* London: 1828. Full calf gilt. Octavo. First English edition. Near fine. $475.00

SPENCE, Lewis. *The Myths of the North American Indian.* London: George Harrap, 1922. Full brown morocco. Top edges gilt. Illustrated. Very good. $240.00

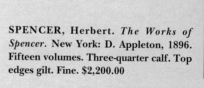

SPENCER, Herbert. *The Works of Spencer.* New York: D. Appleton, 1896. Fifteen volumes. Three-quarter calf. Top edges gilt. Fine. $2,200.00

SPENSER and LOSSING. *History of the United States.* New York: Johnson, Wilson & Co., 1874. Four volumes. Full brown morocco gilt. Illustrated by eminant American artists. Near fine. $650.00

SPENSER, Edmund. *The Faerie Queene.* Ashendene Press, 1923. Original calf. Raised bands with gilt spine. One of 150 copies. Near fine. $1,800.00

SPARKS, Jared. *The Works of Benjamin Franklin.* Boston: Whittemore, Niles and Hall, 1856. Ten volumes. Three-quarter brown calf. Marbled edges. 9½" tall. Near fine. $1,600.00

SPENSER, Edmund. *The Faerie Queene.* London: circa 1909. Two volumes bound in one. 12mo. Contemporary full black morocco gilt. Near fine. $475.00

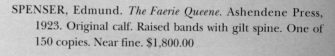

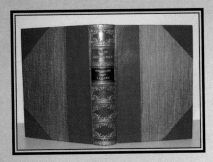

SPIELMANN and LAYARD. *Kate Greenway.* London: Adam and Charles Black, 1905. Three-quarter sky blue morocco by Bayntun. Top edges gilt. Color illustrated. 7½" tall. Near fine. $325.00

SPENSER, J.A. *History of the United States.* New York: 1858. Three volumes. Early twentieth century three-quarter morocco gilt. Quarto. Illustrated with full-page steel engravings and engraved frontispieces. First edition. Near fine. $650.00

ST. JOHN, J.A. *Egypt & Nubia.* London: Chapman & Hall, 1845. Three-quarter tan calf gilt. Illustrated. Near fine. $250.00

ST. JOHN, J.A. *The History of the Manners and Customs of Ancient Greece.* London: Richard Bently, 1842. Three volumes. Full tan calf gilt. Gilt lettered red and green morocco spine labels. Near fine. $550.00

STANFIELD, Clarkson. *Stanfield's Coast Scenery. A Series of Views in the British Channel.* London: Smith, Elder & Co., 1836. Full black morocco. Gilt decorated spines and covers. All edges gilt. Octavo. Illustrated with frontispiece and numerous full-page plates. Near fine. $450.00

SPOFFORD, Ainsworth. *The Library of Choice Literature.* Philadelphia: Gebbie & Co., 1881. Three-quarter tan calf with marbled edges. Illustrated. First edition. 9½" tall. Near fine. $925.00

STANLEY, Arthur. *The History of the Jewish Church.* New York: Charles Scribner's Sons, 1879. Three-quarter tan calf with marbled edges. Illustrated with pull-out maps. 9" tall. Near fine. $425.00

STANLEY, Arthur Penrhyn. *Historical Memorials of Westminster Abbey.* New York: Anson D.F. Randolph & Company, 1882. Two octavo volumes. Three-quarter green morocco gilt by Tout. Raised bands, marbled boards and endpapers. Illustrated with numerous full-page photogravures. Near fine. $450.00

STANLEY, Henry M. *How I Found Livingstone: Travels, Adventures and Discoveries in Central Africa.* London: 1872. Modern three-quarter brown morocco gilt. Thick octavo. Illustrated with full-page illustrations and folding maps. First edition. Near fine. $675.00

STANLEY, Henry M. *In Darkest Africa.* London: 1890. Two volumes. Large quarto. Three-quarter dark brown morocco. First English edition. Illustrated. One of only 250 copies. Near fine. $3,800.00

STANLEY, Henry M. *Through the Dark Continent.* New York: Harper & Bros., 1878. First edition. Two volumes. Three-quarter brown morocco. One hundred and fifty woodcuts and numerous maps. Near fine. $950.00

STEDMAN, Charles. *History of the Origin, Progress, and Termination of the American War.* London: 1794. Two volumes. Quarto. Contemporary three-quarter brown calf. First edition with 15 maps, 11 folding. Near fine. $4,600.00

STAVESHN, Sam. *The Sermon on the Mount.* London: Charles Courtier, n.d., circa 1864. Full green morocco. All edges gilt. Two photos. Highly gilt. Illuminated by Sam Staveshn. 6¾" tall. Fine. $675.00

STEEL, Flora Annie. *English Fairy Tales*. London: MacMillan & Co., 1918. Full red morocco by Bayntun Riviere. Highly gilt spine and covers, all edges gilt. Color plates by Rackham. 8" tall. Fine. $800.00

STEELE and ADDISON. *The DeCoverley Essays*. London: Gay & Bird, 1901. Full dark green by Zaehnsdorf. Top edges gilt. Highly gilt, one of only 60 copies on Japanese vellum paper. Edited by J. Potter Briscoe. 5½" tall. Fine. $550.00

STEEL, A.G., and LYHELTON, R.H. *Cricket*. London: Longmans, Green & Co., 1888. Full blue morocco gilt. Raised bands, gilt spines. 4to. Large paper edition, one of only 250 copies. Illustrated with engravings by Lucien Davis. Near fine. $375.00

STEPHEN, Leslie. *Samuel Johnson*. London: 1888. Contemporary full crushed blue morocco gilt by Bayntun. Octavo. Illustrated with frontispiece portrait of the author and numerous hand-colored plates. Near fine. $450.00

STEPHENS, Alexander. *A Constitutional View of the Late War Between the States*. Philadelphia: National Publishing Co., 1868. Two volumes. Three-quarter butterscotch calf with marbled edges. Illustrated. First edition. 9½" tall. Near fine. $675.00

STEPHENS, James. *Irish Fairy Tales*. London: MacMillan & Co., 1920. Full green morocco by Riviere. Highly gilt spine and cover, all edges gilt. Illustrated with sixteen color plates by Arthur Rackham. First English trade edition. 8½" tall. Fine. $1,100.00

STEPHENS, James. *Irish Fairy Tales*. London: MacMillian & Co., 1918. First trade edition. Full green morocco. Illustrated by Arthur Rackham. Near fine. $1,300.00

STERNE, Laurence. *A Sentimental Journey Through France and Italy*. London: T. Becket and P.A. DeHondt, 1768. Contemporary sprinkled calf. Raised bands, spine compartments gilt with green morocco label. Two volumes bound in one. First edition. Near fine. $425.00

STERNE, Laurence. *A Sentimental Journey Through France and Italy*. London: T. Becket and P.A. DeHondt, 1768. Two volumes. Full tan calf gilt. 16mo. Raised bands with black and red morocco labels. First edition. Near fine. $675.00

STERNE, Laurence. *The Works of Laurence Sterne, with a Life of the Author*. London: J. Johnson, 1798. Ten volumes. Octavo. Modern full mottle calf gilt. Red and black morocco labels. Illustrated with engraved frontispieces plates in each volume. Near fine. $1,400.00

STERNE, Laurence. *The Works of Laurence Sterne*. London: J. Johnson, 1798. Ten volumes. Three-quarter tree calf by Riviere. Yellow edges. 7" tall. Near fine. $1,650.00

STEVENSON, Robert Louis. *A Child's Garden of Verses.* London: John Lane, n.d., circa 1908. Full blue morocco crushed levant by Bayntun-Riviere. All edges gilt. Illustrated by Charles Robinson in black and white and color. First colored illustration edition. 8½" tall. Fine. $900.00

STERNE, Laurence. *The Works.* London: Printed for the Proprietors, 1790. Eight volumes. Contemporary tree calf gilt. Covers with gilt ruled borders, flat spines with blue morocco labels and red morocco volume labels. Marbled endpapers. Four engraved plates. Near fine. $1,800.00

STEVENSON, Robert Louis. *A Child's Garden of Verses.* London: John Lane The Bodley Head 1920. Full blue morocco gilt by Asprey. Illustrated by Charles Robinson . Near fine. $950.00

STEVENSON, Robert Louis. *A Child's Garden of Verses.* London: Longmans, Green and Co., 1885. Original blue cloth gilt. 12mo. First edition. Contains 64 poems. Near fine. $2,100.00

STEVENSON, Robert Louis. *A Child's Garden of Verses.* New York: Charles Scribner's & Sons, 1905. Full tan morocco gilt by Sangorski & Sutcliffe. Illustrated by Jessie Wilcox Smith. Near fine. $1,250.00

STEVENSON, Robert Louis. *A Child's Garden of Verses.* New York: Charles Scribner's Sons, 1909. Three-quarter green morocco gilt. Marbled boards and raised panels. Illustrated by Robinson. Near fine. $625.00

STEVENSON, Robert Louis. *Kidnapped: Being Memoirs of the Adventures of David Balfour in the Year 1751.* London: Cassell and Co., 1886. Full calf. Octavo. First edition. Near fine. $1,600.00

STEVENSON, Robert Louis. *Prince Otto. A Romance.* London: 1885. Contemporary three-quarter blue morocco. 12mo. First edition. Near fine. $500.00

STEVENSON, Robert Louis. *The Complete Works of R.L. Stevenson.* New York: Charles Scribner's Sons, 1900. Twenty-six volumes. Half red morocco gilt. Ribbed gilt decorated spines. Frontis in each volume. Near fine. $3,800.00

STEVENSON, Robert Louis. *The Novels and Tales.* New York: 1909 – 1912. Twenty-seven volumes. Three-quarter red morocco gilt. Thistle edition. Near fine. $3,200.00

STEVENSON, Robert Louis. *The Novels and Tales.* New York: Charles Scribner's Sons, 1895 – 1901. Twenty-six volumes. Octavo. Contemporary three-quarter crimson morocco. Raised bands, marbled boards and endpapers. Near fine. $4,500.00

STEVENSON, Robert Louis. *The Works of Robert Louis Stevenson.* New York: Charles Scribner's Sons, 1921 – 1923. Twenty-six octavo volumes. Three-quarter blue levant morocco gilt over blue cloth boards. Vailima edition, one of 2,090 sets. Near fine. $4,200.00

STEVENSON, Robert Louis. *The Works.* Edinburgh: T.A. Constable for Longmans, Green & Co., 1894. Thirty-four volumes. Edinburgh edition, limited to 1,035 sets. Full green morocco gilt. Silk and leather doublures. Near fine. $8,500.00

STEVENSON, Robert Louis. *The Works.* New York: Charles Scribner's Sons, 1895 – 98. Twenty-two volumes. Octavo. Contemporary full brown polished morocco gilt. Silk endpapers. Near fine. $6,500.00

STEVENSON, Robert Louis. *The Novels and Tales of Robert Louis Stevenson.* New York: Charles Scribners, 1896. Twenty-seven volumes (only three shown). Full sky blue morocco. Top edges gilt. Multicolored leather floral design set in front and back covers of all novels. Tipped in "i.o.u." from, and signed by, Stevenson. 8½" tall. Near fine. $7,500.00

STEVENSON, Robert Louis. *Virginibus Puerisque*. New York: Charles Scribner's Sons, 1893. Full blue morocco. Heavily gilt floral covers by Fletcher Battershall. Top edges gilt. Book plate of the binder who bound the book. Signed by Battershall. First edition. 8" tall. Near fine. $750.00

STEVENSON, Robert Louis. *Treasure Island*. London: Cassell & Co. Ltd., 1892. Full blue polished calf by Bayntun, gilt. Illustrated. Near fine. $750.00

STEVENSON, Robert Louis. *Treasure Island*. London: Cassell & Co., 1883. Small octavo. Full blue morocco. First edition. Near fine. $5,100.00

STEVENSON, Robert Louis. *Treasure Island*. London: Cassell & Company, Ltd., 1883. Three-quarter green morocco. Raised bands and gilt spines. First edition. Near fine. $4,500.00

STEVENSON, Robert Louis. *Works*. Charles Scribner & Sons, 1911. Twenty-seven volumes. Three-quarter red morocco gilt. Near fine. $3,600.00

STEVENSON, Robert Louis. *Works*. London: Cassell & Co., 1906. Ten volumes. Three-quarter blue calf by Bayntun. Ornate gilt on spines. Pentland edition. Near fine. $2,400.00

STEVENSON, Robert Louis. *Works*. New York: 1895 – 97. Twenty-six volumes. With: *Short Stories, Plays, Letters*. Chicago: 1896. Six volumes. Octavo. Contemporary three-quarter green morocco. 12mo. Author's edition. Near fine. $4,500.00

STEWART, W.C. *The Practical Angler or The Art of Trout Fishing. More Particularly Applied to Clear Water*. Edinburgh: Adam & Charles Black, 1857. Small octavo. Modern three-quarter dark brown calf gilt. First edition. Near fine. $375.00

STOWE, Harriet Beecher. *Old Town Folks*. Boston: Fields, Osgood & Co., 1869. Three-quarter tan calf. All edges gilt. First edition. 7½" tall. Near fine. $240.00

STIRLING, William. *Annals of the Artists of Spain*. London: John Ollivier, 1848. Three volumes. Full tan calf. Raised bands and gilt decorated spines with green and red morocco labels. Near fine. $375.00

STOWE, Harriet Beecher. *The Writings of Harriet Beecher Stowe*. Cambridge: Riverside Press, 1896. Sixteen octavo volumes. Modern full brown morocco gilt. Engraved frontispieces. Large paper edition. Near fine. $6,700.00

STOWE, Harriet Beecher. *Uncle Tom's Cabin*. London: 1852. Octavo. Full red morocco. Early illustrated English edition. Near fine. $2,100.00

STOWE, Harriet Beecher. *Uncle Tom's Cabin; or Life Among the Lowly*. Boston: John P. Jewett & Co. Cleveland, Ohio: Jewett, Proctor & Worthington, 1852. Two volumes in one. Octavo. Contemporary three-quarter dark brown morocco. Marbled boards and raised bands. First edition. Near fine. $3,600.00

STOWE, Harriet Beecher. *The Writings of Harriet Beecher Stowe*. Boston and New York: Houghton Mifflin Co., 1896. Seventeen volumes (only five shown). Three-quarter brown calf with top edges gilt. Riverside edition. 7½" tall. Near fine. $4,400.00

STOWE, Harriet Beecher. *Uncle Tom's Cabin*. Boston and New York: Houghton, Mifflin and Co., 1892. Two volumes. Three-quarter blue morocco. Highly gilt spine, top edges gilt. Illustrated by E.W. Kemble. 6½" tall. Near fine. $500.00

STRICKLAND, Agnes. *Lives of the Queens of England*. London: Colburn & Co., 1852. Eight volumes. Full butterscotch calf. Marbled edges. Illustrated. Tipped in signed letter from author. 9" tall. Near fine. $1,750.00

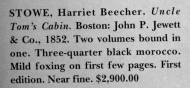

STOWE, Harriet Beecher. *Uncle Tom's Cabin*. Boston: John P. Jewett & Co., 1852. Two volumes bound in one. Three-quarter black morocco. Mild foxing on first few pages. First edition. Near fine. $2,900.00

STOWE, Harriet Beecher. *Uncle Tom's Cabin; Or, Life Among the Lowly*. Boston: John P. Jewett & Co., 1852. Two volumes. Octavo. Three-quarter black calf. Custom cloth and half-calf slipcase. First edition, first issue. Near fine. $8,500.00

STRICKLAND, Agnes. *Lives of the Queens of England, From the Norman Conquest. Published from Official Records.* London: Colburn & Co., 1852. Eight octavo volumes. Full contemporary polished red morocco gilt. Gilt spines and raised bands. Illustrated with a portrait of the author and engraved portraits of every queen. Near fine. $1,900.00

STRICKLAND, Agnes. *Lives of the Queens of England, From the Norman Conquest. Published from Official Records & Other Authentic Documents, Private as well as Public.* London: Henry Colburn, 1853. Sixteen octavo volumes. Nineteenth century red morocco gilt by Bayntun. Illustrated with engraved portraits of every queen. Vignette title pages. Four hundred plates, some hand colored. Near fine. $3,000.00

STRICKLAND, Agnes. *Lives of the Queens of England, From the Norman Conquest.* London: Bell and Daldy, 1864 – 65. Six octavo volumes. Contemporary black morocco gilt. Raised bands, red and green morocco labels. Illustrated with pictures of the court. Near fine. $950.00

STRICKLAND, Agnes. *Lives of the Queens of England, From the Norman Conquest. Published from Official Records & Other Authentic Documents, Private as well as Public.* London: Longman, Green, Longman & Roberts, 1861. Eight octavo volumes. Full contemporary tan calf gilt with raised bands and decorated spines. Near fine. $1,600.00

STRICKLAND, Agnes. *Lives of the Queens of England, From the Norman Conquest.* London: 1841. Six volumes. Octavo. Twentieth century full red morocco gilt by Brentano's. Second edition. Illustrated with engraved frontispiece portraits. Near fine. $1,800.00

STRICKLAND, Agnes. *Lives of the Queens of England.* London: Henry Colburn, 1842. Twelve volumes. Full red morocco gilt. Near fine. $1,500.00

STRICKLAND, Agnes. *Lives of the Queens of England.* London: Colburn & Co., 1851. Eight volumes. Full sky blue morocco by Riviere. Highly gilt spine, top edges gilt. Illustrated. 9" tall. Near fine. $1,450.00

STRUTT, Joseph. *Clic Camena Angel Deod. Or, The Sports and Pastimes of thee People of England….* London: J. White, 1801. Quarto. Contemporary full calf with red morocco spine label. First large paper edition. Illustrated with hand-colored engravings. Near fine. $800.00

STROKE, Elliot. *The Complete History of the Great American Rebellion.* Auburn, New York: Auburn, 1865. Full black calf. Marbled edges. Illustrated. Light foxing. First edition. Very good. $375.00

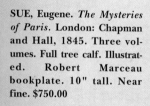

SUE, Eugene. *The Mysteries of Paris.* London: Chapman and Hall, 1845. Three volumes. Full tree calf. Illustrated. Robert Marceau bookplate. 10" tall. Near fine. $750.00

SURTEES, Robert Smith. *Handley Cross; Or, Mr. Jorrock's Hunt.* With: *Hawbuck Grange; Or, The Sporting Adventures of Thomas Scott, Esq.* With: *Mr. Sponge's Sporting Tour.* With: *Ask Mamma; Or, The Richest Commoner in England.* With: *Plain or Ringlets?* With: *Mr. Facey Romford's Hounds.* London: circa 1900. Six octavo volumes. Full red morocco gilt. Illustrated by John Leech and "Phiz" Browne. Near fine. $1,200.00

SURTEES, Robert. *The Sporting Tours.* London: 1853 – 1888. Six volumes. Full tan calf gilt by Riviere. Panels illustrated with gilt sporting devices. Red morocco spine labels. Illustrated by John Leech. Near fine. $1,500.00

SUMNER, Charles. *The Works of Charles Sumner.* Boston: Lee and Shepard, 1870. Twelve volumes. Three-quarter tan calf with marbled edges. First edition signed by the author. 8" tall. Near fine. $1,750.00

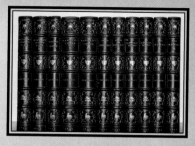

SURTEES. *Surtees' Works.* London: Bradbury, Agnew & Co., 1899. Eleven volumes. Three-quarter navy morocco by Zaehnsdorf. Top edges gilt. Illustrated with hand-colored plates by Leech. The White Friars Press. 10" tall. Near fine. $1,800.00

SWANWICK, Anna. *Goethe's Works.* London: George Bell and Sons, 1879. Eight volumes. Three-quarter butterscotch calf. Highly gilt spine with marbled edges. Bohn's Standard Library. 7" tall. Near fine. $1,300.00

SWIFT, Jonathan. *Gulliver's Travels into Several Remote Nations of the World.* London: Dent, 1909. Publisher's original gilt stamped white buckram binding. Limited edition illustrated by Arthur Rackham, one of only 750 copies. Near fine. $1,100.00

SWIFT, Jonathan. *Gulliver's Travels Into Several Remote Nations Of The World.* London: 1909. Full red morocco by Bayntun. Quarto. Illustrated by Arthur Rackham. Signed limited edition, one of only 750 copies signed by the illustrator. Near fine. $2,100.00

SWIFT, Jonathan. *Gulliver's Travels.* London: 1909. Large paper edition. Three-quarter red morocco gilt. Limited edition, one of only 750 copies. Royal 8vo. Illustrated by Arthur Rackham. Near fine. $1,600.00

SWIFT, Jonathan. *Gulliver's Travels.* London: J.M. Dent & Co., 1909. First trade edition. Three-quarter blue calf gilt. Illustrated by Arthur Rackham. Near fine. $1,500.00

S

SWIFT, Jonathan. *Gulliver's Travels*. London: F.C. and J. Rivington, Printed for J. Walker. Full navy morocco. Marbled edges. 5" tall. Very good. $210.00

SWIFT, Jonathan. *The Works. Containing Additional Letters, Tracts, and Poems, Not Hitherto Published*. Edinburgh: 1824. Nineteen octavo volumes. Contemporary full tree calf. Gilt decorated spines. Second edition of Sir Walter Scott's edition. Near fine. $3,600.00

SWIFT, Jonathan. *The Works. With Notes and a Life of the Author by Sir Walter Scott*. London, 1883 – 84. Nineteen volumes. Octavo. Contemporary three-quarter tan calf gilt. Second edition, one of only 750 copies. Near fine. $3,300.00

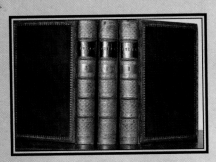

SWIFT, Jonathan. *The Poetical Works of Jonathan Swift*. London: William Pickering, 1853. Three volumes. Full maroon morocco. All edges gilt. The Aldine edition. 6¼" tall. Near fine. $375.00

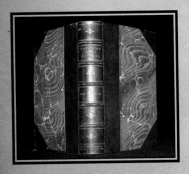

SWINTON, William. *Campaigns of the Army of the Potomac*. New York: Charles Scribners, 1882. Three-quarter brown calf by Launder and MacDonald. Top edges gilt. Illustrated. 9" tall. Near fine. $275.00

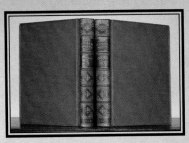

SYMONDS, John Addington. *Studies of the Greek Poets*. London: Smith, Elder & Co., 1873. Two volumes. Full tan calf by Zaehnsdorf. Top edges gilt. 8" tall. Near fine. $325.00

SZYK, Arthur. *The Book of Ruth*. New York: 1947. Tall quarto. Original three-quarter white morocco gilt. Signed limited edition, one of 1,950 copies signed by the author. Color illustrations. $850.00

TAINE, H.A. *History of English Literature*. Philadelphia: Henry Altemus, 1896. Four volumes. Three-quarter tan calf. Top edges gilt. 8" tall. Near fine. $475.00

TALLEYRAND, Charles Maurice de. *Memoirs of Prince de Talleyrand*. London: Griffith, 1891 – 92. Five octavo volumes. Three-quarter red morocco. Raised bands. First English edition. Near fine. $675.00

TALFOURD, T.N. *Tragedies*. London: Edward Moxon, 1848. Full tan calf. Gauffered edges. 6" tall. Near fine. $430.00

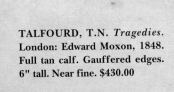

TAURINIUS, Zacharias. *Travels Through the Interior of Africa, from the Cape of Good Hope to Morocco.* London: 1801. Half brown morocco gilt. Octavo. Illustrated. First edition in English. Near fine. $475.00

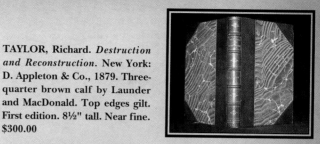

TAYLOR, Richard. *Destruction and Reconstruction.* New York: D. Appleton & Co., 1879. Three-quarter brown calf by Launder and MacDonald. Top edges gilt. First edition. 8½" tall. Near fine. $300.00

TAYLOR, Bayard. *The Poetical Works of Bayard Taylor.* Boston and New York: Houghton, Mifflin & Co., 1894. Full maroon morocco. All edges gilt. Illustrated, The Riverside Press. 8" tall. Near fine. $110.00

TAYLOR, Walter. *Four Years with General Lee.* New York: D. Appleton, 1878. Three-quarter brown morocco by Launder and MacDonald. Top edges gilt. 9½" tall. Near fine. $525.00

TAYLOR, Baynard. *Picturesque Europe.* New York: D. Appleton & Co., 1875. Three volumes (only one shown). Full brown calf. Embossed and gilt covers, all edges gilt. Illustrated first edition. 13" tall. Near fine. $1,350.00

TENNEY, W.J. *The Military and Naval History of the Rebellion in the United States.* New York: D. Appleton & Co., 1866. Full brown calf. Hand-tooled covers. All edges gilt. Illustrated with large pull-out map. First edition. 9½" tall. Near fine. $475.00

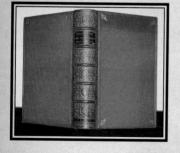

TAYLOR, Edgar. *Chronicle of the Conquest.* London: William Pickering, 1837. Full red morocco by Tout with all edges gilt. Illustrated with color plates, only 25 copies of the color plate edition were printed. Extra illustrated. 8" tall. Near fine. $850.00

TENNYSON, Alfred Lord. *Becket.* London: MacMillan & Co., 1884. Full tan calf with marbled edges. 7" tall. Near fine. $165.00

TAYLOR, Elizabeth. *Authentic Memoirs of Mrs. Clarke.* London: 1809. Nineteenth century brown morocco gilt. Octavo. Illustrated with a hand-colored frontispiece portrait. Second edition. Near fine. $275.00

TAYLOR, George, and SKINNER, Andrew. *Maps of the Roads of Ireland.* Dublin: 1778. Modern full calf. Tall octavo. Illustrated with 288 full page maps. First edition. Near fine. $1,500.00

TENNYSON, Alfred Lord. *Demeter and Other Poems.* London: MacMillan & Co., 1889. Full tan calf with marbled edges. 7" tall. $165.00

TENNYSON, Alfred Lord. *Enoch Arden.* London: 1866. Full green morocco. White silk moiré endpapers and doublures. First illustrated edition by Arthur Hughes. 7½" tall. Near fine. $975.00

TENNYSON, Alfred Lord. *Poems.* London: Henry S. King and Co., n.d., circa 1880. Full blue morocco. Highly gilt spine and covers with all edges gilt. Illustrated. Light spotting. 8½" tall. Near fine. $375.00

TENNYSON, Alfred Lord. *Enoch Arden.* London: Edward Moxon, 1864. Full red morocco. Highly gilt spine and cover, all edges gilt. First edition. 6½" tall. Near fine. $325.00

TENNYSON, Alfred Lord. *The Holy Grail.* London: Strahan and Co., 1870. Full chocolate pebbled calf. Highly gilt spine and covers. Top edges gilt. First edition. 6½" tall. Near fine. $425.00

TENNYSON, Alfred Lord. *Gareth and Lynette Etc.* London: Strahan and Co., 1872. Full red morocco. Highly gilt spine and covers. Gold gilt Bishop coat-of-arms on the front and back covers. All edges gilt. 6" tall. Near fine. $240.00

TENNYSON, Alfred Lord. *The Miller's Daughter.* London: W. Kent, 1870. Chocolate binding. Illustrated by A.L. Bond. Encased in a signed binding by John Leighton. All edges gilt. Highly gilt front cover. 8" tall. Near fine. $375.00

TENNYSON, Alfred Lord. *Idylls of the King.* London: Edward Moxon & Co., 1859. Full red morocco gilt with raised bands. 12mo. First edition, first issue. Near fine. $375.00

TENNYSON, Alfred Lord. *In Memoriam.* London: Hacon and Ricketts, 1900. Full turquoise crushed levant morocco gilt by Otto Schulze & Co. Floral gilt design in red morocco. Housed in a paper-backed cloth wrapper. Near fine. $1,400.00

TENNYSON, Alfred Lord. *The Lady of Shalott.* New York: 1881. Small quarto. Contemporary green morocco. Illustrated by Howard Pyle. Near fine. $475.00

TENNYSON, Alfred Lord. *The Poetic and Dramatic Works of Alfred Lord Tennyson.* Boston and New York: Houghton, Mifflin and Co., 1899. Full tree calf with all edges gilt. Illustrated. 8" tall. Near fine. $220.00

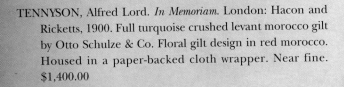

TENNYSON, Alfred Lord. *The Works.* Boston: Dana Estes & Co., 1895. Twelve volumes. Full red morocco, ornate tooling on covers and spines. Edition Deluxe. Near fine. $3,800.00

TENNYSON, Alfred Lord. *The Works.* London: MacMillan & Co., 1911. Full tree calf with gilt crest on cover. Near fine. $250.00

TENNYSON, Alfred Lord. *The Princess, A Melody*. London: Edward Moxon, 1853. Full red morocco. All edges gilt. 7" tall. Near fine. $240.00

TENNYSON, Alfred Lord. *The Works of Alfred Lord Tennyson*. Boston: James R. Osgood & Co., 1871. Ten volumes. Three-quarter calf with marbled edges. Bound by MacDonald & Son. Housed in a custom leather case. 5" tall. Near fine. $750.00

TENNYSON, Alfred Lord. *The Works*. London: Robert Riviere & Son, 1898. Full tan morocco by Riviere. Ornate gilt on spine and covers. Illustrated with early photographs. Near fine. $325.00

TENNYSON, Alfred Lord. *The Works*. London: Robert Riviere & Son, 1898. Tan morocco by Bayntun. Illustrated with early photographs. Near fine. $375.00

THACKERAY, William M. *The Works*. London: Smith, Elder & Co., 1869. Twenty-four volumes. Three-quarter brown morocco. Illustrated. Near fine. $1,700.00

THACKERAY, William Makepeace. *Vanity Fair*. London: 1924. Thick octavo. Mid twentieth century full blue morocco, cover ornately decorated with ten-color inlaid morocco illustration of a scene from the book. Illustrated edition with 16 color illustrations by Charles Combie. Near fine. $975.00

THACKERAY, W.M. *The Virginians*. London: Bradbury and Evans, 1859. Two volumes. Full teal morocco. Highly gilt spine, top edges gilt. Illustrated. First edition in book form. 8½" tall. Near fine. $480.00

THACKERAY, William Makepeace. *Thackeray's Works*. London: Smith, Elder & Co., 1879. Twenty-four volumes (only six shown). Three-quarter red morocco. Top edges gilt. Illustrated by the author. 7" tall. Near fine. $3,000.00

THACKERAY, William Makepeace. *Thackeray's Works*. New York: Lovell, Coryell & Co., n.d., circa 1890. Ten volumes. Three-quarter butterscotch calf. 7½" tall. Near fine. $1,500.00

THACKERAY, William Makepeace. *Vanity Fair*. London: Geroge G. Harrap & Co., 1930. Full red morocco by Riviere. Highly gilt cover, all edges gilt. Color illustrations by Charles Crombie. 9" tall. Near fine. $450.00

THATCHER, B.B. *Indian Biography*. New York: J. & J. Harper, 1832. Two volumes. Three-quarter black calf. First edition. 5½" tall. Very good. $750.00

The Acts of the General Assembly of the Commonwealth of Pennsylvania. Philadelphia: 1782. Contemporary full brown sheep. Folio. First edition. Near fine. $1,100.00

The Aldine Edition of British Poets. London: William Pickering, 1830 – 1852. Fifty-three volumes. Small octavo. Contemporary full polished tan gilt by Zaehnsdorf. Complete set includes works of Milton, Pope, Dryden, Shakespeare, Chaucer, Spenser, Swift, Burns, and Wyatt. Near fine. $6,000.00

The Annual Register, or a View of the History, Politics, and Literature for the Year 1776. London: 1777. Modern half brown calf. Octavo. First edition. Near fine. $850.00

The Travels of Marco Polo. London: J.M. Dent & Sons, 1926. Three-quarter green morocco gilt by Hatchards. Raised bands and gilt panels. With introduction by John Masefiled. Illustrated with ink drawings by Adrian De Friston. Near fine. $450.00

THIERS, Louis Adolphe. *The History of the French Revolution, 1789 – 1800.* Philadelphia: J.B. Lippincott Co., 1884. Five volumes. With: *History of the Consulate and The Empire of France Under Napoleon.* Philadelphia: J.B. Lippincott Co., 1893. Twelve volumes. Seventeen volumes together. Three-quarter blue morocco gilt. Raised bands, spines decorated with Napoleonic emblems. Illustrated. Near fine. $2,800.00

THOMAS A KEMPIS. *The Christian Pattern Paraphras'd: Or, The Book Of The Imitation of Christ.* London: Abel Roper and Roger Clavel, 1697. Contemporary calf. Covers mottled. Raised bands flanked by gilt rules. Engraved frontispiece showing the Crucified Christ. Near fine. $850.00

THIERS, M.A. *The History of the French Revolution.* London: Richard Bentley, n.d., circa 1870. Five volumes. Full butterscotch calf. Illustrated with steel engravings. 7" tall. Near fine. $750.00

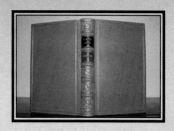

THOREAU, Henry David. *Cape Cod.* Boston: Ticknor and Fields, 1865. Full butterscotch calf by Period Binders. Highly gilt spine, top edges gilt. First edition with original boards and spine bound in. 7" tall. Fine. $1,250.00

THOREAU, Henry David. *Cape Cod.* Boston: 1865. Octavo. Full blue morocco. First edition. Near fine. $1,600.00

THOREAU, Henry David. *The Writings.* Boston and New York: 1906. Twenty volumes. Octavo. Contemporary three-quarter red morocco gilt. Walden edition. Near fine. $4,800.00

THOREAU, Henry David. *The Writings of Henry David Thoreau.* Boston and New York: Houghton, Mifflin & Co., 1893. Eleven volumes. Three-quarter tan calf with top edges gilt. The Riverside edition, The Riverside Press. 8" tall. Near fine. $3,800.00

THOREAU, Henry David. *The Writings.* Boston and New York: Houghton Mifflin and Co., 1906. Twenty octavo volumes. Three-quarter green morocco gilt. Manuscript edition, one of only 600 copies. Near fine. $12,000.00

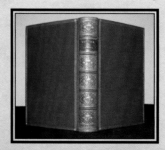

THOREAU, Henry David. *Walden of Life in the Woods.* London: Chapman & Hall, Ltd., 1927. Full rust morocco by Riverside. Highly gilt spine with top edges gilt. Illustrated. 9" tall. Near fine. $450.00

TILLOTSON. *Stories of the Wars 1574 – 1658*. London: S.O. Benton, 1865. Full red morocco. Marbled edges. Illustrated with color, tinted and black and white illustrations. 8½" tall. Near fine. $190.00

THOREAU, Henry David. *Walden. Of Life in the Woods*. Boston: 1936. Tall octavo. Three-quarter calf. Illustrated with photographs by Edward Steichen. Near fine. $575.00

THORNBURY, Walter. *Old and New London*. London: Cassell Petter & Galpin, 1900. Six volumes. Three-quarter red polished calf. Marbled boards and edges. Large 8 vo. Illustrated. Near fine. $850.00

THORNBURY, Walter. *The Life of J.M.W. Turner*. London: Hurst & Blackett, 1862. Two volumes. Three-quarter blue morocco by Zaehnsdorf. Ornate gilt spines, raised bands. Near fine. $475.00

THORNTON, Thomas. *The Present State of Turkey or a Description of the Ottoman Empire*. London: Joseph Mawman, 1809. Two volumes. Three-quarter green morocco. Gilt spines. Illustrated. Second edition. Near fine. $775.00

TOCQUEVILLE, Alexis de. *Democracy in America*. New York: 1904. Two octavo volumes. Three-quarter brown morocco gilt. Near fine. $650.00

TIMBS, John. *Curiosities of London*. London: David Bogue, 1855. Two volumes. Full butter-scotch calf by Riviere & Son. Top edges gilt. First edition, signed by the author. Bookplates of John Barrow and Charles Pilgrim. 6¾" tall. Near fine. $1,200.00

TOCQUEVILLE, Alexis de. *Democracy in America*. London: Longman, Green, Longman, and Roberts, 1862. Two volumes. Contemporary blue half calf over marbled boards. Marbled edges and endpaper. Near fine. $600.00

TOCQUEVILLE, Alexis de. *Democracy in America*. New York: J. & H.G. Langley, 1841. Two volumes. Octavo. Dark brown calf. Near fine. $3,800.00

TOCQUEVILLE, Alexis de. *Democracy in America*. New York: 1838. With: *Democracy in America. Part the Second, The Social Influence of Democracy*. New York: 1840. Two octavo volumes. Full blue morocco gilt. First American editions. Near fine. $5,500.00

TOLSTOI, Count Leo. *Anna Karenina. A Novel*. Philadelphia: MacRae Smith Co., circa 1900. Full wine morocco gilt. Illustrated in color by Helen Grose. Translated from Russian by Constance Garnett. Near fine. $475.00

TOLSTOI, Lyof N. *Novels and Other Works*. New York: Charles Scribner's Sons, 1899. Twenty-two volumes. Three-quarter green morocco gilt. Near fine. $4,500.00

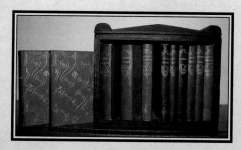

TILT, Charles. *Tilt's Miniature Classical Library*. London: Charles Tilt, 1836. Eleven volumes. Full multicolored morocco. Highly gilt covers. All edges gilt. Housed in a custom wooden box. 4¼" tall. Near fine. $950.00

TIMBS, John. *English Eccentrics and Eccentricities*. London: Chatto and Windus, 1877. Two volumes. Full red morocco by Root. Illustrated, many by hand. All edges gilt. Fine. $900.00

TOLSTOY, Count Lev. N. *The Works of Tolstoy.* Boston: Dana Estes & Co., 1904. Twenty-four volumes (only six shown). Three-quarter blue morocco by Brentanos. Top edges gilt. Illustrated Cabinet edition. Spines faded to green. 8" tall. $3,600.00

TOLSTOI, Lyof N. *Novels and Other Works.* New York: Charles Scribner's Sons. Twenty-four volumes. Three-quarter green morocco over marbled boards. 8vo. Burgundy and red labels. Near fine. $5,100.00

TOLSTOI, Lyof N. *Novels and Other Works.* New York: Charles Scribner's Sons, 1923. Twenty-four octavo volumes. Contemporary three-quarter dark blue morocco. Contains his complete novels. Near fine. $2,900.00

TOLSTOI, Lyof N. *Works.* Boston: L.C. Page & Co., 1904. Fourteen volumes. Three-quarter navy morocco with ribbed gilt decorated spines. Illustrated Library edition. Near fine. $1,800.00

TOLSTOY, Leo. *War and Peace. A Historical Novel.* New York: William S. Gottsberger, 1886. Six small octavo volumes. Original blue cloth. Gilt stamped titles. First edition, first issue in English. Near fine. $4,800.00

TOLSTOY, Leo. *Works.* Boston: 1904. Twenty-four volumes bound in 12. Octavo. Three-quarter red morocco gilt. Near fine. $1,800.00

TOMES, Robert. *Battles of America by Sea & Land.* New York: Virtue and Co., 1861. Three volumes. Three-quarter black calf. Profusely illustrated. First edition. 11" tall. Near fine. $925.00

TOMES, Robert. *The Battles of America by Sea and Land.* New York: Patterson & Neilson, 1878. Three volumes. Three-quarter brown calf. Highly gilt cover with all edges gilt. First edition. 11" tall. Very good. $975.00

TOMES, Robert. *The Great Civil War, A History of the Great Southern Rebellion.* New York: Virtue and Yorkston, 1862. Three volumes. Three-quarter green morocco. Illustrated. First edition. 11½" tall. Near fine. $1,100.00

TOMES, Robert, and SMITH, Benjamin G. *The War with the South.* New York: circa 1866. Three volumes. Quarto. Original publisher's full brown morocco gilt. Early edition. Illustrated with tissue-guarded engraved plates of Civil War scenes and historical figures. Near fine. $1,250.00

TOOKE. *The Life of Catharine II, Empress of Russia.* London: A. Straham, 1800. Three volumes. Three-quarter green calf. Gilt spines, marbled edges. Illustrated. Fourth edition. Near fine. $425.00

TOMES, Robert. *The War with the South.* New York: Virtue and Co., 1862. Three volumes. Full tan calf. Gilt and embossed covers with all edges gilt. Illustrated with steel engravings. First edition. 8" tall. Near fine. $1,300.00

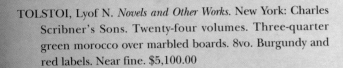

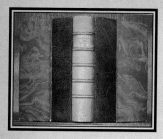

TRANQUILLUS, C. Suetonius. *The Lives of the Twelve Caesars*. London: Henry G. Bohn, 1855. Half green morocco. Top edges gilt, spine faded to brown. 7" tall. Very good. $65.00

TROLLOPE, Anthony. *North America*. London: Chapman and Hall, 1862. Two volumes. Three-quarter tan calf. Pull-out maps. First English edition. 8½" tall. Very good. $475.00

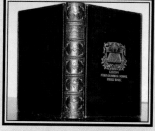

TRENCH, Richard Chenevix. *Notes on the Miracles of our Lord*. London: Kegan Paul, Trench & Co., 1889. Full blue morocco. Prize binding with marbled edges. 7" tall. Very good. $135.00

TROLLOPE, Anthony. *Is He Popenjoy?* London: Chapman and Hall, 1878. Three octavo volumes. Full tan polished calf. Raised bands, gilt decorated spines. First edition. Near fine. $1,900.00

TROLLOPE, Anthony. *The Barsetshire Novels*. Stratford-Upon-Avon: 1929. Fourteen volumes. Large octavo. Contemporary three-quarter green morocco gilt. "Shakespeare Head" limited edition, one of only 525 sets. Illustrated by Charles S. Olcott. Near fine. $4,200.00

TOULOUSE-LAUTREC, Henri de, and CLEMENCEAU, Georges. *Au Pied Du Sinai*. Paris: 1898. Quarto. Modern full brown morocco gilt. Limited edition, one of only 380 copies. Near fine. $8,200.00

TRIGGS, H. Inigo. *Formal Gardens in England and Scotland. Their Planning and Arrangement, Architectural and Ornamental Features*. London: B.T. Batsford, 1902. Three-quarter brown morocco. Gilt spines, raised bands, top edges gilt. Illustrated. Near fine. $750.00

TRISTAM, Outram W. *Coaching Days and Coaching Ways*. London: MacMillian & Co., 1924. Full green morocco gilt by Riviere. Onlay of horses, raised bands, and ornate tooling on cover and spine. Illustrated by Hugh Thomson and Herbert Roulton. Near fine. $1,600.00

TROLLOPE, Anthony. *The Chronicles of Barsetshire*. London: Chapman & Hall, 1887. Eight volumes. Three-quarter blue morocco. Marbled edges. 7¾" tall. Fine. $1,500.00

TROWBRIDGE, J.T. *Cudjo's Cave*. Boston: J.E. Tilton and Co., 1864. Full red morocco. Top edges gilt. First edition, signed by the author. Marceau book plate. 7" tall. Fine. $600.00

TRISTRAM, W. Outram. *Coaching Days and Coaching Ways*. London: MacMillan & Co., 1893. Full red morocco by Bayntun. Highly gilt spine, all edges gilt. 214 illustrations by Hugh Thompson and Herbert Hailton. 7" tall. Near fine. $525.00

TURNER, J.M.W. *The Turner Gallery*. New York: D. Appleton & Co., circa 1880. Two volumes. Folio. Original full brown calf gilt and blind tooled morocco. Illustrated with steel engravings. Near fine. $1,800.00

TURNER, T. Hudson. *Some Account of Domestic Architecture in England from the Conquest to the End of the 13th Century.* Oxford: John H. Parker, 1852. Four volumes. Three-quarter tan calf. Gilt spines, raised bands, and marbled edges. Illustrated. Near fine. $375.00

TWAIN, Mark. *Huckleberry Finn.* London: Chatto and Windus, 1884. Three-quarter red morocco. Marbled edges. 174 illustrations. First English edition. 7" tall. Near fine. $1,100.00

TURNER, G. *Traits of Indian Character.* **Philadelphia: Key & Biddle, 1838. Two volumes. Three-quarter brown morocco. Top edges gilt. First edition. 7" tall. Near fine. $650.00**

TWAIN, Mark. *Life on the Mississippi.* Boston: 1883. Octavo. Three-quarter calf. Housed in a custom half morocco slipcase. First American edition. Near fine. $1,800.00

TWAIN, Mark. *Life on the Mississippi.* Boston: James R. Osgood & Co., 1883. Octavo. Three-quarter brown morocco gilt. Marbled edges and endpapers. First American edition. Near fine. $2,000.00

TWAIN, Mark. *A Tramp Abroad.* **Hartford: American Publishing Co., 1880. Three-quarter brown calf. Marbled edges. 328 illustrations. First edition, later issue. 9" tall. Near fine. $625.00**

TWAIN, Mark. *The Adventures of Tom Sawyer.* Hartford, Connecticut: The American Publishing Company, 1876. First American edition, second printing. Octavo. Original blue cloth stamped in gilt and black lettering. Contained in a quarter blue morocco slipcase. Near fine. $8,600.00

TWAIN, Mark. *A Connecticut Yankee in King Arthur's Court.* New York: 1889. Full calf. Illustrated by Dan Beard. First edition, first issue. Near fine. $1,200.00

TWAIN, Mark. *A Tramp Abroad.* Hartford, Connecticut: American Publishing Co., and London: Chatto & Windus, 1880. Thick octavo. Black morocco gilt. First edition. Illustrated. Near fine. $1,150.00

TWAIN, Mark. *Life on the Mississippi.* **Boston: James Osgood, 1883. Three-quarter butterscotch calf. Three hundred illustrations. Marbled edges. First edition. Very good. $1,150.00**

TWAIN, Mark. *A Tramp Abroad.* London: 1880. Two small octavo volumes. Original brown cloth gilt. First English edition. Near fine. $725.00

TWAIN, Mark. *Adventures of Huckleberry Finn.* New York: Charles L. Webster, 1885. Octavo. Original green pictorial cloth. First edition, first issue. Includes a green half-morocco clamshell box. Near fine. $6,100.00

TWAIN, Mark. *Mark Twain's Autobiography.* **New York: Gabriel Wells, 1925. Two volumes. Three-quarter rust morocco. Top edges gilt. Illustrated. Fine. $425.00**

TWAIN, Mark. *Adventures of Huckleberry Finn.* New York: Charles L. Webster & Co., 1885. Octavo. Black calf. Illustrated by E.W. Kemble. Near fine. $5,400.00

TWAIN, Mark. *The Adventures of Tom Sawyer*. Hartford: The American Publishing Co., 1876. Three-quarter blue morocco. Highly gilt cover. Top edges gilt. Illustrated. First edition. 8¾" tall. Near fine. $8,600.00

TWAIN, Mark. *The Adventures of Tom Sawyer*. London: Chatto and Windus, 1876. First English edition. Octavo. Full brown morocco gilt by Zaehnsdorf. Near fine. $2,750.00

TWAIN, Mark. *The Innocents Abroad, or The New Pilgrims' Progress*. Hartford, Connecticut: American Publishing Company, 1869. Octavo. Three-quarter calf. First edition first issue. Near fine. $3,600.00

TWAIN, Mark. *The Innocents Abroad*. Hartford: The American Publishing Co., 1869. Three-quarter blue morocco. Top edges gilt. 234 illustrations. Original covers and spine bound in rear of book. First edition, first issue. 9" tall. Fine. $2,600.00

TWAIN, Mark. *The Prince and the Pauper, A Tale for Young People of All Ages*. Boston: James R. Osgood & Co., 1882. Octavo. Three-quarter dark brown morocco gilt. Marbled boards and endpapers. First American edition. Near fine. $1,500.00

TWAIN, Mark. *The Prince and the Pauper*. Boston: 1882. Full calf. Octavo. First American edition, first issue. Near fine. $2,100.00

TWAIN, Mark. *The Prince and the Pauper*. New York: Charles L. Webster & Co., 1891. Three-quarter red morocco with top edges gilt. 192 illustrations. 8¼" tall. Near fine. $475.00

TWAIN, Mark. *The Writings of Mark Twain*. New York and London: Harper & Brothers, 1899. Twenty-five volumes (only four shown). Three-quarter red calf. Top edges gilt. Hillcrest edition, illustrated. 8½" tall. Near fine. $7,500.00

TWAIN, Mark. *The Tragedy of Pudd'nhead Wilson*. Hartford: 1894. Full calf gilt. First edition. Near fine. $1,800.00

TWAIN, Mark. *The Writings of Mark Twain*. London: Chatto and Windus, 1899. Twenty-three octavo volumes. Three-quarter green calf. Author's Edition de Luxe, one of only 620 copies signed by the author. Near fine. $9,800.00

TWAIN, Mark. *The Writings*. New York: Gabriel Wells, 1922 – 1925. Thirty-seven octavo volumes. Three-quarter blue morocco gilt. Raised bands. The Definitive edition, one of only 1,024 copies signed by the author: "S.L. Clemens/Mark Twain." Illustrated with full page etchings and photogravures. Near fine. $18,000.00

TWAIN, Mark. *Works*. Hartford: The American Publishing Company, 1899. Twenty-five volumes. Three-quarter maroon morocco gilt. Limited edition, one of only 1,000 sets. Near fine. $8,500.00

TWAIN, Mark. *Works*. New York: Harper & Brothers, 1923 – 24. Twenty-two octavo volumes. Contemporary three-quarter blue morocco gilt. Illustrated with 65 full-page plates. "Mississippi" edition. Near fine. $8,000.00

TWAIN, Mark. *Writings*. New York: 1904 – 07. Twenty-five volumes. Octavo. Contemporary three-quarter burgundy morocco gilt. Hillcrest edition. Near fine. $8,200.00

TWAIN, Mark. *Writings*. New York: Gabriel Wells, 1922. Thirty-five volumes. Full wine morocco gilt. Gilt panels. Signed by the author. Near fine. $17,500.00

TYTLER, Patrick F. *Life of Sir Walter Raleigh*. Edinburgh: Olwen & Boyd, 1833. Three-quarter tan calf. Small 8vo. Illustrated. Near fine. $225.00

T

TYLER, Edward. *Researches in to the Early History of Mankind*. London: John Murray, 1878. Full tree calf with marbled edges. Illustrated. 8½" tall. Near fine. $315.00

UNKNOWN. *The Gift*. Philadelphia: Carey & Hart, 1842. Full tan calf by S. Moore, signed on front cover. Highly gilt spine and cover, all edges gilt. Illustrated first edition. 7" tall. Near fine. $225.00

TYTLER, Margaret Fraser. *Tales of the Great and Brave*. London: W. & R. Chambers, 1895. Full maroon morocco by Relfe. Illustrated prize binding. 7" tall. Near fine. $130.00

UNKNOWN. *The Pentecostal Gift*. Glasgow: James Maclehouse and Sons, 1903. Full tan calf. Marbled edges. Prize binding. 7" tall. Near fine. $150.00

UNKNOWN. *Eucharist, Meditations and Prayers*. London: James Burns, 1843. Full maroon morocco. Hand-painted and gauffered edges, illuminated frontis. 4½" tall. Near fine. $325.00

UNKNOWN. *The World's Famous Places and People*. New York and London: Merrill & Baker, 1900. Thirty-eight volumes (only three shown). Full red morocco. Top edges gilt. Inlaid morocco inner covers with maroon and white leather. Color photo frontispieces. Edition des Aquarelles, one of 26 sets. Color plates. 8¾" tall. Near fine. $5,500.00

UNKNOWN. *Lovely Nights of Young Girls*. London: Erotica Biblion Society, n.d., c. 1912. Three-quarter red morocco. Top edges gilt. Erotic illustrations. Near fine. $400.00

UNKNOWN. *Scotia's Bards*. New York: Robert Carter and Brothers, 1854. Full green morocco. Highly gilt spine and covers, all edges gilt. Illustrated. 9" tall. Near fine. $280.00

UPHAM, Francis W. *The Wisemen: Who They Were; and How They Came to Jerusalem*. New York: Sheldon and Co., 1869. Three-quarter tan calf. Marbled edges. Illustrated with map, inscribed by the author. First edition. 7½" tall. Near fine. $245.00

240

VALE, Joseph G. *Minty and the Cavalry. A History of Cavalry Campaigns in the Western Armies.* Harrisburg, Pennsylvania: Edwin K. Meyers, Printer and Binder. Three-quarter dark brown calf by Launder and MacDonald. Top edges gilt. Illustrated. Near fine. $525.00

VARIOUS. *The Book of English Poetry.* London and Edinburgh: T. Nelson & Sons, 1855. Full green calf with all edges gilt. Illustrated. 6" tall. Near fine. $225.00

VAN DYKE, Henry. *The Works of Henry Van Dyke.* New York: 1920. Eighteen volumes. Octavo. Original three-quarter blue morocco gilt. Avalon edition, one of only 504 sets. Near fine. $3,600.00

VAUGHN, Robert. *Milton's Paradise Lost.* London: Cassell Petter & Co., n.d., circa 1868. Full brown calf. All edges gilt. Illustrated by Gustave Doré. 15" tall. Very good. $875.00

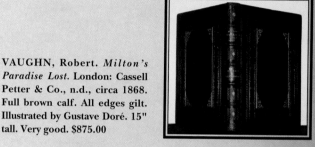

VAN HORNE, Thomas B. *The History of the Army of the Cumberland.* Cincinnati: Robert Clarke, 1875. Two volumes. Three-quarter brown calf by Launder and Mac-Donald. Top edges gilt. With atlas. First editions. 9½" tall. Near fine. $875.00

VAUGHN, Robert. *Revolutions in English History.* London: John W. Parker and Son, 1859. Three volumes. Three-quarter butterscotch calf with marbled edges. 8½" tall. Near fine. $375.00

VAN-LAUN, Henri. *History of French Literature. From the Origin to the Renaissance.* London: Smith, Elder & Co., 1876. Three volumes. Three-quarter calf. Gilt spines with red and green morocco labels. Near fine. $350.00

VAN LAUN, Henri. *The Dramatic Works of Moliere.* Edinburgh: William Paterson, 1875. Six volumes. Full tree calf with all edges gilt. Illustrated. 9" tall. Near fine. $1,400.00

VENN, John. *The Principles of Empirical or Inductive Logic.* London: 1889. Three-quarter calf. First edition. Near fine. $1,600.00

VAN-ESS, William. *The Life of Bonaparte.* London: E. Bumford, 1821. Ten volumes. Three-quarter red morocco gilt. Small 8vo. Illustrated. Near fine. $1,800.00

VERNE, Jules. *The Tour of the World in Eighty Days.* Boston: James R. Osgood and Co., 1873. Translated by Geo. Towle. Full blue morocco, 12mo. First English edition. Near fine. $1,400.00

❧ V ❧

VERNE, Jules. *A Journey to the Center of the Earth.* New York: Scribner, Armstrong & Co., n.d., circa 1890. Three-quarter brown calf by Parsonnet. All edges gilt. Fifty-two illustrations by Riou. Sold by subscription only. Original cloth cover and spine tipped in back of book. Near fine. $375.00. Along with *Off on a Comet.* Circa 1890. Three quarter green morocco. Thirty-six illustrations. Near fine. $375.00

VERNE, Jules. *Around the World in Eighty Days.* London: Sampson Low, 1886. Full maroon morocco with marbled edges. Illustrated. 6½" tall. Near fine. $425.00

VERNE, Jules. *Works of Jules Verne.* New York: Vincent Parke & Co., 1911. Fifteen large octavo volumes. Modern green morocco gilt. Hand-colored frontispieces by R. G. Lancaster. Near fine. $4,200.00

VERNE, Jules. *Works.* New York and London: Vincent Parke & Co., 1911. Fifteen volumes. Prince Edward of Wales edition. Limited edition, one of only 500 copies. Illustrated. Full green morocco, top edge gilt, marbled boards. Near fine. $6,500.00

VERNE, Jules. *Works of Jules Verne.* New York and London: Charles Horne, 1911. Fifteen volumes (only five shown). Full gray morocco. Top edges gilt. Decoree edition, one of 300 volumes. Hand-colored frontispieces, some illustrations signed by the illustrator. 9" tall. Near fine. $5,600.00

VICTOR, Orville. *History of American Conspiracies.* New York: James Torrey, 1863. Full maroon morocco. Marbled edges. Illustrated with steel engravings. First edition. Very good. $325.00

VICTOR, Orville. *The History, Civil, Political and Military of the Southern Rebellion.* New York: James D. Torrey, 1861. Four volumes. Three-quarter brown calf with marbled edges. Illustrated and with maps. First edition. 10" tall. Near fine. $975.00

VIRGIL. *The Aeneid.* Boston and New York: 1906. Two volumes. Large octavo. Contemporary full navy morocco, elaborately gilt decorated spine and covers. Limited edition, one of only 650 copies. Illustrated edition. Near fine. $675.00

VOLTAIRE, Francois-Marie Arouet de. *The Whole Prose Romances.* Philadelphia: 1898. Three octavo volumes. Three-quarter red morocco gilt. Illustrated by Laguillermie and Chevenin. First edition. Near fine. $475.00

VOLTAIRE. *The Works.* New York and Chicago: E. R. Dumont, 1901. Forty-two volumes. Three-quarter green morocco gilt. Raised bands and marbled boards. Illustrated with old engravings and steel plate photogravures. "Ferney Edition," one of only 190 copies. Near fine. $6,500.00

VOLTAIRE, M. *Romances, Novels and Tales.* London: Lackington, Allen and Co., 1806. Two volumes. Three-quarter tan calf. 8" tall. Near fine. $225.00

VULTURE, R. *Praises of God.* Budapest: M.E. Lowv's Son, 1893. Full ivory and celluloid cover. All edges gilt. Written in English and Hebrew. Brass clasps and brass cover trim. Bronze Ten Commandment tablet on front cover. Ivory scroll work diagonal on front cover. 7½" tall. Very good. $825.00

WAFER, Lionel. *A New Voyage and Description of the Isthmus of America.* London: James Knapton, 1699. Modern blue half morocco gilt. Raised bands with gilt ornament in spine panels. Patterned paper sides and endpapers. Illustrated with three engraved plates and a folding map. Near fine. $1,250.00

WAGNER, Richard. *The Rhinegold & The Valkyrie.* London: Heinemann, 1910. Two volumes. Full navy morocco gilt. Quarto. Illustrated. First editions. Near fine. $1,200.00

WALKER, Francis. *General Hancock.* New York: D. Appleton & Co., 1894. Three-quarter navy morocco. Highly gilt spine with top edges gilt. Illustrated. First edition. 9½" tall. Near fine. $350.00

WALKER, Francis. *History of the Second Army Corps.* New York: Charles Scribners, 1886. Three-quarter brown calf by Launder and MacDonald. Top edges gilt. Illustrated. First edition. 8½" tall. Near fine. $350.00

WALKER, James. *The Madonnas of Raphael.* New York: Leavitt & Allen, 1860. Full black morocco with all edges gilt. With tipped in photograph. First edition. 11" tall. Near fine. $550.00

WALLACE, Lew. *Ben-Hur, A Tale of the Christ.* New York: Harper and Brothers, 1880. Three-quarter tan calf. Marbled edges. First American edition. 7" tall. Near fine. $325.00

WALLACE, Lew. *Ben-Hur. A Tale of the Christ.* New York: 1880. Octavo. Three-quarter calf. First edition. Housed in a half morocco slipcase. Near fine. $1,100.00

WALPOLE, Horace. *Letters of Horace Walpole, Earl of Oxford.* London: Richard Bentley, 1857. Eighteen volumes. Three-quarter red morocco by Bayntun. Gilt six paneled spine with raised bands. Marbled endpapers, top edges gilt. Illustrated. Near fine. $3,600.00

WALSH, Robert. *Constantinople and the Scenery of the Seven Churches of Asia Minor Illustrated.* London: Peter Jackson, Late Fisher, Son & Co., 1839. Two volumes in one. Three-quarter tan calf. Quarto. Raised bands. Illustrated with numerous steel engravings of the city. First edition. Near fine. $975.00

WALTON and COTTON. *The Complete Angler.* London and New York: John Lane, 1904. Three-quarter red morocco by Morrell. Top edges gilt. Illustrated. 8" tall. Near fine. $265.00

W

WALTON and COTTON. *The Complete Angler.* London: Henry Kent Causton, circa 1880. Full tree calf by Morrel. All edges gilt. Illustrated. 6½" tall. Near fine. $410.00

WALTON, Izaak. *The Works of the Learned and Judicious Divine Mr. Richard Hooker.* Oxford: University Press, 1850. Two volumes. Full maroon morocco. Prize binding. Near fine. $375.00

WALTON, Izaak, and COTTON, Charles. *The Complete Angler or the Contemplative Man's Recreation.* London: By J.G. for Richard Marriot, 1621. Full speckled calf. 24mo. Raised bands, gilt spine and marbled endpapers. Illustrated. First issue, Third edition. Near fine. $7,200.00

WALTON, Izaak, and COTTON, Charles. *The Complete Angler; or, Contemplative Man's Recreation: being a Discourse on Rivers, Fishponds, Fish, and Fishing.* London: 1842. Octavo. Nineteenth-century full blue morocco gilt. Illustrated with full page engravings and in-text engravings and a fore-edge painting of Izaak Walton. Near fine. $1,200.00

WALTON, Izaak, and COTTON, Charles. *The Complete Angler.* Chicago: A.C. McClurg & Co., 1900. Three-quarter green morocco. Top edges gilt. 7" tall. Near fine. $125.00

WALTON, Izaak, and COTTON, Charles. *The Complete Angler.* London: Elliot Stock, 1896. Small octavo. Full modern marbled calf gilt. Gilt tooled spine, red labels, and marbled endpapers. Reprint of the First edition published in 1653. Near fine. $450.00

WALTON, Izaak, and COTTON, Charles. *The Complete Angler; or, Contemplative Man's Recreation....* London: for John and Francis Rivington, 1775. Full brown calf, raised bands and gilt spine. Small octavo. Illustrated with numerous full-page scenes, copperplate engravings, plates of fishing tackle and various fish. Third edition. Near fine. $600.00

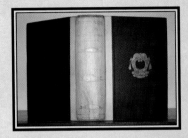

WALTON, Izaak, and COTTON, Charles. *The Complete Angler.* London: J.C. Nimmo and Bain, 1883. One quarter white vellum. Top edges gilt. Illustrated with six original etchings and two portraits by Dammon and 74 woodcuts. 9½" tall. Very good. $425.00

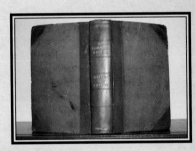

WALTON, Izaak, and COTTON, Charles. *The Complete Angler.* London: Samuel Bagster, 1808. Three-quarter tan calf. Twenty-four copper plates and 17 small copper plates with full-page plates hand watercolored. 9" tall. Very good. $650.00

WALTON, Izaak, and COTTON, Charles. *The Complete Angler.* London: Chatto and Windus, 1875. Three-quarter butterscotch calf. Marbled edges. Illustrated with 60 illustrations by Strothard and Inskipp. 8" tall. Near fine. $425.00

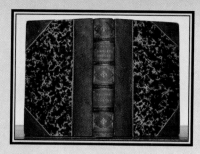

WALTON, Izaak, and COTTON, Charles. *The Complete Angler.* London: George Bell and Sons, 1876. Three-quarter brown calf. Top edges gilt. Illustrated. 7" tall. Good. $185.00

WALTON, Izaak, and COTTON, Charles. *The Complete Angler.* London: Henry Washbourne, 1842. Quarter black calf. Top edges gilt. Illustrated. 8" tall. Near fine. $285.00

WARBURTON, Eliot. *The Crescent and the Cross.* London and New York: Frederick Warne & Co., 1886. Full blue morocco. Highly gilt spine, prize binding with marbled edges. 7" tall. Near fine. $315.00

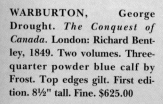

WARBURTON, George Drought. *The Conquest of Canada.* London: Richard Bentley, 1849. Two volumes. Three-quarter powder blue calf by Frost. Top edges gilt. First edition. 8½" tall. Fine. $625.00

WARD, Anna. *A Dictionary of Quotations.* New York: Thomas Y. Crowell & Co., 1883. Full tan calf. Marbled edges. First edition. 8" tall. Near fine. $75.00

WARD, Mrs. Humphry. *Robert Elsmere.* London: MacMillan & Co., 1888. Two volumes. Three-quarter green morocco by MacDonald. Top edges gilt. Book plate of Charles Francis Adams, the great-grandson of John Quincy Adams. 7" tall. Near fine. $320.00

WARD, A.W., and WALLER, M.A. *The Cambridge History of English Literature.* New York and London: 1907 – 1917. Fourteen octavo volumes. Contemporary three-quarter red morocco gilt. Early edition. Near fine. $1,800.00

WARDLE, Col., and DODD, Maj. *The Rival Princess.* London: C. Chapple, 1810. Two volumes. Three-quarter red morocco by Root. Top edges gilt. First edition. 7" tall. Very good. $315.00

WARNER, Charles Dudley. *The Complete Writings of Charles Dudley Warner.* Hartford: The American Publishing Co., 1904. Fifteen volumes. Full green crushed morocco. Raised bands, gilt decorated spines and boards. Red morocco doublures, silk endpapers. Illustrated. Near fine. $4,800.00

WARREN, Albert. *The Promises of Jesus Christ.* London: Day and Son, n.d., circa 1860. Full rust calf. Highly gilt and embossed covers and spine, all edges gilt. Illuminated by Warren. 8" tall. Near fine. $600.00

WASHINGTON, George. *The Writings of George Washington; Being His Correspondence, Addresses, Messages, and Other Papers, Official and Private.* Boston: Charles Tappan, 1846. Twelve octavo volumes. Contemporary full calf. Illustrated with numerous maps, portraits, and facsimiles. Near fine. $2,600.00

WASHINGTON, George. *The Writings of George Washington; Being His Correspondence, Addresses, Messages, and Other Papers, Official and Private, Selected and Published From the Original Manuscripts; With a Life of the Author, Notes, and Illustrations.* Boston: 1855. Twelve octavo volumes. Contemporary three-quarter brown calf gilt. Illustrated with engraved portraits, maps, and facsimiles. Near fine. $1,900.00

WATSON, Henry C. *Thrilling Adventures of Hunters in the Old World and New.* Boston: Kelly & Brothers, 1853. Full black calf with marbled edges. Hundreds of illustrations, some hand colored. Light foxing. First edition. 9" tall. Near fine. $545.00

WEBB, Annie. *Naomi.* London: 1872. Contemporary full red morocco gilt. Square octavo. Illustrated with photographic plates. Near fine. $250.00

WEBB, Daniel. *Observations on the Correspondence Between Poetry and Music.* London: J. Dodsley, 1769. Contemporary smooth calf. Flat spine, gilt ruled compartments with black morocco label. First edition. Near fine. $325.00

WEBSTER, Daniel. *The Works of Daniel Webster.* Boston: Charles C. Little and James Brown, 1851. Full tan calf. Gilt floral embossing to pebbled morocco covers. Top edges gilt. Flat signed by Daniel Webster. Subscriber's copy. 8" tall. Near fine. $1,650.00

WEBSTER, Daniel. *The Works of Daniel Webster.* Boston: Little, Brown & Co., 1860. Six volumes (only two shown). Three-quarter tan calf. Marbled edges. Tipped in letter signed by Daniel Webster. Illustrated. 9" tall. Very good. $950.00

WEBSTER, Daniel. *The Works of Daniel Webster.* Boston: Little and Brown, 1851. Six octavo volumes. Full polished green calf gilt. Illustrated with a portrait of the author. Near fine. $1,100.00

WEBSTER, Noah. *Dissertations on the English Language.* Boston: 1789. Contemporary full calf. Octavo. First edition. Near fine. $1,400.00

WELLS, William V. *The Life and Public Services of Samuel Adams.* Boston: Little, Brown & Co., 1865. Three volumes. Three-quarter tan calf. Marbled edges. First edition. 8½" tall. Near fine. $1,000.00

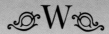

WEIR, Captain R., and BROWN, J. Moray. *Riding and Polo.* London: Longmans, Green & Co., 1891. Full blue morocco. Raised bands, gilt decorated. 4to. Large paper edition, one of only 250 copies. Near fine. $475.00

WESLEY, John. *An Ernest Appeal to Men of Reason and Religion.* London: The Conference Office, 1809. Full tree calf. 7" tall. Very good. $275.00

WEST, Gilbert. *Odes of Pindar.* London: Printed for J. Dodsley, 1766. Three volumes. Full tan calf with all edges gilt. Has a handwritten note from Princess Caroline, a presentation copy. Bookplate of Robert Hoe. 7" tall. Near fine. $1,750.00

WHALLEY, Peter. *The Works of Ben Johnson.* London: D. Midwinter, 1756. Seven volumes. Three-quarter black morocco. From Robert Southey's library, sold by subscription only. 8" tall. Very good. $1,200.00

WHARTON, Edith. *Italian Villas and Their Gardens.* New York: 1905. Full green morocco. Quarto. Illustrated by Maxfield Parrish. First American edition. Near fine. $1,100.00

WHARTON, Grace and Philip. *The Queens of Society.* London: James Hogg & Sons, circa 1860. Six volumes. Three-quarter tan morocco. Raised bands, gilt panels, and marbled boards. Illustrated by C.A. Doyle and the Dalziel Brothers. Near fine. $750.00

WHARTON, Grace and Philip. *The Queens of Society.* London: George Routledge and Sons, 1870. Full tree calf. Highly gilt spine, all edges gilt. Illustrated by Charles Altamont Doyle and the Brothers Dalziel. 7" tall. Near fine. $220.00

WHARTON, Grace and Philip. *The Wits and Beaux of Society.* London: George Routledge and Sons, 1871. Full tree calf. Highly gilt spine, all edges gilt. Illustrated by H.K. Browne and James Godwin. 7" tall. Near fine. $220.00

WHITE, Henry Alexander. *Robert E. Lee.* New York and London: G.P. Putnam's Sons, 1897. Full blue morocco. Prize binding with marbled edges. Illustrated with pull-out maps. 7½" tall. Near fine. $575.00

WHITE, Rev. Henry. *Indian Battles.* New York: D.W. Evans & Co., 1859. Three-quarter brown calf by Starr Bookworks. Highly gilt spine. Rebound spine and endpapers. First edition. 7½" tall. Near fine. $650.00

WHITE, Richard Grant. *Poetry Lyrical, Narrative and Satirical of the Civil War.* New York: The American News Company, 1866. Three-quarter tan calf. Marbled edges. First edition. 8" tall. Near fine. $275.00

WHITTIER, John Greenleaf. *The Complete Poetical Works of John Greenleaf Whittier.* Boston and New York: Houghton, Mifflin and Co., 1903. Full tree calf. Cabinet edition with all edges gilt. 6½" tall. Near fine. $230.00

WHEATLEY, Henry B. *London Past and Present Its History, Associations, and Traditions.* London: John Murray, 1891. Six volumes. Contemporary half green levant morocco. Ornate gilt-decorated spines an covers. Illustrated. Near fine. $2,600.00

WHITMAN, Walt. *Complete Poems and Prose of Walt Whitman 1855 – 1888.* Philadelphia: Ferguson Brothers, 1888. Three-quarter green calf over paper boards. First edition, one of only 600 copies signed by the author. Near fine. $2,800.00

WHITMAN, Walt. *Complete Works.* New York and London: G.P. Putnam's Sons. 1902. Ten volumes. Limited edition, one of only 300 sets. Rebound in full red morocco, gilt panels. Illustrated. Near fine. $3,900.00

WHITMAN, Walt. *Leaves of Grass.* Brooklyn, New York: 1855. Nineteenth-century three-quarter dark green morocco. Marbled boards, edges, and endpapers. First edition, one of only 795 copies signed by Whitman. Near fine. $32,000.00

WHITMAN, Walt. *The Complete Writings.* New York: 1902. Ten octavo volumes. Full dark green morocco gilt. Connoisseur's Camden edition, one of only 200 numbered sets. Illustrated with 40 tissue guarded plates. Near fine. $6,500.00

WHITMAN, Walt. *The Complete Writings.* New York: G.P. Putnam's Sons, 1902. Ten octavo volumes. Original half vellum, gilt decorated. Collector's Camden edition. Illustrated. Near fine. $4,100.00

WHITTIER, John Greenleaf. *An American Slave.* New York: American Anti-Slavery Society, 1838. Three-quarter calf. 18mo. Near fine. $650.00

WHITTIER, John Greenleaf. *Ballads of New England.* Boston: 1870. Original full brown morocco. Octavo. Illustrations by Winslow Homer and other notable artists. First edition. Near fine. $425.00

WHITTIER, John Greenleaf. *The Life and Works of Whittier.* Boston and New York: Houghton, Mifflin & Co. The Riverside Press, Cambridge, 1894. Nine volumes. Large 8vo. Limited artist's edition, one of only 750 sets published. Full dark brown morocco with tan morocco inlay on inside panels and plum colored endpapers. This edition contains 72 hand-colored plates. Near fine. $3,100.00

WHITTIER, John Greenleaf. *The Tent.* Boston: Ticknor and Fields, 1867. Three-quarter olive morocco by Sangorski & Sutcliffe. First edition, first state. 7" tall. Near fine. $320.00

WHITMAN, Walt. *Leaves of Grass.* New York and London: D. Appleton & Co., n.d., circa 1915. Full rust calf. All edges gilt. 8" tall. Near fine. $275.00

WIDENER, Joseph. *Lynnewood Hall. French Engravings of the Eighteenth Century.* Privately printed at the Chiswick Press, 1923. Four volumes. Three-quarter red morocco by Riviere. Folio. Limited edition, one of only 120 copies. Near fine. $3,100.00

WILBERFORCE, Samuel. *Heroes of Hebrew History.* **London: Daddy, Isbister & Co., 1875. Full brown calf by Bickers. Prize binding with red edges. Light foxing to first few pages. 7" tall. Very good. $175.00**

WILDE, Oscar. *An Ideal Husband.* London: Methuen & Co., 1910. Full navy morocco by Bickers. Prize binding with marbled edges. Fourth edition. 6½" tall. Very good. $225.00

WILDE, Oscar. *A Woman of No Importance.* London: 1894. Full red morocco by Bayntun. Octavo. First edition. Near fine. $1,100.00

WILDE, Oscar. *An Ideal Husband.* London: 1899. Full red morocco by Bayntun. Octavo. First edition. Near fine. $1,200.00

WILDE, Oscar. *An Ideal Husband.* London: 1899. Octavo. Full purple morocco. First edition, one of only 1,000 copies. Near fine. $1,250.00

WILDE, Oscar. *Collected Works.* London: Meuthen and Co., 1908. Fourteen octavo volumes. Original vellum gilt. First edition, one of only 80 sets on Japanese vellum. Near fine. $8,700.00

WILDE, Oscar. *Collected Works.* Paris and London: 1908. Fourteen octavo volumes. Three-quarter calf. Edited by Robert Ross. First collected edition, one of only 1,000 sets. Near fine. $2,900.00

WILDE, Oscar. *Complete Writings.* New York: 1909. Ten volumes. Three-quarter green morocco. Limited edition, one of only 1,000 sets. Near fine. $2,800.00

WILDE, Oscar. *For Love of the King; A Burmese Masque.* London: 1922. Full navy calf by Bayntun. Octavo. First edition, one of only 1,000 copies. Near fine. $600.00

WILDE, Oscar. *Lady Windemere's Fan, A Play About A Good Woman.* London: 1893. Full red morocco by Bayntun. Octavo. First edition. Near fine. $1,400.00

WILDE, Oscar. *Poems.* New York: 1913. Three-quarter green morocco gilt. Octavo. Near fine. $300.00

WILDE, Oscar. *The Complete Works of Oscar Wilde.* New York: 1927. Twelve octavo volumes. Three-quarter blue morocco gilt. Connoisseurs' edition. Introductions in each volume by such notable authors as; John Cowper Powys, Walter Pater, W.B. Yeats. Near fine. $2,500.00

WILDE, Oscar. *The Decay of Lying.* New York: 1902. Three-quarter navy calf. Square 12mo. Limited first edition, one of only 1,000 copies. Near fine. $250.00

WILDE, Oscar. *The Happy Prince and Other Tales.* Boston: 1888. Half calf. Small octavo. First American edition. Near fine. $850.00

WILDE, Oscar. *The Poems.* Portland, Maine: 1905. Octavo. Contemporary full blue morocco gilt. One of 750 copies on Van Gelder handmade paper, with frontispiece photograph of Oscar Wilde. Near fine. $750.00

WILDE, Oscar. *The Works.* Boston and New York: 1909. Fifteen volumes. Octavo. Contemporary three-quarter morocco gilt. Edition de Luxe, one of only 1,000 sets. Near fine. $3,400.00

WILDE, Oscar. *The Works.* New York: 1909. Fifteen octavo volumes. Contemporary three-quarter maroon morocco gilt. The Sunflower edition, one of only 1,000 sets. Illustrated. Near fine. $3,800.00

WILDE, Oscar. *The Complete Works of Oscar Wilde.* **Boston: Wyman-Fogg Co., 1905 – 1909. Ten volumes. Three-quarter blue morocco. Top edges gilt. Edited by Robert Ross. Authorized edition. Near fine. $2,700.00**

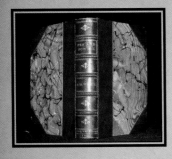

WILKIE, Franc B. *Pen and Powder*. Boston: Ticknor and Co., 1888. Three-quarter brown calf by Launder and MacDonald. Top edges gilt. First edition. 8" tall. Near fine. $400.00

WILKINSON, Sir J. Gardner. *The Manners and Customs of the Ancient Egyptians*. Boston: S. E. Cassino & Co., 1883. Three volumes. Three-quarter butterscotch calf with marbled edges. Illustrated. Dedicated to the Earl of Beaconsfield. 9" tall. Near fine. $675.00

WILDE, Oscar. *The Writings of Oscar Wilde. With an introduction by Richard Le Gallienne*. New York: Gabriel Wells, 1925. Twelve octavo volumes. Three-quarter calf. Limited edition, one of only 575 copies. Near fine. $2,900.00

WILDE, Oscar. *Works*. London: Methuen & Company, 1908. Fourteen volumes. Full green morocco gilt with ribbed gilt decorated spines. Near fine. $2,800.00

WILDE, Oscar. *Works*. London: The Edinburgh Society, 1911. Fourteen volumes. Three-quarter burgundy morocco gilt. Limited edition, one of only 240 sets produced. Near fine. $2,700.00

WILDE, Oscar. *Writings*. New York: Gabriel Wells, 1925. Twelve volumes. Three-quarter green morocco gilt. Large paper edition. Ribbed floral decorated gilt spines. Near fine. $2,400.00

WILKIE, Sir. David R.A. *The Wilkie Gallery*. London and New York: George Virtue, circa 1890. Full burgundy morocco. Raised bands, ornate covers and spines. Folio. Illustrated. Near fine. $875.00

WILKINS, John. A *Discovery of a New World, Or, a Discourse Tending to Prove, That 'Tis Probable There May Be Another Habitable World in the Moon*. With: *A Discourse Concerning a New Planet, Tending to Prove That 'Tis Probable Our Earth Is One of the Planets*. London: John Gillibrand, 1684. Two books bound in one. Contemporary dark speckled calf. Raised bands with brown morocco label. Engraved title page and woodcut illustrations. Fourth edition. Near fine. $1,100.00

WILLIAM, Ward A. *The Electress Sophia and the Hanoverian Succession*. London, Paris and New York: Goupil & Co., 1903. Full red morocco by Riviere. Gilt decorated spine and covers, green silk doublures. Folio. Illustrated. Limited edition, one of only 250 copies. Near fine. $1,100.00

WILLIAMS, George. *Bullet and Shell*. New York: Fords, Howard U Hulbert, 1882. Three-quarter maroon morocco. Illustrated by Edwin Forbs. First edition. Very good. $140.00

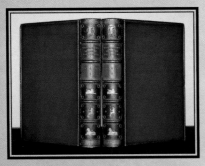

WILKINSON, J. Gardner. *A Popular Account of the Ancient Egyptians*. London: John Murray, 1854. Two volumes. Full sky blue morocco by Bickers. Highly gilt cover and marbled edges. Illustrated. 7½" tall. $675.00

WILLIAMS, Lieutenant-Colonel. *The Life and Times of the Late Duke of Wellington*. London: John Tallis & Co., n.d., circa 1858. Four volumes. Three-quarter black calf with marbled edges. Bordered steel engravings. 11" tall. Near fine. $850.00

WILLIAMS, Benjamin Samuel. *The Orchid-Grower's Manual.* London: 1894. Quarto. twentieth century three-quarter blue calf gilt. Seventh edition, with hundreds of wood-engravings of orchids. Near fine. $750.00

WILLIAMS, D. E. *The Life and Correspondence of Sir Thomas Lawrence, Kt.* London: 1831. Two octavo volumes. Nineteenth century blue crushed morocco gilt by Pomey. Illustrated. First edition. Near fine. $650.00

WILLIAMS, H.W. *Select Views of Greece with Classical Illustrations.* London: 1829. Royal octavo. Contemporary full red pebbled morocco, gilt decorated spine and covers. First octavo edition, with 64 engraved views of Grecian landscapes. Near fine. $1,400.00

WILLIS, N. P. *American Scenery; Or, Land Lake and River Illustrations of Transatlantic Nature.* London: George Virtue, 1840. Two quarto volumes. Full green morocco gilt. Raised bands, gilt dentelles, and marbled endpapers. Illustrated with 117 hand-colored plates by W.H. Bartlett. First edition. Near fine. $3,600.00

WILMER, James. *Events in Indian History.* Lancaster: G. Hills & Co., 1841. Full calf. Large pull-out illustrations, one ripped but piece present. Tape on title page. Foxed. First edition. Good. $375.00

WILLMOTT, Ellen. *The Genus Rosa.* London: 1914. Two thick folio volumes. Three-quarter dark green morocco. Illustrated with 132 full-page color lithographs by Alfred Parsons. First edition. Near fine. $3,100.00

WILSON, Col. *Picturesque Palestine, Sinai and Egypt.* New York: D. Appleton, 1881. Two volumes. Folio. Full brown morocco with blind tooling and ribbed spine. Illustrated by Harry Fenn and J. D. Woodward. Near fine. $1,850.00

WILSON, Colonel Charles. *Picturesque Palestine, Sinai and Egypt.* New York: 1883. Two volumes. Folio. Original full black morocco gilt. First edition, American issue. Near fine. $1,750.00

WILSON, Colonel. *Picturesque Palestine, Sinai and Egypt.* New York: D. Appleton & Co., 1887. Two volumes. Full brown calf. Embossed and gilt covers, all edges gilt. Illustrated first edition. 13" tall. Near fine. $1,850.00

WILSON, Professor, and CHAMBERS, Robert. *The Land of Burns, A Series of Landscapes and Portraits, Illustrative of the Life and Writings of the Scottish Poet.* London: Blackie and Son, 1840. Two volumes. Quarto. Full green calf gilt. Raised bands, gilt decorated spines. First edition. Illustrated by David Hill with full-page illustration, steel engraved plates, and landscape paintings. Near fine. $1,250.00

WILSON, Woodrow. *A History of the American People.* New York and London: 1903. Five large octavo volumes. Three-quarter green morocco gilt. Gilt decorated spines. Near fine. $900.00

WINSOR, Justin. *Narrative and Critical History of America.* Boston and New York: Houghton Mifflin & Co., 1889. Eight volumes. Full navy morocco. Gilt decorated spines with raised bands, marbled endpapers. Illustrated. Limited edition, one of only 550 copies. Near fine. $3,900.00

WINSOR, Justin. *Narrative and Critical History of America.* Boston and New York: Houghton Mifflin, 1889. Eight volumes. Three-quarter green morocco. Raised bands, marbled boards, and top edges gilt. Illustrated. First edition. Near fine. $3,100.00

WILSON, James. *General Grant.* New York: D. Appleton, 1897. Full blue morocco with top edges gilt. Illustrated. First edition. 7" tall. Near fine. $475.00

WINSOR, Justin. *The Memorial History of Boston.* Boston: Ticknor and Co., 1880. Four volumes. Three-quarter butterscotch calf. Marbled edges. Illustrated. First edition. 11" tall. Fine. $550.00

WITHERS, Alexander S. *Chronicles of Border Warfare.* Clarksburg, Virginia: 1831. Contemporary full brown calf. Tall 12mo. First edition. Near fine. $525.00

WOLLSTONECRAFT, Mary. *Original Stories from Real Life, with Conversations Calculated to Regulate the Affections and Form the Mind to Truth and Goodness.* London: J. Johnson, 1791. Sprinkled calf by Courtland Benson. Flat spine with red morocco label. Frontispiece illustration and five engraved plates by William Blake. First edition. Near fine. $2,800.00

WOOD, J.G. *The Illustrated Natural History.* London: Routeledge Warne, circa 1890. Three volumes. Three-quarter green calf, ornate gilt on spines. Illustrated. Near fine. $850.00

WOOD, J.G. *The Illustrated Natural History.* London: Routledge Warne, 1862. Three volumes. Full green morocco gilt. Raised bands, ornate spines and covers. 4to. Illustrated. Near fine. $975.00

WOOD, Rev. J.G. *Insects Abroad.* London: Longmans, Green and Co., 1883. Full tan calf. Prize binding. Marbled edges. With 600 illustrations. 8½" tall. Near fine. $275.00

WORDSWORTH, William. *The Poetical Works of William Wordsworth.* London: Edward Moxon, 1853. Eight volumes. Full navy morocco by Zaehnsdorf. Top edges gilt. 7" tall. Near fine. $1,100.00

WOOSTER, David. *Alpine Plants.* London: 1872 – 74. Two large octavo volumes. Full calf. Illustrated with numerous color plates. First edition. Near fine. $875.00

WORDSWORTH, William. *Poems.* London: 1893. Contemporary full green polished calf. 12mo. Golden Treasury edition. Near fine. $225.00

WORDSWORTH, William. *The Poetical Works of William Wordsworth.* London: Edward Moxon, 1853. Seven volumes. Full butterscotch calf by Root. Highly gilt spine, top edges gilt. 7" tall. Near fine. $1,050.00

WORDSWORTH, William. *The Poetical Works of William Wordsworth.* London: William P. Nimmo, 1876. Brown calf spine with sycamore wood covers. Mauchline cover of Wordsworth on front and Rydal mount on rear. All edges gilt. 6½" tall. Very good. $450.00

WORDSWORTH, William. *Poems.* London: Robert Riviere & Son, n.d., circa 1890. Full red morocco by Riviere. Geometrical inlaid multicolored leather on covers. All edges gilt. 6" tall. Fine. $475.00

WORDSWORTH, William. *Poetical Works.* London: E. Moxon, 1874. Six volumes. Full maroon calf. Small 8vo. Spines are decorated with crests of lions. Centenary edition. Near fine. $850.00

WORDSWORTH, William. *Prose, Poetry and Journals.* London: MacMillian & Co. 1896. Twelve volumes. Three-quarter green calf. Small 8vo. Near fine. $1,200.00

WORDSWORTH, William. *The Complete Poetical Works.* London: MacMillian & Co., 1888. Full red morocco gilt. Introduction by John Morley. Near fine. $275.00

WORDSWORTH, William. *The Poetical Works of William Wordsworth.* London: Edward Moxon, 1836 – 1837. Six volumes. With: *Poems, Chiefly of Early and Late Years.* Seven volumes total. Full red morocco gilt, raised bands and brown morocco spine labels. Very good. $900.00

WORDSWORTH, William. *The Poetical Works.* London: Edward Moxon, 1846. Seven volumes. Three-quarter green morocco gilt with marbled edges. Near fine. $650.00

WRIGHT, Rev. G.M. *China.* London: Fisher, Son & Co., n.d., circa 1843. Four volumes bound in two volumes. Three-quarter red morocco. Illustrated with 124 steel plates, many were executed by Thomas Allon. Very occasional and light foxing. 11" tall. Near fine. $1,500.00

WRIGHT, Rev. G.N. *Life and Campaigns of Arthur, Duke of Wellington.* London: Fisher, Son & Co., n.d., circa 1842. Four volumes. Full navy morocco with marbled edges. Illustrated with pull outs. Light damp staining in Volume 1. 9" tall. Near fine. $525.00

WRIGHT, Marie R. *The New Brazil.* Philadelphia: George Barrie & Sons, 1907. Full red morocco gilt. Raised bands with gilt panels and edges. Quarto. Illustrated. Near fine. $575.00

WRIGHT, Thomas. *The History of Ireland From the Earliest Period to the Irish Annals to the Present Time.* London and New York: The London Printing and Publishing Co., 1900. Three volumes. Three-quarter red morocco. Large octavo. Near fine. $550.00

WYCHERLEY, William. *Miscellany Poems: As Satyrs, Epistles, Love-Verses, Songs and Sonnets.* London: Brome, Taylor & Tooke, 1704. Nineteenth century speckled calf gilt. Raised bands, gilt spine compartments with red morocco labels. All edges gilt. Near fine. $625.00

WYSS, Johann David. *The Swiss Family Robinson.* London: Simpkin, Marshall & Co., 1862. Full tan calf by Hale & Roworth. Prize binding with marbled edges. Illustrated. 6½" tall. Near fine. $275.00

YONGE, C.D. *The Works of Philo Judaeus. The Contemporary of Josephus.* London: Henry G. Bohn, 1854. Four volumes. Full red morocco. Gilt decorated spine and covers. Small 8vo. Translated from the Greek. Near fine. $450.00

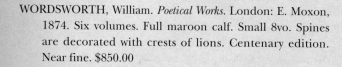

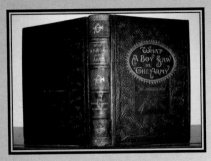

YOUNG, Jesse Bowman. *What A Boy Saw in the Army.* **New York: Hunt & Eaton, 1894. Full red morocco. Embossed covers. Spine layed down. One hundred illustrations by Frank Beard. First edition. 9½" tall. Near fine. $240.00**

ZANGWILL, Israel. *Works.* London: 1925. Fourteen octavo volumes. Original three-quarter red morocco gilt. Illustrated by Alfred A. Wolmark. Limited "Edition de Luxe," one of only 1,000 copies. Near fine. $1,500.00

ZIMMERMAN, Dr. William. *A Popular History of Germany.* **New York: Henry Johnson, 1878. Four volumes. Three-quarter butterscotch calf. Over 600 illustrations. 11¼" tall. Fine. $550.00**

ZOLA, Emile. *Works.* Philadelphia: George Barrie & Son, 1890. Twelve volumes. Three-quarter red morocco. Raised bands, gilt decorated spines. Illustrated. Limited edition, one of only 1,000 copies. Near fine. $2,400.00

ZOSIMUS. *The New History of Count Zosimus, Sometime Advocate of the Treasure of the Roman Empire to Which Is Prefixed Leunclavius's Apology for the Author.* London: Joseph Hindmarsh, 1684. Late eighteenth century flamed calf. Flat spine gilt in compartments. Near fine. $1,100.00

GLASSWARE & POTTERY

6321	Carnival Glass, The Best of the Best, Edwards/Carwile	$29.95
6326	Collectible Cups & Saucers, Book III, Harran	$24.95
6344	Collectible Vernon Kilns, 2nd Edition, Nelson	$29.95
6331	Collecting Head Vases, Barron	$24.95
6830	Collector's Encyclopedia of Depression Glass, 17th Ed., Florence	$19.95
6629	Collector's Encyclopedia of Fiesta, 10th Ed., Huxford	$24.95
5609	Collector's Encyclopedia of Limoges Porcelain, 3rd Ed., Gaston	$29.95
5677	Collector's Encyclopedia of Niloak, 2nd Edition, Gifford	$29.95
5842	Collector's Encyclopedia of Roseville Pottery, Vol. 2, Huxford/Nickel	$24.95
6646	Collector's Ency. of Stangl Artware, Lamps, and Birds, 2nd Ed., Runge	$29.95
5680	Collector's Guide to Feather Edge Ware, McAllister	$19.95
6124	Collector's Guide to Made In Japan Ceramics, Book IV, White	$24.95
6559	Elegant Glassware of the Depression Era, 11th Edition, Florence	$24.95
6126	Fenton Art Glass, 1907 – 1939, 2nd Edition, Whitmyer	$29.95
6320	Gaston's Blue Willow, 3rd Edition	$19.95
6127	The Glass Candlestick Book, Vol. 1, Akro Agate to Fenton, Felt/Stoer	$24.95
6648	Glass Toothpick Holders, 2nd Edition, Bredehoft	$29.95
6329	Glass Tumblers, 1860s to 1920s, Bredehoft/Sanford	$29.95
6562	The Hazel-Atlas Glass Identification and Value Guide, Florence	$24.95
5840	Heisey Glass, 1896 – 1957, Bredehoft	$24.95
5913	McCoy Pottery, Volume III, Hanson/Nissen	$24.95
6135	North Carolina Art Pottery, 1900 – 1960, James/Leftwich	$24.95
6335	Pictorial Guide to Pottery & Porcelain Marks, Lage	$29.95
5691	Post86 Fiesta, Identification & Value Guide, Racheter	$19.95
6037	Rookwood Pottery, Nicholson/Thomas	$24.95
6448	Standard Encyclopedia of Carnival Glass, 9th Ed., Edwards/Carwile	$29.95
6476	Westmoreland Glass, The Popular Years, 1940 – 1985, Kovar	$29.95
5924	Zanesville Stoneware Company, Rans/Ralston/Russell	$24.95

DOLLS, FIGURES & TEDDY BEARS

6315	American Character Dolls, Izen	$24.95
6317	Arranbee Dolls, The Dolls That Sell on Sight, DeMillar/Brevik	$24.95
6319	Barbie Doll Fashion, Volume III, 1975 – 1979, Eames	$29.95
6221	Barbie, The First 30 Years, 2nd Edition, Deutsch	$24.95
6134	Ency. of Bisque Nancy Ann Storybook Dolls, 1936 – 1947, Pardee/Robertson	$29.95
6451	Collector's Ency. of American Composition Dolls, Vol. II, Mertz	$29.95
6546	Collector's Ency. of Barbie Doll Exclusives, 3rd Ed., Augustyniak	$29.95
6636	Collector's Ency. of Madame Alexander Dolls, 1948 – 1965, Crowsey	$24.95
5904	Collector's Guide to Celebrity Dolls, Spurgeon	$24.95
5599	Collector's Guide to Dolls of the 1960s and 1970s, Sabulis	$24.95
6456	Collector's Guide to Dolls of the 1960s and 1970s, Vol. II, Sabulis	$24.95
6452	Contemporary American Doll Artists & Their Dolls, Witt	$29.95
6455	Doll Values, Antique to Modern, 8th Ed., DeFeo/Stover	$14.95
6635	Madame Alexander Collector's Dolls Price Guide #30, Crowsey	$14.95
5611	Madame Alexander Store Exclusives & Limited Editions, Crowsey	$24.95
5689	Nippon Dolls & Playthings, Van Patten/Lau	$29.95
6336	Official Precious Moments Collector's Guide to Figurines, Bomm	$16.95
5253	Story of Barbie, 2nd Ed., Westenhouser	$24.95
6642	20th Century Paper Dolls, Young	$19.95
4880	World of Raggedy Ann Collectibles, Avery	$24.95

JEWELRY & ACCESSORIES

6122	Brilliant Rhinestones, Aikins	$24.95
6323	Christmas Pins, Past & Present, 2nd Edition, Gallina	$19.95
4850	Collectible Costume Jewelry, Simonds	$24.95
5675	Collectible Silver Jewelry, Rezazadeh	$24.95
6453	Collecting Costume Jewelry 101, Carroll	$24.95
6468	Collector's Ency. of Pendant & Pocket Watches, 1500 – 1950, Bell	$24.95
4940	Costume Jewelry, A Practical Handbook & Value Guide, Rezazadeh	$24.95
5812	Fifty Years of Collectible Fashion Jewelry, 1925 – 1975, Baker	$24.95
5330	Handkerchiefs: A Collector's Guide, Guarnaccia/Guggenheim	$24.95
6464	Inside the Jewelry Box, Pitman	$24.95
5695	Ladies' Vintage Accessories, Bruton	$24.95
1181	100 Years of Collectible Jewelry, 1850 – 1950, Baker	$9.95
5232	Plastic Jewelry of the 20th Century, Baker	$24.95
6337	Purse Masterpieces, Schwartz	$29.95
6039	Signed Beauties of Costume Jewelry, Brown	$24.95
4850	Unsigned Beauties of Costume Jewelry, Brown	$24.95
6923	Vintage Jewelry for Investment & Casual Wear, Edeen	$24.95

FURNITURE

3716	American Oak Furniture, Book II, McNerney	$12.95
1118	Antique Oak Furniture, Hill	$7.95
6474	Collector's Guide to Wallace Nutting Furniture, Ivankovich	$19.95
3906	Heywood-Wakefield Modern Furniture, Rouland	$18.95
6338	Roycroft Furniture & Collectibles, Koon	$24.95
6343	Stickley Brothers Furniture, Koon	$24.95
1885	Victorian Furniture, Our American Heritage, McNerney	$9.95

ARTIFACTS, GUNS, KNIVES, TOOLS, PRIMITIVES

1868	Antique Tools, Our American Heritage, McNerney	$9.95
1426	Arrowheads & Projectile Points, Hothem	$7.95
6021	Arrowheads of the Central Great Plains, Fox	$19.95
5685	Indian Artifacts of the Midwest, Book IV, Hothem	$19.95
6130	Indian Trade Relics, Hothem	$29.95
6565	Modern Guns, Identification & Values, 15th Ed., Quertermous	$16.95
6567	Paleo-Indian Artifacts, Hothem	$29.95
2164	Primitives, Our American Heritage, McNerney	$9.95
6031	Standard Knife Collector's Guide, 4th Ed., Ritchie & Stewart	$14.95

PAPER COLLECTIBLES & BOOKS

5902	Boys' & Girls' Book Series, Jones	$19.95
6623	Collecting American Paintings, James	$29.95
6553	Collector's Guide to Cookbooks, Daniels	$24.95
1441	Collector's Guide to Post Cards, Wood	$9.95
6627	Early 20th Century Hand-Painted Photography, Ivankovich	$24.95
6936	Leather Bound Books, Boutiette	$24.95
6234	Old Magazines, Clear	$19.95
3973	Sheet Music Reference & Price Guide, 2nd Ed., Guiheen/Pafik	$19.95

TOYS & MARBLES

2333	Antique & Collectible Marbles, 3rd Ed., Grist	$9.95
6649	Big Book of Toy Airplanes, Miller	$24.95
4945	G-Men and FBI Toys, Whitworth	$18.95
6633	Hot Wheels, The Ultimate Redline Guide, 2nd Ed., Clark/Wicker	$29.95
6466	Matchbox Toys, 4th Ed., 1947 to 2003, Johnson	$24.95
6638	The Other Matchbox Toys, 1947 to 2004, Johnson	$19.95
6340	Schroeder's Collectible Toys, Antique to Modern Price Guide, 9th Ed	$17.95
6650	Toy Car Collector's Guide, 2nd Ed., Johnson	$24.95

OTHER COLLECTIBLES

5814	Antique Brass & Copper Collectibles, Gaston	$24.95
1880	Antique Iron, McNerney	$9.95
6447	Antique Quilts & Textiles, Aug/Roy	$24.95
1128	Bottle Pricing Guide, 3rd Ed., Cleveland	$7.95
6345	Business & Tax Guide for Antiques & Collectibles, Kelly	$14.95
3718	Collectible Aluminum, Grist	$16.95
6342	Collectible Soda Pop Memorabilia, Summers	$24.95
5676	Collectible Souvenir Spoons, Book II, Bednersh	$29.95
6625	Collector's Encyclopedia of Bookends, Kuritzky/DeCosta	$29.95
5666	Collector's Encyclopedia of Granite Ware, Book II, Greguire	$29.95
5906	Collector's Guide to Creek Chub Lures & Collectibles, 2nd Ed., Smith	$29.95
6558	The Ency. of Early American Sewing Machines, 2nd Ed., Bays	$29.95
5683	Fishing Lure Collectibles, Vol. 1, Murphy/Edmisten	$29.95
6141	Fishing Lure Collectibles, Vol. 2, Murphy	$29.95
6328	Flea Market Trader, 14th Ed., Huxford	$9.95
6458	Fountain Pens, Past & Present, 2nd Edition, Erano	$24.95
6631	Garage Sale & Flea Market Annual, 13th Edition, Huxford	$19.95
2216	Kitchen Antiques, 1790 – 1940, McNerney	$14.95
5603	19th Century Fishing Lures, Carter	$29.95
6322	Pictorial Guide to Christmas Ornaments & Collectibles, Johnson	$29.95
5835	Racing Collectibles, Editors of Racing Collector's Magazine	$19.95
3443	Salt & Pepper Shakers IV, Guarnaccia	$18.95
6570	Schroeder's Antiques Price Guide, 23rd Edition 2005	$14.95
5007	Silverplated Flatware, Revised 4th Edition, Hagan	$18.95
6647	Star Wars Super Collector's Wish Book, 3rd Ed., Carlton	$29.95
6632	Value Guide to Gas Station Memorabilia, 2nd Ed., Summers/Priddy	$29.95
5925	The Vintage Era of Golf Club Collectibles, John	$29.95
6036	Vintage Quilts, Aug/Newman/Roy	$24.95
4935	The W.F. Cody Buffalo Bill Collector's Guide with Values, Wojtowicz	$24.95

This is only a partial listing of the books on antiques that are available from Collector Books. All books are well illustrated and contain current values. Most of these books are available from your local bookseller, antique dealer, or public library. If you are unable to locate certain titles in your area, you may order by mail from COLLECTOR BOOKS, P.O. Box 3009, Paducah, KY 42002-3009. Customers with Visa, MasterCard, or Discover may phone in orders from 7:00 a.m. to 5:00 p.m. CT, Monday – Friday, toll free 1-800-626-5420, or online at www.collectorbooks.com. Add $4.00 for postage for the first book ordered and 50¢ for each additional book. Include item number, title, and price when ordering. Allow 14 to 21 days for delivery.

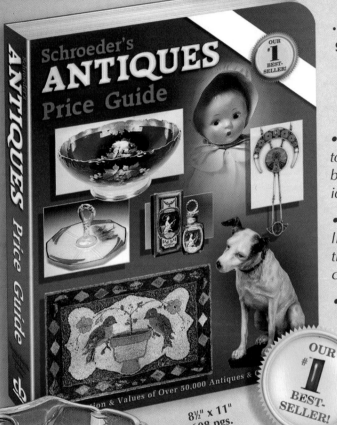